Management for Professionals

The Springer series Management for Professionals comprises high-level business and management books for executives, MBA students, and practice-oriented business researchers. The topics span all themes of relevance for businesses and the business ecosystem. The authors are experienced business professionals and renowned professors who combine scientific backgrounds, best practices, and entrepreneurial vision to provide powerful insights into how to achieve business excellence.

Xiaodong Ma

Methodology for Digital Transformation

Implementation Path and Data Platform

Springer

Xiaodong Ma
Suzhou Guoyun Data Technology Co., Ltd.
Beijing, China

University of Science and Technology
of China
Hefei, China

ISSN 2192-8096 ISSN 2192-810X (electronic)
Management for Professionals
ISBN 978-981-19-9113-4 ISBN 978-981-19-9111-0 (eBook)
https://doi.org/10.1007/978-981-19-9111-0

Jointly published with China Machine Press Co., Ltd.
The print edition is not for sale in China (Mainland). Customers from China (Mainland) please order the print book from: China Machine Press Co., Ltd.

Translation from the Chinese Simplified language edition: "数字化转型方法论: 落地路径与数据中台" by Xiaodong Ma, © 机械工业出版社 2021. Published by 出版社: 机械工业出版社. All Rights Reserved.

This Springer imprint is published by the registered company Springer Nature Singapore Pte Ltd.
The registered company address is: 152 Beach Road, #21-01/04 Gateway East, Singapore 189721, Singapore

Preface

In recent years, the growth models of traditional industries have been disrupted by modern digital technologies, particularly the mobile Internet, Internet of Things (IoT), cloud computing, and big data. The relentless impact of digitalization has meant that digital drivers have now become the key to solving the development bottlenecks across all industries and an essential means for accelerating their growth. The Artificial Intelligence of Things (AIoT) applications in all industries are gaining traction in the research and development (R&D) field by employing data as the primary resource and cloud storage as the logistical support. There is a constant deep dive into the exploration of autonomous driving, "City Brain," medical imaging, intelligent speech interaction, and other fields. Regardless of the exploration of AIoT or mining of the big data technology applications, they are all primarily based on data, which continually enriches people's work and lives.

Today, data intelligence services are ubiquitous among industries, and there are pressing needs for digital transformation in all industries. The new model of Alibaba's "large digital platform, small front-end platform" has provided a template for many companies to carry out digital transformation. Different companies have varying business logic, technical strengths, and backgrounds, so it is challenging to completely replicate Alibaba's data platform construction model. Without proper professional guidance on digital transformation as well as the construction and implementation of the data platform, it will only miserably backfire if any company just copies wholesale from the transformation model of another company.

The purpose of authoring this book is to empower the company managers, R&D personnel, business staff, data practitioners, and data technology enthusiasts to have a better understanding of the significance of digital transformation, fully understand the technical structure of the data platform as well as grapple with the construction methods of the data platform.

By combining theoretical and practical approaches, this book aims to show how companies can achieve digital transformation utilizing a suitable data platform, providing readers with practical guidance on implementing and creating such a platform.

This book is divided into eight parts.

Part I (Chaps. 1–2): *Why Do You Implement Digital Transformation?*

Part II (Chaps. 3–5): *When Do You Implement Digital Transformation?*

Part III (Chap. 6): *What Is Digital Transformation?*

Part IV (Chap. 7): *Should You Implement Digital Transformation?*
Part V (Chap. 8): *Who Is Responsible for Digital Transformation?*
Part VI (Chaps. 9–15): *How Do You Implement Digital Transformation?*
Part VII (Chaps. 16–19): *Critical Tools of Digital Transformation—Data Platform*
Part VIII (Chaps. 20–24): *Case Studies of Digital Transformation*

Through the eight parts above, this book dissects the path to digital transformation layer by layer and clarifies the critical components of digital transformation for its readers. Scan the QR code below to get more information about this book.

QR Code

In pursuing a perfect manuscript by the author, there may be some inadequate parts. Thus, the author would like to seek positive criticisms and rectifications from the experts, teachers, and readers.

The publishing of this book has garnered strong support from Fuchuan Yang, Chief Editor of China Machine Press, and the author would like to express his gratitude here.

Beijing, China Xiaodong Ma

Contents

Part I
Why Do You Implement Digital Transformation?

Digital transformation is the mainstream of modern development. Regardless of the varying reasons why all industries are actively investing in digital transformation, the companies still need to dive deep into the evolving industries and grasp the primary user needs to constantly adapt and change with the times and needs of the consumers. For different types of companies, there are other paths to implement digital transformation. Some may adjust their growth strategies, and some may raise their operating efficiencies. Some may even elevate their user experiences—to find a method suitable for themselves to achieve a successful transformation.

Part I of this book describes the elements driving companies toward digital transformation. And then, we analyze how digitalization disrupts the traditional industries from a macroperspective. In the final part, we discuss the common misconceptions during digital transformation. The purpose of this section is to allow the readers to understand the significance and value of digital transformation and be fully aware of the general trends of digital transformation.

The Significance of Digital Transformation

1

Before implementing digital transformation, companies must understand its significance and future challenges. This Chapter profoundly analyzes the five drivers from the three dimensions of internal environment, external environment, and technical empowerment, as well as the most significant dividend of digital transformation—Dividend Beyond Conformism.

1.1 Five Drivers of Digital Transformation

The five drivers of digital transformation are as follows: the demographic dividend is disappearing fast, persisting trade conflicts between China and the U.S., consumption upgrading, reinforcement of the protection and oversight of the ecosystem, and newly evolving technologies, as shown in Fig. 1.1.

1.1.1 The Demographic Dividend Is Disappearing Fast, and Innovative Development Is Inevitable

The demographic dividend has been disappearing fast with a constant decline in birth rates, an apparent aging population trend, and a labor shortage in China in recent years. The direct impacts on the companies are a labor shortage and ever-increasing labor costs, as shown in Fig. 1.2.

This phenomenon has forced companies to look forward to new digital technologies for innovation and change. Though many companies across the wide-ranging industries have made several attempts in this area, there were only a few success stories. For example, replacing manual labor with industrial robots to perform labor-intensive, high-risk, and procedural tasks; replacing systematic, highly

X. Ma, *Methodology for Digital Transformation*, Management for Professionals,
https://doi.org/10.1007/978-981-19-9111-0_1

Fig. 1.1 Five drivers of digital transformation

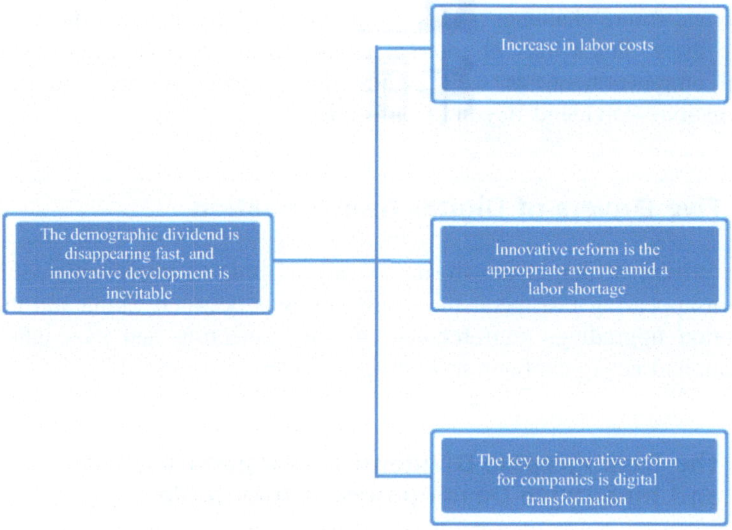

Fig. 1.2 Driver 1 of digital transformation—demographic dividend is disappearing fast

repetitive, low-value manual labor with intelligent RPA robots; improving efficiencies and savings on labor costs with data intelligence, artificial intelligence, and other new technologies.

While companies are employing new technologies for innovation and change, they are essentially undergoing digital transformation in the most basic form. The core elements of digital transformation are technology and data. The best choice for corporate transformation is undoubtedly the digital solution represented by the data platform construction. As the companies have accumulated a large volume of data through their daily activities such as operations, product, production, sales/marketing, customer services, and user interactions, they can seamlessly connect the internal and external data with data intelligence technology, build a data circulation mechanism and support the needs of frontline business departments at all times. Coupled with free circulation and intelligent application of data within the internal departments of the companies, it would continually stimulate the employees in the innovation of data applications and unearth the user needs and new business opportunities hidden beneath the data.

1.1.2 Persisting Trade Conflicts Between China and the U.S. Drive Corporate Restructuring

Since the explosion of Sino-U.S. trade conflicts in the spring of 2018, it had continued persistently for nearly three years. On the one hand, the U.S. has imposed higher tariffs on more than 1000 Chinese imports. It was a double whammy for domestic manufacturers with meager profits. On the other hand, the broadening of Chinese export controls by the U.S. has also affected the growth and survival of certain manufacturers in China.

In summary, the Sino-U.S. trade conflicts certainly harmed all Chinese companies. The most apparent issues caused by the tariff adjustment include escalating procurement costs, barriers to imports and exports, and investment restrictions.

Although the Chinese industrial structure has constantly been subject to adjustments and the structure of exports has also been continually improving, the Chinese exports are comprised mainly of highly replaceable labor-intensive products, which were lacking in international competitiveness. Amid the escalating trade conflicts, companies should transform their growth models, anticipate the potential losses incurred from the trade conflicts and make firm preparation well in advance.

And companies should also adopt a long-term vision, employ new digital technologies in their digital transformation, increase R&D investment and independent innovation, proactively nurture their independent brands with core technologies, and ensure product quality. Besides, companies should employ digital operations to elevate service quality, strengthen product competitiveness, and meet domestic and international market demands. Companies should also unearth the value hidden beneath the data, empower the businesses, expand their product range and increase their market share. In addition, companies should also build a versatile team with the core of empowering their businesses and optimize their corporate management structures and operating models with digital transformation, as shown in Fig. 1.3.

1.1.3 A Higher Market Supply Than Demand Enhances Consumption Upgrading

With the surge of Chinese national disposable incomes amid strong economic growth, consumers have more choices nowadays. Consumers have become more

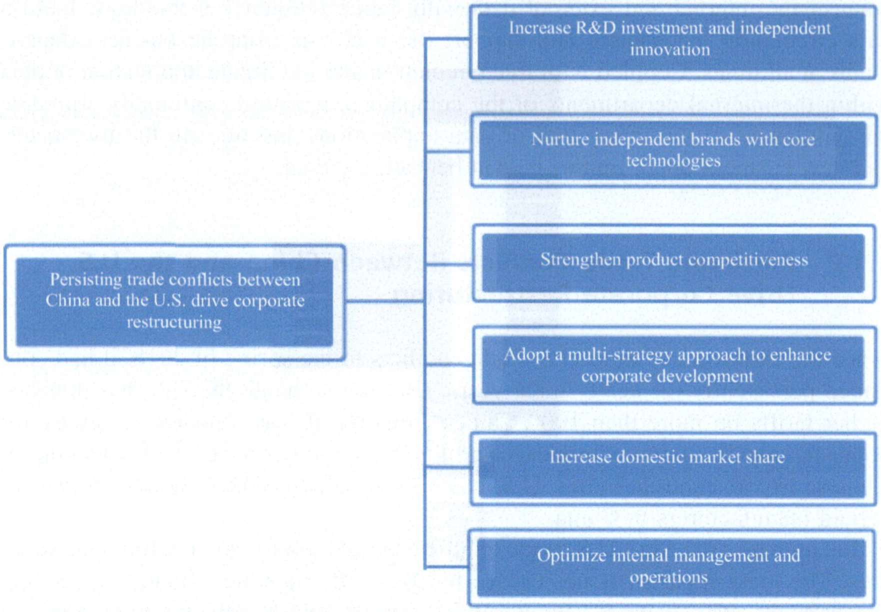

Fig. 1.3 Driver 2 of digital transformation—persisting trade conflicts between China and the U.S

rational in their choice of goods. They are not only concerned about the product quality and prices, but also the brand equity beneath the goods as well as the pre-sales and after-sales services and other user experiences. Many consumers are no longer satisfied with standardized services and are more willing to pay for personalized and customized services.

All of the above are clear indications of consumption upgrading. Consumption upgrading is the result of a higher market supply than demand. As more companies compete in the market, there is a significant change in the relationship between supply and demand, as shown in Fig. 1.4.

Consumption upgrading has shattered the winning ways of traditional companies. In the past, companies could meet market demand by engaging in large-scale, standardized, mass, automated production. Today, this business model can no longer meet the individual needs of consumers. More companies are considering providing personalized, customized goods and services to consumers. In response to this evolving demand, companies can use two methods—The first way is to provide the same goods and services while employing a more refined digital marketing approach to obtain higher user growth. The second way is to restructure the product development and innovation models with the users at its core. Through extensive data analysis, we can understand the user needs and match different goods and services based on varying user profiles so that companies can be sustainable in the competitive market. This approach is a transformation of products with digital technology, and it can provide more precise, demand-oriented goods and services for users.

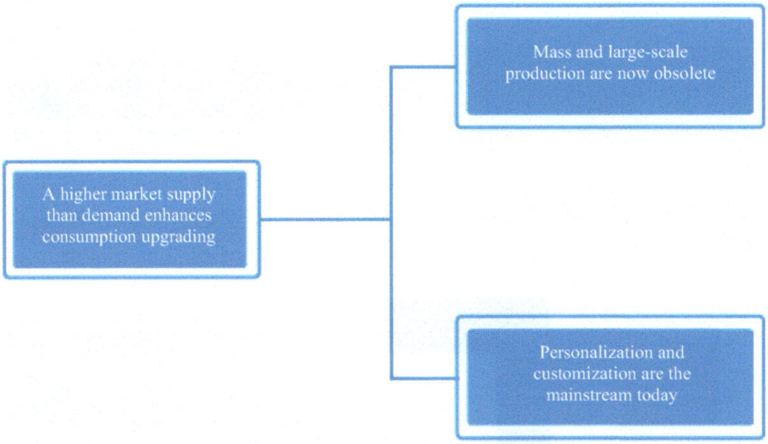

Fig. 1.4 Driver 3 of digital transformation—consumption upgrading

In addition, companies can also apply digital capabilities to a broad spectrum of activities such as production process, operational efficiency, and management quality to achieve digital transformation as a whole.

1.1.4 A Stark Urgency in Ecological Protection Creates the Need for Companies to Transform

In the past, the famous saying "Pollute the environment first before managing it" has become a "shortcut" for domestic companies in their quest for corporate growth. Some companies sacrificed the natural environment in their "constant pursuit of growth". For example, indiscriminate mining has caused environmental pollution around the factories, and industrial waste has caused widespread littering of heavy metals in the rivers. China has endured through the growth phase with tightening resource constraints, severely polluted emissions, overloading of the urban environment, and low ratings for its industries.

In recent years, the central and local governments have constantly strived to raise the requirements for environmental protection. The past rugged development concept has been virtually phased out. Companies need to prepare proper planning for the production, distribution, allocation, and consumption processes, and also employ innovative technologies as essential back-end support to drive transformation for traditional industries and achieve sustainable green development objectives, as shown in Fig. 1.5.

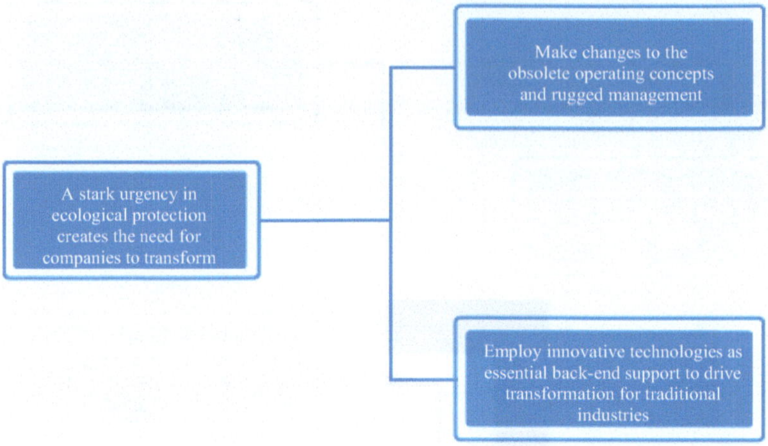

Fig. 1.5 Driver 4 of digital transformation—reinforcement of oversight of ecological protection

As the old way of development at the expense of the environment is no longer viable, companies face new challenges. If companies want sustainable and long-term growth, they must abide by the national initiatives and move in tandem with ecological protection. The two forces of technology and innovation are indispensable during this process. And it is also the objective of digital transformation to seek development with technology and innovation.

Companies must transform their operating models through digital transformation to achieve "environmental operations". Furthermore, companies may perform streamlined operations and reduce waste with digital technologies by building an enclosed loop of data collection, transmission, storage, processing, and feedback.

They may also seamlessly eliminate the data barriers between different levels and departments of the companies by utilizing the data platform. Creating a global data center may uncover the modules in each linking phase that can streamline operations and utilize the same production materials in the past to produce more finished goods to achieve intelligent operations and management. On the other hand, companies can also precisely forecast sales by utilizing digital technologies, achieving the principle of "using sales of goods to replace production" to cut down warehouse inventory.

On top of that, companies can also expand their digital capabilities to the ecological adjustment of businesses, evolving technologies, product creation, brand creativity, and other areas, uncover the possibilities of more streamlined operations and improve the overall operational efficiency and profitability of the company consequently. Digital transformation is not only a wise move to respond to environmental protection in the modern era, but it is also a core element of long-term sustainable growth for all companies.

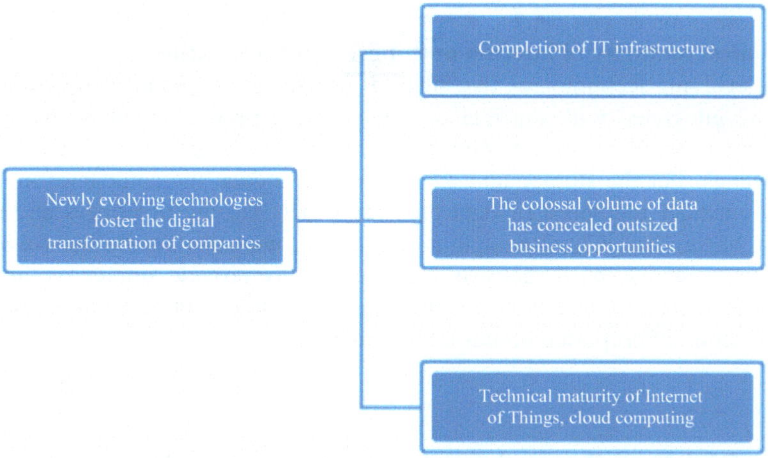

Fig. 1.6 Driver 5 of digital transformation—new evolving technologies

1.1.5 New Technologies Foster the Digital Transformation of Companies

Digital technologies have specified several conditions for traditional companies to roll out digital transformation, as shown in Fig. 1.6. The maturity of technical requirement shall lay the foundation for companies to change their business models.

Regardless of the collaborative development of multiple internal departments of the companies, the construction of an external sales network, the precise implementation of marketing strategies, or even the escalation of customer experience, every phase of the business decision and execution process is correlated to the digital capabilities beneath the new technologies.

1. **Completion of IT infrastructure**
   Companies have completed the IT infrastructure consisting of the operating system, software applications, network/communications, and data management. Implementing these infrastructures can help companies to achieve data interoperability and provide solid environmental support for data mining and analysis.
2. **The colossal volume of data has concealed outsized business opportunities**
   With the increasing application of new technologies such as mobile Internet, the colossal volume of data collated from the individual consumer-end to the product-end of the companies and then to the industrial production-end has brought immense value to the society and economic growth of the country. The volume of data collected by humans in the past few years was equivalent to the total collected over the past few centuries. As different dimensions of the data

can all be accessed, it has provided an abundance of digital assets for the digital transformation of companies.

3 **Technical maturity of internet of things, cloud computing**
New evolving technologies like Internet of Things and cloud computing have deeply integrated with the real economy. Every production phase has generated a large volume of data embedded within the companies with the Internet of Things. For the storage and analysis of these data, the companies must not only consider the speed of data processing but also the timeliness and sensitivity of the data. Cloud computing can help companies handle the volume of data generated in each scenario and dynamically provide storage, computing, network resources, and fast response. Thus, cloud computing technology is the cornerstone of corporate digital transformation.

1.2 Dividend Beyond Conformism—Biggest Dividend of Digitalization

In the past, most companies have survived mainly from dividends derived from open markets. Some fearless entrepreneurs were the first few to seize the opportunities to expand their market share. Within the last 20 years, however, the factors of production, such as labor, and resources, have been rapidly changing. As these changes reach the technological singularity in the next few years, the companies that have relied on dividends derived from the open market in the past have still not engaged in any innovation. They still operate traditionally as usual. These companies are both large in size and very slow in their movements. While they still appear to be the industry's leading companies, their market share is sharply declining. However, these companies can maintain their businesses within a certain period.

A formula is often used in corporate operations management: Labor Costs + Resources Costs + Other Costs = Total Costs. Today, labor costs are continually on the uptrend, and the costs of the resources used by companies are also rising. If traditional companies still engage in their traditional operating protocols, they may end up with negative profits. Under such circumstances, the market would have a huge business opportunity. In other words, using new ways to facilitate the transformation has created a winning formula for business success.

There are two types of transformation. The first type is the application of the latest technologies by startups to raise efficiencies, reduce labor and resources costs, achieve profitability and become the industry's new leaders. The second type is a second rejuvenated entrepreneurship by traditional companies, utilizing digital transformation to provide a new lease of life for their businesses.

Whether it is the startups disrupting all industries or the second rejuvenated entrepreneurship by the traditional companies, it is fundamentally the use of digital means to lower labor and resources costs, raise efficiencies and achieve profitability. Among them is a concealment of a considerable dividend, namely the

"Dividend Beyond Conformism," proposed by the Economist, Fan He. Although it may seem that everyone is working on their assignments, most are "Conformists" in the company. All you need is to be a little more hardworking to enjoy this special dividend.

Those companies that keep relying on the old singular profitability model without transformation concepts are "Conformists." In contrast, those companies brave enough to innovate and use new technologies can employ digital means to grasp the new opportunities in the market and unearth the "Dividend Beyond Conformism."

Every industry contains a vast "Dividend Beyond Conformism." It is worthwhile to use digital technologies to reshape their business models. "Dividend Beyond Conformism" is a new type of dividend derived from a company's digital transformation, and it is also the most significant dividend brought about by the transformation itself. Through digital transformation, companies can employ new technologies to identify new business opportunities in areas where others have often neglected, precisely position themselves in the market, quickly take appropriate actions and consistently work on their plans for the long term. Company leaders with long-term visions can lead their teams to implement second rejuvenated entrepreneurship and regain their position at the peak of profitability in the whole industry. "Dividend Beyond Conformism" can help old companies to maintain or leap into the leading position in the industry amid the turbulent digital waves.

Those new startups would face intense competition from the old companies. With the immense pressure to survive in the industry, it is much easier for startups to find the "Dividend Beyond Conformism," creating highly effective digital capabilities and disrupting the whole industry with light battleground equipment.

Three Types of Digital Disruptions to Traditional Companies

2

Digital transformation has long been a consensus among companies at home and abroad, and the proliferation of digital disruption to the traditional industries has inspired more companies to be passionate about digital transformation. This Chapter comprehensively outlines the analysis in detail of how digitalization disrupts the traditional industries from the three dimensions of strategic level, efficiency level and user experience, and discusses the misconceptions of digital transformation.

2.1 Disrupting Traditional Industries from the Strategic Level

By disrupting traditional industries from the strategic level, the key is in the transformation of a company with a new business model. In other words, the outcome of a digital transformation is reshaping a company's business model. Take an example of a customer from Guoyun Data. The customer is a renowned retail company, and it has been consistently ranked No. 1 in the industry. As a famous brand, however, the company can only sell its products to C-users via the supply chain and distributors, and it can merely sell its goods and cannot directly obtain user data.

When the company transformed its previous business model to a digital model of S2B2C and converted itself from a company with a famous brand to a platform merchant, the sales of its goods substantially surged. The specific measures are introduced in more detail in Chapter 22 (Fig. 2.1).

The transformation of this business model is entirely built on top of the digital capabilities, which we call digital intelligence business.

Disrupting the industries from the business models (or strategic level) requires a substantial accumulation of industrial experiences and resources by the company and firm reserves of digital capabilities. Consequently, many companies do not

X. Ma, *Methodology for Digital Transformation*, Management for Professionals,
https://doi.org/10.1007/978-981-19-9111-0_2

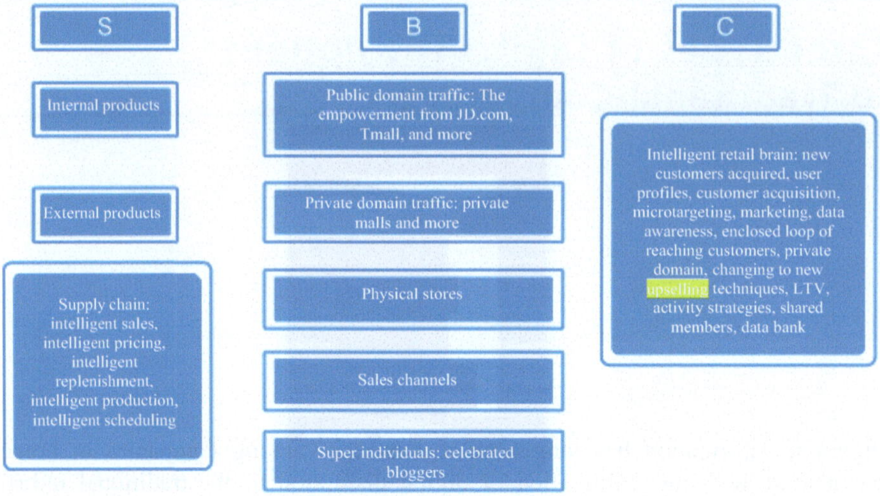

Fig. 2.1 Digital business model

fare well in their digital transformation. There are few successful cases of transformation for companies in the traditional industries from the perspective of the business models.

2.2 Disrupting Traditional Industries from the Efficiency Level

Apart from disrupting business models from the strategic level, the companies can also achieve the objectives of digital transformation from the efficiency level. The critical issue of disrupting traditional industries lies with the efficiency of transformation. While keeping the same products and strategies (i.e., business models) constant, the companies are implementing a transformation based on efficiency. The modern father of management education, Peter Drucker, once said, "A decline in costs of more than 30% is known as disruption."

If the companies want to disrupt the traditional industries from the efficiency level, they can begin to step in by escalating their efficiencies on the one hand. As shown in Fig. 2.2, the daily operations of a specific retail company often experience multiple operational phases, including traffic, customers, product services, factory productions, and warehousing logistics, each of which involves a multidimensional operation. Improving the efficiency of a single phase does not affect the company's overall efficiency. When the efficiency of each phase is improved, the overall efficiency is affected. As exhibited by this formula of Traffic x User × Product × Production × Logistics × Others = Efficiency, if the efficiency of each phase of the company has improved by 1.1, then the overall efficiency of the 10 phase shall improve by 2.56 times. Likewise, if the efficiency of a single phase is improved by 1, the overall efficiency is still 1, as shown in Fig. 2.3. As the diagram shows below, there are significant differences in overall efficiency between every phase and a single phase.

Furthermore, disrupting traditional industries from the efficiency level can also begin by lowering costs. The company costs include the costs of many phases in a business life cycle, including customer acquisition, delivery, and production. If the cost of a specific product of a company is $10, the cost in each of the 10 phases has been reduced by 1 to 10%, or if the cost in each phase has been reduced by $0.1, the final cost would be reduced to $9, as shown in Fig. 2.4. Companies with low costs are more likely to stand out in a highly competitive market, enabling them to build their core competencies.

Companies can begin from the operations perspective to elevate the efficiencies of their daily operations and shore up their market competitiveness as a result.

There were many cases of disrupting traditional industries from the efficiency level. As the efficiency of any phase in the operational chain of the company can be improved, it is possible to disrupt the whole industry.

Take an example in the sales phase. In the past, the sales team used to sell their products through door-to-door visits and telephone calls. Assuming the sales team meets 10 potential customers, and maybe 8 of them do not need the products, the final sales transaction is only 2 based on verbal persuasion during the sales process.

To date, companies use digital tools to generate profiles for their customers. These profiles can help the sales team understand the customer's needs in advance and propose targeted solutions for them. During home visits, the sales team can utilize this solution to negotiate more effectively and achieve a higher customer conversion rate. Take a particular scenario of having the same sales team with constant capability, motivation, and working hours, who have also met 10 potential customers. But these 10 potential customers are carefully selected by the company's digital platform, which accurately predicts an 80% chance of closing a sale. In addition, the sales team can also devise personalized solutions and customized consultations for their customers with the digital tools provided by the company, rather than adhering to regular, standardized sales techniques. A total of 7 deals are made in the end.

From the example given above, under constant conditions, there are only 2 sales transactions without digital empowerment while there are 7 sales transactions with digital empowerment. Hence the efficiency of a sales team has increased by 3.7 times.

Apart from raising efficiency in the customer acquisition area, the companies can also improve efficiency in other phases like delivery, and production, escalating the overall operating efficiency.

The efficiency in different phases and roles of the company can be substantially elevated with digital empowerment. When the efficiencies of many phases in a company are higher than the industry average, the company gets several times higher efficiency than the traditional industries, disrupting the other companies in the same industry.

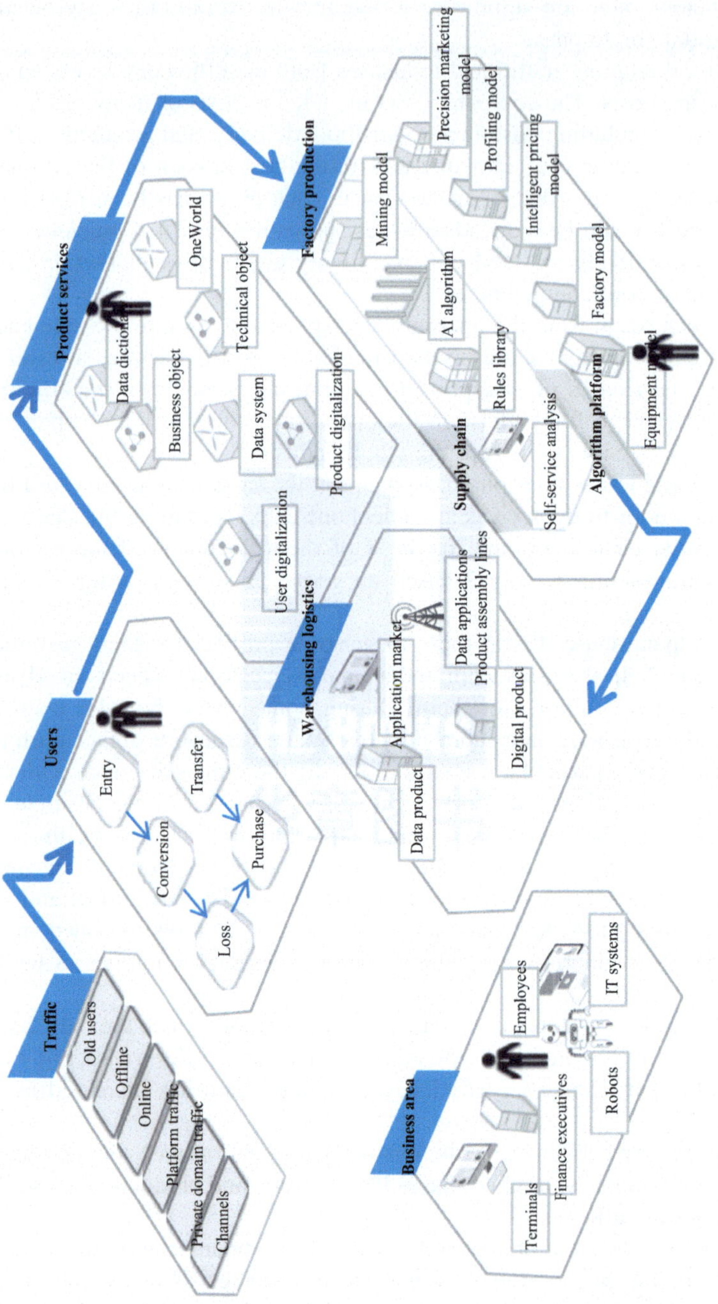

Fig. 2.2 Disrupting traditional industries from the efficiency level

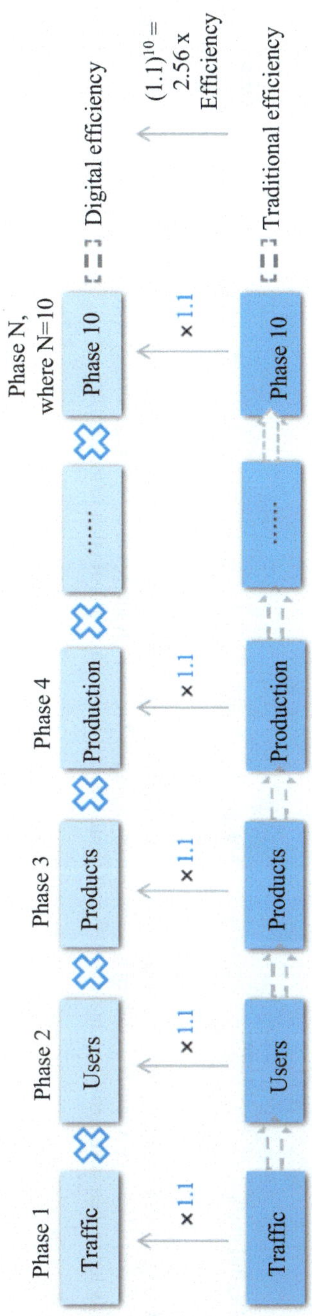

Fig. 2.3 Digital efficiency formula. *Note* If there are 10 critical phases, where N=10 and each phase has improved its efficiency by 1.1, the cumulative effect of the 10 phases is 2.56 (improved digital efficiency). However, while the traditional efficiency improvement is on a single node submerged in all 10 phases, there is no effect on the overall efficiency

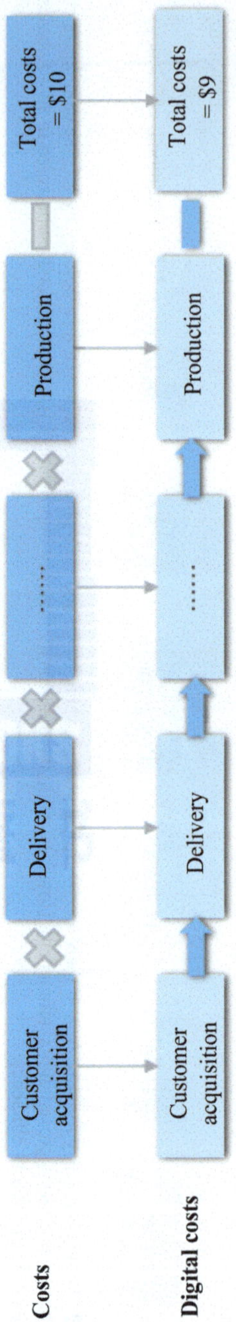

Fig. 2.4 Digital cost formula. *Note* The overall cost effect is insignificant when one or two costs are reduced. If the cost of each phase is reduced cumulatively, the overall cost advantage would be significant. If companies can utilize the cost advantages to expand their scale of operations, reinforce relevant measures, and virtuously lower their costs again to achieve a 30% cost reduction, that is known as a disruption to the industry

In conclusion, not only can companies disrupt the traditional industries from the strategic level, but they can also improve their efficiencies in different operations, achieving efficiency improvement and enhancing their market competitiveness.

2.3 Disrupting Traditional Industries from the User Experience

In disrupting traditional industries' user experience, the key is to enhance the user experience under the circumstances of no significant changes in the business model and operating efficiency to capture a larger market share.

It is widespread when the market supply is more significant than the demand. In such a scenario, the consumers would be spoilt for choices since the market is flooded with excess goods. As a result, the consumers would turn their focus to the user experience.

What is a good user experience?

When you need it, it would immediately appear in front of you. That is an example of a good experience.

The products and services provided by mobile payment are the same as that provided by banks. However, the convenience of mobile payment has disrupted the payment methods of credit cards and cash. Hence, it has also disrupted the whole banking industry.

Let's take a look at another example. As some e-commerce merchants or logistics companies have offered services like the next-day or same-day delivery of parcels, even if their unit prices are slightly higher than other platforms, the users are more willing to buy into their services. These services' fulfillment largely depends on the large volume of data intelligence technologies. In the offline situation, if the goods are not in the warehouses, they cannot be purchased and delivered. Data intelligence technologies can help retail companies pinpoint the exact location of the goods at all times and rearrange the logistical routes. By doing this, the turnover of goods has been lowered with data intelligence technologies. Many users have selected the next-day delivery option of the goods because they love the unique feature of receiving their goods quickly. That is also another classic example of disrupting traditional industries from the user experience.

Disrupting traditional industries from the user experience has significantly reduced the company's customer acquisition cost and substantially reduced the costs of customer loss and user growth. Consequently, companies can strive to focus on providing better user experiences for the customers to disrupt the whole industry.

So, what is the value of a good user experience?

When buying a product, consumers can experience some personalized services delicately designed by the merchant. Companies can diplomatically deliver their corporate values with this method. Today, good user experience has become a new marketing model. It can bring about higher business value for companies.

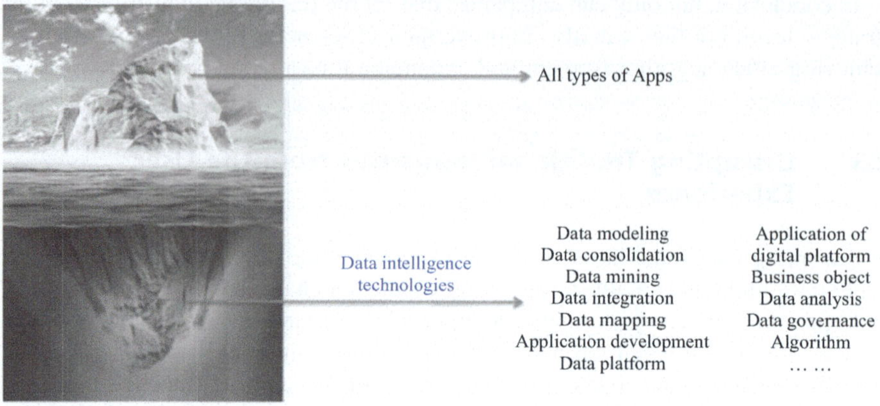

Fig. 2.5 Data intelligence beneath the user experiences

To provide good user experiences for the users, companies would need to showcase their products and services on the screen of the internet (such as all types of Apps) and superior data intelligence technologies to meet the user experience needs of thousands of individually unique consumers, as shown in Fig. 2.5.

Most of the time, when some companies embrace the internet, they only identify all types of applications sitting on top of the "iceberg" while neglecting the colossal volume of data intelligence technologies sitting beneath it. These technologies decide whether companies can provide the core values of a good user experience.

Take the example of Taobao. In Taobao, I worked with their technical teams to conduct intelligent processing based on the consumers' different usage habits, non-use periods, and usage areas. Although users may find that there have been no significant changes to the main interface of Taobao for a long time, different users view the interface in a completely different way. That is the effect of "thousands of individually unique consumers," which has been accomplished by the data intelligence technologies of the Taobao teams.

With the ever-changing and evolving technologies, the user experiences in every industry likely are significantly enhanced in the future, breeding a new wave of opportunities to disrupt the industry.

2.4 Two Misconceptions of Digital Transformation

While discussing digital transformation, some companies believe that a transformation is achieved by correctly using appropriate IT technologies. And some companies also believe that digital transformation only needs to restructure the business models, and it is not essential to bring in new technologies. These two completely biased perceptions are the two most common misconceptions of digital transformation.

1. **Technologies drive digital transformation**

Many companies maintain that technologies drive digital transformation, which is not valid. Although technologies play an essential role during digital transformation, it does not mean that companies would only need the correct deployment of technologies to achieve digital transformation.

Regardless of the Industrial Revolution, Information Age, or the Digital Era, transformation and growth are mainly driven by the overwhelming needs of society. These types of needs represent the interests of the broad user base. It also reiterates that the fundamental of all businesses is to understand the users' needs. If companies want to understand the users' needs, they need to begin from the user's perspectives and use data to dissect the user needs to provide personalized products and services.

How do companies gain insights into their user profiles? Data must be applied to every phase, such as R&D, production, and marketing. And decision-making is solely dependent on data. That is also the essence of digital transformation. As a result, digital transformation is driven by the users.

In addition, users would have higher expectations from the companies when they experience more personalized services. If a company cannot meet the users' needs, the users would switch to another service provider. A real example is a bank. In the past, it was commonplace for everyone to process their banking needs at the bank counters. To date, however, more people are accustomed to processing their banking needs with their mobile phones. That is a testament to the users' higher expectations with the implementation of digital transformation by the banks. If the banks cannot meet the user's needs in a timely manner, they may be in danger of bankruptcy. It would then drive the banks to implement digital transformation from the user's perspectives. Digital transformation is not driven by technologies, but rather it is driven by the users.

Faced with the personalized needs of the users, companies need to dissect their users into different layers, groups, and categories, providing different products to different users at different periods. Most importantly, it is very critical for companies to achieve the objective above, especially the To C companies. Though they cannot provide one-to-one service for many customers, they can not only precisely understand the user needs by analyzing the user profiles with data but also rapidly provide matching services. Companies must provide products and services to their users at the core, which is also the key to driving digital transformation.

The fundamentals of businesses are to understand their users with their core of creating and transmitting values. Companies can only uncover their business core with insights of understanding their users.

2. **Misconception 2: Digital transformation is only a restructuring of the business models**

Some companies figure that digital transformation is only a strategic issue and merely the restructuring of their business models. This biased view is incomplete as it does not encompass the fundamentals of digital transformation.

There are many theories in the market discussing the true meaning of digital transformation. What is digital transformation? Most of the listed examples were discussions about restructuring business models, which were strategic disruptions. Take a look at Didi and Uber, for example. Apart from disrupting industries from the strategic level, transformation can also be achieved by boosting efficiencies and user experiences.

With the rapid development of internet technologies in mainland China, companies have few opportunities to transform and innovate their business models because those equipped with internet technologies have become pioneers in trying all sorts of business models. For traditional companies, there are very few success stories of digital transformation that begin with the transformation of their business models. Whether it is appropriate for companies to implement digital transformation by transforming their business models would still require further discussion and analysis. The industrial fields in which traditional companies can transform their business models have been disrupted in the past decades.

Many believe that digital transformation is only suitable for those industries with the opportunity to transform their business models. Transforming business models is only one of the ways of digital transformation. If companies only depend on transforming their business models to achieve the efficiency objective, it is more challenging to transform their businesses digitally. The reason is that some companies business models have already matured, and there is no more room for any possible transformation. Instead, the same objective can be achieved by raising efficiencies or enhancing user experiences.

Part II
When Do You Implement Digital Transformation?

When should companies implement digital transformation? Right now, or wait for a while more? The answer is to do it right now.

Digital transformation is an unstoppable and inevitable wave of change. The strong push for the "Construction of New Infrastructure" initiative and the abrupt new coronavirus pandemic in 2020 have forced companies to implement digital transformation immediately.

Digitalization has fastened the pace of industrial evolution, giving rise to new service models and operating concepts.

Digitalization has disrupted the industrial leaders of the traditional generation and incubated new industrial giants.

Digitalization has driven industrial innovations, disrupted the competitive order, and given birth to new industrial players.

Regardless of the impact of digital transformation on the whole industry, companies need to understand the modern trends of digital transformation and its current advantages and disadvantages.

Consequently, this section first describes the necessity of digital transformation for companies. It then concisely lists the timeline for digital transformation so that different companies can grapple with the valuable opportunity to begin their digitalization journeys, achieving their digital objectives with less time. It also provides a timeline for the reference of digital transformation in each industry so that the readers are fully aware of the urgency of digital transformation for all companies.

New-Born Species of Digitalization 3

Digitalization has brought about outsized changes in all industries. This Chapter demonstrates the urgency of digital transformation for companies from three perspectives: acceleration of industrial evolution with digitalization, the birth of new industrial giants, and new industrial players.

3.1 Digitalization Accelerates the Industrial Evolution

In modern society, most people can get their daily necessities without stepping out of their houses. The ongoing use of WeChat, online video, communications, and entertainment applications has constantly met the mental health needs of people at large. The internet has comprehensively infiltrated the ordinary lives of most people.

3.1.1 The Prevalence of Digital Intelligence Speeds Up the Obsolescence of Industries

What is the objective of digital intelligence? It is to meet the needs of people who strive to have a better life with new methods based on developing relevant industries using digital technologies.

Digital intelligence is reflected in every aspect of our lives and is evidence of industries' rapid evolution. In the present era, innovations are commonplace to disrupt traditional industries. For example, electronic toll systems have gradually replaced the toll operators. The birth of self-serviced banks has raised serious concerns from bank employees over their "iron bowls"; self-serviced supermarkets have caused unemployment among personal shoppers and cashiers; intelligent robots have slowly supplanted the customer service representatives from call centers…

X. Ma, *Methodology for Digital Transformation*, Management for Professionals,
https://doi.org/10.1007/978-981-19-9111-0_3

3.1.2 Leading Industries of Digital Companies

In the digital era, the rapid development of the Chinese economy shows an enormous consumption potential that attracts both domestic and foreign companies. And digital capabilities have become the core competitiveness of all companies and a modern trend across all industries, especially in the internet, media, government, and capital-intensive industries. It does not indicate that all companies benefit from it, and only those embracing digitalization become the next generation of leaders in their respective industries. These companies include new companies that employ digital technologies as their foundations and those old traditional companies with active investments in digital transformation.

The new companies that employ digital technologies as their foundations are the first to benefit from the digital era. Compared with traditional companies, these companies will more proactively deploy digital technologies to expand their business capabilities and capture market share quickly. The pace of development for these types of companies has far surpassed the industrial average. As shown in Fig. 3.1, the average growth rates of GMV (gross merchandise value) of new brands of flavorful food, nutritional food, beverages, and cosmetics industries during the "Double 11 Shopping Carnival" (the Chinese Singles' Day) in 2019 were 8.5, 13, 15.9 and 3 times higher than that of the industrial average as a whole, respectively. In addition, the promising growth of companies empowered by digital technologies has also sparked new enthusiasm for other companies in the quest to implement digital transformation.

The growth rates of the old traditional companies with active investments in digital transformation have also surpassed other companies in the same industry. During the "Double 11 Shopping Carnival" in 2019, the average growth rate of the flavorful food industry was 22%, while the average growth rate of GMV of the old traditional companies with active investments in digital transformation was 41%, 1.9-fold that of the industrial average. The average growth rate of GMV in the nutritional food industry was 17%, and the average growth rate of GMV of the old traditional companies with active investments in digital transformation was 31%, 1.8-fold that of the industrial average.

3.2 Digitalization Drives the New Industrial Giants

Many companies have always wished to implement digital transformation quickly and successfully with the final objectives of raising efficiencies and lowering business costs. To achieve this objective, each company must put much effort and financial resources in place. With the gradual adoption of digital transformation among all companies, new industrial giants are generated within the respective industries.

Companies must implement digital transformation if they want to become industrial giants. Strategy, business, operations, and organizational structure transformation are critical during the digital transformation process. The digital

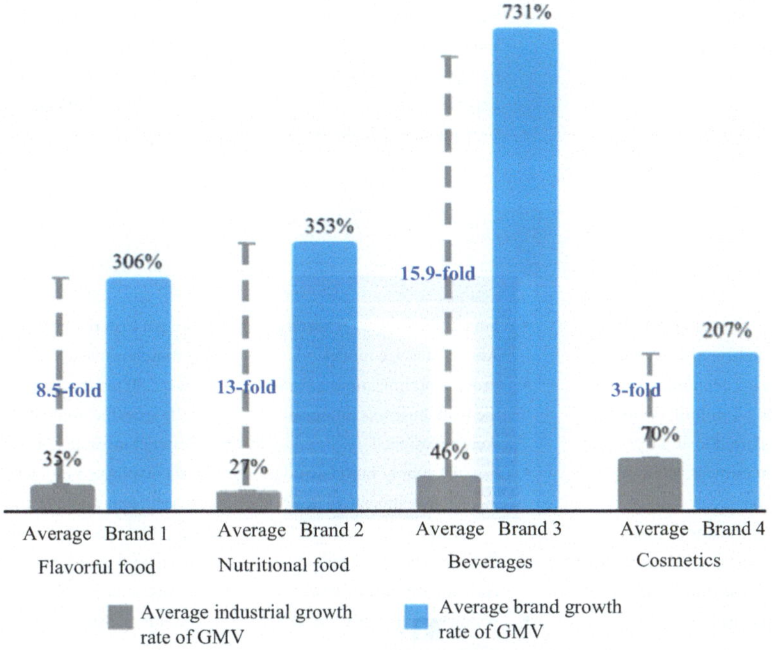

Fig. 3.1 The growth rate of digital companies has far surpassed that of the industrial average

transformation of a particular foreign bank is a successful example of digital transformation in the financial sector.

The digital transformation milestones of a particular foreign bank included 3 phases of merger and consolidation, superior operations and digitalization, and comprehensive channels, as shown in Fig. 3.2.

First, the bank merged with another in other business fields, expanding its customer base and improving its multi-channel service concept. At the same time, the bank transferred millions of its customers to a standardized IT platform backed by the model of scaling up its businesses and reducing costs. It was the first step of digital transformation for the bank.

After that, the bank changed its original service model, employing the standardization of the "Directly Above" service model, redesigning and optimizing most of the business processes such that the daily banking activities were more straightforward, convenient, transparent, and the supplies were more rational.

Last but not least, the bank derived a unique, comprehensive channel experience with its core concept of "providing digitally innovative products and services." Its teams adopted agile working methods to achieve the transfer at ease between different channels, as well as the digitalization of everything and the effects of more personalized and appropriate products and services.

In the digital transformation process, the bank significantly lowered labor costs and simultaneously raised efficiencies.

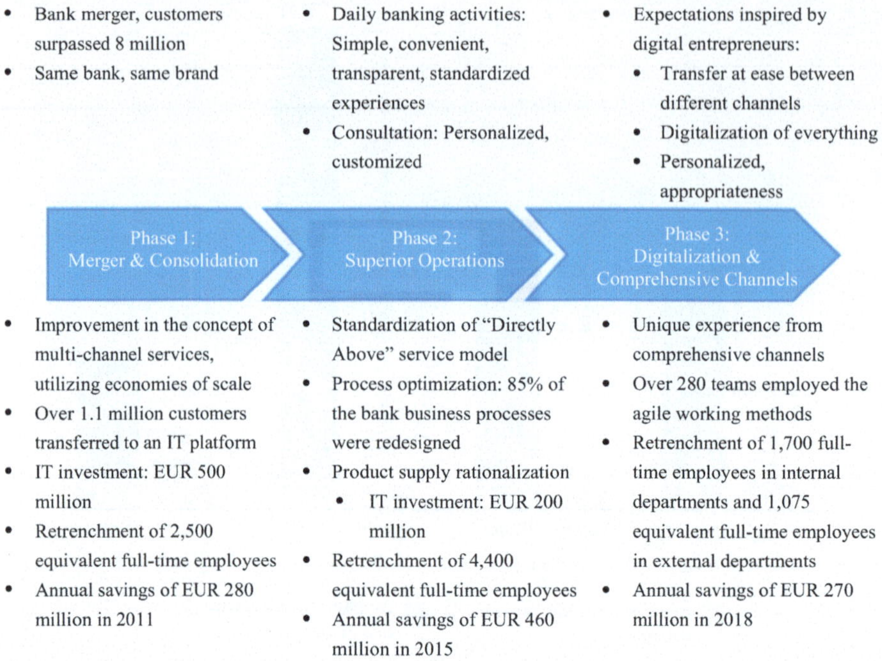

Fig. 3.2 Digital transformation milestones of a particular foreign bank

To date, the businesses of the bank span across the globe, and its branches are scattered around many countries. It has become the new generation of bank giants in the financial sector around the world. Its implementation path and methodology of digital transformation have also become a sampling template for many global companies.

In retrospect, every major revolution would create a batch of new industrial giants. And the previous traditional industrial leaders would quietly exit from the economic battleground as they could not keep up with the rapid development pace. Under the new wave of digital transformation, companies in all industries should grasp the opportunities, select the correct methods and actively implement digital transformation.

3.3 Digital Transformation Boosts the Newly Emerging Industrial Companies

In the digital era, data processing technology is developing at an unprecedented pace. Data has become the core resource of competition among companies, and they capture more market share by utilizing digital technology. A drive for digital transformation in an active way inevitably boosts market competitiveness and also disrupts the competitive order, even bringing about a new generation of new industrial players.

In the traditional consumer markets, there was a wide range of varying service categories of companies. It was a remarkable phenomenon in which every company in all different industries was freely competing and flourishing in different forms and styles. And the number of companies falling under the same service category (often known as peers) was large, with intense competition simultaneously. For example, many gaming brand technologies with R&D and marketing as their objectives have very similar technical competencies, and there is little to differentiate between them, making it harder to stand out in the ultracompetitive markets.

Today, companies can utilize deep data resources and technical capabilities to fasten the pace of digital transformation, develop products that meet the user needs and be the first to capture the vast consumer markets to break the competitive deadlock. The development of digital technologies encourages talented people who are adept at innovations or startups to participate in market competition, transforming them into new industrial players. Under the oversight of the markets, these new industrial players capture a particular market share with price discounts, and even provide free products and services to achieve their objectives. These companies regularly intensify their R&D capabilities and optimize their products and services to maintain market share and creative vitality.

In summary, digital transformation drives companies to employ new technologies to raise their product quality and service levels, enhance the innovative capabilities of all industries to bring about a new batch of new industrial players, and make significant changes to the competitive order of the markets.

4 Two Primary Reasons to Speed Up Digital Transformation

In Chap. 1, we analyzed and discussed the five drivers of digital transformation. The strong drive of the new initiative of the "Construction of New Infrastructure" in China is a new motivation to push for digital transformation. The abrupt new coronavirus pandemic in 2020 has had grave impacts on the global economic growth and the lives of the Chinese people, and it has also forced many companies to actively seek viable alternatives, further accelerating the pace of digital transformation.

4.1 The "Construction of New Infrastructure" Initiative Has Sped Up the Pace of Digitalization

During the Industrial Revolution, the traditional construction of basic infrastructure was mainly referred to as the project "Basic Infrastructure of Railway and Public Roads." In other words, it referred to several construction projects for the railway, public roads, airports, seaports, and water conservancy facilities.

In the digital era, the definition of the construction of basic infrastructure has also changed. "Construction of New Infrastructure" is fundamentally the construction of basic intelligent infrastructure. It primarily refers to constructing basic software and hardware related to data, including networks, data platforms, cloud computing platforms, and basic software. The "Construction of New Infrastructure" is based on the concept of innovations and development, driven by technologies and having an information network as its foundation. As a central pillar of support and foundation of economic growth for the future, the "Construction of New Infrastructure" accelerates digital transformation for companies.

X. Ma, *Methodology for Digital Transformation*, Management for Professionals,
https://doi.org/10.1007/978-981-19-9111-0_4

1. **The traditional construction of basic infrastructure has driven the economic growth of the country**

The traditional construction of infrastructures such as high-speed rail, highways, and airports are constantly improving. On top of narrowing the distance between cities and villages, the construction of these basic infrastructures has also provided convenience to the lives of urban and rural people, created massive employment opportunities, driven the economic exchanges and development of different regions, and proactively enhanced the social and economic development of the country.

2. **The "Construction of New Infrastructure" speeds up the pace of digital transformation for companies**

As a new generation of information technology empowers the traditional manufacturing sector to transform and upgrade, the "Construction of New Infrastructure" has also brought about new scenario applications. In particular, under the severe impact on the national economy and society by the new coronavirus pandemic in 2020, there has been a critical focus on constructing new infrastructure in the medical field, including medical information.

Apart from the construction of new infrastructure in the medical field, the other "Construction of New Infrastructure" includes the construction of basic infrastructure in critical industries such as 5G, ultra-high voltage, intercity high-speed rail and intercity rail transport, industrial internet, electric vehicle charging stations, big data centers, and artificial intelligence that affect the livelihoods of the people. All these are the application directive of the "Construction of New Infrastructure" in general. In the big data centers, IT equipment manufacturers, IDC integrated service providers, cloud computing companies, and software companies can strengthen their collaboration and achieve a win–win under the strict guidance of the "Construction of New Infrastructure."

The development of the "Construction of New Infrastructure" has not only reinforced the awareness of the people toward digital technologies but has also provided firm support in transforming traditional industries with big data and uncovering new market opportunities. For example, the emergence of new phenomena such as the sales of goods in live streaming sessions, social e-commerce merchants, car sharing, and autonomous driving have been closely associated with the "Construction of New Infrastructure."

A strong push for the "Construction of New Infrastructure" undoubtedly speeds up the pace of digital transformation for companies. The profitability of companies, on the one hand, is somewhat limited during an economic downturn. But if the companies can proactively use digital technologies with the underlying "Construction of New Infrastructure" to implement a digital transformation, they can overcome the obstacles faced during their development phase. In addition, the push for the development of the initiative of the "Construction of New Infrastructure" has also, to a certain extent, driven the progress of integrating digital technologies into each industry. Integrating digital technologies with each industry does not only refer to the basic construction of network technologies. However, it has a deeper meaning. It is a deep dive into the various internal departments of the companies in the industry, profoundly integrating digital technologies with the business and facilitating the development pace. First, it can help companies implement digital technologies in different industries. Second, it can also help companies uncover new business opportunities.

In conclusion, developing the "Construction of New Infrastructure" has expanded the application scope of digital technologies, fastening the pace of digital transformation for companies.

4.2 The New Coronavirus Pandemic Spurs the Pace of Digitalization for Companies

At the beginning of 2020, the new coronavirus pandemic outbreak severely dampened the spring festival's joyful spirit. The national economy and livelihoods of the people virtually came to a standstill during this sudden pandemic. The delay of work resumption was commonplace, opening school hours, and many industries, particularly the food and beverage, tourism, movie, and other cultural entertainment industries, were in a dire state. Some companies closed down with long sustained periods of mandatory closure.

With the heavy economic losses incurred during the pandemic, companies started integrating digital technologies with their operations management, achieving a lower cost structure with higher efficiencies through digital transformation.

Under the constant pandemic threat, it was not the first time companies had taken the initiative to transform themselves. During the SARS outbreak of 2003, Alibaba rolled out Taobao in tandem with the market trends, developed an e-commerce platform, and accelerated the development of the e-commerce industry in China. Similarly, many online activities have been carried out during this new coronavirus pandemic, gradually pushing the momentum for many companies' digital transformation.

During the pandemic, the tourism industry was hit hard with ever-plunging revenue. It created an urgency for the tourism industry to develop a new strategy for survival purposes. Many tourism companies successfully employed online broadcasting tools, including live streaming, cloud tourism, and online sceneries, to continue their businesses. It enhanced tourism products' exposure, raised the user penetration rate, and promoted many other business products. All these creative efforts have warmed up the momentum for tourism recovery post-pandemic. As the employees could not return to work in the manufacturing industry amid the raging pandemic, production had to be suspended. The supply of raw materials was also disrupted by the malfunctioning supply chains, resulting in delayed production schedules. Despite all challenges, some companies engaged in remote control management via the big data platform of IoT to ensure smooth production momentum.

Moreover, many companies in mainland China have also been proactively using digital technologies to seek new business opportunities and provide more online activities for their users. For example, they have been actively developing data platforms in the travel and medical sectors, providing timely support for the prevention and control of the coronavirus. They used big data technologies to share medical information in real-time, utilized positioning technology to obtain the exact location of any individual and employed network technologies and intelligent terminals to deploy telemedicine services.

When Do You Implement Digital Transformation?

5

When do companies begin with their digital transformation? The answer is that the earlier, the better, while the best is to start right now. So, are there any references for the transformation timeline? This Chapter examines this issue in detail.

5.1 Opportunities for Digital Transformation

Today, some companies have successfully implemented digital transformation. Some may have just started, while some may have already firmly progressed into their next phase of business growth. The majority of the companies, however, have still not engaged in any transformation at all. That is because there is a timeline for a massive explosion of digital transformation in every industry. The digital penetration rate is different for every industry, so the timeline for implementing digital transformation is thus different. Take a look at the retail and finance industries. These two industries have already experienced digitalization in a much earlier period of time. Many companies in these industries have been implementing digital transformation now. While the digital penetration rate for traditional industries like agriculture is relatively lower, these traditional industries still have to begin with their digital transformation.

So, when do companies begin with their digital transformation? Do you take the lead to start the process first If the majority of the companies in the same industry still have not started with their digital transformation? The answer is definitely. That is akin to the principle of "get it when you arrive first." When most companies within the same industry have not started with their digital transformation, some companies may have tried doing it first. Although the outcome may be a success or a failure, the daring company would have a better chance of disrupting the industry if it is successful in its digital transformation.

X. Ma, *Methodology for Digital Transformation*, Management for Professionals,
https://doi.org/10.1007/978-981-19-9111-0_5

Companies that have not started with their digital transformation must grasp the opportunities fast. The first step is to consolidate the unique conditions and strengths of digital transformation and immediately engage in the transformation.

5.1.1 Price Scissors Theory

Digital transformation is a long-term project. Companies must start to implement digital transformation now. From the long-term perspective, companies can benefit from implementing digital transformation and gain sustainable improvement in their efficiencies, optimization of their management, innovation of their product offerings, and growth of their businesses. Companies must implement digital transformation at the earliest possible and gain superior advantages of having early digital capabilities and be ahead of those companies that have yet to carry out any digital transformation or have started the transformation slightly later. As depicted in Fig. 5.1, the price scissors theory shows that as time passes, the labor cost of companies is increasingly higher while the digital cost is increasingly lower. Before the intersection of digital and labor costs, the labor cost is lower than the digital cost. Maybe it is because some companies are reluctant to grasp the opportunity to implement digital transformation. If companies are waiting until the inflection point (intersection point) before they begin their digital transformation, they lag behind other companies. There is a time lag for digital transformation before the companies can see its actual effect. After the digital cost and the labor cost converges at the inflection point, the labor cost of companies is higher than the digital cost. Some companies believe that "they can replace digital transformation with additional staff, which is cheaper than technological investment." That is an incorrect viewpoint. Once the inflection point is reached, companies' digital capabilities significantly empower and enable their business growth.

A company's digital transformation is a process of spiral development, and it is a newly emerging idea that needs to undergo several processes. Likely, there are few successful digital transformation stories, and many companies cannot find any

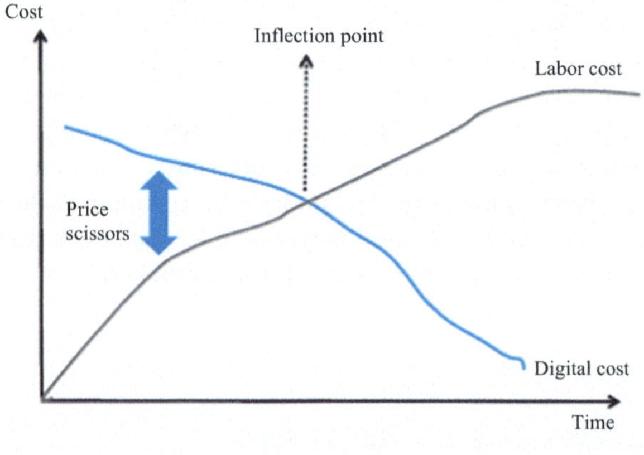

Fig. 5.1 Price scissors theory

prior references for guidance. Or there may be some successful digital transformation stories, but because there are significant differences in the development scale and strength between the companies, the likelihood of having any viable references is lower. As a result, companies must go through a spiral development process of independent exploration, continual trial-and-error, and rectification based on their specific conditions coupled with integrating their mature external experiences.

During this process, some companies may have the mistaken view that they can emulate the successes of other companies to achieve a successful digital transformation directly. On the contrary, every company must go through every phase of digital transformation. Undoubtedly, learning from the past experiences of others may help companies to avoid common mistakes. However, all companies must go through the different development milestones based on their specific conditions, independently explore and overcome the obstacles "without circumventing each process." While the companies are learning from others, the successfully transformed company has more efficient working methods.

Consequently, the earlier a company begins its digital transformation, the better it is for its business growth. Your company may not be reaping much of the rewards in the initial phase of digital transformation, but the organizational structure, digital concepts of your employees, and digital culture of the company, among others, are constantly evolving. In addition, digital transformation is also a trial-and-error process. If companies can transform earlier, they can find and rectify their issues and step into the right track of digital transformation earlier.

5.1.2 Matthew Effect of Digitalization

The Matthew Effect is sometimes summarized by the saying, "the strong get strong, and the weak get weak." The Matthew Effect of digitalization refers to the phenomenon where the overall capability of a company that uses digital technologies is often stronger than another company that does not use any. This company does not only get stronger over time. Likewise, the overall capability of a company that uses digital technologies earlier is more substantial than another that uses digital technologies later. The latter company only gets stronger over time, as shown in Fig. 5.2. That is because data has long been a factor of production that companies cannot afford to ignore.

To date, data is a new factor of production equal to other traditional factors such as land, labor, capital, technology, and other resources. It signifies that data, like any other factor of production, including land, labor, capital, technology, and other resources, can empower and enable company operations. Data, as a new factor of production, has two differences in comparison with labor.

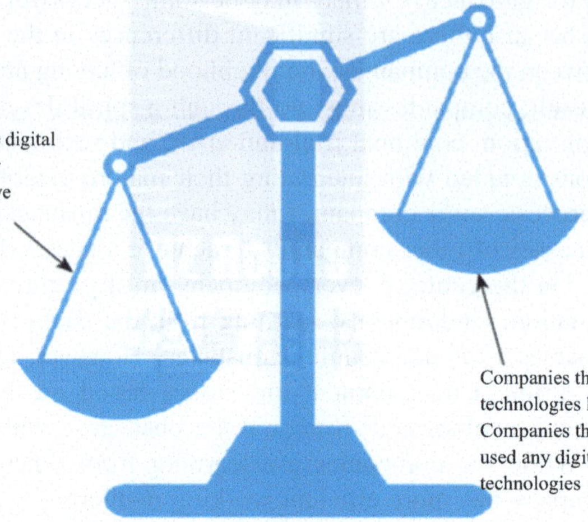

Fig. 5.2 Matthew effect of digitalization

The first difference is the advantage of accumulation. As the scale of a company gets large, it would need more labor. However, the marginal cost[1] of the company does not go down, the labor cost gets high, and the management cost is also higher. As a factor of production, the cumulative effect of labor is not apparent. After the company markedly invests in digital technologies, it utilizes a large volume of data. And it also creates more data as a result. Similarly, the digital technologies employed are also increasingly matured; the cost of single data technology gradually declines, and the effects of using the data rise exponentially. As a new factor of production, data have accumulated advantages.

The second difference is the advantage of scalability. As a traditional factor of production, it is difficult for labor to develop and manage the business at scale. If a company wants to achieve a specific development scale by increasing labor, it must first find suitable talents and the leadership of the people who can manage them. It is challenging for the company to a certain extent. And it is difficult for the company to develop these talents with standard operating protocols, just like digital technologies. This model of achieving an expanded development scale by increasing labor often hits a roadblock further ahead. The marginal cost of digital technologies is 0. If a company grows from 1 to 10 factories by utilizing digital technologies, there is more room for technological improvement, while intelligent efficiency is high. Thus, data has the advantage of scalability as a new factor of production.

[1] 1 Marginal cost is the increase in total cost from producing one additional item (or item purchased).

As data contains the advantages of accumulation and scalability, once the company has appropriately employed data and digital technologies, its digital transformation progresses faster than its peers with better effects. That leads to more confidence and resources invested in digitalization, and the company's overall digital capabilities become even more vital. The process of digital transformation is similar to the Matthew Effect. As long as companies have correctly deployed digital transformation, they are more robust over time. On top of that, there are increasingly more benefits that companies can reap from deploying digital technologies. Hence, it leads to more investments, and companies can quickly capture their market share, surpassing their peers and becoming the new industrial giant.

5.2 Timeline for Reference of Digital Transformation for Each Industry

From the internet industry, which is the birthplace of data, to the telecommunications and financial industries, which have begun the exploration of digital operations, to the retail, entertainment, real estate, automobile, education, energy, and pharmaceutical industries, which have actively embraced digitalization, there is often a timeline for a massive explosion of digital transformation in every industry. But these timelines may not be consistent with the actual development. Thus, we can only make a forecast based on the industry attributes, growth conditions, and development regulations.

Each industry initiates a wave of digital transformation. But there is a sequential difference in the respective timeline for the transformation. As shown in Fig. 5.3, the ICT, media, and financial industries were the pioneers in initiating a digital transformation. Entertainment, leisure, retail, trading, and other consumer industries were ranked second. Public utility, government, medical, education, and other relevant industries were ranked third. High-end manufacturing, oil and gas, manufacturing of essential products, chemical, pharmaceutical, and other capital-intensive industries were ranked fourth. Agriculture, personal and local services, hotel services, construction, and other localized industries were the last to start the digital transformation.

Suppose companies want to keep pace with the waves of digital transformation. They need to understand the latest trends in the digital transformation of their industries, devise digital transformation solutions promptly and deploy their plans to ensure proper execution.

5.3 Misconceptions of Digital Transformation: If the Cost of Adding Staff Is Low, Then the Solution Is to Add More Staff

There are some misconceptions about digital transformation among companies. These companies believe that arranging more employment positions and staff is

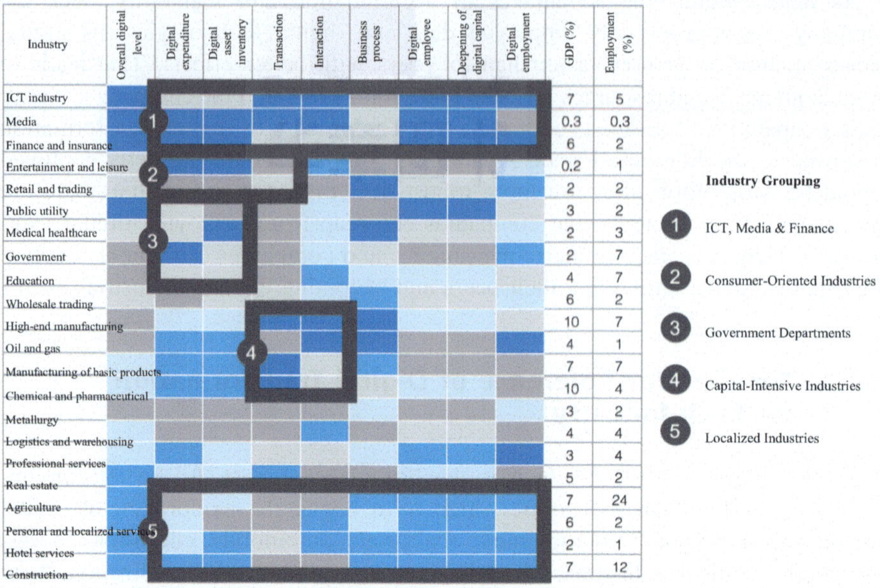

Fig. 5.3 Each industry successively begins digital transformation

more economical than installing digital technologies. Hence, they pursue the strategy of adding more staff to resolve the issue. The companies only consider saving costs for digital transformation, but not the enduring values created by digital technologies that transform the paradigm shift of traditional industries, working methods, and processes. Moreover, they have also neglected the Matthew Effect of digital transformation.

These are the following disadvantages in comparing adding staff and employing digital technologies.

First, employee turnover results in the loss of resources and capabilities. If companies do not have comprehensive processes or systems to sustain their resources or capabilities, it causes bottlenecks in the business workflow, and many processes need to start over again. However, employing digital technologies helps companies generate specific digital capabilities, which do not disappear with significant employee turnover.

Second, the additional deployment of employees does not increase the effectiveness of digital transformation. Digital transformation is optimizing processes, raising efficiencies, and innovating businesses by integrating digital technologies and business needs. It involves every department and module of companies and extracts conventional rules and values with a colossal volume of data. The conclusion is, though, more scientific yet convincing. The arrangement of employees is solely dependent on the personal experiences of the superiors, and there may be an inevitable omission in the job placement. It is hard to judge the effects of staff addition and digital transformation.

Last but not least, digital transformation enables a sustainable effect for companies to improve efficiencies, optimize management, innovate products and develop businesses, and continually empower the companies. Consequently, it is an outright mistake for companies to harbor the misconception that adding staff lowers the costs of employing digital technologies and inevitably affects their digital transformation.

Part III
What Is Digital Transformation?

When companies clearly understand why they need to have a digital transformation, and when they start their digital transformation, they also need to understand the specific contents of digital transformation.

Digital transformation creates intelligent business operating systems and helps companies accumulate digital capabilities. It is a systematic process whereby each phase and role has to be materially adequate. On top of being a trial-and-error process, digital transformation is also an exploratory process into the future. Digital transformation includes six indispensable elements. Only with the understanding of digital transformation can companies avoid unnecessary paths to a successful digital transformation.

The Elements of Digital Transformation

6

The digital transformation of companies is a process of creating intelligent business operating systems. And this is a systematic process. This Chapter examines and describes the digital transformation in detail.

6.1 Intelligent Business Operating System—Building Digital Capabilities

Before implementing digital transformation, companies need to build intelligent business operating systems. Intelligent business operating systems are the basic capabilities of all industries. The results of data analysis direct the business behaviors of companies, while the business behaviors also generate data that continue to be fed into the data analysis that directs the business behaviors again. By repeating the cycle, a dynamic and cyclical state of operations is thus formed between the data and business behaviors, helping companies to achieve the objectives of digital transformation and obtain extraordinary results. Intelligent business operating systems can disrupt the existing non-intelligent, non-dynamically evolving, unsustainable growth, as shown in Fig. 6.1.

6.1.1 The Importance of an Intelligent Business Operating System

If companies want to be successful in their digital transformation, they must first understand the significance of the structure and construction of the intelligent business operating system.

X. Ma, *Methodology for Digital Transformation*, Management for Professionals,
https://doi.org/10.1007/978-981-19-9111-0_6

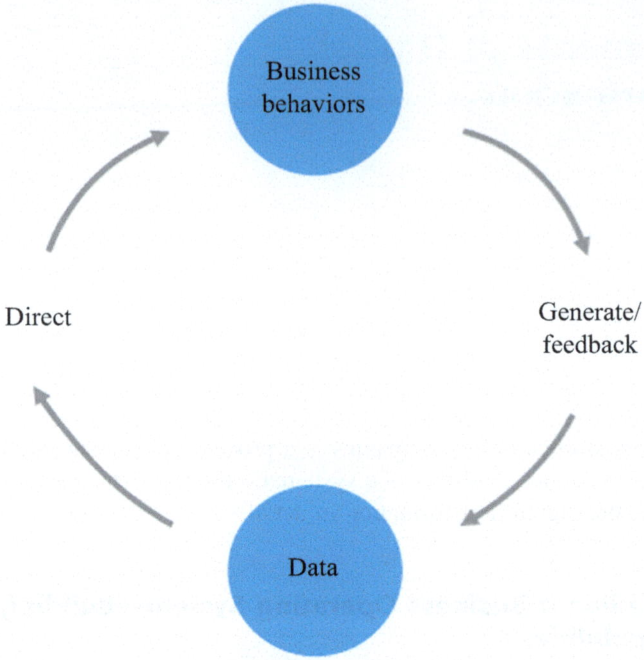

Fig. 6.1 Intelligent business operating system

1. **Structure of the intelligent business operating system**

Digital transformation is primarily constructing "intelligent business operating systems" for companies. Its structure is shown in Fig. 6.2.

Digital transformation is continuous learning, iterating, and integrating. It directs that an intelligent business operating system is also a dynamically matching structure. Figure 6.2 shows that the intelligent business operating system's underlying technical architecture depends on the data platform's construction. As a strong pillar of the applications platform in the upper layer, the data platform is the main engine for creating intelligent R&D, operations, and supply chains. Under the support of the underlying architecture of the data platform, companies construct intelligent applications after sorting out the market indicators of distributors' data, financial indicators of profitability, and team indicators of organizational relationships.

These intelligent applications form the core of an applications platform. Under the foundation of these intelligent applications, companies still need to employ the leadership capability model if they want a successful transformation. The leadership capability model consists of two parts, namely strategy and execution. Market analysis, business design, and strategic positioning form the inner core of the strategy. Talents, organization, and corporate design drive execution. The data platform,

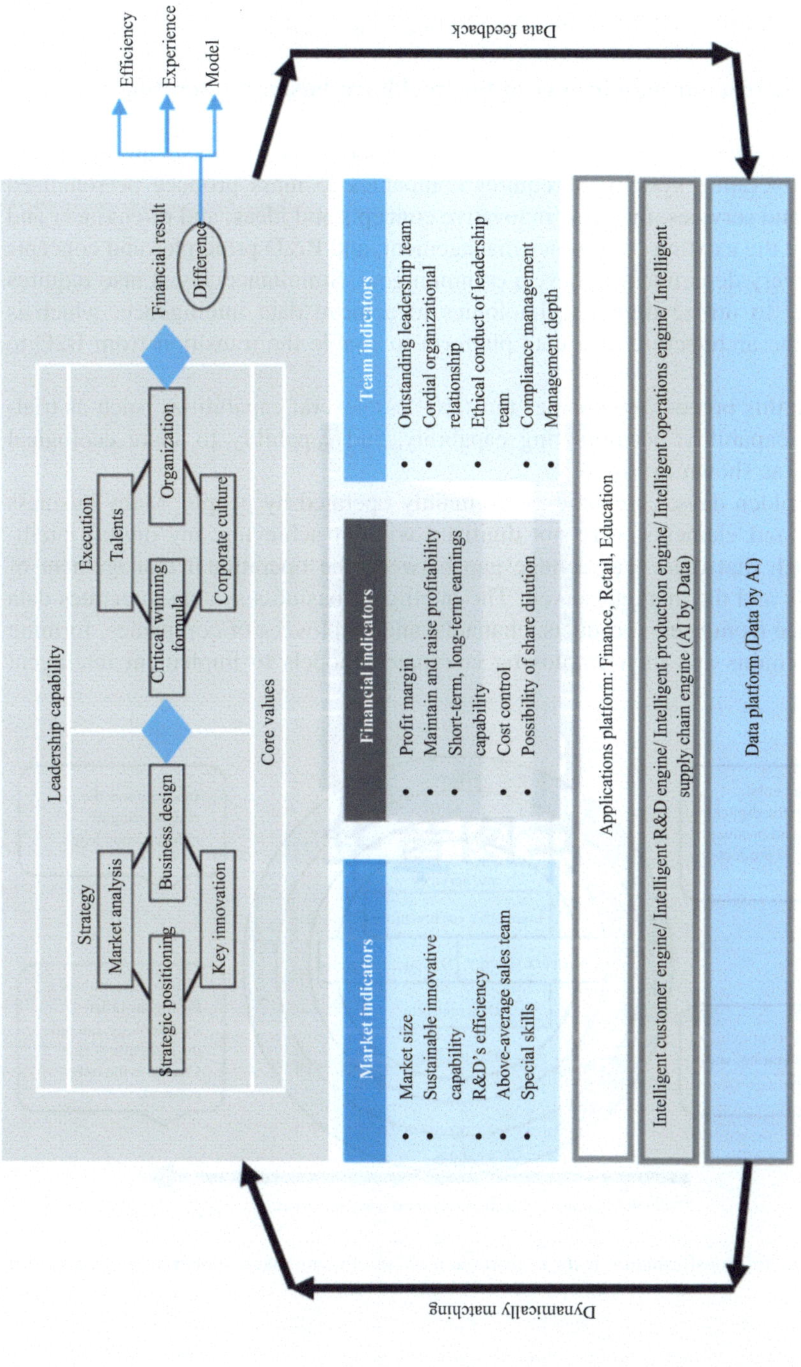

Fig. 6.2 Intelligent business operating system: data platform × applications platform

applications platform, and leadership capability are the three critical components that enable companies to achieve their digital transformation objectives, acquire digital capabilities and attain measurable financial results.

2. **The construction significance of the intelligent business operating system**

The fundamental purpose of digital transformation is to create an intelligent business operating system. It requires companies to mass produce personalized products and services, integrate innovative concepts and ideas, and re-engineer and restructure the existing operations, management, and R&D principles and concepts to unify every department to have a common goal. Simultaneously, it also requires companies to utilize digital technologies to achieve data intelligence, which is building the architecture of a data platform to enable the transition from B2C to C2B.

During this process, companies must possess several capabilities, such as trial-and-error capability, accumulating capability, and capability to share ecological resources, as shown in Fig. 6.3.

In the olden days, companies were mainly operated by people. Many business decisions and elements were not digitized without achieving any digital intelligence, such that there was a huge gap between the operational management of companies and the markets served. The intelligent business system integrates data intelligence from users, products, channels, and employees of companies, forming dynamic chains and then employing automated models to implement intelligent

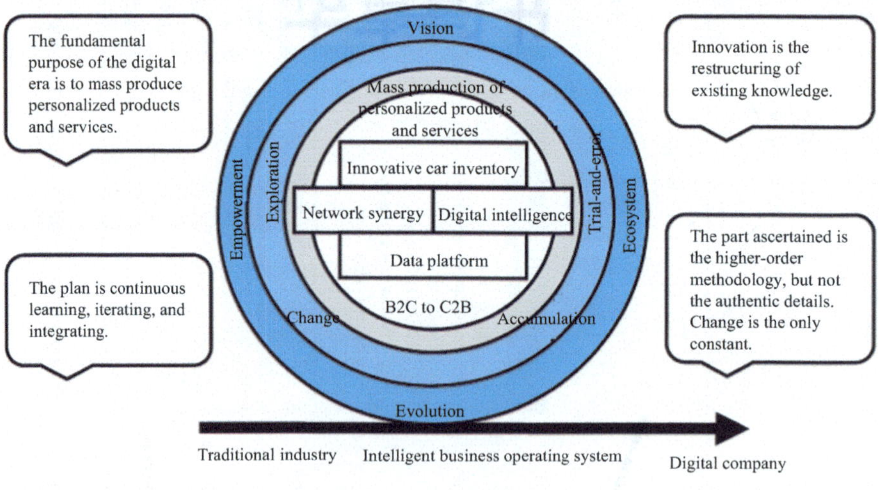

Fig. 6.3 Digital transformation is the construction of "intelligent business operating systems" for companies

operations. The intelligent pricing application in the retail industry has resolved the issue of pricing millions of SKU,[1] for example.

First, the intelligent pricing application consolidates and collates the upstream and downstream data in the sales, production, supply chain, raw materials, competitors' data, and logistics data before analyzing and intelligently processing them, providing dynamic pricing references for companies. In addition, it also adjusts the pricing frequency, which was only implemented quarterly or annually in the past. It can intelligently adjust product prices based on different periods, raw materials, and markets, helping every company in each channel get first-hand market reference prices and promptly keep up with the market changes. It has also altered the old competitive techniques of depressing prices at all costs and undercutting competitors to maintain revenue, and it continues to safeguard profit growth for the whole industry.

The intelligent pricing application is mainly based on the total data integration in a company, and these data have been entirely and seamlessly interconnected in the data platform. In the data platform, the technical staff builds many models to facilitate the business employees to integrate all data for analysis and implement intelligent pricing.

The benefits derived from this pricing model are so huge that it was impossible to attain with labor long ago. It relies on the highly efficient operational capabilities of the intelligent business operating system. The intelligent business operating system manages data in a highly efficient and intelligent way, reducing the placement costs of IT staff, providing motivation and drive for the sustainable development of companies, and saving a considerable chunk of labor costs.

6.1.2 Relationship Between the Intelligent Business Operating System and Digital Transformation

Building an intelligent business operating system is the only way to achieve digital transformation for companies. The purpose of digital transformation is to nurture a cyclical and dynamically matching capability to raise efficiencies and obtain benefits. And an intelligent business operating system can generate this type of capability.

An intelligent business operating system contains digital twin technology. What is digital twin technology in this context? It is both the consecutive collation and intelligent analysis of the operational data of companies and a virtual representation of a product in a digital system model. It can carry out simulation tests and validation on the real-time digital counterpart of the product to enhance the product's value. In addition to improving the reliability and usability of the product,

[1] 2 SKU, Stock Keeping Unit, is a unique code of a sales product consisting of six numbers. Every product in the sales phase must have it.

digital twin technology can simultaneously mitigate the R&D and manufacturing risks.

The intelligent business operating system seamlessly integrates and interconnects all companies' upstream and downstream data and builds models used to test the business operating conditions. And then, it feeds the outcomes into the real scenarios for critical adjustments, optimizing the business operating conditions. With repetitive feedback of the outcomes derived from accurate adjustments to the various models, the models convert the outcomes into data with a dynamically matching method, and the updated data continues to serve the models again. Through repetitive cycles day in and out, it forms a sustainable, intelligent capability. These are the fundamentals of an intelligent business operating system.

The intelligent business operating system can help companies accumulate the experience of using digital infrastructure to cope with future changes and challenges to business competition.

6.2 The Barrel Theory Applies to Digital Transformation

Many companies are used to understanding digital transformation from the information technology perspective, and they have no idea that digital transformation is a strategic, systematic, long-term, and demanding task. Akin to the barrel theory, there are six indispensable elements of digital transformation, namely data, applications, talents, tools, experiences, and digital platforms, as shown in Fig. 6.4. Any shortfall in one of the six indispensable elements significantly affects the effectiveness of digital transformation for companies.

Digital transformation for companies is a progressive spiral development process. A shortfall in indispensable elements in the arduous digital transformation journey substantially affects the progress and outcome. During digital transformation, for example, if companies only focus on technological investments and overlook the reasonable allocation of talents, it is difficult to have good results in the data-enabled business. The transformation objectives also fall short for many companies. If companies are complete in all six indispensable elements in their transformation deployment, would there be any chance for them to succeed in a digital transformation? During the digital transformation process, companies must timely observe each element's development scale and applications level by the current conditions, quickly make up for any shortfall, adjust the pace and scale of any element that may have run ahead prematurely, and avoid overinvestment in any single element.

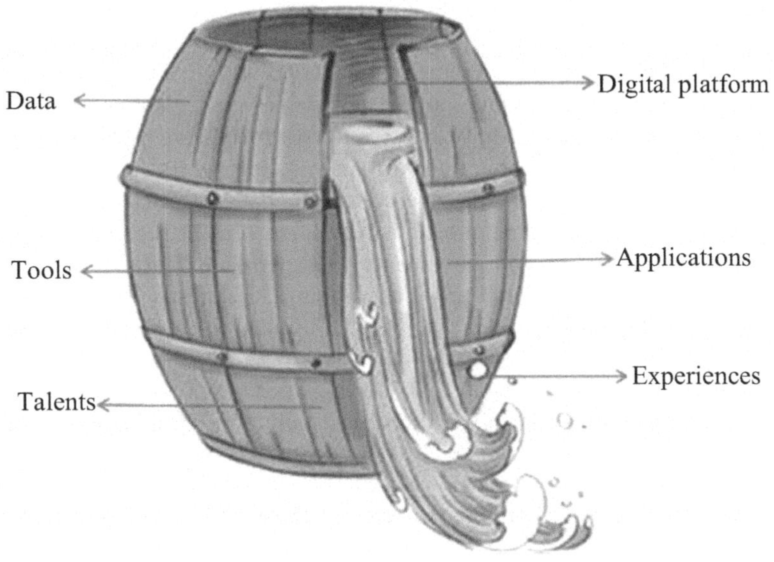

Fig. 6.4 The barrel theory of digital transformation

6.3 Digital Transformation Is a Systematic Project

In reality, digital transformation for companies is a systematic and innovative revolution, including strategy development, data governance, technology upgrade, product innovation, organizational change, and management change.

Since some companies lack overall knowledge about digitalization, they cannot achieve the "comprehensive combination of a point, line, and plane" during transformation.

Merely relying on the underlying data governance and focusing on the procurement of all information equipment and systems to complete automation, intelligent production lines, and the construction of factories would only result in an overlay of several intelligent applications and the deployment of intelligent products. For companies, this type of digital transformation is selective but not comprehensive. By unilaterally zeroing in on the additions of all kinds of data tools and the placement of high-quality talents, it may only "cure the symptoms on the surface but not the root cause of the disease." Hence, companies can only unlock the values of data-enabled businesses if they achieve data applications in all dimensions.

If companies are unable to use the data reasonably, their digital operations rest on the superficial layer of statistical analysis without reaching the application of deep DT. Consequently, companies must not only concentrate their efforts on the equipment of information technology infrastructure, but they must also focus on digital technologies and businesses, as well as the deep integration with organizational structure, production processes, and management models. Companies should re-examine the importance of their digital growth strategies and profoundly understand the digital transformation from the strategic level of their development to keep pace with the digital era's operational concepts and growth directives.

Apart from completing the tasks above, companies must also pick out the logical relationship between data and businesses to ensure they are on the right path in applying data intelligence. Digital transformation requires full deployment across a broad spectrum of areas, including data collection, data governance, data mining, data analysis, and intelligent applications. Companies must seamlessly interconnect and share data through data governance to accumulate digital assets, integrate the shared data and accumulated applications into an enclosed loop and generate data from applications. Then the data could be utilized to fulfill users' needs and decrease costs efficiently.

In summary, digital transformation is a systematic but not an isolated issue. The lack of any phase or factor leads to companies' failure in digital transformation.

6.4 Six Indispensable Elements of Digital Transformation

Digital transformation is a systematic project. There are six specific elements of a systematic project: data, applications, talents, tools, experiences, and digital platform, as shown in Fig. 6.5.

6.4.1 Data

In the process of digital transformation, companies need not only internal data but also need external data as well. Companies generate large volumes of data during their production processes. These are the companies' internal data, and they are stored in different departments without seamless interconnection. The data in the same department can be stored in different data warehouses, and technical walls must be broken down to create seamless interconnectivity between these data. If the internal data of companies cannot be interconnected, the business department is not able to correlate and integrate the different sets of data and fail to uncover the data value in a deeper layer.

In the digital era, if companies want to grasp business opportunities, they require not only internal data but also external data support. Long ago, companies were not used to integrating and using external data. Nowadays, amid the splashing waves of digitalization, companies would have little choice but to place more emphasis on these external data.

There could be many reasons for the lack of data. First, there may be specific data issues in the internal departments of companies.

(1) The internal data review is unclear, and companies do not have concise data asset management and system.
(2) The value of the internal data assets is not clear.

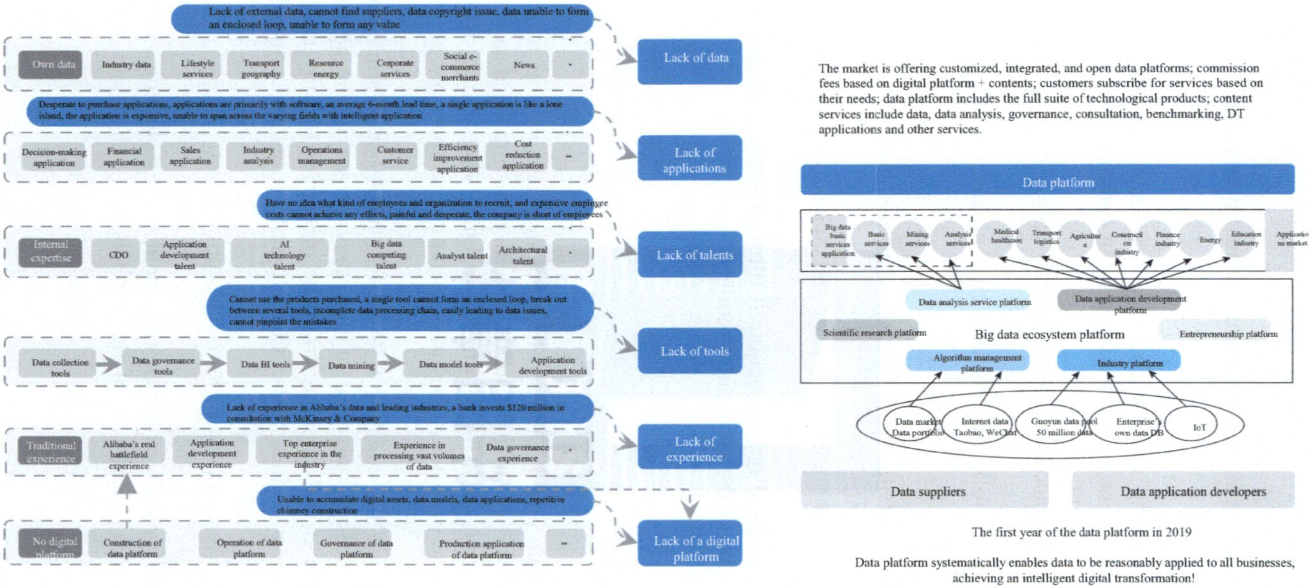

Fig. 6.5 Six indispensable elements of digital transformation

(3) The data has not formed any enclosed loop resulting in companies failing to employ the data assets fully.
(4) The data has not reached the standards of OneWorld,[2] and data standards are inconsistent.
(5) Companies dare not easily use data without quality assurance.
(6) As part of the data assets are in the hands of the suppliers, companies cannot use them flexibly and autonomously.
(7) Data assets are lacking in protecting risk control systems (technical skills, legal skills, management skills), resulting in an external leach of data without creating any data advantages.
(8) Data is lacking in the accumulation and build-up of enduring values.

Second, there are also the following issues with companies' general understanding and use of external data.

(1) Lack of awareness of the types of data that companies themselves should acquire and supplement.
(2) Companies are unclear about the sources and channels through which external data is acquired.
(3) Even when the external data is acquired through various channels, the data copyright issue makes the companies harder to use the data.

6.4.2 Applications

The application of data intelligence can help business departments to resolve the demand issue. However, companies often encounter incomplete data intelligence applications during digital transformation. The technical investments of companies do not reflect the value of different business scenarios, so there are no changes to the business results.

Companies often use the common CRM, ERP, and other information systems to collect data. But this is only one of the many phases in the application of corporate data, and it is still far away from the objectives of fully utilizing data to improve management, reduce costs, raise efficiencies, and accomplish record-breaking revenue.

There are three reasons for the lack of data applications.

Reason 1: As the growth model of the application technology is too traditional and the development cost of the application is also high with lagging

[2] 3 OneWorld is one of the steps for data governance, enabling the interconnectivity and interoperability of data with partners through the OpenAPI approach.

response, it is straightforward to generate a data silo. The development of corporate applications is customized chiefly, which is generally expensive with a long development cycle. No data is shared between applications, resulting in isolated data islands.

Reason 2: It is the overinvestment in IT technologies and underinvestment in digital technologies. Without controlling the application of data, digital technologies utilize the data produced by IT software to empower businesses and optimize their business values.

Reason 3: The data platform of companies cannot develop applications, and thus it cannot accomplish the actual application of data intelligence. Suppose the application developed by the company cannot directly generate business value but only generate a large volume of data for reporting purposes. The company can refer to Chapter 7.1 to assess the level it is currently at to put in place a compatible development plan for the application of data intelligence and develop an application of data intelligence that can directly generate value.

6.4.3 Talents

The incessant waves of the digital economy have forced companies to quickly devise a digital strategy from the various scenarios such as workflow, business model, conceptualization, and application as early as possible. "Data-driven business" is not a slogan, and the first step in its implementation is building a team of talents.

A complete data system requires not only high-level talents who would master the data strategy but also middle-level and basic-level talents who are familiar with the technology, application, and algorithm, as shown in Fig. 6.6.

First, considering high-level talents, many companies may have changed several CTOs during digital transformation. As every CTO has a different opinion toward digital transformation, they have different emphases in executing their companies' digital transformation solutions. It may constantly revolve around a

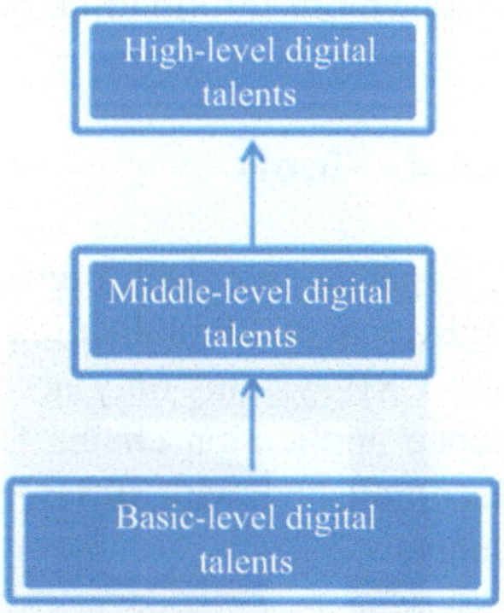

Fig. 6.6 Schematic diagram of digital talents

particular phase of digital transformation without any progress. Besides lacking a suitable CTO, companies often lack a CDO of high-end talents. Primarily responsible for driving digital transformation, a CDO creates new business opportunities by employing digital technologies. There are two aspects to the requirements of this role. First, it is the understanding of the rationale behind a digital transformation solution, while second, it is the exceptional competency in the principles of technology and the logical relationship in business. These two qualities can effectively drive the finer details of digital transformation and empower businesses with data.

Second, considering middle-level talents, the middle level needs to resolve the issue of transforming data to create digital products and empower the business. This process requires middle-level talents to drive the transformation tasks in each business scenario and ideally enable the technical and business departments to collaborate.

Lastly, companies must form a battling team of talents with different expertise considering basic-level talents. Talents with different personalities, work habits, professional expertise, and skill sets can coordinate various aspects of the tasks based on the project requirements to achieve higher working efficiency. There is often a particular phenomenon in allocating and placing basic-level talents. On the one hand, there may be enough talents in one aspect, for example, too many programmers, while on the other hand, there is an acute shortage of data analysts, product managers, and algorithm engineers who are multi-faceted talents and understand both the business and technology as well. Any unreasonable allocation of talents in a company cannot empower the frontline business in a highly efficient manner.

Among them, there is a larger requirement for middle and basic-level talents. Companies can build their training systems and nurture suitable talents, allocating appropriate multi-faceted talents and making ready preparations with systematic talented teams.

Companies must have digital talents in the first place to achieve a digital culture and drive the application of digitalization with a specific base and scale of talents. Therefore, constructing a team with digital talents is of utmost importance for companies.

For more information, please scan the QR code on the Preface.

6.4.4 Tools

Companies may lack digital tools to use the data properly. Informatization is not equivalent to digitalization and business intelligence. The deployment of CRM and ERP systems only accomplishes the data collection phase in the data intelligence application chain. The other phases in the complete chain cycle must be accomplished with different tools, including data processing, mining, and data analysis.

Digital tools can enhance the efficiency and quality of corporate management, provided they are built on a comprehensive foundation of a tool system. There are many different types and formats between various digital tools, so a data enclosure cannot be formed if these types and formats are not standardized. Misusing these digital tools may lead to mistakes in the analysis results, and it would be difficult to pinpoint whether there are issues in the data integration or data analysis phase.

Consequently, companies must not only build a tool system consisting of different phases, but they must also enable the formation of a data enclosure between different digital tools under the basis of data sharing to achieve data-driven businesses.

6.4.5 Experiences

Companies that lack experience in data operations face many difficulties in its usage. Most companies that have achieved a successful digital transformation with a successful data platform have enriching experiences in data operations. Take Alibaba, which proposed the concept of a data platform, as an example.

The concept of a data platform has been proposed by Alibaba, which participated in countless real battles and constantly transformed the construction of big data under the waves of digital transformation. The construction of Alibaba's data platform relied solely on the powerful data processing capability of Alibaba. Most importantly, ordinary companies do not have the applications development capability and data governance capability of a top-rated company in the industry like Alibaba. They are often "at a total loss" while facing a massive volume of historical data. As they do not understand the application scenarios and data values of big data, they find it very hard to figure out the application requirements of big data accurately and fail to achieve the values behind self-diagnosis and data mining for the company's growth.

The business department cannot specify the data requirements clearly, while the data technical department cannot help the business department explore the value of data in the short term. The decision-makers of companies may believe that the investment in digital technologies is not justified as compared to the results. To a certain extent, it would make companies procrastinate and adopt a cautious stance toward digital transformation. It not only affects companies to explore opportunities in the digital era but also impedes them from relying on digital transformation for technical accumulation and data application capabilities.

Suppose companies want to salvage this type of scenario. They must rely on their professional data team to construct application scenarios for big data, enabling the business employees to understand the actual value of data, continually enhancing the application capability of business data, and accumulating the experiences of digital transformation.

6.4.6 Digital Platforms

Companies can segregate data assets, construct models, and accumulate data applications with a digital platform. Suppose companies only keep getting more applications without constructing a digital platform. It leads to duplicated construction with many isolated data chimneys such that the internal and external data is not shared and seamlessly interconnected, and the data application capability cannot be accumulated.

A data platform can help companies seamlessly interconnect and integrate their internal and external data, thus achieving data analysis and applications in all domains. The business department can freely enjoy the data services on top of the digital platform, while the back-end technical department also does not need to crack its brain for the simple requirements of the front-end business. It can, however, retain a tremendous amount of energy to develop application products of higher levels. The business department can resolve these basic requirements independently with the digital platform.

The data platform is the core of digital transformation for companies. Companies would not be able to implement digital transformation smoothly without constructing a data platform.

Nonetheless, some companies still fail in their digital transformation, even with the complete construction of the above. Why is that so? There are three reasons as follows:

1. **Data does not circulate virtuously and dynamically**

Although some companies have performed segregation and construction of the six indispensable elements above, their data is in a static state, and a virtuous circle cannot be formed as a result. In addition, it also cannot be updated and flowed back, and it cannot provide a dynamic data analysis in a real-time manner for the front-end business.

2. **Data lacks systematic management**

Though some companies have completed the pre-governance of data, some questions remain unanswered. For example, the data of each module exists independently, exhibiting a dotted distribution without any interconnection or business logic relationship between different datasets. However, the data of each business module is standardized, there is no multiplier effect between them, and the efficiency generated is only used in each independent business module or business department. There is absolutely no presentation of the actual value of all data.

3. **Data usage is in an "atypical mode"**

Some business modules are usually more critical or have a higher market share. As the data applications of these modules are more frequent and concentrated, the data quality is also better. While these have provided significant help for the growth of critical businesses, there are also some issues. As the data governance of these business modules is slightly better, the value of empowering the business is also correspondingly higher.

Companies emphasize data governance in these areas while neglecting data governance in other ones. Despite the value of data empowerment in these critical business modules being increasingly more robust and the data-driven intelligent operations also increasingly more professional, the data applications of the other business modules are fragile. As the data applications of these single, independent businesses are gradually improving over time, it is increasingly difficult to integrate the data with other business modules. To maintain data empowerment of these business modules, companies constantly invest heavily and enter a vicious circle in the end. That is an "atypical mode" of data usage in companies.

Digital transformation is a long-term project that entails a complete strategic deployment by companies revolving around the core of "data-enabled businesses." To achieve digitalization, companies must not only focus on constructing the items above, but also pay attention to data operations, data management, and data usage. Companies can only achieve "business intelligence (BI)" and enjoy a successful digital transformation if all the aforementioned elements operate smoothly and seamlessly.

Part IV
Should You Implement Digital Transformation?

As digital transformation has become a type of industrial mainstream nowadays, there are real concerns over the following questions.

Should companies implement digital transformation?

What developmental stage must a company be at before implementing digital transformation?

What are the requirements for digital transformation?

What are the noteworthy issues during the digital transformation process?

To resolve the issues above, companies must determine their levels of digitalization first by the degree of digital operations and the employment of digital testing and assessment models and then perform segregation over the areas of strategic development, management system, organization structure, human resource to assess their competencies for a transformation and ascertain whether to implement digital transformation in the end. On top of that, companies must also avoid common misconceptions about digital transformation, so they do not miss the opportunity to perform a much-needed transformation.

Self-assessment of Digital Transformation

7

After understanding the significance of digital transformation, companies must decide whether to implement digital transformation. This Chapter helps companies to determine whether they should implement digital transformation from the perspective of their levels of digital operations and their degree of readiness for digital transformation. Furthermore, companies must also avoid the four major misconceptions before deciding on any digital transformation.

7.1 Digital MAX Maturity Model and Assessment

Should companies implement digital transformation?

What developmental stage must a company be at before implementing digital transformation?

In answering the two questions above, we need to understand that data and technology tools are not equivalent to the level of digital operations. Using Excel does not mean a low level of digital operations, while using big data, BI, digital platforms, and other tools does not mean a high level of digital operations.

The roles and values of data displayed in corporate management are the standard benchmarks to measure the level of digital operations. Companies can determine their digitalization levels using a professional Digital MAX Maturity Model to decide whether to implement digital transformation and devise a solution suitable for their needs.

7.1.1 Six Levels of the Digital MAX Maturity Model

Digital MAX Maturity Model contains six levels from levels 0–5, as shown in Fig. 7.1.

X. Ma, *Methodology for Digital Transformation*, Management for Professionals,
https://doi.org/10.1007/978-981-19-9111-0_7

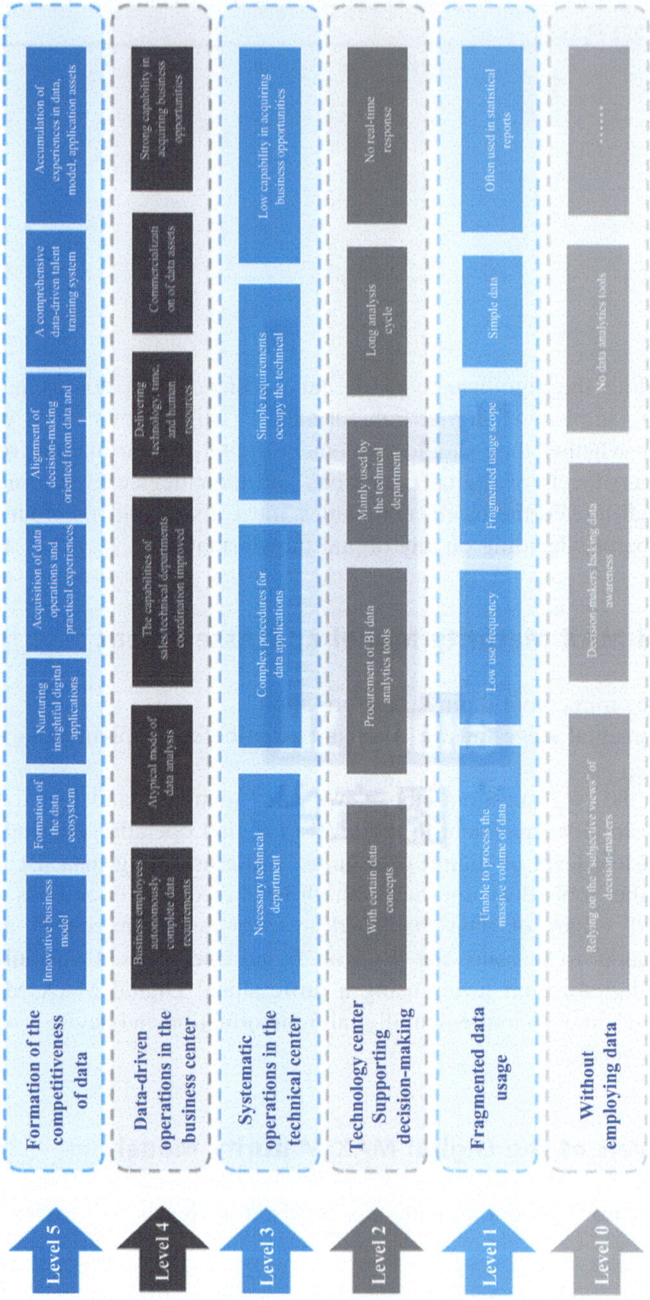

Fig. 7.1 Six levels of the digital MAX maturity model

Level 0: Without employing data and relying entirely on the responsible person's subjective decision-making.
Level 1: Employing Excel storage and analyzing data with fragmented data files and a low volume of data.
Level 2: Implementing data analysis by relying on the technical department.
Level 3: Systematically applying the data and utilizing data-supported businesses with technology at its core.
Level 4: Digital operations with technology at its core and data empowering the businesses.
Level 5: Data leads and directs the business, empowering the business with innovation and transformation.

From the six dimensions of the Digital MAX Maturity Model, ranging from Level 0 of without employing data to Level 5 of leading and directing the businesses with data, we can classify the digitalization levels of companies, help them quickly understand their digital shortcomings and ascertain the necessity for digital transformation, look for the key and penetration points in the construction of digitalization, and reasonably devise a digital transformation solution to achieve digital transformation successfully and rapidly.

7.1.2 Assessment of the Levels of Digital Operations

After understanding the Digital MAX Maturity Model, companies can assess their levels of digitalization to ascertain the necessity for digital transformation and devise a solution suitable for their development. The following depicts the six levels of the Digital MAX Maturity Model.

1. **Level 0 company**

A Level 0 company has the following characteristics: It has not adopted any data analysis into its daily operations, and the decision-makers lack data awareness. It also does not employ any data analytics tools and has no concept of the application of data in its daily operations.

2. **Level 1 company**

The staff of each department and the upper management of a Level 1 company have used data analysis in a fragmented way. The business department of certain companies uses the most common Excel tool to analyze data. But the frequency of use is relatively low, with few employees using it. Even though companies may have over 10 departments, only 1 department uses the Excel tool to perform data analysis. Under this scenario, the analysis results can only be used by that department, and a domain-wide data analysis cannot be achieved. And it also cannot help the upper management to draft and prepare business initiatives and directives from the corporate perspective. It is, however, likely that some employees in specific departments use data analysis. But the data used are often those in contact with those employees in their daily work. Hence, the analyzed results may be very biased. Besides, the assistants of the upper management may also need to perform data analysis to provide analysis reports to the upper management. The data used by the assistants mainly originate from the companies' IT systems, for example, the data from the tabulation of sales revenue. These data analysis results are usually microscopic in perspective, failing to provide references to the decision-makers in a macroscopic way. Consequently, the Level 1 company still has not formed the habit of using data systematically. It only uses data as a means of consideration in a temporary manner.

Although the Level 1 company has already started to use the Excel tool to meet the requirements of specific data analyses, data applications are far too few. While Excel has its advantages, it also has its disadvantages as well. The advantages of using Excel include relatively low maintenance costs, basic query and calculation functions, and able to restrict user access and amend permissions. Once the volume of data becomes too large for Excel to handle, the query and calculation speed decline. Hence, it cannot manage its roles demanded by the users. And the requirements of the data structure are also more straightforward. Thus, the Excel tool used by the Level 1 company cannot support the data systems in the corporate world.

3. **Level 2 company**

The data usage of a Level 2 company has surged from the personal level to the corporate level. This type of company uses BI analysis tools to perform data analysis to support decision-making in upper management. But the primary user comes from the technical department. The applications of these BI analysis tools include corporate operational reports and upper management. Compared to the Level 1 company, the Level 2 company has performed data operations at the corporate level with scale and organization. The most common basic statistical data analytics tools for operational reporting are Excel and BI (Business Intelligence). BI and Excel have become the first choice among companies with data concepts in performing data analysis because they have reporting analysis and interactive capabilities that can concisely display data dynamics.

It requires collaboration between many departments to use BI analysis tools, as shown in Fig. 7.2. When the business staff has requirements for data analysis, the IT staff must first be responsible for the cleaning and interconnectivity of data, then submit the collated data to the data analysis department. The data analysis department gets the relevant results and feedback from the business department. Ultimately, it provides a basis for business staff to make appropriate business decisions, supporting the company's operations. The erratic cycles of generating the analysis of as little as two weeks or as long as a few months cannot promptly respond to the business staff's requirements, let alone when the requirements are larger and more complex.

Fig. 7.2 Data application model of Level 2 company

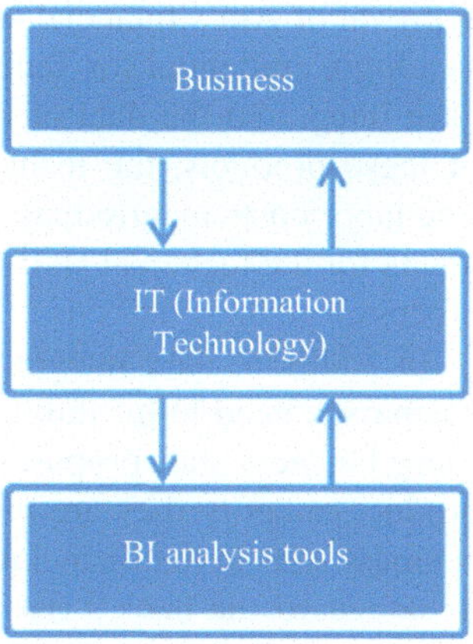

As these BI analysis tools have high technological barriers to entry, only the technical staff use and maintain them, and they cannot comprehensively encompass the company's daily management.

4. **Level 3 company**

A Level 3 company constructs a systematic data operations system by employing technological support at its core. The technical team in this type of company is the leading value creator for data, which also helps achieve the business department's requirements. This type of technical team has a particular scale, often resolving some general data issues and mainly supporting some critical departments of the company. With such a company's high costs of data operations, it cannot achieve data operations for all employees.

When the volume of data of a company reaches a particular scale, it is difficult to resolve the root of the issue by solely relying on data analysis. Data governance is critical at this juncture. Consequently, the construction of the systematic data operations architecture and its application to the business units, in the end, is the unique signature of the operations of a Level 3 company. The technical units support this type of company's digital transformation and generate fewer low-level applications.

For a Level 3 company, data governance is the fundamentals of data operations. Companies would mostly use BI (data analysis)—ETL (extract, transform and load)—DW (data warehousing) models to create a toolbox from the whole process of data governance to data analysis to implement data governance. As each process requires a transitional phase for data integration, companies must be equipped with a strong, professional technical team.

While maintaining each type of IT or DT product of the company, the technical department would often find that the data between many products are closely interconnected. Take an example of the personal credit card information generated during the payment with Alipay. The same data can also be used in the loan approval of Ant's financial services. The WeChat account information can be used as a login credential for Tencent Video. Why is this possible? Alibaba and Tencent have integrated the data of their every product. Before the integration of the data of these products, the technical staff needs to maintain the relevant apps' data. The labor costs incurred are higher as a result. And there are also specific requirements for the technical staff's professional competency during the data governance process.

In addition, data integration, data maintenance, and data-enabled companies' businesses need to go through complicated processes, as shown in Fig. 7.3. First, every business staff proposes different requirements for data analysis based on the product category they are in charge of and the user preferences. For example, the business staff in the financial industry need to assess their clients' credit conditions to safeguard the bank's risk assessment capability. According to the needs of the business staff, the data analysis department builds models.

Then, the technical department codes the data analysis department's modeling language and verifies the final codes' accuracy. Lastly, the business staff achieves business value through these models or applications. This type of data-driven business model is a single-oriented cycle, which requires going through many operations in various departments.

As it can be seen, companies need to be equipped with a professional technical team and data analysis team to complete the proposal of needs, construct models, and conduct tests on the whole process. In this process, the business staff only propose the data analysis requirements, while technical staff must invest a lot of

Fig. 7.3 Model of data-driven business

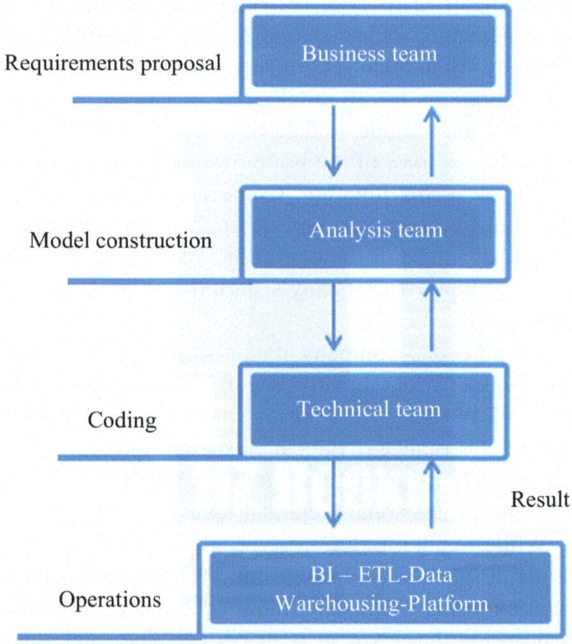

time and energy in the implementation phase. For the technical staff, some data analysis requirements are fundamental and straightforward. Take an example of the daily statistical analysis. The business staff can utilize professional data analytics tools to access the data to generate an automatic analysis without having the technical staff expend energy and time in this area. If the technical staff are busy tackling these simple requirements all year round, they would not be able to invest more energy into developing higher-order applications, thus failing to enable the digital transformation of companies. This type of data operations model with technology at its core often lead to "endless grievances" from the technical staff. While data usage has not penetrated the core businesses, the depth of data usage is also inadequate.

5. **Level 4 company**

The Level 4 company forms the data operations system with business at its core. In other words, the primary purpose of each department using data is to enable the business. This type of company has formed a virtuous circle for the data, achieving the build-up of data assets and the objectives of a data-enabled business. These companies change the data operations model with the technical team at its core, mining the data value to build a more comprehensive data platform. The frontline business staff can autonomously complete 80 percent of the data requirements. That is a feature of the data operations in a Level 4 company, as shown in Fig. 7.4.

The construction of a data platform has shattered the single-oriented data analysis model for the Level 3 company. The business staff do not need to go through many departments or numerous phases like before to fulfill the analysis requirements, and they can directly utilize the data and information prepackaged by the

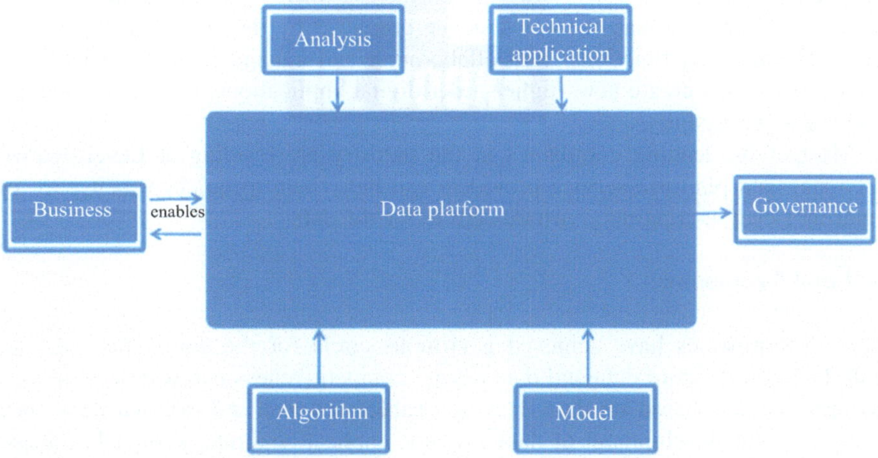

Fig. 7.4 Model of data-enabled business

data platform and analyze the data with the BI analysis tools provided by the data platform.

Before the business staff can autonomously analyze the data, the data platform has provided an answer to specific simple data analysis requirements. As shown in Fig. 7.4, the data platform enables the whole data chain of the company and empowers the cyclical circulation of data. It stores and expands the development of the developed data, models, algorithms, applications, and other "assets" of the company and develops a shared model, ensuring that the technical, data, and business departments can directly access it at any time. It benefits the business staff, and the technical staff can achieve data governance, model R&D, algorithm construction, and application R&D through the data platform.

With the construction of a data platform, the business staff can easily and conveniently use the data. When there are significant data analysis requirements from the business staff, they can directly resolve their issues via the data platform without relying on the technical and data analysis staff. It has enabled large data analysis requirements and stimulated the inspiration for more applications, but it has also saved enormous time for the technical and data analysis staff. The technical staff can focus their energy on the segregation of data assets directly impacting the business, achieving the commercialization of data assets, and building data-driven earnings growth.

If we say that Level 3 companies meet the business requirements through data analysis to raise the efficiency of capturing business opportunities, then Level 4 companies make data-driven business decisions. The business staff constantly adjusts their concentration to enhance further the efficiency of capturing business opportunities. Besides, constructing a data platform alters the technical department's past perceptions of concentrating on improving technical capabilities while neglecting to enable the business. Today, the central component of the technical department is to serve the business department, proactively transforming their functions and quickly driving business growth. In addition, the business department can also reap the convenience produced by the technical department in transforming its functions. By collaborating and enhancing their capabilities, both departments create new, higher-order digital applications, helping companies transform successfully.

Most of the leading companies in the industry are residing at Level 3. Professional data platform service providers can help them to quicken their pace of entering Level 4, creating a virtuous circle for the data.

6. **Level 5 company**

Level 5 companies have achieved a virtuous circle for the data. They can not only build on the core data and data assets' competitiveness but also develop new business models based on data. Having enabled internal and external data, they complete their development of data strategy, application strategy, model strategy, and algorithm strategy. Over 60 percent of employees can use the data to achieve business value. The new models created by the data have generated a certain amount of investment returns. This type of company that can achieve "data-driven growth" is called the Level 5 company.

In the internal departments of this type of company, there is complete integration between semi-automated data, fully-automated decision-making capability, human judgment, and decisions. The seamless interconnectivity of internal and external data has formed a data ecosystem, continually driving companies to implement digital transformation. After experiencing several years of digital operations compared with their peers, they have produced their unique data assets and ecosystems with the autonomous algorithm, modeling, and application assets. The depth and number of applications of such assets are prominent in the industry. As the business roles differ, the digital applications under R&D are also different, and the scenarios applied to vary. The different roles in companies can rapidly acquire relevant data with lower costs. Data operations have dived deep into the development milestone of Level 5 companies. The data security strategy has been created in the internal department of companies, rolling out data applications. Simultaneously, due to the complete data operations concept and practical experiences of companies, the training systems and processes of the data talents are more comprehensive. As a result, the concept of "practically nurturing talents, who in turn support the real implementation" has flourished with the virtuous circle, providing perpetual energy for the digital transformation of companies.

In summary, companies can assess their levels of digital operations with Digital MAX Maturity Model and Assessment to ascertain the multi-level leapfrog strategy in their next step. It is a matter of progressing level by level or engaging in a multi-level leap. If companies want to engage in a multi-level leap, they need to consider the resources and capabilities required to achieve the targeted level and progress steadily, avoiding failure in such an attempt.

Reminiscing on the digital development of companies in the past decade, leading companies in the industry mainly were residing at Level 3. Even some companies have already reached Level 3 in a much earlier period. In the internal departments of companies, there are at least dozens of staff or hundreds of staff solving data problems. The high cost of data maintenance still has not produced any higher-order applications for data.

The data usage of companies is still stuck at a low level, while the data operations are in deep trouble, unable to form a virtuous circle. Companies must determine their upgrading strategy according to their circumstances in this scenario.

For more information, please scan the QR code on the Preface.

7.2 Nine Dimensions of the Digital Self-readiness Model

Before deciding whether to implement a digital transformation, apart from assessing the level of their digital operations with the Digital MAX Maturity Model and Assessment, companies still need to consider whether they have the requirements for transformation. It requires companies to prepare a comprehensive review of

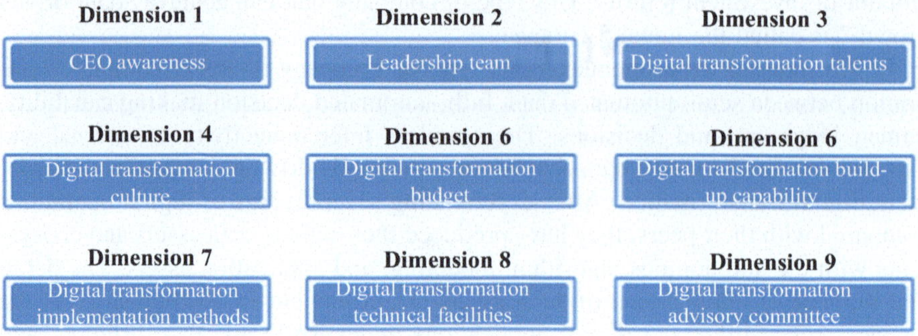

Fig. 7.5 Nine dimensions of the digital self-readiness model

the internal and external circumstances, sort out the capabilities of digital transformation and complete the assessment of the Digital Self-Readiness Model. The assessment can be carried out from nine dimensions, namely CEO awareness, leadership team, digital transformation talents, digital transformation culture, digital transformation budget, digital transformation build-up capability, implementation methods, technical facilities, and advisory committee, as shown in Fig. 7.5. The Digital Self-Readiness Model can help companies identify their capabilities and opportunities in digital transformation to ascertain their determination for digital transformation and draw up a solution suitable for themselves.

7.2.1 Whether the Leaders Have Any Awareness of the Digital Transformation

Before using the Digital Self-Readiness Model to assess the companies' capabilities for a transformation, the first step is to evaluate whether the CEO (the highest-ranking individual in the company) is aware of digitalization. The CEO must designate several phases, including decision-making, control of critical points, and role assignment, as shown in Fig. 7.6. Digital transformation can only be effective if the top leaders in a company have a deep awareness of digital transformation.

Company CEOs must also be well prepared for common issues during the digital transformation process. For example, how each department cooperates and coordinates, how to determine the KPIs for the staff participating in the digital transformation, and how to inspect and accept the different phases of digital transformation, among others. These issues would need to be initiated by the company CEOs. From the company perspective, the CEOs must clearly understand the digital transformation process and always be prepared for a long-term stance.

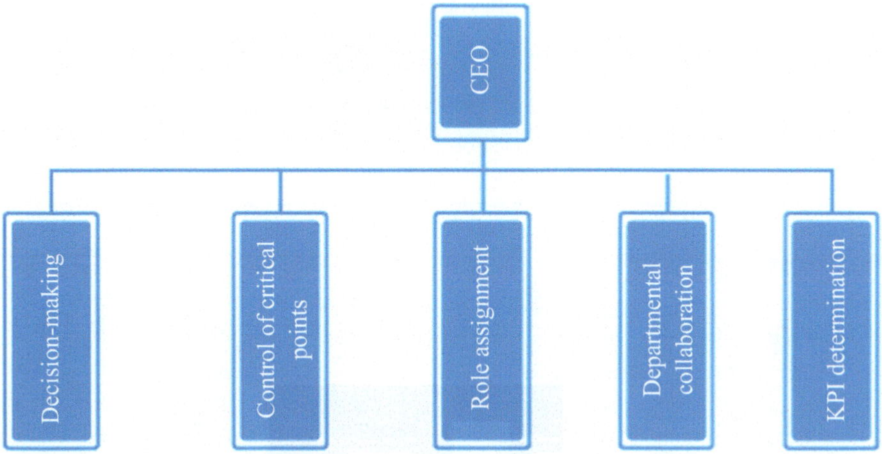

Fig. 7.6 Dimension 1 of the digital self-readiness model: leaders' awareness of the digital transformation

7.2.1.1 Whether the Company Has Any Digital Leadership Team

After clearly understanding digital transformation, company CEOs must build compatible leadership teams, as shown in Fig. 7.7. As digital transformation disrupts the existing operating models of companies, it may also affect the interests of certain groups. As a result, it is crucial to building a leadership team with coherent awareness and understanding of digital transformation.

Digital transformation would involve the KPIs of all departments in a company. The leadership team may need to think about how the responsible staff in each department can provide support for digital transformation based on completing the designated tasks. Before any digital transformation, companies must build an appropriate leadership team and consider whether the roles of the team members are complementary, whether the understanding of digital transformation is coherent, and other issues. Although different companies in different industries may need a leadership team with different roles, it must, however, include the Chief Executive Officer (CEO), Chief Digital Officer (CDO), Chief Technology Officer (CTO), Chief Operating Officer (COO), and other critical designations.

Among these varying positions, the CEO shall be the critical person to control the whole situation and is also responsible for the outcome of the digital transformation. The CDO is responsible for driving and executing the transformation work. The person in such a position would require a deep understanding of the business, technical competency, and outstanding coordination capability. It is indispensable for the CDO to possess the technology, business, and coordination capabilities. Otherwise, it is tough to help companies to drive digital transformation rapidly and effectively.

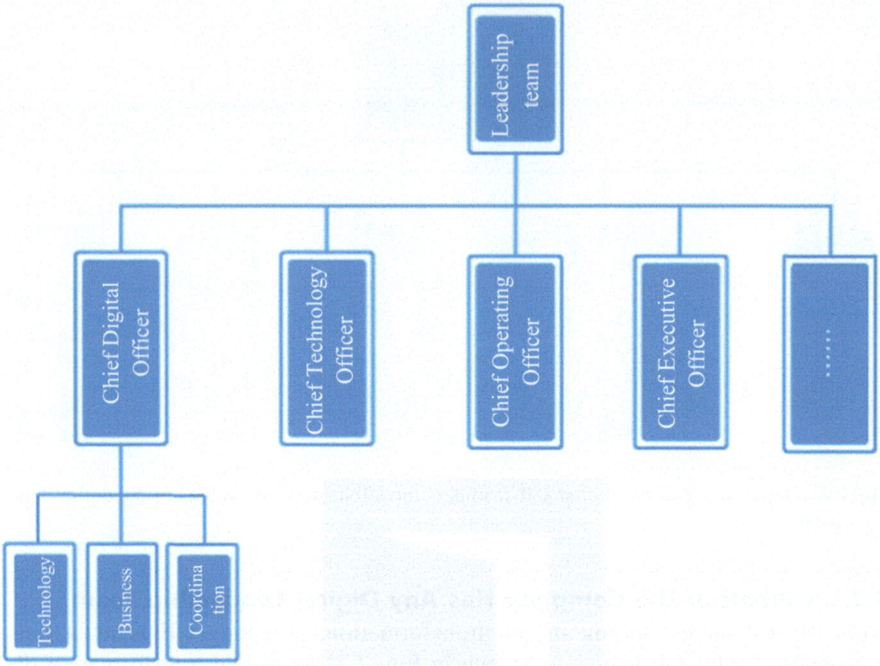

Fig. 7.7 Dimension 2 of the digital self-readiness model: build a digital leadership team

7.2.2 Whether the Company Has Any Digital Transformation Talents

When companies have ascertained that their CEOs are aware of and understand digital transformation and have a digital leadership team, they still need to assess whether they have a certain number of digital transformation talents, as shown in Fig. 7.8.

During the assessment, companies must consider setting aside digital talents at their basic level and nurture leaders to drive the technology, business, and data work in their digital transformation. Companies need talents such as digital product managers, analysts, and business engineers during the digital transformation process.

In addition, there are four aspects of consideration while building a pool of talents in the organization of a digital transformation team.

(1) Only set aside adequate and completely equipped personnel: For the provision of endless backup support for the digital transformation of companies.
(2) Reasonable building of talent pools with suitable candidates: On the one hand, a uni-functional team cannot unleash the full effects of a whole company,

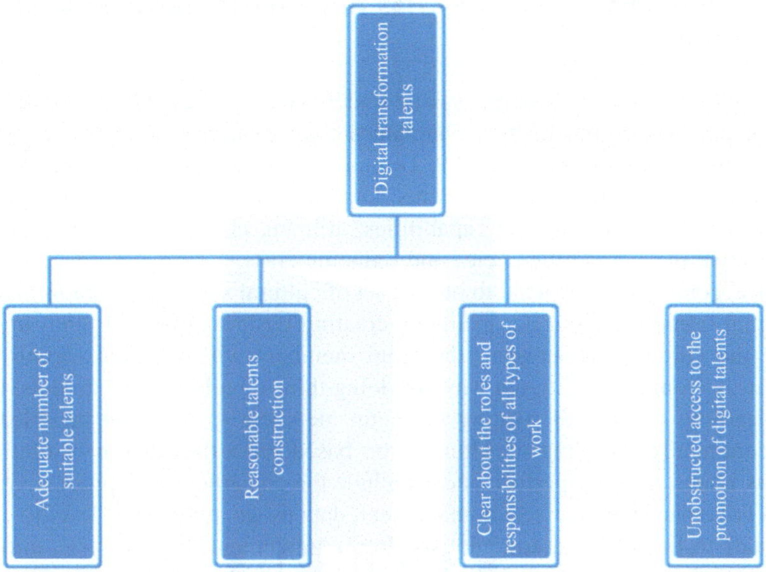

Fig. 7.8 Dimension 3 of the digital self-readiness model: digital transformation talents

failing to form an enclosed loop of talents. On the other hand, a multifunctional team can cooperate and coordinate to accomplish the tasks.

(3) Clear and concise roles and responsibilities of each designation: If there are no clear and concise roles and responsibilities for every team member, it is tough to unleash the full effects of each designation. And it would fail to drive companies' digital transformation successfully.

(4) Unobstructed access to the promotion of digital talents: During the digital transformation process, companies must build a comprehensive talents promotion system to nurture talents from the basic to the middle level so as to set aside the core support for digital transformation.

Companies need to consider building human resources in the digital transformation team. Some of the issues that companies need to consider include whether the existing human resource system can identify and build a digital team, whether the human resource model, screening channel, and criteria required in the construction of a digital transformation team are ascertained, and how to retain the talents, how to nurture and promote talents, among others.

7.2.3 Whether the Company Has Any Digital Transformation Culture

Apart from assessing the awareness and understanding of the CEOs, digital leadership team, and digital talents, companies must evaluate whether they have a digital culture, as shown in Fig. 7.9. Digital culture is a business-oriented, data-driven awareness of resolving problems. Digital transformation is a disruption of the traditional, tested rules and capabilities, utilizing new technologies to achieve the objective of raising efficiencies and reducing costs.

Hence, companies also need to build a set of cultural systems before implementing digital transformation. For example, creating business-oriented innovations to inspire the culture, encouraging the team members with material incentives to break away from the traditional ways of doing things, building new models; building a learning culture, motivating the team members to maintain their learning drive continually; building a cultural vibe based on a data-driven resolution of business issues, specific performances include the construction of process systems of data governance, data assets management, data usage at the basic level to enable more staff to be able to autonomously, freely implement data analysis, nurturing the awareness of the staff to use data to resolve the business issues, forming a cultural vibe with "a paradigm shift in the concept of data meeting the business needs" to help the companies to achieve data innovations.

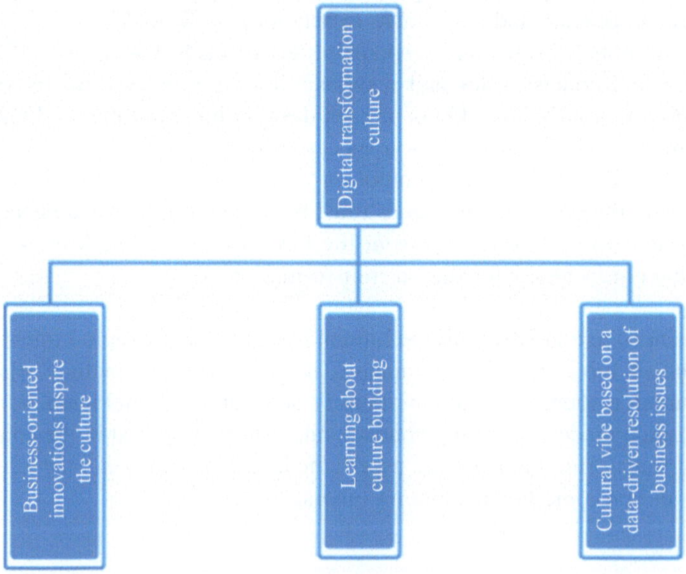

Fig. 7.9 Dimension 4 of the digital self-readiness model

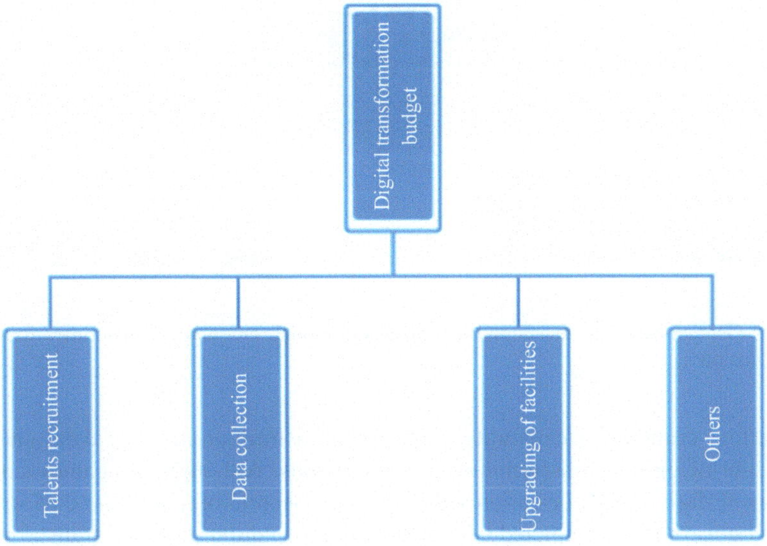

Fig. 7.10 Dimension 5 of the digital self-readiness model: digital transformation budget

7.2.4 Whether the Company Has Prepared Any Digital Transformation Budgets

Companies need to prepare the financial budgets for their digital transformation accurately. The different phases of digital transformation, such as talent recruitment, upgrading of facilities, and data collection, all involve the support of a financial budget, as shown in Fig. 7.10. Based on the survey and understanding of implementing a digital transformation, companies must estimate the spending required in the transformation process to ensure seamless execution without misallocation of expenditure. Companies must also estimate the time and spending required in digital transformation and ascertain the financial costs and time required to achieve the right objectives.

7.2.5 Whether the Company Has Any Cumulative Capabilities of Digital Transformation

Companies need to have specific cumulative capabilities to activate a digital transformation quickly. Capabilities, including data and user digitization, product digitization, organizational digitization, and conceptual systems, are companies' capabilities in implementing a digital transformation. It can be seen as the fundamentals of a quick activation of a digital transformation by companies, as shown in Fig. 7.11.

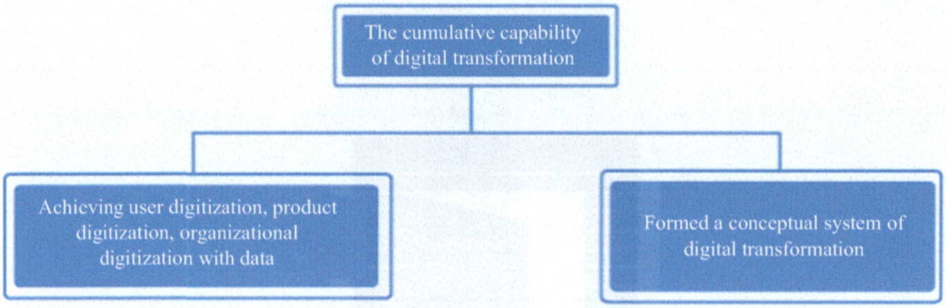

Fig. 7.11 Dimension 6 of the digital self-readiness model: cumulative capabilities for digital transformation

The first cumulative capability of digital transformation is the data, and data is the soul of digital transformation for companies. Although companies can also implement digital transformation with nothing concrete on hand, the data integration and governance completed before the implementation of digital transformation would exert a multiplier effect on the outcome in the later stages.

User digitization, product digitization, and organizational digitization are also crucial. Digital capabilities are achieved through several elements, including users, products, and organizations. These digital capabilities can help companies create new business models and operating techniques. If companies do not have sufficient cumulative capabilities, they would have to invest heavily in labor and materials to gather such capabilities after digital transformation.

On top of that, the experiences derived from digital transformation are also companies' cumulative capabilities that are the critical foundation to help companies quickly activate digital transformation. If companies have not tried any digital transformation, do not have any successful application case study, or lack the trial-and-error experiences of digital transformation, they would have to begin from scratch in their digital transformation. Companies that have gathered specific trial-and-error experiences from past digital transformation efforts can quickly activate it without wasting time.

Lastly, companies must determine whether they are equipped with a conceptual digital transformation system. In the operating processes of companies, over time, they would accumulate some professional knowledge, concepts, and theories, among others. Some companies may even have professional processes and concepts. This conceptual system's cumulative effect can help companies quickly embark on the right track of their digital transformation, untangle "confusions," improve their efficiencies in the seamless interconnectivity of data, sort out data assets, and empower businesses backed by data.

7.2.6 Whether the Company Has Any Implementation Methods for Digital Transformation

The digital transformation methodology is the key indicator of the completion of digital transformation for companies, as shown in Fig. 7.12. In the digital transformation process, determining the implementation steps and whether the company has any implementation methodology decide on the final directive and the smooth progress of the digital transformation. The digital transformation methodology must be concise and capable of forming an enclosed loop, while it must not be dotted and fragmented conceptual knowledge. When companies are driving these critical measures, fragmented conceptual knowledge cannot guide the whole transformation process to form a virtuous circle, an enclosed feedback loop, and coherent dynamic status. Even though companies may have performed well in certain phases of digital transformation, they may fail to drive their business growth in the end.

Companies must focus on constructing the six significant maps in the digital transformation process. First, the digital team must sort out the strategy map based on the growth objectives and plans of the company. Second, it must segregate the businesses according to the strategy map and separate the circular flow between businesses and their critical points to construct a business map. The technical and business teams also need to analyze which sections in the business map can be made more efficient and which sections are not appropriately configured to split or convert. Last but not least, the digital team must also sort out the data based on the business map and integrate the data of all businesses within the companies as well as the data backflow to form a holistic view of the overall data sources and

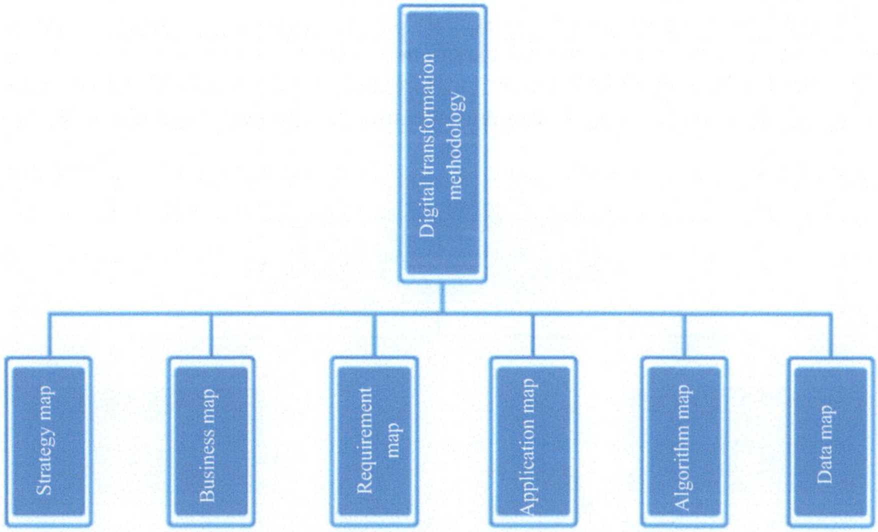

Fig. 7.12 Dimension 7 of the digital self-readiness model: digital transformation methodology

data flow and "draw up" a data map. While sorting out the business and data maps, companies can also derive more maps such as algorithm maps, application maps, and requirement maps to reinforce the company's strength of the digital transformation and safeguard the transformation effects. Before implementing digital transformation, companies need a professional team to sort out a concise transformation plan and devise a 1–3-year execution plan consisting of the six dimensions of strategy, business, demand, application, algorithm, and data. Afterward, they may draw up the corresponding acceptance criteria for the critical points of the transformation plan so that the digital transformation team can fully control the whole process with ease and confidence.

7.2.7 Whether the Company Has Any Technical Facilities for Digital Transformation

Besides preparing the tasks given above, companies must also consider whether their technical facilities can meet the technical needs of the whole digital transformation process. From data governance in the early stages to business data response in the later stages, it critically requires a robust and agile technical infrastructure architecture, as shown in Fig. 7.13.

The IT facilities created by the companies in the construction process of informatization could not flexibly respond to the ever-changing data needs of the digital era. The basic technical architecture built by companies in the information age was complicated and could not be easily modified with inferior scalability and poor adaptability. It resulted in the companies' back-end technical architecture being unable to perceive the front-end business requirements, thus failing to achieve digital innovations.

In addition, as the front-end user scenarios of companies are constantly changing, the data, users, and technical experiences generated are also accumulating with complex back-end technical architecture and inferior scalability, such that it is impossible to integrate new data and accumulate technical capabilities. With a

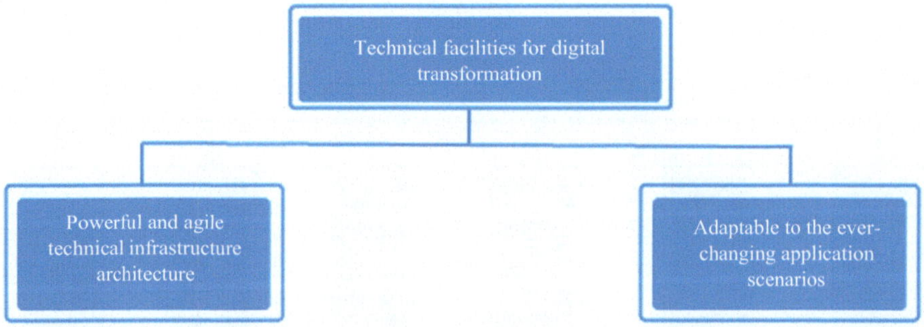

Fig. 7.13 Dimension 8 of the digital self-readiness model: technical facilities for digital transformation

continuous staff turnover, the newly generated data assets and technical capabilities cannot be retained, and the intangible losses cannot be underestimated.

Hence, digital transformation can be implemented only if the front platform of the technical infrastructure of companies is versatile, the digital platform is powerful, and the back-end platform is stable. Suppose the technical infrastructure of companies is traditional, and they do not have cost-reducing and efficiency-enhancing capabilities and cannot respond to the versatile fluctuations of the front-end business. In that case, companies must upgrade their facilities to a technical infrastructure supportive of digital transformation. After upgrading their back-end infrastructure, companies acquire substantial processing and application capabilities with more data volume and continual accumulation of models and algorithms. By doing this, the outcome of the digital transformation is comfortably assured.

7.2.8 Whether the Company Has Any Advisory Committee for Digital Transformation

On top of their own technical and economic capabilities, companies still need the support of a professional expert team during the digital transformation process, as shown in Fig. 7.14. The advisory committee for digital transformation can deliver an appropriate training system for companies to help the basic, middle, and high levels members improve their digital awareness. The advisory committee can provide professional recommendations on the digital transformation process's critical issues to avoid misunderstandings. The advisory committee can also fully monitor the course of the digital transformation from the professional perspective, assist in determining KPIs for the critical points, and devise the acceptance criteria for the transformation results to help companies safely navigate the whole digital transformation process.

Some companies, however, believe that digital transformation does not require the guidance of an advisory committee, and that is not true. Digital transformation requires assistance from digital transformation consultants and other professionals to identify the resources needed for digital transformation and tailor a digital transformation solution suitable for the company's development. Creating a digital transformation advisory committee can significantly save costs and time in trial and error efforts.

Besides, there is no competition between the advisory committee and the company. In a more precise way, it is more like a partnership between them. Apart from customizing a set of digital transformation solutions for companies, the advisory committee also shares the risks and benefits of digital transformation and covers the inadequacies of companies in digital transformation.

It is challenging for a company to achieve digital transformation by recruiting people on a large scale. First, the labor cost of the company would increase substantially. Second, it is easy for employees to have different views without

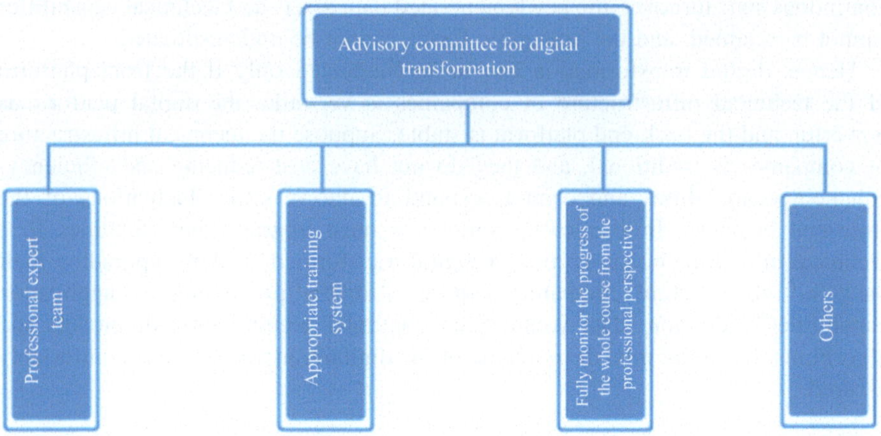

Fig. 7.14 Dimension 9 of the digital self-readiness model: advisory committee for digital transformation

a common idea, and they cannot concentrate on their tasks in the digital transformation process. With a digital transformation advisory committee, companies can drive their employees on the right track through the digital transformation advisory committee and quickly achieve success in digital transformation. Suppose companies do not seek professional assistance and blindly implement digital transformation without a concise logic. They would likely fall short in their digital transformation efforts and waste a large volume of financial and material resources, affecting the morale of their employees.

In summary, companies need to assess their capabilities and readiness for digital transformation from different dimensions, such as strategy, system, organization, and resources.

If companies want to proceed with their digital transformation, they must assess their readiness in the nine dimensions above and comprehensively evaluate their capabilities and resources to prepare them for the challenges ahead. If companies do not have proper preparation and begin their digital transformation recklessly, they are entirely clueless about the appropriate steps for a successful digital transformation and execute the processes in an unstructured manner.

For more information, please scan the QR code on the Preface.

7.3 Four Misconceptions About Digital Transformation

When companies understand their digital levels based on the Digital MAX Maturity Model and their capabilities based on the Digital Self-Readiness Model, they should be clear about their decisions to implement digital transformation. The four misconceptions about digital transformation are as follows:

7.3.1 Misconception 1: There Is No Necessity for Digital Transformation as Their Profits Are Currently Ideal

Some companies may think their current profits are ideal and do not need to plan for digital transformation. Other government agencies, universities, and financial institutions may think that their foundations are solidly intact and that they do not have to spend time and effort implementing digital transformation.

It is hardly imaginable that digital transformation is a long-cycle transformational change. As a force of technological change, it is constantly penetrating all industries. Those companies that are slow to change are gradually phased out in the fierce and competitive market. This phenomenon may not only apply to companies alone. Government agencies, higher education institutions, and financial institutions are not spared either. They should also proactively dive deep into the concepts and methodology of digital transformation and take necessary actions simultaneously. The digitalization of the government improves the efficiency and quality of government services. Digitalizing the financial institutions provides more convenient payment options and personalized financial products for the consumers. The digitalization of higher education institutions helps universities develop professional courses that are more appropriate for learning and teaching and cultivate social talents.

Digital transformation is an enormous, long-term project, and it is in the best interest of companies and various organizations to lay out their plans for such a move.

7.3.2 Misconception 2: Digital Transformation Is Only for the Leading Companies

The objective of a digital transformation is to achieve corporate intellectualization and differentiation. Intellectualization is to build business processes, enhance user experiences, and raise service efficiencies. The objective of differentiation is to utilize business restructuring and create new data-driven models to provide customers with better experiences, services, and products. From the perspective of serving customers and improving the competitiveness of products, digital transformation is not directly correlated to the size of a company. It is imperative to change the traditional way of doing things in management and marketing to compete in the ever-changing competitive market. Digital transformation is necessary.

For companies, digital transformation brings about a set of digital optimization methods that can help them adjust their operational concepts and streamline their channels and corporate management. Digital transformation can enable companies to have a more innovative organizational structure that is helpful for their future growth. In light of the continuous waves of digitalization, if small and medium enterprises (SMEs) have not actively deployed and implemented their strategies to keep up with their competitors, they would lag behind them or even totally exit from the market. On the contrary, if SMEs take the initiative to grapple with the business opportunities to implement digital transformation promptly, capitalize on the advantages of the nimbleness of SMEs and quickly switch their market focus, they could likely seize a larger market share first with a faster response than their bigger counterparts.

Hence, digital transformation is a necessary condition in the modern era of corporate development.

7.3.3 Misconception 3: Leading Companies in the Industry Do Not Require Digital Transformation

In the eyes of some industry-leading companies, digital transformation is not necessary for their development. Many large companies are still using traditional, outdated production and operational methods.

Although they have advantages in their resources, this type of advantage is limited in scope. On top of the data resources not being effectively applied, there are also silos between data. Though they can maintain the company's current operations, it is only limited to this function. Breaking away from any bottlenecks in the company's development is increasingly difficult.

For these companies, the Dividend Beyond Conformism is an opportunity to be seized. The leading companies in the industry have more advanced technologies, abundant capital, and rich customer resources to better understand the types of services customers need. Besides, their organizational structure is clear and concise, and they only need to disrupt their efficiencies to obtain more market opportunities and consolidate their market leadership.

For the standardized industrial revolution in the past, companies depended on large production scale and broad sales channels to seize market share. They built barriers to entry and captured huge market share by utilizing these advantages. Given the current personalized needs of each customer, akin to the concept of "a thousand faces with a thousand people," different customers need different personalized services, however. The real test of the consumer market is no longer the scale of the company, and it is instead the provision of personalized services for the customers by utilizing technologies and products. That is a complicated issue facing companies now. Even if some companies provide personalized services to their customers, they incur very high costs.

Hence, industry-leading companies also need to undergo digital transformation. They can create more value with less cost, making breakthroughs to circumvent obstacles and improve industrial upgrading.

7.3.4 Misconception 4: As There Are Few Success Stories of Digital Transformation Among Companies, There Is No Need for Any Digital Transformation

Some companies that have not yet implemented digital transformation may think it is unnecessary to implement it because there were few success stories. There were also no particularly successful digital transformations in the industry or substantial precedents that would spark industrial attention.

That is a mistake. Because of this misunderstanding, many companies "cannot see, cannot understand, cannot appreciate and cannot keep pace with" digital transformation. That is, they "cannot see" the power of digital transformation; they "cannot understand" how to implement a digital transformation, and they "cannot appreciate" the merits of having digital transformation because they cannot see and understand. Thus they "cannot keep pace with" the other companies. Digital transformation is a continuous process of trial and error. Likely, some industry-leading companies are still constantly exploring digital transformation and have yet to reap the rewards and benefits of digital transformation. If other companies are still waiting for these companies to achieve a successful digital transformation before deciding to implement one, these companies may have already lost a golden opportunity.

Consequently, companies must devise a customized digital transformation solution based on their unique characteristics because different companies have different products and operations conditions. They could not rest on their laurels even without digital transformation success stories.

Currently, there are two types of digital transformation: one is a progressive type, and the other is a penetrative type.

1. **Progressive digital transformation**

Most companies suitable for progressive digital transformation are rich in resources and have unique labor, capital, and land advantages. Their organizational structure is characterized by many departments, long business chains, and centralization. These companies have redundant functions, so they are unsuitable for directly transitioning to digital transformation. They need a progressive approach, accumulating experiences one step at a time and driving the completion of digital transformation in a spiral manner. Digital transformation is a long-term project, and it is hard to see the effects of digital transformation in the short term. But with a long-term accumulation of experiences spanning from changes in quantity to quality, these companies may enjoy superior benefits compared to those without digital transformation. In this process, companies only need to ensure they are on the right track in digital transformation before getting the desired results after a specific accumulation of experiences.

2. **Penetrative digital transformation**

Another type of company can employ the penetrative approach to drive digital transformation based on the characteristics of their industry. They can disrupt and innovate simple processes and short business chains in their internal departments. Some apparel companies can quickly produce a batch of clothes in 5–15 days, surpassing the usual 20-day production cycle typical among their peers. The essence of market competition lies in full control of time. Companies with the right conditions can adopt a penetrative digital transformation.

Part V

Who Is Responsible for Digital Transformation?

After companies decide whether to implement digital transformation after assessing their current conditions and capabilities, the leaders of these companies need to consider the following questions.

How to build a leadership organization for digital transformation?

How to recruit talents and build an organizational structure after determining the leadership organization?

Who is responsible for digital transformation? Who are the ones responsible for the execution of digital transformation?

How to determine the KPIs for digital transformation to ensure that the transformation is adequately executed during the digital transformation process?

A successful resolution of these issues can help companies to achieve a clear division of labor and responsibilities in the deployment of digital transformation; thus, ensuring the execution is proper and on target.

8 The Main Driver of Digital Transformation

In the following section, we shall describe the directors spearheading digital transformation. How does a board of directors drive digital transformation? How does a CEO construct an organizational structure, recruit and retain talents, and determine digital transformation KPIs? How does a CDO continually drive digital transformation? The list goes on.

8.1 How Does a Board of Directors Drive the Company to Implement Digital Transformation?

The digital wave is spearheading the development of all industries, pivoting the importance of technology in the business arena, thus unlocking more new products and services and bringing significant value to society and the economy at large. Digital transformation is of vital importance to all companies. It disrupts the competitive order in the industries, rolls out new products and services with intelligent applications of digital technologies, and builds new business models, achieving the seamless interconnectivity of people, objects, and scenarios, and breaking away the information barriers isolating different departments and creating more business opportunities to maintain their market positions in the foreseeable future.

When companies have decided to implement a digital transformation, the board of directors, the highest decision-maker within the organization, must first understand the significance and influences of digital transformation before making the right decisions, leading the organization to significant adjustments and ascertaining the growth directive of the organization.

X. Ma, *Methodology for Digital Transformation*, Management for Professionals,
https://doi.org/10.1007/978-981-19-9111-0_8

8.1.1 Three Challenges of Digital Transformation Facing the Board of Directors

Digital transformation is a significant source of business innovation for most companies today and in the future. Companies need to re-evaluate their business models and services. As the highest decision-maker within the organization, the board of directors faces three significant challenges under the onslaught of the digital waves, as shown in Fig. 8.1.

1. **Understand the significance and influences of data-driven business**

Before deciding on implementing digital transformation, the board of directors' attitude, the organization's highest decision-maker, is of utmost importance.

That is because it is closely associated with supporting resource deployment, approving financial budgets, and constructing talent teams during the digital transformation process if the board of directors understands the reasons for digital transformation, whether to implement a digital transformation, and when to begin the digital transformation, how to drive digital transformation, what kinds of results after digital transformation, and other issues, the transformation tasks can be executed appropriately to achieve the final objective, as shown in Fig. 8.2.

2. **Raise the priority of digital strategy to counter the competitive order in the future**

The enormous energy of digital transformation is reflected in the development of transforming industries. Hence, the board of directors needs to make timely decisions about the direction of the company, including the devising of a digital

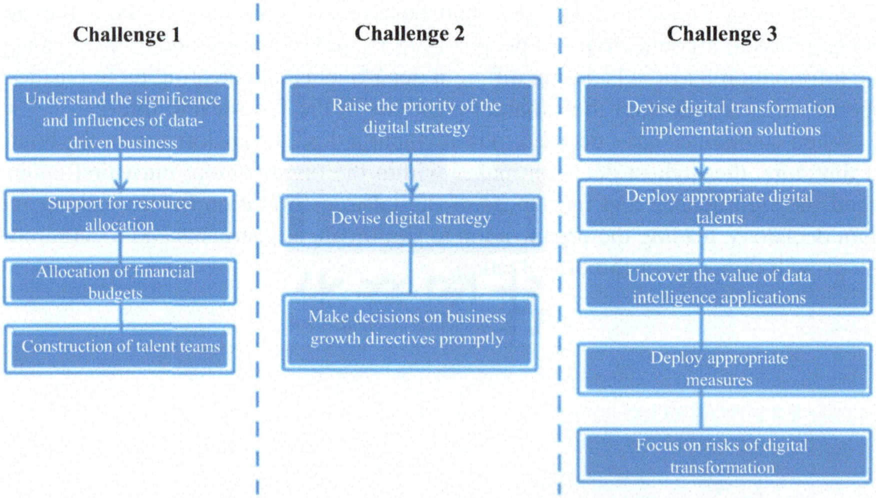

Fig. 8.1 Three challenges of digital transformation facing the board of directors

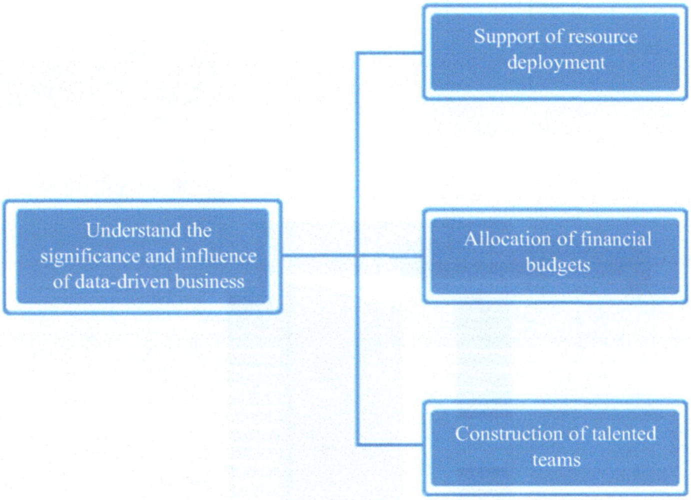

Fig. 8.2 Challenge of digital transformation facing the board of directors: Significance and influences of data-driven business

strategy, which is elevated to the top strategic position of the company, so that the whole company can actively explore the path of digital transformation with united actions, as shown in Fig. 8.3.

3. **Devise digital transformation implementation solutions to enhance customer experience and raise the quality of products and services**

After the board of directors has devised the digital strategy, they need to drive the digital transformation solution based on the strategy.

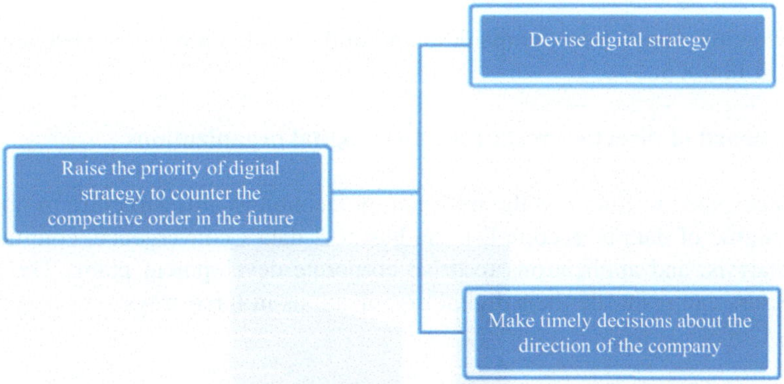

Fig. 8.3 Challenge of digital transformation facing the board of directors: prioritize digital strategy

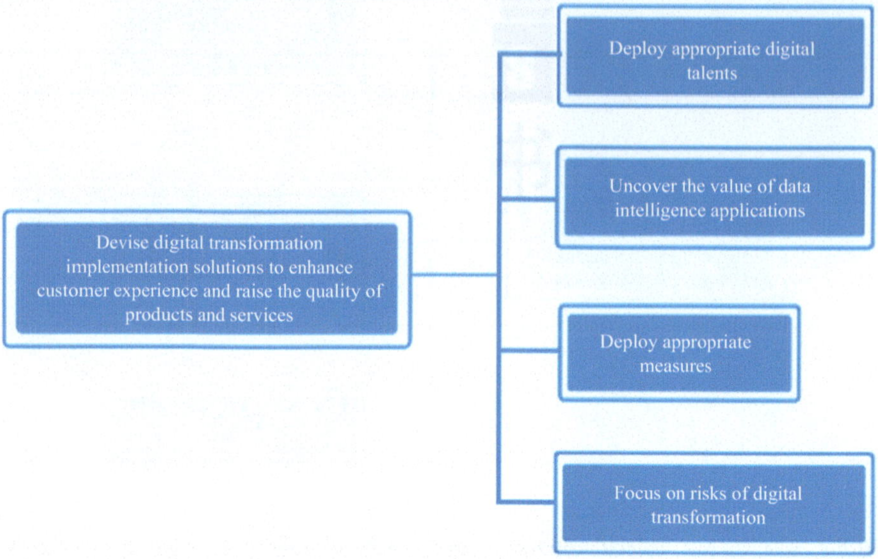

Fig. 8.4 Challenge of digital transformation facing the board of directors: devise digital transformation implementation solution

The frontline team will better accomplish the objectives in each phase of the digital transformation according to the implementation solution to ensure positive results. In the digital transformation process, the board of directors should also deploy appropriate digital talents, uncover the value of data intelligence applications, and implement relevant measures to focus on the risks of digital transformation, as shown in Fig. 8.4.

8.1.2 How to Build Digital Competitive Advantages

The following details how companies can build digital competitive advantages, as shown in Fig. 8.5.

1. **The board of directors reshuffles their digital organizations**

Companies need to fully use the information technology infrastructure to obtain a large volume of data to accomplish the business data's convergence, communication, analysis, and applications to drive corporate development plans. The board of directors can reshuffle their digital organizations in three ways.

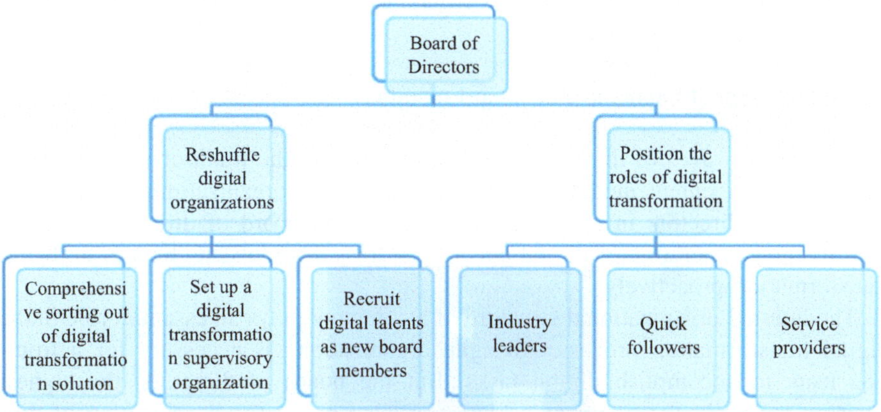

Fig. 8.5 Building of digital competitive advantages

(1) A comprehensive review of the digital transformation program

As the highest level of the organizational structure, the key focus of the board of directors lies in policymaking rather than implementation. In the digital transformation process, however, the board of directors not only needs to understand the significance of policymaking, but they also need to understand the implementation process and results of digital transformation so that they can roll out measures promptly and adjust the direction of the transformation. Hence, the board of directors needs an execution team to conduct a comprehensive review of the transformation program, including strategy development, financial budgets, talent deployment, technology provision, and schedule control, to ascertain the strategy and objectives in different phases of the digital transformation.

(2) Set up a digital transformation supervisory organization

Once a company's digital transformation has begun, it requires more effort to follow up and analyze the results. The board of directors can thus set up a digital transformation supervisory organization to follow up and understand the digital transformation's progress and results to provide more references for their subsequent digital measures.

In addition, the board of directors, and the digital policymaker, are not directly involved in the specific implementation of the digital transformation. The execution results of the frontline team should be collated and audited by the leaders in the middle management. Hence, the board of directors needs to differentiate and evaluate the digital business capabilities of the direct leaders of the frontline team to ascertain their competencies to connect and control the transition from traditional to digital business.

(3) Recruit digital talents as new board members

The incessant waves of digitalization disrupt not only the traditional, tested business and management models but also the traditional organizational structure of the board of directors in all companies. Hence, the board of directors needs to recruit a new generation of digital talent to address the constant changes in digital transformation proactively.

The internal organizational structure of a company plays an essential role in the digital transformation process. An agile organization[1] is necessary for a front-line team to accomplish digital tasks. But the board of directors, the highest decision-maker in the company's hierarchy, also needs the participation of digital professionals, thus enabling the policy-making process to be more scientific, objective, and practical. The board members, who have past experiences in digitalization, challenge the traditional organizational structure of the board of directors and construct operating models and methods to drive digital businesses within the board and across the companies.

2. **Position the roles of digital transformation**

In the digital transformation process, companies of varying sizes reside in different development phases. E-commerce giants with robust digital technologies and a large volume of user data can be regarded as the leaders in digital transformation. In the long digital transformation journey, there are bound to be many companies with varying degrees of transformation.

Whether large companies or SMEs, companies that want a successful digital transformation must deeply understand their conditions. Whether they are striving to be an industry leader, a quick follower, or a service provider that focuses on product R&D and service creation as well as provides solutions for digital transformation, the board of directors needs to consider all factors carefully and make a final decision. There are three common types of corporate positioning as follows:

(1) Industry leaders

Large internet companies that ride on the new digital waves drive value creation in the industry in the digital transformation process. They are essential in creating value driven by consumers, services, assets, and products. The industry leaders in digital transformation review the significance of interconnection between people,

[1] [4] An agile organization has an organizational structure akin to the operational models of the Special Forces. It is a fully functional team that responds and adapts quickly to the changes in the marketplace, executes strategic plans strongly, and innovates continually.

businesses, and products and use the idea of value creation to be the measure of success in digital transformation.

New companies can permanently disrupt the traditional growth models regardless of the fast-growing internet industry or a slow-growing traditional industry. It is not an exception, even for digital transformation. The new companies that rely heavily on the deep integration of digital technologies and businesses compete with those which are reluctant to innovate and change in the marketplace. The new digital companies redefine the traditional industry and continuously renew industry knowledge.

(2) Quick followers

There are many followers of digital transformation chasing after industry leaders. These followers can quickly identify the digital advantages of the leaders and focus on their core digital initiatives. By learning from the relevant measures and integrating them with their corporate characteristics, they can quickly create new business markets and develop a system with defensive capabilities against other competitors in the industry.

(3) Service providers

Apart from the industry leaders and quick followers, there is another type of corporate positioning known as service providers. Service providers do not have the robust digital technologies of the industry leaders and are also not dominant in the market. They are still far away from the leading pack, with a significant distance away from the quick followers. In the macro environment of digital transformation, service providers only rely on a small market share to complete the digital transformation by themselves.

With the proliferation of emerging technologies, service providers must provide products that meet market demand and deploy the appropriate products to avoid the rapid disruption of digital technologies on their products and business systems. Companies that are content with developing a single product without enhancing the relevant services find it hard to gain a strong foothold amid the waves of digital transformation.

Companies must make a definitive decision in implementing digital transformation based on their unique business characteristics and market positioning. It is a critical factor that decides whether the particular company eventually becomes an industry leader, a quick follower, or a service provider. Regardless of the varying roles, all companies must begin to take action now. Industry leaders must constantly enhance their businesses and products with digital technologies and uncover the value in digital transformation. The followers must monitor the market trends and industry development and analyze and learn from the digital transformation initiatives employed by the leaders to recalibrate their pace of digital transformation and unlock the business value. The service providers must focus on product

R&D and the creation of services to maintain their market competitiveness amid the digital waves.

8.2 How to Build a Leadership Organization for Digital Transformation

Amid the onslaught of digital waves across all industries, the traditional top-down hierarchical approach to management cannot meet the business requirements of the new era. In the business environment of the digital era, there are inevitably more demanding requirements in terms of the speed of response to customer needs, the accuracy of services provided, and the personalization of customer experience. Achieving these requirements needs a large amount of investment in data analysis.

Companies need to create new organizational structures to meet the solid analytical requirements and the ever-changing data-driven objectives to build a leadership organization that can quickly adapt to digital development. The objective of the leadership organization is to help companies achieve a successful digital transformation. Formed by a group of personnel with different skillsets that enable digital transformation, it aims to enhance business creativity and the speed of response to customers.

The leadership organization in the digital era should demolish the old, rigid hierarchical structure within the companies, enrich the corporate resources, reinvigorate the intrinsic vitality of the team, and devise a sharing mechanism so that companies can quickly adapt to the changes in the marketplace in a more versatile way.

Companies can first understand the limitations of the current hierarchical leadership structure before building a leadership organization for digital transformation.

8.2.1 Understand the Limitations of Hierarchical Leadership

While it may not be possible to predict the exact value digital transformation bring about, digital transformation requires companies to be more agile, faster in decision-making, more substantial in engagement, and more significant in innovation and autonomy. In contrast, the traditional hierarchical leadership structure focuses on reporting and accountability systems, risk management, resource optimization, and progressive improvement. This outdated management approach in the industrial revolution is utterly incompatible with the digital development model with unique agility, responsiveness, customization, and personalization features. If companies do not make any changes, it affects the progress of digital transformation.

8.2.2 Build a Digital Leadership Organization

Just as every industrial revolution would disrupt social production and lifestyle by introducing new organizational structures and management models, digital transformation also proposes new requirements for companies' organizational structures and business models. Digital transformation is not a short-term project but a long-term program involving a multi-dimensional approach to companies' organizational structures, management, and operating models. Consequently, companies must achieve success in their digital transformation. They must implement a top-down digital strategy and construct a project-based, skill-based, scenario-based organizational model to inspire the digital transformation team's creativity and enhance the businesses' agility.

1. **Build a digital leadership organization with the CEO (highest-ranking individual in a company) as its core**

In today's ever-changing business landscape, companies need a leadership organization to counter the pressure of digital transformation. In this digital organization, the CEO is the number one person responsible for digital transformation, who is led by the board of directors and oversees the work of the CTO, CIO, CDO, and COO. The division of labor among the CEO, CTO, CIO, CDO, and COO differs for each individual. Their job descriptions should be specified before the implementation of digital transformation to provide firm assurance for the execution of a digital transformation, as shown in Fig. 8.6.

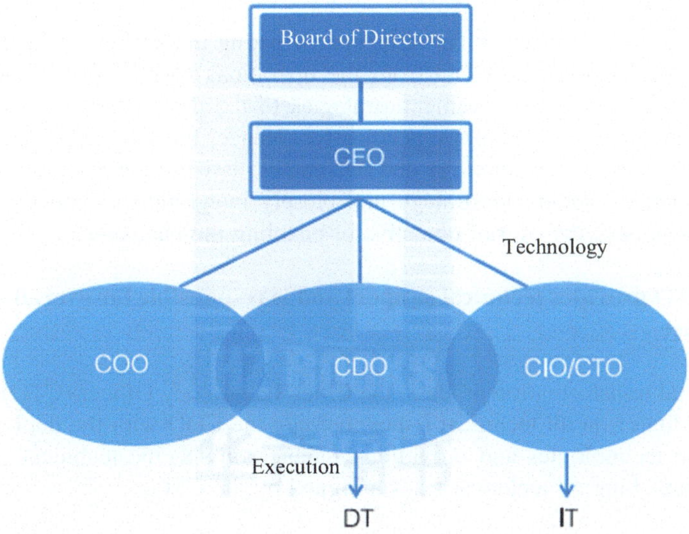

Fig. 8.6 Digital leadership organization

The CEO, the company's top decision-maker, must lead the digital transformation strategy, provide advice to the CDO to drive and implement a digital transformation, organize and allocate the human and financial resources, construct a leadership organization and verify the results. The CEO also must acknowledge the technical architecture construction and data-enabled businesses undertaken by the CTO or CIO and coordinate the interconnecting issues between technologies and businesses. The digital transformation of companies should be built on a foundation with the CEO at its core, balanced by the CDO, COO, CTO, or CIO to form a leadership organization with mutual collaboration.

2. **The CDO is responsible for the implementation of digital transformation**

The Chief Digital Officer (CDO), the implementation leader in digital transformation, leads the digital transformation team to complete the variable objectives from data to business. In the overall perspective, CDO is responsible for the progress of digital transformation, including the beginning of execution, the push for progress, and the acceptance test of results. The CDO reports to the CEO with equal seniority with the CIO, CTO, and COO, cooperating with them to collectively achieve data-enabled businesses' objectives.

3. **The CIO is responsible for information technology, system maintenance, and operations**

Chinese companies often combine the CIO and CTO job descriptions; only one is the responsible person. If their job descriptions in the two positions are dissected in finer detail, it would not be surprising that there are some differences in their responsible areas.

The Chief Information Officer (CIO) participating in the digital transformation can assist and support the CDO from the operations of information technology and provide technical improvement strategies to the digital transformation team from the information technology perspective. Hence, the CIO must be equipped with the knowledge of technology and businesses, assisting the CDO in deploying the organization's technical strategy and closely integrating it with the business strategy to achieve the overall objective of enabling the businesses.

4. **The CTO provides technical support and is responsible for overall technical guidance**

In the digital transformation process, the Chief Technology Officer (CTO) acts as a strong facilitator on all technical issues, helping the CDO with the deployment of appropriate technologies and providing guidance on specific technical problems, and accomplishing all technical tasks assigned by the CEO.

5. **The COO is responsible for sorting out the multiple business lines and the provision of business requirements**

The digital transformation of companies aims to utilize digital technologies to improve operating efficiency and management level, enabling the business to be more innovative. Hence, the COO needs to sort out the products and services in varying dimensions, functions, categories, and levels during the digital transformation process, concisely determine the business lines of companies, collate the needs of each business, and lay down compatible objectives of the digital transformation.

Meanwhile, the COO also needs to address the following issues: whether the digital transformation solution fits with the company's earlier business plans, whether the marketing plans and management can be more intelligent, and whether the sales performance can be improved. In particular, the COO needs to balance the relationship between the technical and business departments during the digital transformation process so that both departments can communicate and cooperate closely.

The construction of a digital leadership organization provides resources for the digital teams to create connecting interfaces in multiple fields, such as technology, systems, and business, reshaping the entire digital leadership organization. In addition, it enhances agility and versatility among leaders in different fields, enabling channels for information sharing and resource collaboration among digital teams, breaking down information silos and resource barriers, and providing a platform for communication and collaboration.

The organizational roles above, including the CDO, COO, CTO, or CIO, can be appropriately adapted to an organization's actual situation, such as a company or a bank. If the CIO has the capability of a CDO, it can be performed by one person as long as the transformation objectives are met.

8.3 How Does a CEO Build a Leadership Organization for Digital Transformation

Every organization has a position of the "highest-ranking individual." For example, the president of a bank, the university dean, or the company CEO are the highest-ranking individuals in their respective organizations and are responsible for their organizations' daily operations. For convenience, we refer to the highest-ranking individual as the CEO herein. In this section, we describe how to build a leadership organization during the digital transformation process in each organization, using the CEO of a company as an example.

The CEO of a company needs to have complete control of the operations internally while dealing with all kinds of partnerships externally. A company's digital transformation depends on the CEO's decisions and promotional campaigns. Hence, it is critical for the CEO to build a leadership organization for digital transformation. The CEO needs to understand the importance of organization construction, the factors for consideration while building the organization, and the vital roles and capabilities in the digital transformation process.

8.3.1 The Role that a CEO Plays in Digital Transformation

1. **Definition of CEO**

The CEO (Chief Executive Officer) is the highest-ranking individual responsible for a company's daily operations, and the CEO is also known as the chief executive officer, general manager, or top executive officer. In the digital transformation process, the CEO must finalize the digital transformation solution from the strategic perspective, build a leadership organization and coordinate the resources of all departments to support the steady progress of digital transformation.

2. **Job duties of the CEO in digital transformation**

- Make decisions on all critical operational matters, including the development of solutions, financial budgets, operational goals for digital transformation, and the expansion and reduction of digital business scope.
- Control the direction of the company's digital transformation and develop digital strategies.
- Participate in the decision-making of the board of directors and implement the board resolutions.
- Lead the company's day-to-day business activities aligned with the digital transformation objectives.
- Appraise the senior management responsible for the digitalization of the company.
- Report regularly to the board of directors over the business conditions and the results of different phases in the digital transformation and include the results of digital transformation in the annual report and submit them to the board of directors.

Hence, the company's CEO must proactively lead the direction of digital transformation, drive the entire company in a united front to march toward the goals of digital transformation, resolve the issues faced by the CDO and other staff along the long journey of digital transformation, and verifying the progress and results of digital transformation to calibrate and refine the pace and direction promptly during the digital transformation process.

8.3.2 How Does a CEO Build a Leadership Organization for Digital Transformation

As the highest-ranking individual in a company, the CEO plays a crucial role in the success or failure of the company's operations. In the digital transformation process, the CEO should, on the one hand, understand the necessity of building a leadership organization and, on the other hand, learn to build leadership in an organization for digital transformation, as shown in Fig. 8.7.

1. **Necessary to build an organizational structure**

An organizational structure refers to the overall structure of an organization. It is the fundamental component of organizing resources, building processes, managing businesses, and implementing management within the company because of many factors such as corporate management requirements, positioning of management control, management models, and business characteristics.

Constructing the team's organizational structure can enable the whole team to collaborate more systematically and standardized, thus improving the team's working efficiency. Building an organizational structure requires sorting out the team's functional structure and delegating the specific job descriptions according to the roles and positions of every team member. Hence, an endorsed organizational structure is essential in the operational process and is a core component of the whole team.

2. **Factors to be considered in the building of an organizational structure**

The pressure faced in achieving a successful digital transformation is enormous. Under the onslaught of heavy pressure, what are the factors the CEO must consider while building an organizational structure?

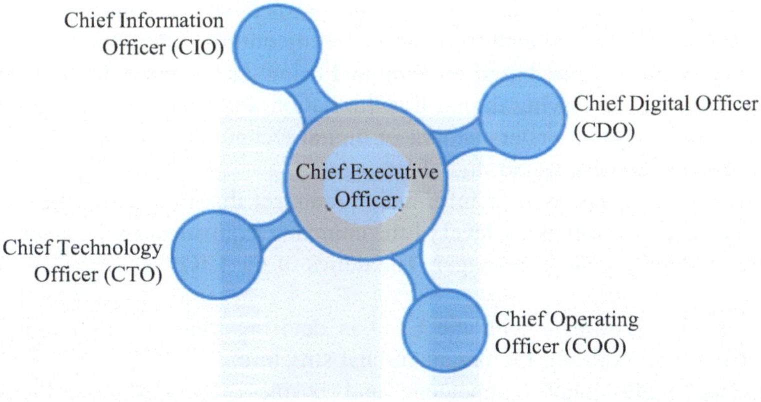

Fig. 8.7 How does a CEO build a leadership organization for digital transformation

(1) Leadership. Leadership is divided into several components, including leadership qualities, leadership knowledge, leadership behaviors, and leadership strategies. It is one of the most critical parts of the organizational structure.
(2) Budgetary cost control. Each department's production and operational activities are checked and monitored according to the standardized revenue and expenditure specified in the budget to ensure that all activities and departments achieve their specific goals. By doing this, reasonable profitability and the use of resources can be attained. Hence, costs and expenses must be subject to strict and effective control.
(3) Strategic planning. The long-term objectives of the organization must be put in place and implemented. Having proper plans for specific tasks is essential from a macro perspective.
(4) Technological level. As technology is fast evolving nowadays, the CEO must be aware of the latest technological developments in the industry to develop policies that meet the current level of technological advancement and fit into the company's growth.
(5) Business model. The operating model can be integrated into the current business model to protect it against the risks that the digital business may face in an ever-changing environment and integrate digitalization into the product design and process to ensure an orderly and stable advancement of digitalization.

During the implementation of a digital transformation, many senior executives desire to transform their companies into successful digital companies in the shortest time possible. The transformation path, however, is not easy. It takes a long time, a strong will, and strict time management and planning.

3. **Determine the core personnel for digital transformation**

It is key to selecting the right employees to be the core personnel in digital transformation. What kind of person can be core personnel? The best candidates for core personnel are the CIOs, CTOs, COOs, and CDOs, who are responsible for the leadership in the digital businesses of their respective companies.

The role of a CDO is to lead the team in sorting out the different business lines, refining the business value based on data, and using data to solve business issues. As a pivotal figure in driving digital transformation, the CDO, who reports to the CEO, must have a good understanding of digital technology and deep knowledge of the company's business and digital strategies.

A CIO/CTO is a new type of information manager that falls under the category of the highest decision-making level of the company, equivalent to the level of vice president or deputy general manager. The duties of the CIO/CTO are as follows:

(1) Proactively coordinate with the CEO in devising plans for digital business strategies and building the organizational structure.
(2) Enhance professional competency and business knowledge and play an important leadership role in developing a digital business.

(3) Ensure that the technical components of digital business are included in the budget.
(4) Assess the skill sets of the entire team and lead the team to actively address the business and technological challenges under the premise that the entire team has adapted well to the new platform for digital business.

The most critical issue faced by companies in the digital transformation process is the complexity of data. Data has become as complicated as business and technology. The core personnel must focus on execution while having the capabilities to provide proper solutions.

8.4 How to Hire and Retain Talents

Talents are the most critical component in the process of digital transformation. Regardless of how perfect the CEO's digital transformation plan is, it needs to be implemented by digital talents.

1. **Selection criteria for digital talents**

The ability to attract, select and retain digital talents is pivotal to a successful digital transformation of companies. Digital talents must understand and master technology, data, and business to enable business innovation. As there is a shortage of such people with comprehensive capabilities, companies can combine talents with individual capability in technology, data, and business to achieve business innovation as a team, as shown in Fig. 8.8.

During the selection process for digital talents, companies must be aware that the selection of digital talents should not be driven solely by technical competencies as their core criteria but rather by the common objectives of digital

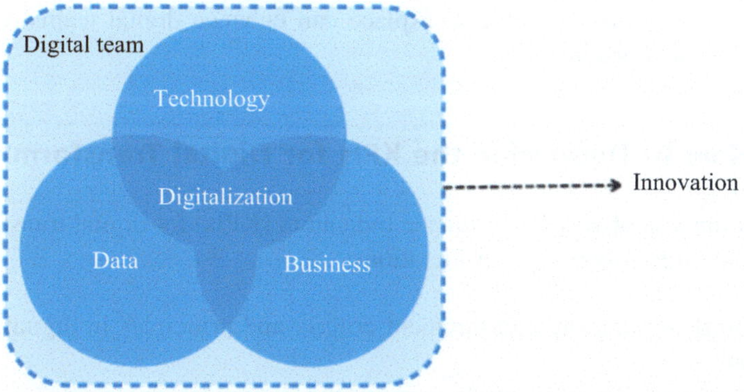

Fig. 8.8 Digital team enables digital transformation

transformation. In this aspect, the CEO needs to clearly articulate it to the board of directors and get their support.

2. **Build a digital workplace**

A digital workplace not only improves the productivity of team members but also increases their levels of participation in projects. Technology can be utilized to create a digital workplace. These technologies include data analytics tools, cloud office software, and algorithms based on employees' behaviors, which can be deployed in the digital workplace, thus changing how employees work and enhancing their creativity and efficiency. The digital workplace is a new way of accomplishing traditional work that facilitates business innovation. Digital teams losing a digital workplace vanish their ability to innovate digitally, and the digital talents are quickly assimilated into the traditional talents.

While building a digital workplace, the digital transformation leaders should not only focus on the essential IT systems, but instead, they should focus on improving the employee experience, interactions, and corporate performances as their objectives. It must not be driven solely by technology. The digital workplace needs to contain cloud-based applications to support remote work, ease of data access, and professional data analytics tools to enable self-service data analysis services. At the same time, leaders can utilize data analytics tools to effectively manage employees so that companies can use data to provide feedback on how well employees are performing, improving management efficiency. In addition, the social aspect of a digital workplace must be conducive to fostering the spirit of collaboration and innovation between team members.

The provision of an engaging digital work experience for all employees requires not only the efforts of the IT department but also the collaboration between other business departments to develop work processes according to the actual business scenarios and needs.

The future of work consists of more innovative work experiences. Building a digital workplace is one of the methods to achieve it. Integrating the appropriate technologies with a suitable workplace can enhance digital teams' creativity, collaboration, and productivity.

8.5 How to Determine the KPIs for Digital Transformation

The determination of Key Performance Indicators (KPIs) for digital transformation involves the three following considerations:

(1) How to determine the measurement criteria and principles in digital transformation?
(2) How to assess the company benefits of the digitalization process?
(3) How to build strategic capabilities for the future?

8.5.1 Determination of Criteria and Principles of KPIs for Digital Transformation

As the steering leader of business operations management, the CEO needs to determine the measurement criteria and principles for KPIs of digital transformation before initiating the digital transformation process. Banks, for example, need to abide by two principles in determining KPIs for digital transformation. The first type is the determination of revenue-based KPI, while the second type is the determination of KPI based on strategic capability. Revenue-based KPI aims to improve the current and future revenue of the bank with digital transformation, as shown in Fig. 8.9. KPI based on strategic capability aims to enhance the strategic capability of the bank in the future, including capturing business opportunities, efficiency enhancement, and data applications capability.

Regardless of the revenue-based KPIs or KPIs based on strategic capability, they should encompass all phases of digital business development. Companies can devise indicators for revenue growth and improvement of strategic capability at different phases to drive the digital business development process.

In addition, the objectives of the different phases of development should be determined in the early phases of digital business development rather than during the implementation process. The early phases should be thorough, comprehensive, and reasonable planning.

Lastly, the digital business indicators should not be too few or too many. On the one hand, if there are too few indicators, it is not easy to control the work boundaries without clearly indicating responsibilities during the whole project process. On the other hand, if there are too many indicators, the actions are restricted

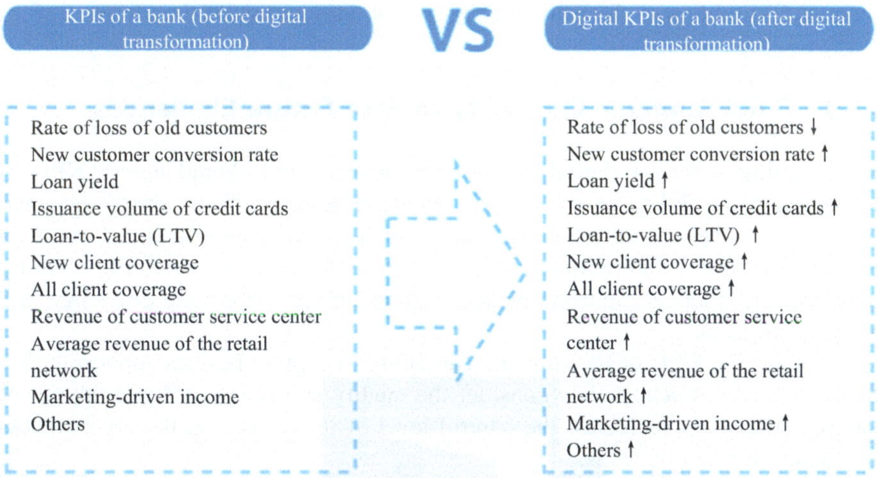

Fig. 8.9 Revenue-based KPIs for banks

with excessive responsibilities, significantly affecting the positioning of the various roles in the data team.

The KPIs for digital transformation are designed to evaluate the digital transformation process of a company, which results in performance improvement. The changes in performance can be reflected in the KPIs of the company. Digital business development can only be guided by a clear definition of the measurement criteria for digital transformation, helping companies to recalibrate their measurement criteria at any time according to the changes in business and industry. It is however noteworthy that these KPIs are not always static, and they are complementary to other performance indicators of the company.

8.5.2 Quantify the Digital Returns in All Sectors

In the digital transformation process, the CEO needs to ascertain the principles to determine KPI and work with the senior executives from different departments to quantify the revenue-based indicators brought about by digitalization in each department. While working with these senior executives, the CEO needs to develop a set of KPIs to assess the current business model of the digitalization process. KPIs can help the CEO evaluate the efficiency of the digital business and streamline the digital model promptly. The KPIs of digital transformation in the sales segment can help companies to focus on their sales operations, measuring the percentage of sales based on digital channels and assessing the effect of digitalization on the company's sales performance.

The CEO can set digital goals and KPIs for different aspects of the business operations and management, including operations, supply chain, products, and customer service. For example, companies can reduce their inventories from 2 billion to about 500 million in the warehousing section in a particular time frame.

8.5.3 Build Strategic Capability to Face Future Challenges

While setting KPIs for digital transformation, the CEO should devise KPIs of the strategic capability to face future challenges, apart from setting revenue-based KPIs. These strategic capabilities can help companies gain or maintain market share in the future and sustain their growth. Strategic capability includes many aspects, such as capturing business opportunities, improving efficiency, and applying the data.

While setting KPIs of the strategic capability to capture business opportunities, the CEO can comprehensively consider the quality and speed of data analytics of unexpected hotspot incidents, the control level of incidents, and the effectiveness of utilizing traffic dividends.

While setting KPIs of the strategic capability to improve efficiency, the CEO can consider the customer acquisition aspect. Suppose a company uses a digital customer acquisition method and gets a higher customer acquisition capability than its competitors, while the efficiency of each customer acquisition process is enhanced. Using this method, the company can set the KPIs of strategic capability based on customer acquisition capability.

While setting KPIs of strategic capability for data applications, the CEO can comprehensively consider the quality and quantity of data applications and the feedback length. The CEO, for example, can consider how many people are using data to solve their problems, how efficient the data is in solving business problems, and how short the response is. These are all factors for consideration in the KPIs of strategic capability from the data applications aspect.

Strategic capability is often intangible, and it cannot be seen directly. But strategic capability gradually is built into the company's organizational structure and business growth, subtly affecting the whole company's business growth digitally. In the development process, companies must focus on performance and revenue in the short term while concentrating on their core strategic capabilities in the long term.

8.5.4 Five Noteworthy Points in Determining KPIs

In the digital transformation process, companies need to consider the operating effectiveness of the team members. Setting KPIs differently from daily operating KPIs for digital transformation is necessary. There are five noteworthy points for companies in the determination of KPIs.

1. **KPIs for digital transformation are not corporate KPIs**

Digital business objectives are different from the KPIs of daily operations. They are not mutually replaceable and have common goals of expanding the business and pursuing revenue. They revolve around revenue growth, cost reduction, and profit enhancement. The difference lies in the approach to achieving the goals. Digital businesses emphasize using new digital technologies synergized with businesses to achieve cost reduction, efficiency improvement, and revenue enhancement. While implementing proper measures to achieve digital business goals, companies should also maintain the KPIs for daily operations to assess the digital business progress and opportunities to reflect the differences between digital and non-digital revenue with revenue and profit indicators.

2. **KPIs for digital transformation are only temporary**

KPIs have a time frame. Companies should create a time horizon while setting KPIs for digital transformation with start and end times. The end time for digital transformation can be adjusted to the progress. Besides, the end time also urges the team members to stay on track with their digital tasks. When a company has completed a digital transformation, original KPIs may change. Specific renewable digital indicators, for example, can be added to the corporate KPIs and become permanent business indicators to further direct digitalization efforts.

3. **Digital transformation should set a balance of indicators**

Digital transformation does not imply that all business models have to be digitalized and setting up too many digital interactive models can have a negative influence. The digital transformation KPIs should be balanced between employees and customers, and each KPI should have a point of balance to avoid excessive digitalization. With the advancement of digitalization, the balancing point may also change. The KPIs for digital transformation should be set to align with the business characteristics of the company.

4. **Key indicators are only shared across multiple departments**

Although many specific indicators exist in a company's digital transformation, some key indicators can only be shared with multiple departments. The different dimensions of indicators involved in the production process, including production indicators, data analytics indicators, yield optimization indicators, indicators to reduce consumables, and inventory maximization indicators, can be key indicators to describe the digitalization level of the production process and shared with multiple departments. As other single indicators are insufficient to represent the progress of digitalization, they do not need to be shared. Apart from sharing key indicators, companies should also set clear and measurable goals for each critical phase of digital transformation.

5. **KPIs for digital transformation should calculate the current market share and forecast the future market size**

While companies may refer to the corporate KPI models when setting KPIs for digital transformation, they often only consider tracking incremental progress and revenue.

Digital businesses, however, can permanently disrupt business models creating entirely new opportunities. Thus, KPIs for digital transformation should be set to take into account the goals in the execution progress and assess the indicators for companies to pursue innovative growth opportunities. KPIs can help the CEO understand the company's current revenue and market share, providing a reference for future market development so that companies can adequately quantify the new business models and prepare for emerging business opportunities.

For more information, please scan the QR code on the Preface.

8.6 How to Drive the Advancement of Digital Transformation

As the steering leader of companies, the CEO is responsible for all operations management and may not fully commit himself to digital transformation tasks. Companies can hire a CDO to serve as the main driver of digital transformation, responsible for the overall coordination of the digital transformation tasks. The CEO needs a brainstorming session to define the digital transformation strategy, unify the top-down digital transformation thinking and then assign implementation tasks for the CDO. The main task of the CDO is to supervise the digital transformation team to achieve the goals of data-enabled businesses and proactively drive the implementation of the digital transformation campaign, as shown in Fig. 8.10. The CDO also faces many challenges during the implementation phase.

1. **Types of capabilities a CDO should possess**

In the digital transformation process, the CDO can only understand how to lead the team to achieve the goals and uncover the business value if the CDO can understand how the business requirements are achieved and the essence of data-driven businesses.

(1) Digital capability

The primary duty of a CDO is to transform traditional businesses into digital businesses and drive profitability growth. The CDO must understand how to utilize intelligent tools, platforms, technologies, services, and processes to create new business value. Hence, the digital capability of a CDO refers to the capability to identify and understand digital trends, develop a deep understanding of the industry development and current business issues and find appropriate solutions. Besides, the digital capability of the CDO is also a subtle sense of market development, ever-changing technological trends, and the current survival state of companies.

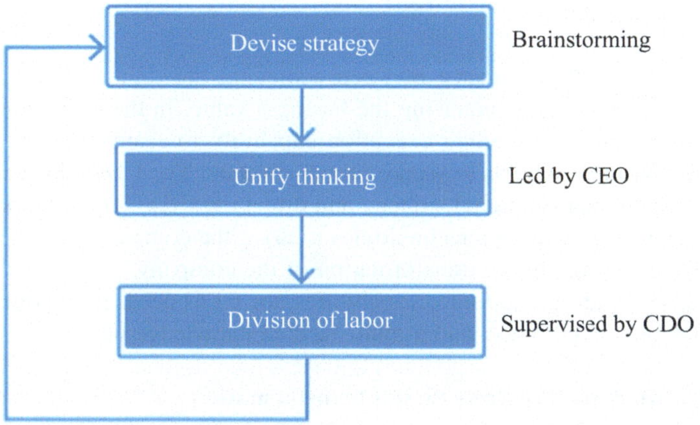

Fig. 8.10 How to drive the advancement of digital transformation

(2) Understanding of strategies

The CDO must understand the significance of profound strategic renewal and the initiatives, why the company is developing such a strategy, and how the digital strategy differs from the prior strategy. The CDO can only better control digital transformation progress by understanding these critical points.

(3) Business capability

The CDO must think about business continuity, understand the advantages and disadvantages of the old businesses, and understand the significance and effects of business innovation through digitalization. To a certain extent, they need to understand the deployment of different business lines and the need for digital transformation in different products and services. All these require the CDO to broaden and deepen his business knowledge.

(4) Capability to differentiate technologies

The CDO also needs to monitor the ever-changing technological trends and the latest use of technologies. In addition, the CDO not only needs to understand the advantages and disadvantages of the information technology architecture in the past but also to understand the development trends, characteristics, costs, and functions of the new technology architecture, such as the data platform as well as consider the alignment between this new technology architecture and the company's strategy. The specific details of the use of technologies can be assigned to the CIO/CTO.

(5) Execution capability

The CDO must strike a balance between achieving the digital strategy, driving technological change, and enhancing the business value. In the execution process, the CDO must have outstanding execution capability to seamlessly integrate the old and new business models to secure proper revenue. The CDO also needs to be guided by the company's digital strategy and direct the CIO/CTO to work together with the COO, employ digital technologies to drive the company's business value, and steadily boost the digital transformation of the company.

Apart from the abovementioned capabilities, the CDO needs a superior mindset, rich management experience, and a multi-faceted knowledge base.

2. **Devise a work plan to drive digital transformation**

The CDO should set a work plan for the digital transformation team to ensure that the strategic goals are aligned with the actual implementation of the digital transformation. The CDO must also devise a 2–3-year strategic plan for the digital transformation team and guide their pace of development. Devising a strategic plan for digital transformation will better guide the CDO in leading the team to effectively complete the work plan and accelerate the pace of digital transformation for companies.

3. **A clear description of the responsibility and authority of the CDO**

Companies need to clearly describe the CDO's responsibilities in coordinating the organization and the authority in various aspects of management and control, governance, analysis, and applications of data assets.
Companies should delegate the authority to the CDO in coordinating the organization, enabling the CDO to have the authority to coordinate various departments and personnel in the process of achieving the strategic goals of digital transformation. There must be a regular reporting mechanism from the CIO/CTO and COO to CDO and CDO to CEO such that the CDO can understand the level of cooperation between each department promptly, while the CEO can also regularly understand the implementation process and results of digital transformation at the same time.

Companies also need to have a clear description of the responsibility of a CDO. Setting meaningful performance indicators is perhaps one of the difficulties in assessing this role, especially those associated with business performance. As it is more difficult for most digital transformation companies to correlate the data and business metrics, companies must set clear, measurable business-related benchmarks that define the performance and responsibility of the digital transformation team led by the CDO. There must not be too many indicators for responsibility as it would make the work boundaries unclear. If there are too many indicators for responsibility, the CDO is overwhelmed with excessive burdens and becomes stressed with fatigue. If there are too few indicators for responsibility, the CDO has too little responsibility and cannot control the pace of the digital transformation. The CDO can only showcase his potential and capabilities with effective indicators for responsibility.

The CDO needs to take full responsibility for the types, qualities, permissions, access paths, acquisition methods, and technical models of the data assets. Otherwise, the CDO finds it hard to drive the implementation of digital transformation.

8.7 Common Misunderstandings of Digital Transformation from the CEO

It is inevitable to make mistakes in the digital transformation process. Some rather bad decisions by the board of directors, CEO, and CTO may create many misconceptions about digital transformation.

Some CEOs of companies believe they can entirely hand over the digital transformation task to others without participating in the process. Some CEOs believe that they can hold the people in charge of the digital transformation accountable, and their lack of involvement does not affect the effectiveness of digital transformation. And some CEOs also believe they can replace the people in charge of the digital transformation if they make mistakes to compensate for any losses incurred during the digital transformation process. These are all misconceptions about digital transformation.

1. **The CEO does not participate in the digital transformation task**

The job of a CEO is to lead digital transformation. As the highest-ranking decision-maker in a company, the CEO needs to understand the logical overview of digital transformation, including the implementation paths, staff arrangement, resource allocation, fund allocation, and deployment effects of technology. At the same time, the CEO also needs to get the right people to implement the tasks based on his understanding of the critical points of digital transformation in some specific projects. Hence, the CEO should not be indifferent to digital transformation but also deeply understand the significance of transformation and control the direction of digital transformation.

2. **The CEO can make up for the losses incurred by holding the people in charge accountable during digital transformation**

Some CEOs may hold the people in charge of digital transformation accountable after they have assigned the tasks to them. From an employee's perspective, the maximum loss is merely losing his job. But for the companies, the losses incurred from mistakes made in digital transformation are not as simple as firing an employee.

That is a common misunderstanding many companies face during the transitional phase of digital transformation. Digital transformation is a new phenomenon. Firing the people in charge of digital transformation after making mistakes does not compensate for the losses incurred; apart from deducting the time and financial costs, any mistakes in digital transformation damage the cost of credibility. There would be a lull period of a year or two without any positive or negative effects on digital transformation. It may make everyone in the company lose confidence in their digitalization efforts. In conclusion, no one can pay for a company's credibility costs.

3. **Mid-course personnel changes do not influence digital transformation**

Some companies dedicated to digital transformation, in particular some board of directors and CEOs with decision-making authority, believe they can change the personnel in charge at any time during the digital transformation. And the mid-course personnel changes do not influence digital transformation progress. Once the digital transformation has begun, it involves all the company's core systems. Any mid-course personnel changes significantly influence the progress of digital transformation.

(1) Mid-course personnel changes do not correct the mistakes made in the directive of digital transformation.

The CEO must carefully select the personnel in charge of digital transformation. There are significant differences between digital transformation and informatization. If the right personnel is not selected carefully, companies may have to bear the consequential costs of wasting time, economic costs, and failure to achieve the expected results of a digital transformation. After making personnel changes, moreover, companies face a new predicament. As the prior personnel in charge have been steering digital transformation on the incorrect path for some time already, it is challenging to change its direction in the first instance.

(2) Staff misplacement results in financial losses and waste of resources

Digital transformation is a process that involves the placement of key talents in key positions and key departments. Large companies have different departments and functions, and their job priorities are also different. If companies engage in staff misplacement during digital transformation, mid-course personnel changes only bring about more enormous economic losses and waste resources.

(3) Noteworthy points in the placement of personnel in digital transformation

In the digital transformation process, companies must ascertain the three following points concerning personnel placement.

(1) What types of talents are needed for digital transformation?
(2) What types of capabilities do the talents require to have in digital transformation?
(3) What types of experiences do the talents require to have in digital transformation?

There is a huge cost to bear in the trial-and-error of digital transformation. Mid-course personnel changes will not only alter the organizational structure of digital transformation but may also lose some potential business opportunities.

4. **Digital transformation falls under the category of IT department**

If the CEO believes that digital transformation is the sole responsibility of the IT department without coordination from the business, management, and operations departments, then the company may be directly stepping into the incorrect path for its digital transformation. The CEO, who is leading the digital transformation team, cannot harbor such a view. CEOs are the highest-ranking individuals in a company with the authority to make business decisions. If they believe digital transformation only concerns a particular department without coordination or involvement of other departments, their digital transformation is doomed to fail miserably.

Digital transformation should be a holistic process of strategy deployment, team arrangement, resource allocation, technical configuration, and demand planning. It is a multi-faceted implementation process that cannot solely rely on the technical architecture of the IT department. The IT department perceives digital transformation from its perspective and often neglects the needs of the business, operations, management, and other departments. It cannot perceive and deploy its resources from a holistic perspective.

5. **It is acceptable to replicate the digital transformation program from other companies**

Some CEOs directly replicate the digital transformation program from other companies while leading the digital transformation efforts without making necessary customization based on their company's characteristics. Many companies have not seen any significant results after implementing digital transformation for nearly half a year. The most common reason was that they had used the wrong approach and construction ideas and did not have customized solutions based on their characteristics.

Hence, the CEO must customize the transformation program based on the company's growth phase and attributes of the industry in which it falls without relying solely on the company programs of other successful digital transformations. Usually, a digital transformation program should deliver value in the early phases of implementation, and it should not take too long for one to see the results. It is a common misconception here. Many people believe that digital transformation is a long-term process, and it is very common not to see any results in the short term. Companies have chosen the wrong approach right from the start of the digital transformation process. A digital transformation program is never an instant solution, and it requires constant adaptation and recalibration of the processes based on the growth characteristics of the company.

Part VI

How to Implement Digital Transformation?

After building an implementation team, the next step is to define the implementation plan for digital transformation. Companies should ascertain the specific implementation methodology and avoid the risks of failure in digital transformation. Hence, it is imperative to understand the risks of failure in digital transformation, master the methodology for successful transformation, and determine its implementation path.

Failures of Digital Transformation 9

The KPIs for digital transformation are divided into two parts: capability and performance. Capability refers to the ability to build an intelligent business operating system and enhance the ability to uncover business value, while performance refers to digital transformation results. A poor transformation result is akin to a transformation failure. This Chapter provides a reference for the digital transformation of companies from the perspective of failures.

9.1 Four Types of Non-linear Growth Curves Depicting Failures of Digital Transformation

Many factors determine the success of the digital transformation of companies. Any failure in one factor or part of the process can result in digital transformation failure. In general, however, the digital transformation path of a company has a spiral shape. Figure 9.1 shows the four types of non-linear growth curves of corporate failure in digital transformation with the horizontal coordinate of time and the vertical coordinate of business value generated by digital transformation. Over time, companies move through different phases of the transformation process, including digital technology/systems, scenario experience implementation, and industry integration. As time passes, the personalized characteristics of the digital transformation of companies become more distinctive. Each company has a different development path. By mastering the four types of non-linear growth curves depicting failures of digital transformation in advance, it can avoid the risks of failure and hit the target precisely.

1. **Growth curve of Type 1 company—ending at the system predicament**

When Type 1 companies first start their digital transformation, they invest more energy and money. They are confident in the transformation results, believing that

X. Ma, *Methodology for Digital Transformation*, Management for Professionals,
https://doi.org/10.1007/978-981-19-9111-0_9

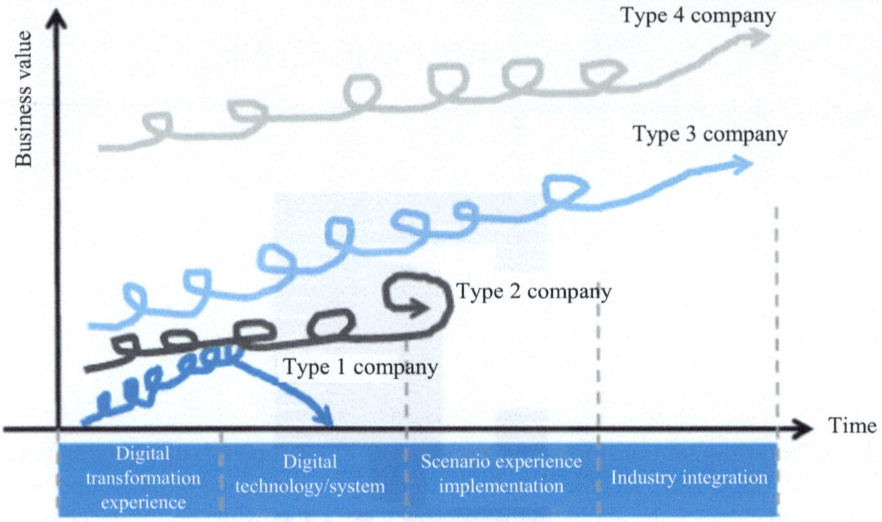

Fig. 9.1 Four types of non-linear growth curves

digital transformation is a way to save the company or an opportunity to overtake other competitors. They do not understand the digital transformation from a systematic approach, however. Hence, the starting point of the transformation is low. The digital team of the companies can only keep on maintaining the trial and error practices, and they cannot move forward.

This phenomenon indicates that the company has reached a point of congestion or bottleneck in its digital transformation. Under this scenario, companies may have lost the confidence to succeed in their digital transformation, failing to find a way around the dilemma until they finally give up on the transformation.

2. **Growth curve of Type 2 company—ending at the technical predicament**

The starting point of the transformation for Type 2 companies is high. On top of having excellent consulting resources for the transformation, they also know how to learn from the experiences of other companies. They steadily cross the digital system predicament and reach the technical phase. After reaching the technical phase, they keep revolving around this section. They may have tried for many years but still cannot overcome the technical predicament.

These types of companies are very dedicated to digital transformation. They always feel that they are not investing enough in technology. Hence, they keep investing more in traditional IT technologies. It is difficult for traditional IT technologies to generate new DT applications and digital transformation requires investment in DT technologies.

These companies may give up their digital transformation in the technical predicament phase or continue to struggle and fall into the IT loop.

3. **Growth curve of Type 3 company—inadequate mining of scenarios**

Type 3 companies with a spiral development have traversed the system and technical development phases. Though they are rewarded with high business value, they still fail in their digital transformation.

These types of companies have better technology systems and transformation systems. But as the mining of scenarios is not deep enough, they cannot pull away from their competitors. That is often the result of a lack of digital talent. As companies are short of digital talents, it becomes difficult for them to carry out business innovation in a batch and assembly line manner.

At this stage of development, companies need a large pool of digital talents with business knowledge to carry out business innovation. Companies should also create an innovative institution with a new creative incentive scheme to build a comprehensive talent, culture, and incentive system.

4. **Growth curve of Type 4 company—failure to deal with the inflection point of transition**

The pace of development for Type 4 companies is quick. But the pace of digital transformation begins to slow down after their labor and technology costs reach an inflection point. These companies fail to deal with the inflection point, failing in the end.

These companies have robust technological competency. In the initial phase, their pace of digital transformation is quicker. In the middle and later phases, however, they are still primarily figuring out the correct path, which consumes much time and eventually affects digital transformation results.

Companies with a high starting point in digital transformation usually have learned from proven digital transformation experiences, and they may have prepared for the resources required for digital transformation and circumvented the early pitfalls. These companies begin to generate high business value in the initial phase of the digital transformation process.

By reviewing the four different paths above, the most intelligent way for companies is to learn from proven digital transformation experiences and employ advanced technologies simultaneously. Equipped with scenario-based implementation experiences, companies continually integrate with the industry, gradually invest their resources, and wait patiently for digital transformation results. If companies want to achieve a successful digital transformation, they still need to take note of the following points.

(1) Focus on costs

The digital transformation process of companies is a constant process of trial-and-error which includes the financial cost, opportunity cost of time, and cost of confidence. The opportunity cost of time is the most critical of all. If companies do not get satisfactory business value during trial and error, it will not only undermine the confidence of the digital team but also consume a lot of opportunity cost of time. The trial-and-error cost comes from the overall perspective of the transformation and continues to increase along with its progress. Hence, it is of utmost importance that companies quickly utilize the proven experiences of digital transformation to enhance business value in the initial phase of the process, minimizing the cost of trial and error as much as possible.

(2) Take note of the time lag of trial and error

At a certain phase of digital transformation, companies may still be exploring trial-and-error, and they may not perceive the business value for a while. The business value sustainably grows if the trial and error method is successful. Companies should not rush through the digital transformation process and wish for a quick hit; instead, they should proceed with the program one step at a time. They certainly need to take note of the concept of time lag.

(3) The Matthew Effect—the better the transformation results, the greater the investment

The Matthew Effect of digital transformation for companies reflects the cumulative advantage of economic capital; companies have to invest more for better transformation results. Consequently, they have more confidence in the results of digital transformation. In Fig. 9.1, the faster the spiral curve turns upward, the more the company invests. There also be higher value enhanced by the transformation as well. If companies do not invest in digital transformation initially, it is too late to start investing when they see other companies are getting better results. Companies should focus on investment in digital transformation as early as possible.

(4) Take note of the price scissors issue

When other companies' labor and technology costs reach the inflection point of price scissors, it is too late for companies to catch up. If companies do not prioritize their investment in digital transformation in the early phases, they still progress slower than other companies even after spending much time on the transformation, and they always lag.

9.2 Six Types of Failures in Digital Transformation

This Chapter describes the six types of failures in digital transformation, helping companies mitigate the risks of failure.

Failure 1: Incorrect direction
Some companies embark on their digital transformation in the wrong direction right from the beginning or begin in the right direction and steer off the right track after some time, resulting in a decoupling between technology and business, which follow a different growth trajectory individually. The reason may be the company management does not adequately monitor the digital transformation efforts, failing to rectify the digital team's transformation path promptly.

What can be done under this scenario? One way is to review the entire digital transformation process, dissect and analyze all issues, streamline the implementation process of the entire digital team and rectify the direction of the transformation. Another way is to adopt the digital transformation program proposed by the consulting firm and recalibrate the specific implementation process according to the actual situation.

Failure 2: Companies keep trying because the digital transformation technology path is incorrect
The second type of digital transformation failure for companies is the incorrect technical path engaged, which requires the digital team to keep repeatedly trying, leading to a bottomless, dead-end cycle for the transformation efforts.

(1) Lack of integration between technology and business

This phenomenon is relatively common in many companies. The business staff do not appreciate the value of the technical staff's products and have no idea how to specify the requirements. The lack of integration between the parties is the main reason companies are slowly getting off the right track in digital transformation.

(2) Issues with the technology infrastructure

Companies are implementing their concepts of digital transformation with technology. But there are issues with the technology infrastructure. Why is the data platform so popular? The most common reason for digital transformation failure is the considerable investment in IT, resulting in isolated data chimneys. Whenever the business department has a requirement, the IT department produces a system for them. Over time, more management software is installed in the company, such as CRM and ERP. The data platform is a type of technical support. It supports implementing innovative businesses with a poor description of their requirements, thus making up for the issues with the corporate technology infrastructure.

Failure 3: The low business value generated by digital transformation cannot empower businesses.
The third scenario of digital transformation failure for companies is the solid technical capability but weak output and low business value. Many strong companies have more comprehensive technical capabilities and purchased many advanced

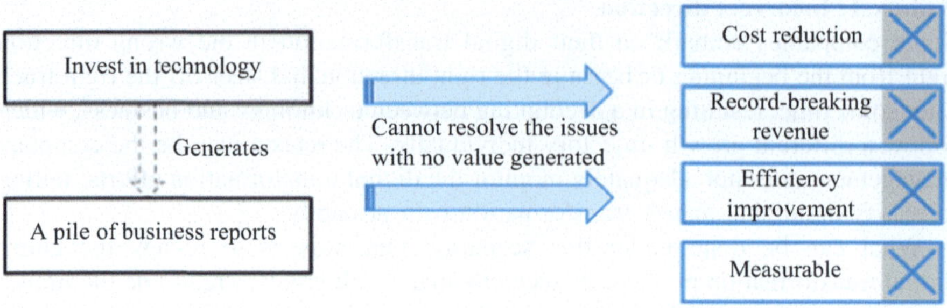

Fig. 9.2 The low business value generated by digital transformation cannot empower businesses

technologies. In the end, however, they only produce a pile of reports that cannot directly generate business value, as shown in Fig. 9.2.

The technical services of such companies are aimed at the managers. While a digital company has to empower the frontline staff, there is little empowerment.

Failure 4: Lack of a comprehensive digital transformation system
Digital transformation is a long-term and continuous process of trial and error. Companies not only need to have a complete system to minimize the cost of trial and error but also need to perceive digital transformation from a macro perspective. Companies should be aware of the pitfalls experienced by other companies in their digital transformation process and summarize the key takeaways from valuable lessons learned to avoid making the same mistakes. Even for companies with the same business model, their transformation priorities are different at different phases with different organizational capabilities and leadership styles. Companies must have proper knowledge and skillsets in every phase of the process. As a long-term project involving the participation of many departments, digital transformation requires collaboration and coordination across the companies. Companies should have a transparent system to continually identify and solve issues in each phase of the process and constantly recalibrate the work focus of the entire team.

Failure 5: Inconsistencies from top to bottom of the corporate hierarchy
Digital transformation is a digital capability of companies for their future. In this transformation process, companies may face several issues of inconsistencies from top to bottom of the corporate hierarchy.

(1) Inconsistency in thinking and views

The top management they have their views and visions. But the CEO and the board of directors may not always be clear about the awareness of the digital transformation path from the middle and lower levels of the corporate hierarchy. Although some companies are substantial, only a few ponder the digital strategy.

(2) Inconsistency in capabilities

There is only a minority of staff who genuinely possess the future strategic capability of a company.

(3) Inconsistency in KPIs

The KPIs for digital transformation in each department is different. While many companies are chanting the slogan, "Digital transformation is fundamental," every department still employs the traditional ways in the implementation process because they can accomplish the KPIs effortlessly.

(4) Inconsistency in interests

Companies disrupt the prior order of personal interests during the digital transformation process, thus disturbing the interests of some company staff. A common phenomenon is that some former staff may no longer be suitable for their current jobs after a successful digital transformation. Companies must deal with the relationship between varying roles at this juncture. As it involves a mixture of technology and business, companies often find it hard to find a clever solution. Companies have planted this conflicting seed at the beginning of digital transformation. Large and not market-oriented companies are particularly concerned about this issue.

(5) Inconsistency in attitude

If the leaders in the middle and lower levels of the corporate hierarchy do not understand the thinking of their CEO, the corporate attitude is not consistent.

Failure 6: Lack of digital talents
The lack of digital talents also leads to digital transformation failure.

(1) Lack of talents who possess experience in digital transformation

In the digital transformation process, companies are not short of technical talents; they, however, are short of talents with experience in digital transformation, particularly those experienced senior executives. This type of personnel can help companies significantly shorten the trial and error cycle and quicken the push for digital transformation.

(2) Lack of digital operations talents

Business staff with a digital mindset are companies' digital innovation sources. Digital talents use the awareness of data to solve business issues, achieving business innovation. Looking for talents that can synergize business and data awareness is pivotal.

(3) Digital talents do not form an enclosed loop

Companies' data analysis and mining must form an enclosed loop to drive their digital transformation. From the lower to middle to higher levels of the corporate hierarchy, companies cannot get effective results by only accomplishing staff placement, and these talents must form a reasonable enclosed loop to achieve the expected results.

10 How to Achieve Digital Transformation at Low Costs

The profit margins of many industries have declined, especially SMEs in the manufacturing industry in recent years. Faced with many headwinds like rising labor costs, outdated management, lack of innovation, and low operational efficiency, some companies have closed and declared bankruptcy. Despite the declining economic conditions compared to prior years, the consumer sector is still maintaining robust demand, creating opportunities for companies to tap and lead in this segment. How can companies achieve digital transformation at low costs with declining profits in the industry? What types of obstacles will companies face in the process of achieving digital transformation? How can businesses driven by digital technologies meet the diversified needs of consumers? This Chapter introduces the approach to achieving digital transformation at low costs. Figure 10.1 illustrates the principles of digital transformation at low costs.

10.1 Bigger Resistance for Data-Driven Businesses

With the rapid growth of big data, IoT, artificial intelligence, and 5G technology, the one-stop service of digital technology provides convenience to the work and lifestyle of people. And to a certain extent, it also uncovers more digital intelligence needs of the consumers. Nowadays, applying digital technology is pivotal to developing companies' core competitiveness. Any inadequate use of data resources makes it harder for companies to achieve digital transformation. There are many existing issues, including data barriers, isolated data chimneys, and a lack of standardized data formats between each department of the company. At the same time, companies may find it hard to look for suitable data suppliers due to the sticky issue of data copyright. Lacking the synergy with external data, companies cannot carry out the data presentation from the overall perspective. The internal and external data in the company cannot form an enclosed loop, making it more challenging to uncover data value. The factors above lead to an increase in the cost

X. Ma, *Methodology for Digital Transformation*, Management for Professionals,
https://doi.org/10.1007/978-981-19-9111-0_10

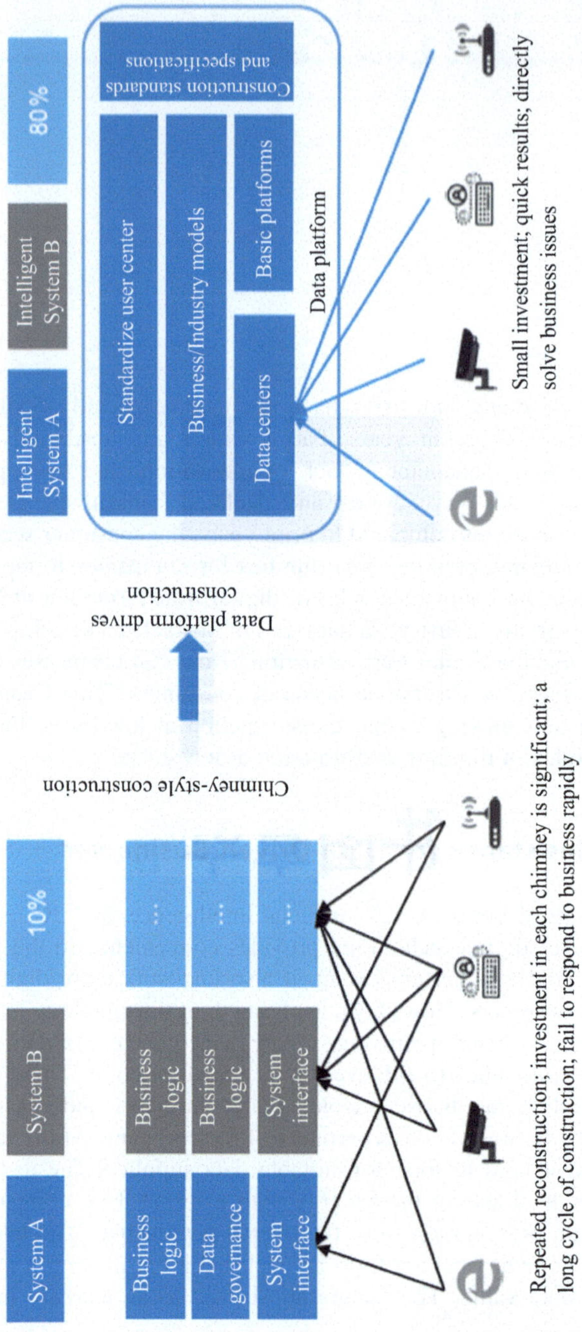

Fig. 10.1 The data platform model can reduce costs and achieve digital transformation rapidly

of data intelligence applications for companies. Coupled with the lack of professional technical talents and the support of technical systems makes it even more challenging to achieve a successful digital transformation.

Companies lacking in digital transformation talents, technologies, and methodologies can utilize the strength of data intelligence service providers to accomplish digital transformation at several levels, from the formation of data assets to the construction of data technology architecture.

10.2 Recipe of Success to Achieve Digital Transformation at Low Costs

Companies can employ digital technology to drive their businesses and meet the diversified needs of consumers, achieving the goal of reducing costs and improving efficiency. The recipe for success is constructing a data platform, companies' core digital transformation component.

1. **Standardized data platform architecture**

A data platform can help companies seamlessly interconnect the data of varying business departments and standardize the user center by constructing a standardized data processing application architecture. The basic platform in a data platform has a certain degree of scalability, and it can promptly adjust the underlying architecture according to the front-end businesses' needs. The data platform can change the phenomenon of excessive systems and high procurement costs in some companies, thus reducing the operational cost of companies to a certain extent.

2. **Professional digital talents**

Professional data intelligence service providers can help companies create a standardized technical architecture and nurture their professional digital talents in providing digital transformation services. Regardless of the data analysts, IT architects, or business analysts, they can provide companies with professional advice on digital transformation.

3. **Provision of references for digitalization experiences**

Data intelligence service providers have accumulated enriching practical experiences while providing digital transformation services to varying industries. Despite the different business logic across all industries, the data governance model beneath is very similar. Data intelligence service providers can help companies create data intelligence departments, organize digital operations training, nurture digital talents, and direct companies to a standardized data platform for management by scaling up their operations and reducing average costs to improve employee efficiency and reduce labor costs.

Companies implementing digital transformation can build a data platform by utilizing the strength of the data intelligence service providers. It is a small investment with fast results. By doing this, it can shorten the trial and error period and reduce the relevant cost. The data platform can help companies to optimize their business processes, reduce operating costs and rationalize the supply of products, thus enhancing the market competitiveness of companies.

10.3 Misconception of Digital Transformation: Experience Cannot Be Reused

As humanity advances from the information age to the digital era, digitalization has become part and parcel of the social economy. But some industries are still unfamiliar with the concept of digital transformation.

For the several questions of how to implement a digital transformation, when to implement a digital transformation, and how to build the technical architecture of digital transformation, companies need to constantly explore their road to discovering digital transformation and seek suitable answers. Some companies believe that there are no substantial precedents of digital transformation, and they cannot learn from the experiences of other successful companies. Meanwhile, if there are some matured digital transformation samples, companies can comprehensively refer to them and learn from the experiences of technical architecture construction and resource allocation.

1. **The importance of reusing digital transformation experiences**

Reusing digital transformation experiences is not simply a replication but adapting it to suit individual digital transformation programs by drawing on other companies' past experiences according to corporate characteristics. Reusing valuable digital transformation experiences can enhance the digital transformation knowledge for companies and diminish the cost of trial and error in digital transformation.

2. **Reusing the contents of digital transformation experiences**

Reusable contents include applying value creation, building the data platform architecture, building agile organizations, and coordinating with all departments to accelerate growth.

3. **Noteworthy points while reusing the digital transformation experiences**

While reusing the experiences of successful digital transformation, companies should take note of the two following points.

First, it is pivotal for companies to ensure that the basic infrastructure of the data platform is constructed. Companies should select the right data platform to ensure the data platform architecture is built precisely right from the beginning, avoiding any possible rework in the future. Companies can quickly build an intelligent business operating system by utilizing the basic infrastructure of a data platform.

Second, companies must continually reuse the capabilities of their data platforms. The capability of a data platform can be reused, and companies can use the data platform architecture to carry out different kinds of businesses.

11 Six-Map Planning Method of Digital Transformation

The six maps in the planning method of digital transformation include the strategy map, business map, requirement map, application map (data intelligence), algorithm map, and data map. Companies can sort out the business map according to their strategy map. The requirement map is generated from the business map. After sorting out the requirement map, the application map (data intelligence) is formed by integrating the digital transformation path. The algorithm and data maps are needed to create the application map (data intelligence), as shown in Fig. 11.1.

The six-map planning method of digital transformation can help implement digital transformation from six different perspectives, ensuring that every step of the digital transformation is equally effective.

11.1 Strategy Map

With the development of the new generation of DT technology, it is a critical path for companies to utilize digital transformation to seize market share and attain higher strategic growth. The first step of a digital transformation for companies is to sort out the strategic direction and create a strategy map. By sorting out the strategy map, it involves strategic objectives, performance goals, types of KPIs, growth approach of KPIs, and growth value of KPIs, among others.

Take an example of a bank. If the bank wants to increase its profit to CNY 100 million next year, it can divide its ultimate goal into smaller goals at each level, evaluating and allocating the resources required for different modules. The annual revenue, for example, can be broken down into revenue goals driven by marketing, revenue goals of the customer center, and revenue goals of the retail network. That is the path to sorting out the strategy map.

X. Ma, *Methodology for Digital Transformation*, Management for Professionals,
https://doi.org/10.1007/978-981-19-9111-0_11

Fig. 11.1 Six-map planning method of digital transformation

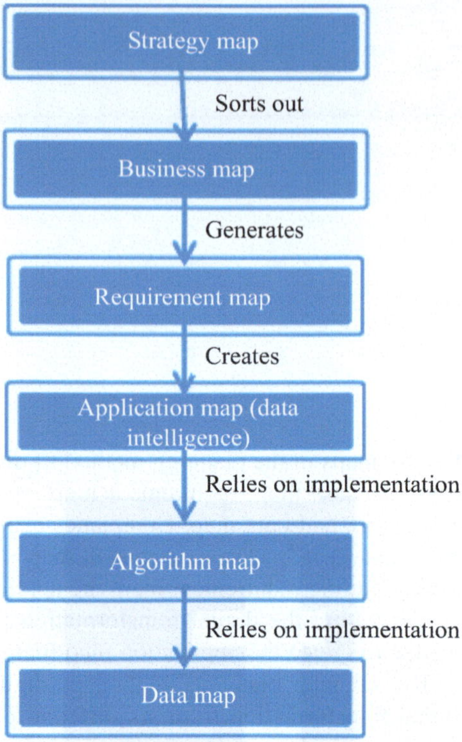

In addition, companies should be aware of including the participation of the board of directors, the CEO, and key executives while organizing their strategy maps. The strategy map is not a static concept. It requires to be updated and recalibrated by companies annually. However, the overall architecture does not change at large.

11.1.1 Sort Out Existing Strategies, Define New Strategic Goals, and Drive United Actions

While building a strategy map, companies must sort out their plans for the next three to five years, define new strategic goals and determine the implementation steps of driving the strategy from the top to bottom corporate hierarchy to galvanize a high degree of focus on strategic actions. Take the example of a bank drafting its strategy map. Its strategic vision for the next three to five years is "to expand its retailing business greatly and significantly increase its profit contribution to the bank," while its strategic path is "to dive deep into customer operations, enrich its products and services, drive improvement in its production capacity and accelerate the channel transformation." It also streamlines the implementation path to achieve its strategic objectives, as shown in Fig. 11.2.

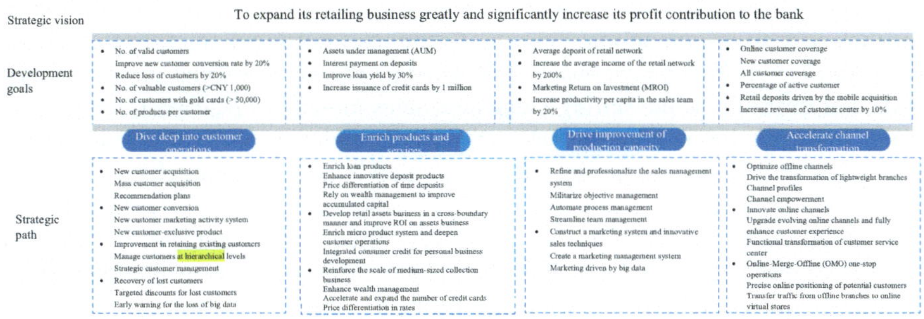

Fig. 11.2 Strategy map sorted out by a certain bank

In sorting out the strategy map, the two following scenarios may occur: The first scenario is that the business models are not disrupted by digital technologies, such as disruption in efficiency and experience. The other scenario is that digital technologies drive changes to business models, such as strategic disruption leading to a digital strategy.

Consequently, while considering the achievement of their annual performance goals and organizing their strategy maps, companies must first ascertain where they should begin to transform, be it from a strategic transformation, efficiency, or empirical transformation. Companies must develop a strategy map based on the transformation perspective. We will not first discuss strategic and empirical transformation but focus on how companies can transform their efficiencies and organize their strategic maps.

The specific digital terms, such as industrial internet, S2B2C companies, new retail, and new finance, advocated by modern people, are all representatives of the era of digital disruption. Most industries have not changed their contents, goals, or product features. Only their ways of doing business have changed. Traditional industries have always been depending on manual operations. Nowadays, however, they rely on digital capabilities. When the same thing is done differently, achieving a multiplier effect, this new way of doing things disrupts the old way, thus generating a new business. That is a classic demonstration of efficiency disrupting traditional industries.

11.1.2 Summarize the Strategic Objectives and Vision

While companies must sort out their strategy maps and determine their strategic goals, the implementation path, pace of implementation, and implementation methods of the strategic goals are equally important too.

After completing the internal and external strategies, companies need to summarize their new strategic goals and visions. Companies need to dissect strategic goals into several goals in different phases and ascertain the existing goals and secondary goals. For example, while setting the annual sales targets for next year, retail companies must determine how the sales target is completed this year. We can set a reasonable annual sales target by integrating market development, changes in suppliers, and other external circumstances. The annual sales target is further divided into smaller parts according to the month, department, and other dimensions, and then the target for each phase is thus ascertained while the implementation path of the sales target in different phases is determined.

Once the overall strategic goals and milestones are set, companies still need to clearly understand the implementation path to achieve the relevant goals to be aligned with the appropriate strategic implementation path and executive strategies. It is to ensure that the strategic goals can be carried out in an orderly and firm manner according to the plans simultaneously.

11.1.3 Allocation of Labor, Financing, and Other Resources to Achieve the Strategic Objectives

In sorting out strategic maps and achieving strategic objectives, companies must mix and match their corporate resources, particularly their human resources. They also need to assess the staff capabilities, the total number of staff, and the talent structure to devise a concrete strategy. While driving and executing the strategy map, companies can better explore their business/innovative revenue/operational models with digital technologies.

11.2 Business Map

After defining their digital strategies and devising a consistent top-down strategy map, companies can organize their business maps by the latest digital strategies and operational models, and derive the algorithm map, data map, and application map (data intelligence) in sequential order. The business map is the action plan for companies to achieve the objectives of the strategy map, including business processes and methods. Companies can only be very clear about which business processes can be optimized and restructured only after sorting out their business maps.

If companies have businesses of varying dimensions, especially their core business, they should dissect the relevant initiatives at the early phase of planning, sort out the existing business structure, and analyze the existing issues and obstacles, as shown in Fig. 11.3.

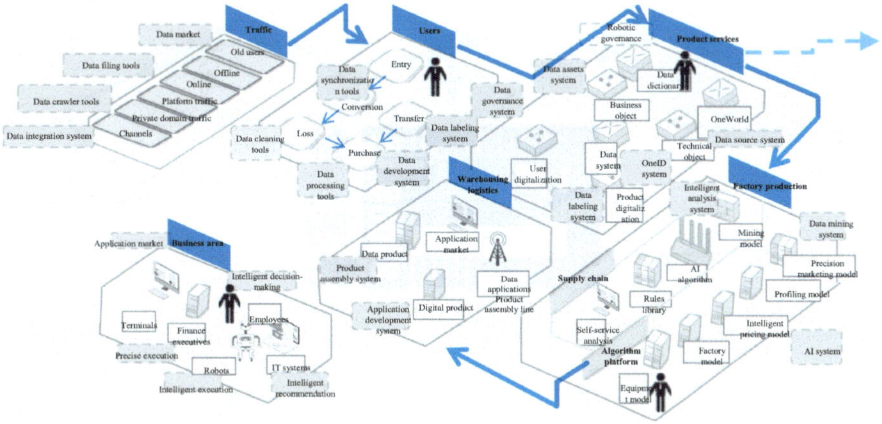

Fig. 11.3 Business map

The middle management of companies must be involved in sorting out their core business. They can first organize their key businesses and critical phases, including the business departments pending to be optimized, the organizational structure pending to be adjusted, and the intelligent applications of data pending to be achieved, among others. When retail companies are sorting out their business maps, for example, certain key businesses may encompass tens of thousands of categories of office products. Among these categories, there are sub-categories and varying product models. Apart from these product categories, the key business segments of such companies may also include customized and after-sales services. These are all core businesses of such companies. They must carefully prioritize the tasks and phases required to be performed while sorting out their business maps.

After completing the organization of their business maps, companies can employ digital technologies more efficiently and cost-effectively to achieve their strategic goals.

11.3 Requirement Map

Today, companies have a more insightful understanding of data-enabled businesses. The ultimate objective of implementing digital transformation for companies is to employ digital technology to meet business needs, achieve business innovation, acquire more customer resources and increase corporate revenue. After sorting out their business maps, companies can further develop a set of systems to meet the business requirements—requirement map, as shown in Fig. 11.4.

Companies can set milestones for their requirement maps according to their business maps to prioritize each requirement in the digital transformation, ensuring a perfect fit of resource allocation at all levels.

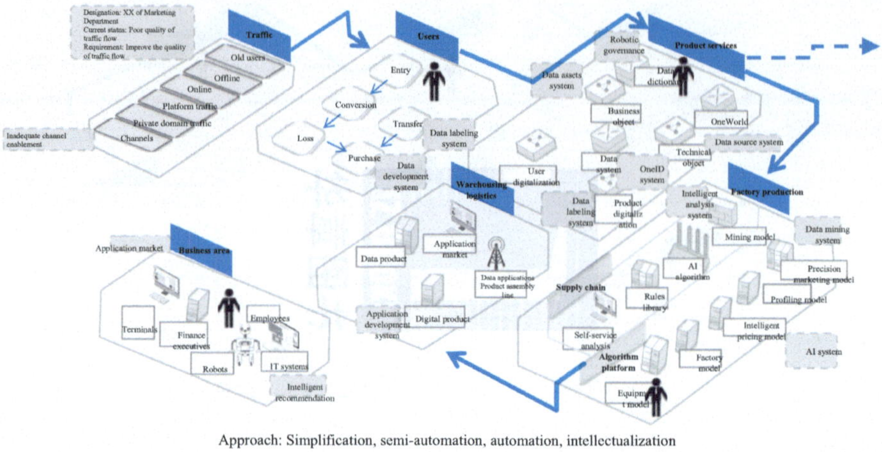

Fig. 11.4 Requirement map

1. **Devise the requirement map and ascertain the principles of requirement order**

While devising the requirement map, the CEO needs to understand the needs of the business team and figure out what types of business value the customers need. For example: What basic functions are required by the business management system? What are the types of input and output formats? What kinds of interactions can be achieved with the users? What are the principles of business processing? Before developing the requirement map, all of these must be sorted out on the business map.

The requirement map is not a subjective decision by the relevant staff. And instead, it is a set of requirements identified by the business logic that needs to be addressed urgently. It requires the participation of the business department and the coordination of the technology and other departments.

Many companies may have a misconception, believing that the business department must only raise the requirements. Hence, these companies passively wait for the business department to raise such requirements that the technical department fulfills.

The consumer market is constantly changing. The requirements proposed by the business department are often creative ideas, which very seldom become specific requirements. The business department may experience certain pressure while proposing their requirements because it takes a long process to meet such requirements before they become viable projects in the end. With a long cycle, this implementation process slowly demoralizes the business department, keeping them away from creative innovation.

Hence, the best solution is for the digital team to identify the business requirements and organize them into products that can be implemented digitally. The digital team undertakes the value and tasks of business innovation by accomplishing it from the digital perspective. Now, companies can offer specific incentives to encourage the digital team to implement the business department's requirements proactively.

2. **The No.1 individual participates in determining the sequential order of the requirement map to ensure a close follow-up on the resources.**

It requires the digital transformation team's joint participation with key decision makers, such as the CEO (i.e., the No.1 individual), to devise the requirement map. Decision makers must begin the digital transformation from a holistic perspective, ensuring that companies' limited resources are prioritized to be used urgently in the requirement map during the first six months of digital transformation. The No.1 individual must categorize and prioritize the requirements, allocating the limited resources to the critical requirements to achieve the most effective resource allocation. That is a crucial step to provide further assurance and support to the digital transformation team.

11.4 Application Map (Data Intelligence)

Modern society is traversing a technological transformation from the information age to the digital era. As the core resource of the modern era, data is the fuel of digital transformation for companies. The digital transformation team must resolve many issues, including how to use data resources and digital technologies to achieve the goal of digitalization, automation, and intellectualization of the operations and management of companies. Companies can construct a comprehensive, detailed application map (data intelligence) with the two following points to achieve high efficiency in the use of data, as shown in Fig. 11.5.

1. **Devise data application plans, create application environment and enhance application system**

In the digital transformation process, companies need to devise and reinforce the data application plans, in other words, to create an application map to better achieve the intelligent application of data. From the perspective of enabling businesses, the digital transformation team must select the appropriate scenarios to generate and solve business issues, collect the requirements, integrate the data resources concerning these scenarios, and sort out the processes to create different dimensional categories of data applications.

While sorting out the application map (data intelligence), companies can construct a scalable data application environment by utilizing data technologies, build

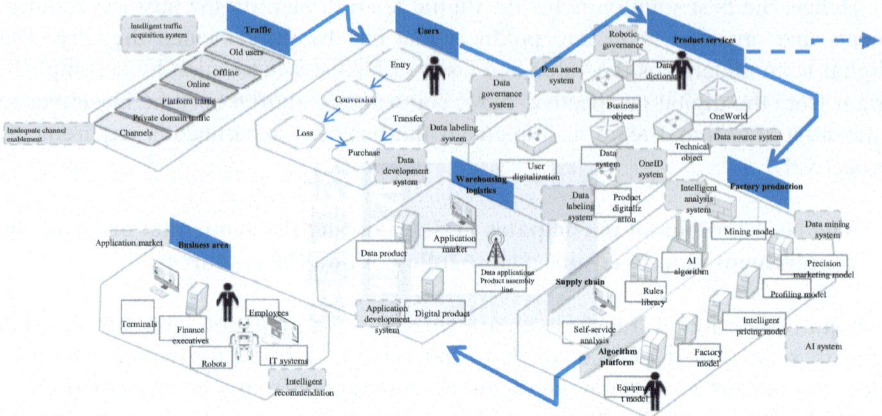

Fig. 11.5 Application map (data intelligence)

a data platform with data applications at its core, and dissect/share/allocate data resources in varying dimensions to facilitate the business staff. Then the companies may deploy the data resources, enhance operational capabilities and improve the efficiency of data applications.

The digital transformation team must also enhance the company's data application system, revolve around the acquired data resources and showcase the value hidden beneath the data through data collection, processing, storage, analysis, mining, visualization, and security verification to reinforce the capability of creating record-breaking revenue.

2. **Construct an application map (data intelligence) to meet the multi-dimensional business requirements**

The digital transformation team needs to revolve around the data intelligence application logic, organize the data and requirements generated in each stage of the entire product life cycle, and create a data intelligence application system, helping companies to determine the fields and modules of the data intelligence applications and providing directions and opinions for the planning of data intelligence application solutions.

The application map (data intelligence) must be versatile and adjustable according to the changes in business requirements, always meeting the ever-changing business requirements and driving sales growth.

Given the different business issues, companies can construct several application maps, helping the operations department to achieve data-enabled businesses.

An application map differs from the frontline execution schedule, such as a daily work log. The application map provides a concise overview of the goals, investment, project task volume, and other digital transformation indicators. The CDO or CEO and the board of directors can keep track of important matters, such as digital transformation progress, by quickly browsing through the application map.

11.5 Algorithm Map

Companies increasingly need data analysis for their sales and service quality, and the algorithm plays a critical role in data analysis. The use of decision trees, logistic regression and linear regression, and cross-validation can help companies to improve the accuracy of precision marketing, user profiling, monitoring, and early warning.

With the development and enhancement of algorithms, algorithm applications have become powerful competitive tools for all companies. Algorithms are widely used in many industries, including new retail companies' customer precision operations systems, which utilize algorithms to develop an early warning model for potential customer loss and cross-selling. Likewise, the government public security departments also employ algorithms to study criminal behaviors, predict the crime rates of specific regions and build safe communities.

Companies can organize professional algorithm teams to build algorithmic data models and algorithm maps with algorithmic businesses and applications, as shown in Fig. 11.6.

11.5.1 The Significance of Constructing the Algorithm Map

Before building the algorithmic model and constructing the algorithm map, companies must first understand its significance.

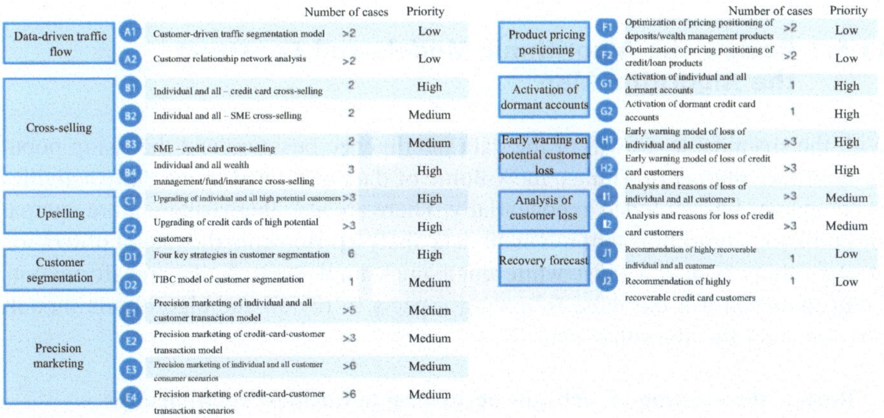

Fig. 11.6 Algorithm map (using the bank as an example)

1. **Enhance market competitiveness of companies**

Constructing an algorithm map can help companies make more accurate analysis decisions and improve their competitiveness in the market. In the building of user profiles, for example, companies use algorithms to implement group segmentation, find the unique characteristics of different groups of people, build loss of customer models, analyzing the reasons for the loss of customers by labeling the consumer behaviors as potential risks of losing the customers to facilitate the operations team to make adjustments to the marketing plans promptly and retain the customers with practical approaches.

2. **Avoid wasting resources**

With the creation of an algorithm map, companies can organize, categorize and store the previously developed algorithms to avoid any loss of algorithms and duplication of development due to staff turnover. The algorithm map can help the digital transformation team fully understand the algorithmic resources within and beyond the company to support the next step in data governance and applications.

3. **Facilitate the deployment of digital solutions for companies**

Companies can only provide solutions for the next step in deploying talents and resources by determining the actual contents of data resources and algorithmic models, among others. That is the laying of a cornerstone for the recalibration of the organizational structure. Constructing and applying the algorithm maps can help companies to spur the scope and efficiency of using algorithms internally, enabling algorithmic applications to be more intelligent and driving the pace of digital transformation.

11.5.2 Review the Algorithmic Models and Construct the Algorithm Map

With the sustainable growth of the data intelligence business and the rising popularity of the Internet of Things, the volume of data generated in the daily activities of companies has exploded exponentially. There are also increasingly more companies utilizing algorithms to implement data analysis. Boosting the rate of utilization of algorithms is also a must while companies implement digital transformation. Companies can use the three following aspects to review the algorithmic models and construct the algorithm map.

1. **Review the existing algorithms according to business relationships**

The algorithm map is an algorithmic planning map organized according to business relationships. The algorithm map can be divided into statistical models, mining models, AI models, industry models, function libraries, and algorithm libraries. Among them, statistical models such as decision trees, K-means clustering, and factor analysis are created using statistical methods, which can be applied to group classification, customer segmentation, and satisfaction surveys. Companies can sort out the model maps of different business lines according to business relationships.

2. **Emphasize the supplementation of algorithmic models and intelligent R&D**

While constructing the algorithm map, companies can use the algorithm model management framework to arrange algorithms, develop, and supplement any shortfall in algorithmic models, providing great convenience in the next step of algorithmic applications. At the same time, companies can record the key processes during the compilation of the algorithm map to determine which algorithms can be automated and then embedded in the automated decision modules in all business processes. In addition, companies can also supplement any shortfall in algorithmic models for companies or all organizations according to their digital transformation requirements.

3. **Put in place an open, shared, and iterative algorithm map sharing mechanism**

In the digital transformation process, companies need to standardize the compilation of the existing algorithms according to the complete workflow, segment them into different categories, and create an algorithm map. Under this foundation, an open, shared, and iterative algorithm map sharing mechanism is developed for the team members of the digital transformation to use at any time.

11.6 Data Map

After completing the various maps, such as strategy, business, requirement, application (data intelligence), and algorithm maps, companies need to draw a further data map, as shown in Fig. 11.7. The data map, a data assets management tool in the form of diagrams, can standardize the query and management of all data collated in the data platform.

With the proliferation of business data in all industries, companies are increasingly concentrating on the value of data-enabled businesses. The importance of the data platform is extraordinarily highlighted. Companies need to build a data platform to manage and plan the data based on their data maps to achieve cost reduction objectives with technology, efficiency improvement in applications, and business empowerment.

Data is an indispensable asset in all industries. In the application process, companies need to begin from three areas, including data resource planning, data category review, and data model management, to develop a set of comprehensive data maps to lay the foundation for the subsequent use of the data platform architecture to achieve the objective of data-enabled businesses.

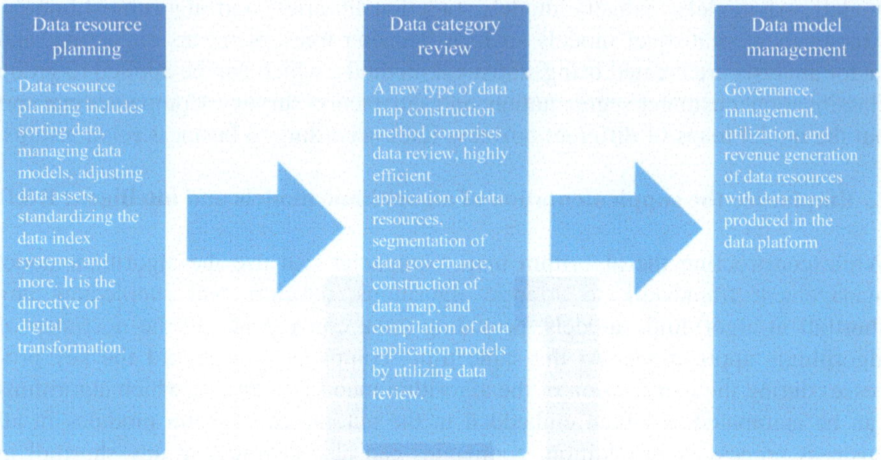

Fig. 11.7 Construction path of a data map

1. **Map out plans for data resources to ensure the results of data applications**

To build a data map, companies must first map out plans for internal and external data resources, including sorting out the types of data, managing data models, adjusting data assets, and standardizing data index systems, among others.

Data resource planning is crucial in constructing data maps and building data platforms. In mapping out plans for data resources, managers and technical staff must work together closely to examine and analyze the business requirements and ascertain the data resources required to ensure the expected results of data applications.

2. **Review data to raise the efficiency of data applications**

After planning internal and external data resources, companies need to review the data to improve the efficiency of data applications.

(1) Review data and apply them in a highly efficient manner

After completing the compilation of the strategy map, business map, requirement map, application map (data intelligence), and algorithm map, companies clearly understand the digital transformation work schedule for the next six months. The digital team can get an overview of the data conditions of companies and map out reasonable plans for data that require governance.

These different types of data can be used to create a data map, which is used to sort out the highly efficient data application model. The highly efficient data application model can help the digital team quickly match up the data with the prior requirements of the business staff, identify the areas in which the data can be appropriately applied, and uncover the relevant data issues to enhance the effectiveness of data, thus reflecting the value of data assets.

(2) The misconception about the data application model

The traditional data application model begins with the organization of the data map, which is used to construct the application system. Meanwhile, leaders often neglect to integrate the data application model with the actual data conditions, solely relying on their personal experiences to create the data maps. In the traditional data application model, the data team spends significant time on data governance, cleaning, and management, resulting in developing data applications that do not promptly meet some business requirements. The companies cannot achieve the strategic and business values of their investment.

The new type of construction method for data map: use data review → segment data governance → construct data map → sort out data application model can help companies effectively enhance the efficiency of mining data value.

3. **Manage data models to improve data quality**

Companies can manage data models by constructing data maps to solve the issues of inconsistency in the development of data maps and data models such that there is a perfect fit between the application of data models and data resources, boosting the utilization rate of data resources, as shown in Fig. 11.8.

There are bound to be data errors in the application process, such as exceptions and coding logic errors that lead to incorrect data results. Hence, it is necessary to enhance the data quality and ensure data accuracy. Companies must ensure the direction for data quality and devise a comprehensive data improvement plan. Second, they need to analyze, assess, clean and monitor the data, install an early warning system for data errors and implement multi-dimensional data control to ensure data quality.

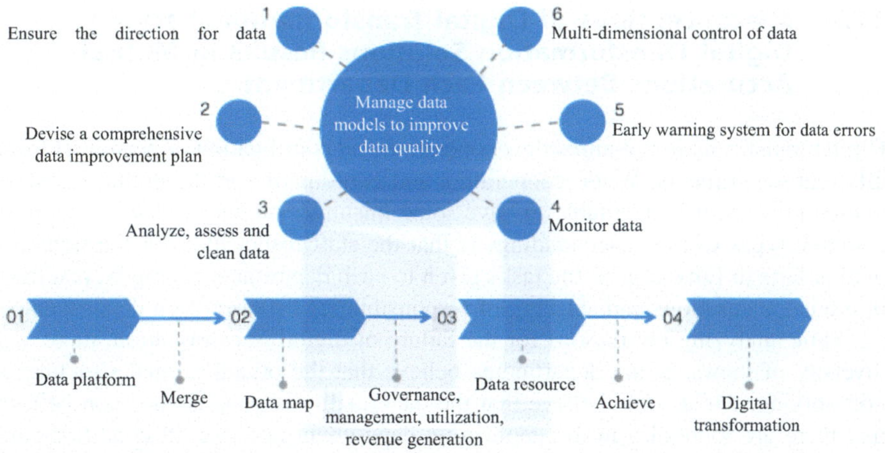

Fig. 11.8 Construction model of a data map

As the extensive data platform system constructed under the traditional data application model is a bit outdated, it cannot meet the customers' needs. Consequently, companies need to build a data platform to produce the data map, which is used to manage the data resources.

After creating the strategy map, business map, requirement map, application map (data intelligence), algorithm map, and data map by the companies, a data utilization system for digital transformation is developed. When companies need models and algorithms in different directions and types of data resources, they can utilize the six maps to quickly achieve a good fit, enhancing the value of data utilization.

The correct approach to building the six maps during the digital transformation of companies is to sort out the strategy, business, requirement, application, algorithm, and data in the hierarchical order from top to bottom. Some companies, however, sort out these resources using the bottom-up approach, which begins with what types of data are available, what types of algorithms are available, and what types of requirements and processes to achieve. This sorting approach is aligned with the technical concepts, and a certain misconception exists.

As the bottom-up approach of sorting out data resources has a long cyclical period with significant technical investment, it is easy for companies to deviate from the right track while sorting out the data from the bottom layer. When the CEO is unclear about the digital transformation process, it easily becomes a data model of "construct, govern and apply." The priority is to carry out data construction and governance before implementing data applications.

Constructing the six maps under the data platform structure can help companies accurately match the relevant talents in the organizational structure in the next step of the digital transformation, quickly achieving the transformation goals and enabling the data to empower the businesses.

11.7 Misconceptions of Digital Transformation: Lacking Digital Transformation Solutions Results in Mutual Accusations Between Each Department

Digital transformation requires the cooperation and coordination of personnel from different departments. While cooperating and coordinating in the digital transformation process, it is inevitable to have some misunderstandings. One of the most common types of misunderstandings is that the staff responsible for the transformation fails to fully control the tasks given to each department promptly, resulting in mutual accusations and shirking of responsibilities between each department.

While analyzing the reasons for the failure of digital transformation, there is a diversity of views. Some departments believe that the organizational structure is not working, while some believe that the data quality is poor. Some even believe that there are loopholes in the application department and that all conditions are not adequately ready. In short, they have all attributed the failure of digital transformation to a range of problems that occurred during the transformation process.

However, these problems do not exist at the beginning of the project, and they only occur during the specific implementation. At this juncture, companies need an experienced partner to guide them, advising them of the problems they may face and the solutions to solve them to ensure the desired transformation outcome.

Undoubtedly, there are many unexpected issues during the digital transformation process. For example, the shortage of data or the resistance faced in accessing the data during the digital transformation process; the business department is too preoccupied with other businesses to focus on the transformation project; or they begin the implementation of digital transformation without really understanding it; lack of outstanding AI engineers in the algorithms field, among others.

In the digital transformation process, another problematic node or phase may lead to the failure of the entire project, resulting in the shirking of responsibilities between each department. The business department believes the failure of the project is attributed to the issues in the technical department, while the technical department believes that the issues faced during the transformation are the responsibility of the business department. It may end up with the companies failing to pinpoint the root of the problem and hold up the potential opportunities.

Under this scenario, companies can perform the two following solutions at large. The first solution is the self-scrutinization of the internal departments, from the technology to the business department. But this method is rather time-consuming and labor-intensive, and many companies may not have this capability of self-scrutinization. The second solution is to hire experienced personnel externally. These professional personnel helps companies to scrutinize and investigate the root of the problem, devising a set of reasonable digital transformation solutions such that every person in the different departments is aware of the goals in each phase of the digital transformation.

12 To Whom Should Digitalization Be Empowered?

The key to a successful digital transformation lies in empowering frontline employees. Digital transformation can also empower the sales team, enhancing the efficiency of the sales staff and improving the precision of their services. It can empower the operations team, shrinking the decision-making time and creating a more precise implementation solution. It can empower the product managers, helping them to create products that better meet the consumer needs with their personal experience and data support. It can empower the finance team, helping them to set reasonable performance indicators, and enhance the overall operating efficiency of companies. It can empower the management team, boosting the efficiency of the management team in three hierarchical levels: senior management, middle management, and lower management. In addition, digital transformation can also improve the stickiness of all companies in the ecosystem, helping every company, particularly the core company, achieve more revenue.

12.1 Digital Transformation Empowers the Frontline Employees

In the past, there were two types of disposition in companies' operations.

The first type is the disposition to emphasize the empowerment of managers but not the frontline employees. It leads to the situation of not meeting the needs of the frontline employees, thus failing to enhance the efficiency of these employees. The management of companies not only fails to delegate authority to the frontline employees, but it also fails to equip their frontline employees.

The second type is the disposition to control and order the employees by the management of companies. For example, the management systems such as CRM, and ERP, installed by companies only increase the workload of the frontline employees, failing to empower the frontline employees.

X. Ma, *Methodology for Digital Transformation*, Management for Professionals,
https://doi.org/10.1007/978-981-19-9111-0_12

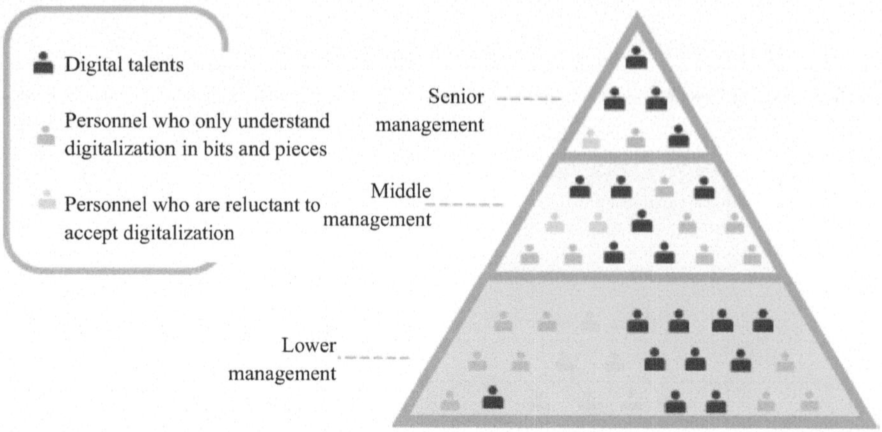

Fig. 12.1 Schematic diagram of the digital density of companies

Today, with the gradual increase in the orientation and fields of DT applications, companies can ultimately empower frontline employees with DT applications. For example, empowering the sales team to get more profits for companies is something that cannot be achieved in the IT era.

Companies implementing digital transformation should empower their frontline employees, who generate the most business value, determine whether companies can continue the large-scale division, and enhance efficiencies. The frontline employees can use the data platform to segment the applications and improve business.

As shown in Fig. 12.1, the senior, middle and lower management of companies are distributed with different digital talents, personnel who only understand digitalization in bits and pieces, and personnel who are reluctant to accept digitalization. The percentage of digital talents in a company is known as "digital density." The higher the digital density, the more influential the digital transformation is.

Many companies, however, face a dilemma where the CEO is the only digital talent in the senior management, while most middle management is personnel who only understand digitalization in bits and pieces. Most of the lower management are personnel who are reluctant to accept digitalization. As shown in Fig. 12.2, this is a distorted distribution of digital density.

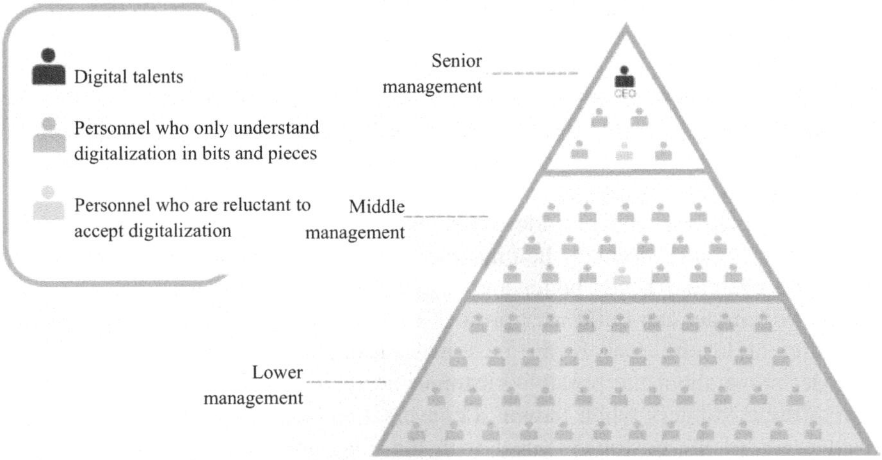

Fig. 12.2 Schematic diagram of a distorted distribution of digital density

12.2 Digital Transformation Empowers the Sales Team

The essence of digital transformation is to shift from a product-oriented to a customer-oriented approach. Empowering the sales team is equivalent to using advanced digital technologies to quickly provide customers with the products and services they want, driving business operations with customer demand and thus enhancing sales effectiveness.

Due to the streamlining of business scenarios and ever-changing customer experiences, there are more customer segmentation and management requirements for the 2C sales team. Similarly, due to the complicated partnership in the corporate service market, the 2B sales team must accurately assess the effectiveness of the partnership. Digital transformation can also help the sales team address the needs above.

A long time ago, the sales team might need to visit 10 customers daily. Among them, 8 potential customers cited no purchasing need. Only 1 potential customer was successfully converted to an actual customer out of the remaining 2, and the successful conversion rate was shallow.

Nowadays, companies can develop customer profiles, analyze them and summarize the recommendations with a data platform. Instead of using the same standardized sales pitch and offering the same products and services, the sales team is transformed to use a personalized sales approach to improve the sales closing rate and enhance efficiency.

12.2.1 How Does Digital Transformation Empower 2C Sales Revenue?

Sales revenue is a company's livelihood, providing the necessary fuel for the company's healthy growth. But sales revenue is also the most uncertain component in companies. As the market is continually changing with constant intense competition, there is always uncertainty in the economic environment.

The data platform can provide the sales team with real-time, comprehensive data from the entire domain, helping the sales team complete data analysis to understand customer needs better and implement precision marketing. The sales team, for example, can build user profiles with the data platform, classify groups into different layers, analyze the customer preferences, perform analogies, and make decisions about the possible customer needs to quickly create a solution to impress the customers while having a conversation with them. Then, the personalized needs of the customers meet with the company products and services to achieve the correct goal due to the understanding of customer needs. That is the role played by the data platform for 2C sales revenue. It is akin to "a pair of eyes" dissecting through the heart of the customers for the sales team.

In addition, the ensuing tasks undertaken by companies are premised on implementing a deep understanding and prediction of customers by the data platform. They are based on customer requirements regardless of intelligent planning, production scheduling, supply chain, warehousing, or procurement.

With the increasing popularity of mobile applications, the business department of 2C companies often needs to work with segmented business scenarios, changing customer experiences, and multi-dimensional operating modules. In particular, the sales team in 2C companies working scenarios are more complex. It is rather difficult to precisely push the key buttons of the customers by depending on traditional empirical decisions. The capabilities of digitalization can exactly meet these needs.

The decision-makers in 2C companies make references to data for their management and strategic decisions. The data application is at a more macro level. And the data application for frontline employees is more refined. More importantly, the data assets are directly invested in resolving specific business needs.

The sales team can rely on digital technologies to implement data applications for customer segmentation. More specifically, it provides the sales staff with a list of potential customers through intelligent segmentation after analyzing the external sales data. This list contains the potential needs of the customers as well as the corresponding sales strategies. The intelligent customer segmentation application enables the sales team to avoid ineffective and inefficient telemarketing and on-site visits, significantly improving labor efficiency and reducing the costs of trial and error. The intelligent segmentation application employed by the sales team can effectively identify potential customers, enhance the sales closing rate, and to a certain extent, it promotes digital transformation for companies.

12.2.2 How Does Digital Transformation Empower a 2B Sales Company?

2B companies can analyze partnership efficiency with product data in the corporate service market. In the production and operating processes, 2B companies often collaborate with channels and other companies providing different products and services. Two parties work together to provide services for a common target customer. Their relationships are not constant superior-subordinate relationships but more complex partnerships. During the collaboration period, 2B companies are usually unable to assess the settlement period, collaboration results, and contract renewal of partnership. Companies implementing digital transformation can determine the key issues above through their data platform.

The sales team of 2B companies can develop intelligent applications in the data platform, enter the relevant data of their partners, understand the basic information and operating conditions of their partners, seamlessly interconnect the internal data, and even integrate them with the external data of the whole network to devise an early sales warning model to carry out countermeasures in advance, avoiding huge losses. As companies have different preferences for business risks, the business department can build an early warning model by seamlessly interconnecting the internal and external data to address the potential risks.

The intelligent application of digital technology can empower the sales staff in 2B companies, improving their efficiencies and avoiding risks.

12.2.3 The Value of Digital Transformation for Sales Revenue

When many business lines of companies generate a large volume of data, it is necessary to integrate the data across the whole domain and develop a standardized management and application platform to achieve effective data interconnectivity and value exploration among different business departments. This type of data management application platform is a key outcome of digital transformation for companies. Digital transformation can empower the sales team with digital operating capabilities and alter the traditional sales marketing model and concept, preventing the sales team from relying on subjective judgment that can lead to poor marketing decisions. Digital transformation primarily utilizes digital technologies and data analysis to help the sales team achieve product sales objectives.

From the perspective of a sales staff, digital transformation has the four following types of value.

1. **Help the marketing team to innovate**
   In the digital transformation process, the entire marketing solution must be product-centric and devised from the perspective of the interaction between the consumers and products, utilizing the technical infrastructure of digital transformation—the data services and operating capabilities of the data platform to generate creative content to achieve data empowerment truly.

2. **Refine and streamline the sales solution**
   Digital transformation must complete the data interconnectivity of R&D, production, sales, services, and other processes, summarize the data across all domains for the sales and marketing departments, provide data references for the sales staff to develop annual sales programs and help the sales department to streamline the implementation of marketing programs.
3. **Enhance the sales KPIs**
   One of the key components of implementing marketing policies is the intensity of sales execution. Most marketing budgets also rely on sales execution to showcase their value. Digital transformation can help companies improve the effectiveness of their marketing investment, generating profit growth while saving marketing costs for them. That is the most desired outcome for companies and the value exhibited by digitalization in the marketing field. It is also the ultimate goal of the frontline team in the sales department that they are constantly striving to achieve.
4. **Boost the business response speed and elevate the customer satisfaction level**
   A business unit, including the sales department, can create marketing and business scenarios based on data-based operations. They can utilize powerful multi-dimensional data resources, robust technical architecture, a diversified range of data services/data products, and multi-functional data analytics tools to effectively predict consumer habits, facilitate the business staff to make predictions, and boost the response intensity to customer needs.

12.3 Digital Transformation Empowers the Operations

The operating solutions constantly change from traffic to consumer operations and e-commerce to new retail. As an essential merchandising phase, operations play a critical role, and precise execution of operating strategies can help companies shrink decision-making time.

The traditional operating model is single-faceted and inefficient. Whether building its operations department or outsourcing the operations team, it can only meet the needs in one dimension. There are rich dimensions of operations from the perspective of products, services, and brands. And today, most companies have multiple channels and methods of operations, including public domain operations, private domain operations, membership operations, and traffic operations. Hence, the operations department must focus on dynamic tracking of user profiles, mining data value effectively and developing operating models to avoid missing business opportunities. There are three core components of intelligent operations, namely fast feedback, fast response, and the formation of a dynamic enclosed loop for feedback and response. In traditional marketing empowerment, most operations staff put up the requirements fulfilled by the technical staff. This type of marketing empowerment model is slow to respond to the market, incurring high costs

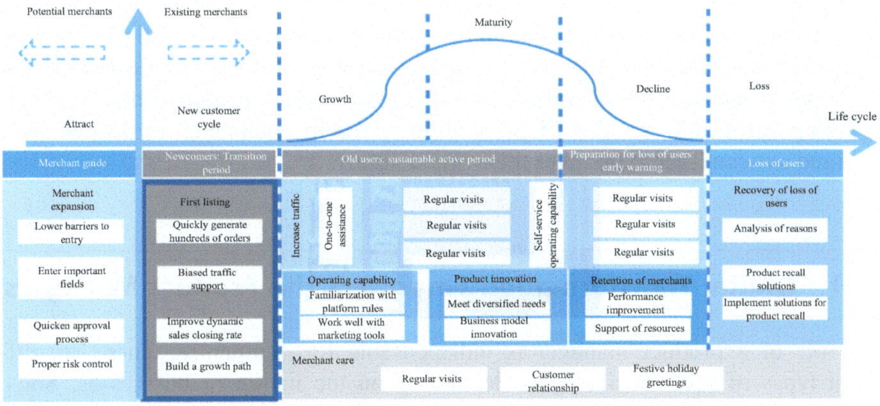

Fig. 12.3 Digitalization empowers operations

and unable to form an enclosed loop. Companies need to continually integrate new technologies and innovative thinking if they want to raise their brand awareness and sales growth simultaneously and fulfill the various requirements of operations. Digitalization can empower operations in two ways, as shown in Fig. 12.3.

1. **Digitalization optimizes the operating capability in the early phase of activities**
   In the digital transformation process, the operations department can enhance the capability of creating multiple business scenarios through the data platform, sustainably and constantly optimize the operating capability and resolve the single-faceted issues of traditional operating models.
   Companies can utilize the data platform to seamlessly interconnect the whole chain of data, which directs product marketing strategies. While planning the marketing activities, the operations department can develop regional group profiles through the data platform, understand the sources of customers in the region and appropriate marketing platforms, and devise different programs for stores in different regions. That is the value digitalization provides to the operations department in the early phase of activity planning.
2. **Digitalization provides intelligent services for the entire operating life cycle**
   In reality, digitalization can provide data intelligence services revolving around the whole work cycle of operations. One example is meeting the needs of decision-making in a high-frequency mode. In the sustainable implementation process, the marketing campaigns must be dynamically recalibrated in real-time according to user conditions. One of the most iconic needs is intelligent pricing. While integrating the internal pricing rules for the operations department with the external pricing rules for customers, the intelligent pricing application can help companies adjust their competitive pricing strategies promptly to

align with their competitors' products for large marketing campaigns. The high-frequency responsiveness capability of intelligent pricing can help companies quickly replenish inventory, boost sales revenue and ensure sustainable profits.

While meeting the operational needs of the operations department for marketing across all domains, digitalization can help companies to deepen their brand awareness and uncover their brand equity.

12.4 Digital Transformation Empowers the Product Managers

The role of a product manager is indispensable for companies. There are different types of product managers depending on the nature of businesses. Some examples include B-end product managers who focus on business growth, C-end product managers who focus on user growth, and product managers who build internet applications. Digitalization can empower product managers in product development.

Today, the disrupting waves of digitalization have made it difficult for product managers to create popular products with consumers by solely relying on their working experiences. To a large extent, they need a colossal amount of data support, such as market size research, feasibility study, and analysis of key user needs. This data support can provide a product design concept for the product managers.

In the digital era, there is an urgency for product managers to create product designs with references to the data.

A traditional company first proposes an idea for a product during the product design process. After that, it conducts R&D, followed by design. After completing the product design, the product is tested with several different solutions. Different product participants are assigned to submit improvement recommendations for the product. Ultimately, the company leaders or product managers make the final decisions. When the product is launched after the development phase, the data department provides user data to the product managers, who can continue to improve the product. Sometimes, however, the product managers do not even browse through the data and continue to work as usual. In this scenario, if there is an issue with the product, the company would not be able to figure out the root of the problem—whether the problem lies with the operations, sales department, or the product itself. The product team lacks systematic data for references throughout the entire production chain. Some products may already have issues during the decision-making process.

What would the result be if the product managers designed the products with the concept of digitalization and flexibly used data during the entire process? The product managers devise a set of design solutions according to market demand. They are unsure which is the best solution to choose from while discussing the market research. They can use intelligent A/B solutions to test the product at this juncture. In other words, the design solution is dispatched to some target users to observe which solution is the most suitable for them. Product managers can directly view the data about the use of the product through the data platform, implementing adjustments and improvements to the product at any time. By designing products with digitalization, product managers ensure higher product precision, avoiding the bias incurred by prior reliance on empirical decisions.

(1) The design solution reduces the cost of trial and error in product development after being tested in the market.
(2) Feedback data can be obtained as soon as the product is launched, helping the product development team to develop products that are truly suitable for the users quickly.
(3) When a system is formed for developing products using data, the product launch cycle becomes increasingly shorter while the success rate also increases.

The traditional product development model is no longer comparable to the digital product development model of the modern day. Utilizing data intelligence, product managers can develop products with a holistic range of support, fully understanding the development milestones of the products. If product managers still rely on their natural abilities to design products in the modern days, it may not be a wise move. They can only enable their products to stand out prominently if they comprehensively utilize data intelligence.

In the digital transformation process, product managers must analyze user needs and mainstream technology trends through the data platform, swiftly integrate them with companies' growth initiatives, and plan, deliver and operate data intelligence products, converting their ideas into final products from concept to reality.

12.5 Digital Transformation Empowers the Finance Team

As the gatekeeper of corporate value management, the data application capability of the finance team is the sole determinant of whether companies can get the highest efficiency with the most reasonable efforts. Hence, the finance team can employ data to improve work efficiency, setting reasonable performance indicators for members of every team.

The financial system of companies is to consolidate, summarize and analyze all finance-related data generated from all areas of the business process, reflecting the current state of the company's operations and forecasting the business development. The financial system is essentially a data system. Against the backdrop of digital transformation, the finance team employs digital technologies to collate all data generated in the business process and integrate them into the financial work scope to produce financial statements in an efficient and real-time manner, reflecting the current state of the business operation of companies.

With the construction of a data platform, companies can rely on the relevant functions to automatically add statistics to enable an intelligent financial system. Relying on the data platform, the finance team can easily access the auto-generated data and apply them to the more essential tasks. With the use of key performance indicators, the finance team can determine the exact allocation of the financial funds, issuing an early warning for the financial indicators. That eliminates the reporting errors for manual warning and saves labor in manually collating the data.

12.6 Digital Transformation Empowers the Operations Team

The key to improving the execution of all company employees lies with the directive control of the decision-makers in the senior management, the policy drive of the middle managers, and the execution results of the frontline employees. The management team's organizational structure comprises the decision-makers in senior management, middle managers, and all employees. The operations team must work closely with each other if companies want to achieve digital transformation. In the digital transformation process, the operations team should consider companies' future growth from several dimensions, such as strategic planning, early warning model, and precision profiling. Digitalization can empower the operations team in the three following ways.

1. **Digitalization optimizes the strategic execution process**
   The senior management decision-makers devise medium to long-term digital development strategies. The middle managers assign frontline employees to gradually carry out digital transformation in pilot projects in each department. Companies may utilize the data platform technology to digitalize all processes and provide comprehensive, real-time data operational reports, enabling the decision-makers in the operations team to recalibrate and optimize the strategic deployment from the real-time, dynamic and holistic perspective so that companies are always in a state of continual evolution, continual learning, and continual adaptation. Companies can only maintain their lead at the forefront of the competition in this way.
2. **Digitalization optimizes the path of the operation**
   Companies implementing digital transformation must create an implementation path for the operation steam, from goal setting to process execution to goal attainment. The highest ranking officer to the frontline employees can all view the operating conditions of the companies.
3. **Manage data intelligence**
   The most common report used by the operations team is the monthly operating report. Before the implementation of digital transformation, retail companies

needed to extract and analyze the data manually, which was both time-consuming and prone to making errors, and the work efficiency was very low. With the strong support of digital technologies, however, the operations team can utilize the data platform to gain access to operational data in a dynamic and real-time manner. The intellectualization of operational reporting significantly trims the cost of manual data analysis and the cost of trial and error, sending a timely reminder to the frontline teams and regional managers to react appropriately and precisely grasp the business opportunities.

12.7 Digital Transformation Empowers the Ecosystem

When companies grow more robust, they have many supply chains. The companies in these supply chains rely on the core companies for their development. The better these companies develop, the more they rely on the core companies. The stronger both parties stick together, the more revenue they get. That is a virtuous circle of development of the business ecosystem.

As Jack Ma said, "The IT Age was a period of the concept of self-interest, while the DT Era is based on a selfless idea." The DT Era enables others to benefit from achieving a win–win situation.

Nowadays, core companies not only play a role as partners but also as ecosystem builders. They enable digitalization to empower other companies, helping collaborative companies to get more benefits and enhancing the stickiness of each company within the ecosystem. For example, the production process, business process, user operations, product sales, and others in companies' supply chains are directly enabled by data. They can also deliver financial services to companies in the supply chain, helping them to find consumers better.

To date, many companies want to finance the supply chain, but there are very few success stories. The reason is the lack of systematic control of the upstream and downstream supply chains and the lack of digital infrastructure support, leading to the high costs of financing projects in the supply chain. As the results are far from ideal, the ecosystem cannot be empowered successfully.

13 How Does a CDO Execute Digital Transformation?

In the digital transformation process, the CDO is responsible for executing the decisions made by the CEO and devising a detailed plan for digital transformation.

The position of a CDO originates from the requirements of digital transformation for companies, and this is a strategic position that concerns companies' future growth. The job responsibilities of this position include the drive to integrate the traditional organization, operating models, and digital technologies of companies through the reinforcement of interaction and data flow between the internal departments, suppliers, and customers. In the digital era, although the senior management and board of directors have a specific cognitive awareness of the value of data, they still miss the critical points about enabling businesses to uncover data value.

13.1 The First 200 Days of Digital Transformation

As the key driver of digital transformation for companies, the CDO must determine the capital and objectives before implementing digital transformation.

Preparing adequate capital decides a successful drive for digital transformation for companies. Hence, the CDO must adequately plan for the capital required for the digital transformation, ensure a ready pool of capital during the transformation process, and devise his KPIs.

Having precise objectives is also key to having a correct path of digital transformation for companies without deviating from the right track. The CDO can find the transformation's correct direction by constructing the six maps.

During the digital transformation drive for companies, the CDO must first communicate with the relevant stakeholders in the various departments, including technology, data, business, management, and other departments, gradually ascertaining how to achieve the business goals with management and data deployment.

X. Ma, *Methodology for Digital Transformation*, Management for Professionals,
https://doi.org/10.1007/978-981-19-9111-0_13

Besides, the CDO also needs to understand the approaches used to measure the value of data assets and devise a comprehensive execution plan, ensuring key preparation for the digital transformation during his tenure.

13.1.1 Devise a Comprehensive Execution Plan for the First 200 Days

The CDO must plan for the implementation path of digital transformation according to the budget, avoiding overspending. At the same time, the CDO must also focus on the data applications and organize the data governance and business analysis team together for close coordination and collaboration to validate whether the data has provided any value to the businesses.

In addition, the CDO also needs to invest a certain period in communicating with the primary stakeholders of the various teams, including management, technology, business, and data teams, creating and achieving the KPIs of value-realization of businesses together with them.

1. **Prepare well in advance to lay the foundation for the ensuing drive**

In the first week of his job assignment, the CDO must perform much preparation to lay the foundation for the ensuing drive.

(1) Reinforce the relationships between team members. The CDO must build a partnership with the digital team members, proactively motivating the employees.
(2) Understand the organizational structure. The CDO can clearly understand the organizational relationships with an organizational structure diagram, comprehending the key leadership roles in the internal organization, particularly the relationship between the CIO and CTO.
(3) List out the key stakeholders. The CDO must sort out the key stakeholders, laying a solid foundation for the ensuing communication and achieving KPIs.

2. **A full description of the 200-day execution plan**

The 200-day execution plan for digital transformation devised by the CDO is the beginning of building a partnership and conveying the data-driven business goals with other departments. The CDO must communicate with other departments and determine the assessment benchmarks and processes to execute the plan. The CDO must use common business languages in the communication process and avoid complex technical terms. Furthermore, the CDO must also make use of specific illustrations to convey the message that "data concisely is the key asset of companies," explaining how data can help the operations, business growth, and revenue

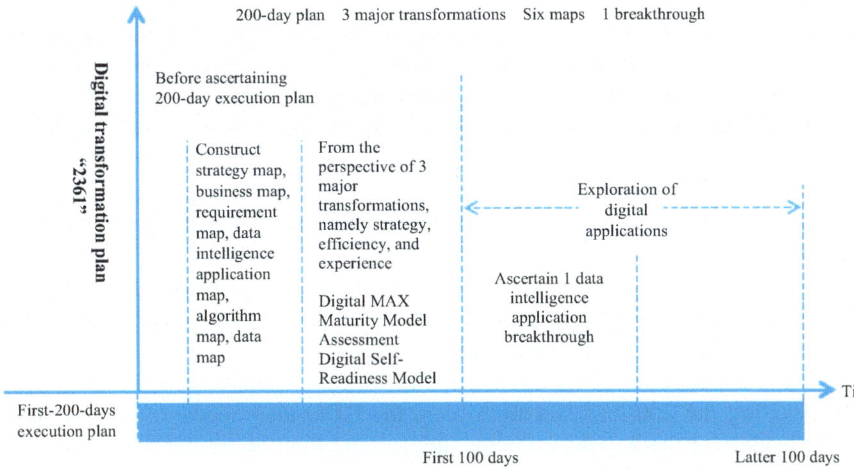

Fig. 13.1 Execution plan for the first 200 days of digital transformation

generation for companies to all departments to showcase the alignment of the execution plan for digital transformation and the strategic objectives of companies, as shown in Fig. 13.1.

(1) Assess his digital level. While devising the 200-day digital execution plan, the CDO must first evaluate the digital phase the company is currently located in, the types of digital level the company is required, and the need to upgrade to which level according to the Digital MAX Maturity Model Assessment.
(2) Assess his level of self-readiness. The CDO must utilize the Digital Self-Readiness Model to assess the preparation of the company for its digital transformation, ascertain whether the company is ready to implement a digital transformation, any lack of resources, and how to make up for the shortfall quickly.
(3) Build digital leadership. The purpose of building digital leadership is to ascertain the acknowledgment and dedication of the senior management toward digital transformation. The views initiated by the board of directors are paramount to the smooth progress of digital transformation. The board of directors must decide on the perspective from which it executes digital transformation, whether it is the perspective of strategy, efficiency, or experience transformation. It ultimately decides how the CDO would execute digital transformation. The members of the digital leadership must have an insightful understanding of the execution process of digital transformation, at least to a certain specific cognitive awareness, with proactive coordination.
(4) Determine the transformation method. At the beginning of the execution of a digital transformation, the CDO must start from either the perspective of strategy, efficiency, or experience transformation.

(5) Construct the six major maps. After determining the digital transformation perspective, the CDO needs to construct the six major maps, critically sorting out the strategy, requirement, business, and application maps. These four major maps are the foundation of the algorithm and data maps.
(6) Construct the digital execution team. After completing the work above, the CDO needs to construct a digital execution team according to the execution plan, including constructing the middle management architecture under the leadership of the senior management and the deployment of frontline employees.
(7) Build a data platform with five elements of the digital platform. The next step for the CDO is to carry out the specific execution, and the key lies in the construction of technical architecture.

While devising the 200-day execution plan, the CDO also needs to communicate with the leaders of the key departments, understand their operating conditions and satisfaction levels toward the corporate data, and comprehend the business issues and data applications problems required to be resolved quickly to sort them out and prioritize them in order.

Besides communicating with the leaders of each department, the CDO also needs to communicate with the members of the digital transformation team, understand the challenges faced in their work, comprehend the level of data governance of the team, and recognize the attempts by the team members to uncover the value of data in all areas and the obstacles they faced.

1. **Noteworthy points of the 200-day execution plan**

Data is an essential resource for companies and using it effectively can help companies boost their revenue and reinforce their risk management. Hence, the CDO must take note of the following points while devising the 200-day plan.

(1) Transfer the value of data-enabled businesses to the varying departments, including IT, legal affairs, human resources, finance, business, and data department, and clarify the significance of value-realization from data to the relevant participants.
(2) The CDO needs to understand companies' data quality from the CTO/CIO.
(3) The CDO needs to sort out the organizational structure of the data governance team, ensuring a perfect fit of responsibilities for every role.
(4) As the key driver of digital transformation for companies, the CDO needs to accumulate relevant knowledge through continuous learning, constantly upgrading his capabilities.

13.1.2 Determine the Goal-Setting Outcomes of Each Phase

After developing a 200-day work plan, the CDO must monitor the execution of the plan and make timely adjustments, if necessary. A series of assessment indicators must also ascertain the plan execution results. Consequently, the assessment result is the testing benchmark (touchstone) of the execution plan for the digital transformation of companies.

1. **Ascertain the transformation perspective and construct the six major maps**

The CDO must consolidate all pivotal items, including digital level testing, preparation readiness self-check, determination of transformation perspective, construction of six major maps (refer to Fig. 13.2), and digital platform architecture to evaluate the results of the plan execution. The CDO must prioritize the six areas 3 to 6 months before the execution of the plan: data quality, project rationality, characteristics of the information management system, data migration, budget application, and the use of data assets.

After determining the assessment results, the CDO must also assess data quality, including the ERP information system, CRM information system, key financial system, and data quality application in the sales and marketing systems.

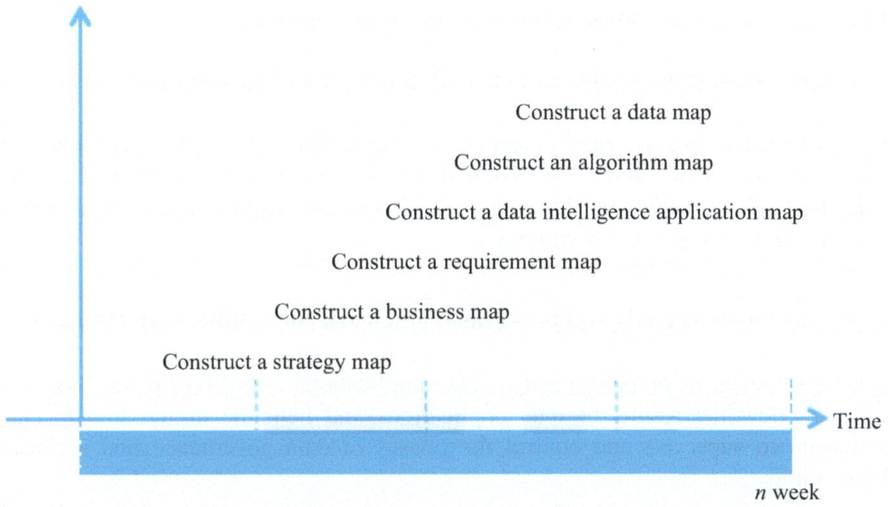

Fig. 13.2 Construction of six major maps of digital transformation

2. **Sort out the business relationships and goals**

The CDO must seek the team members' opinions according to the business urgency to ascertain the processing methods and delegate responsibilities. Besides, the CDO must also communicate with the leaders of the business department, building an open and collaborative relationship to understand the needs of the business department in the initial phase and during digital transformation. The business department is responsible for providing a clear data-enabled business path so that the CDO can quickly lead the digital transformation team to meet their needs.

3. **Utilize the DT infrastructure**

A mature data platform can help the CDO optimize different data types. The CDO can utilize the data platform to look up the data source, including rules of data use, strategic planning, data application plan, and operating manual for data applications.

13.1.3 Execute a 200-Day Plan

After completing the development and preparation of the 200-day plan, the actual implementation has officially begun. In the execution process, the CDO must take note of the execution and acceptance of the six major items.

1. **Prepare data strategy documents and develop 3 to 5 prioritized items**

The CDO needs to sort out the data strategy execution documents, prioritize the goals that must be accomplished first, and deploy the critical action plans. In addition, the CDO must also get the relevant stakeholders' support and communicate the data strategy's execution strategy.

2. **Set the business goals and build the framework compatible with the data**

The CDO needs to prepare a list of data applications aligned with the business goals to view the results of data applications and help the digital transformation team to supervise and control the phases of data governance and analysis applications.

3. **Define the roles and responsibilities of every member of the digital transformation team**

While executing the 200-day plan, the CDO must also define the roles and responsibilities of every member of the digital transformation team, including data managers, data scientists, data architects, and business analysts.

4. **Create an environment that is favorable to business data applications**

While executing the plan of data-enabled businesses, the CDO must create an environment that is aligned with the execution of digital strategy and value-realization of business, develop data governance policies, principles, benchmarks, and guidelines, and draw up execution policies that are measurable, operable, relevant and time-limited in advance. A good data policy must be clear, simple, and aligned with the data automation application.

5. **Assess the maturity of companies in the areas of data governance and uncover business value**

The maturity and experience levels of companies in data governance and uncovering business value are far too low because they do not focus on the value of data assets in the initial phase of digital transformation. The CDO must understand the levels of data governance and companies' applications in advance to lay a solid foundation for the ensuing expansion and development.

6. **Develop a meeting mechanism for regular communication with senior management**

While executing the digital transformation tasks, the CDO must listen to the demands of the senior management at any time, ensuring that the digital transformation results are aligned with the goals of the initial plan to safeguard the data governance and analysis teams to achieve their business goals.

13.1.4 Assess the Effectiveness of the Execution of the 200-Day Plan

The digital transformation of companies is a very tough assignment. The key to the entire digital transformation is assessing the results of business data applications. The CDO can create a benchmark approach under the guidance of various managers such as the CEO, CFO, and CMO to measure key data assets' actual and potential values.

1. **Select a meaningful benchmark for success to assess the execution progress**

While assessing the execution of the 200-day plan, the CDO must compile the benchmark index, monitor the execution results, and set measurable, operable, relevant, and time-limited goals as far as possible. At the same time, the CDO must also create a benchmark for success and improvement goals, accurately conveying them to the members of other departments.

2. **Use a data evaluation model to measure the execution results**

The CDO can lead the team to develop specific data indices according to the business processes and regularly assess the execution results with the data evaluation model.

3. **Assess the accuracy and consistency of data**

While assessing the execution results, the CDO must also evaluate the accuracy of the data source and the consistency of their applications, mitigating the loss of customers.

4. **Monitor the progress of processes and projects**

The CDO must compile concise, regular progress reports and list out the projects being discussed earlier with the leaders of each department, enabling the project manager to understand the key points of the 200-day execution plan and ensuring that the data governance and analysis tasks are on the right track within the stipulated timeframe.

5. **Compile two100-day quarterly reports**

After completing the testing of the execution plan and determining its results, the CDO can compile the investigation findings into two100-day quarterly reports. The report's indices and deliverables can provide companies with targeted operating recommendations.

For more information, please scan the QR code on the Preface.

13.2 The Key Capability of a CDO Is Communication

Though many companies have set up the designation of a CDO, the CDO must get strong support from every department to do his work smoothly and drive the relevant projects. The CDO must position himself as an evangelist who builds a shared vision with the senior management and department heads, driving a successful digital transformation for companies.

13.2.1 Two Key Areas for a CDO to Strengthen His Communication Capability

While driving digital transformation, the CDO must be equipped with good communication capability. There are two key areas to strengthen communication capability.

1. **Set measurable goals and make a commitment**

The CDO can set measurable goals and commit to achieving the goals within a certain timeframe. Timely delivery with a pledge of commitment can gain the trust of others. Consequently, it reduces the headwinds and obstacles in the course of work.

2. **Get strong support from the stakeholders**

As digital transformation may disrupt the interests of some personnel, the CDO must constantly communicate and discuss with the stakeholders, getting them to know the value of digital transformation and the possible future results to gain their acknowledgment and support.

13.2.2 Understand His Skill Deficiencies and Reinforce the Construction of the Team

Apart from reinforcing communication with the two methods above, the CDO must also understand his skill deficiencies and reinforce the construction of the team.

1. **Self-examination and improvement**

Besides helping companies to uncover the potential and competitive advantages of the data assets with data analytics, the CDO must also implement governance over key information assets, improve the relationship between customers, suppliers and partners through the exchanges of information assets, and participate in the cost-performance analysis, helping companies to raise their productivity. These job responsibilities exert high demands on the capabilities of the CDO. Hence, the CDO must continually self-examine, discover his deficiencies, and constantly improve himself during communication and goal achievement.

2. **Reinforce the construction of the team**

While improving his capabilities, the CDO must also concentrate on the construction of the team and develop relevant work plans according to the team members' personalities at the same time.

13.3 How Does a CDO Lead His Team?

The CDO must dive deep into several issues, such as team collaboration and resource allocation, leading his team to support the digital transformation initiative further.

1. **Empowerment of technical digital platform**

The response capability of the front-end business depends on the management operating capability, execution efficiency, and accuracy of requirements of the business team; the empowerment of the technical team. The CDO must provide the best support for the technical team, build a technical architecture suitable for the business department and technical team, showcase the dynamism of technology, and deploy it in advance for the business.

2. **The technical team must keep pace with the business growth**

Under the foundation of the technical architecture of the data platform, the CDO must proactively interconnect the online and offline data and overcome the restrictions of data to achieve the integration and presentation of global data, and even profoundly uncover models, delivering more meaningful technical guidance in the prediction of consumer behaviors.

3. **Create dual digital platforms for data applications**

After completing the construction of the data platform architecture, the CDO must maintain both the stability and scalability of the system, delivering more space to maneuver in the area of business innovation. At the same time, the front-end business data can be dynamically updated and free-flowing through the data platform while completing the different phases of governance, integration, storage, and complete presentation online. Integrating and governance the colossal data volume can provide more support for constructing an application platform. It is a manifestation that the CDO must delegate the respective tasks to the data, technical, and application teams, enabling these three parties to build data assets and create intelligent applications jointly.

13.4 How Does a CDO Purchase Appropriate Digital Platforms and Tools?

With the deepening of digital transformation for traditional industries, the past operating model that mainly relied on empirical decisions has steadily become a new model comprising profound statistical analysis of consumers with intelligent data tools. Consequently, digital technologies with iterative and updating features in many areas are becoming increasingly popular with many companies. In light of the complexity of data analytics tools in the corporate market, companies often find it hard to differentiate suitable data analytics tools for their usage. It is paramount to understand the confusion of purchasing software and choose the most appropriate digital platform and tools. Appropriate digital platforms and tools must meet the following requirements.

1. **Align with the corporate development**

When equipping a digital platform and tools, the first issue is alignment with corporate development. Companies of varying scales and sizes may choose different digital platforms and tools. Take an example of a large-scale e-commerce giant. As it is often equipped with many features of the internet and has real experiences with digital technologies, it undoubtedly has more options. In addition, companies can also utilize the technical capabilities of the service providers to purchase digital platforms and tools suitable for their business requirements.

2. **Align with the user requirements**

A digital platform and tools must be selected according to the targeted users. Some users are ordinary business staff. Hence, the presentation of analytics methods, algorithms, and models must be very user-friendly that only requires some simple operating steps. As professional data analysts use the tools, they must be configured with more complex modules according to their requirements.

3. **Align with the usage requirements**

The original intent of purchasing a digital platform and tools differs for many industries. Some industries do not require a large volume of data but stronger support in storing and managing data. Some industries require a larger volume of data with a significant focus on value creation with data analysis. Hence, they concentrate more on the analytics modules. Some industries even use data platforms and tools to optimize their reporting documents, improving warehousing capability with data. Consequently, traditional industries must consider their application objectives before procuring a data platform and tools.

4. **Good scalability**

If a company has a small scale with low data volume and flat, functional requirements, it does not have a pressing need for a digital platform. But with the rapid growth and expansion of the business, the original digital platform purchased may not be able to keep pace with the demanding requirements of corporate development. Purchasing a new digital platform is required to meet future growth and challenges, leading to a waste of resources without any control over costs.

Companies must procure a scalable digital platform that can meet personalization requirements and offers superior operating and maintenance services. It can seamlessly interconnect the traditional data management software in the internal departments of companies and smoothly access external data. Simultaneously, it also showcases certain scalability to meet the data analytics requirements of the constantly growing company.

5. **Reasonable price**

The traditional industries may feel that it is expensive to procure a digital platform and tools, and they believe that popular branded software is a superior product. In reality, software procurement depends on its suitability for the company. It must meet the requirements of the company in the following areas: the functions of the software are aligned with the business requirements, the cost performance of the software, memory computing power, simple operating procedures, advanced technologies, after-sales, operating, and maintenance services. SMEs, in particular, must procure a digital platform and tools based on their financial capabilities.

13.5 How Does a CDO Manage the Quality of Data?

As the driver of digital transformation for companies, the CDO plays a proactive leadership role in utilizing data as assets. The CDO must have a deep understanding of the quality of data, which determines the results of data intelligence applications.

The phenomenon of having errors in data applications due to poor quality of data that leads to the failure of deeply uncovering the business value and the spike in transformation costs is commonplace in the modern world. Despite such unnecessary failure, the leaders of some companies are still hesitant to prioritize the quality of data.

Apart from the lack of focus on the data quality, the data team only focuses on the logic and authenticity between data and fails to optimize the data quality from the perspective of business requirements. This type of working model also cannot safeguard the quality of data.

Hence, the CDO, CTO/CIO, and other relevant leaders from various departments must develop standardized specifications to manage data quality in the digital transformation process.

(1) Standardize data quality and business indicators and develop an accountability system for managing data quality.
(2) Build a data analytics model to examine the existing quality of data and the future results of data applications, enhancing the quality of data in uncovering business value.

(3) Outline the rates of return between the total costs for managing the quality of data and the business value realization from data applications, providing references for the recalibration of data quality management and budget application.

13.5.1 Standardize Indicators and Develop Quality Accountability

The leaders of many companies do not have a deep understanding of the importance of data quality, neglecting the rising costs due to the poor quality of data during digital transformation. Poor quality of data leads to errors in the analysis decisions. Besides, no one is accountable for the data errors with a lack of accountability system and data tracking system. The data managers or a company CDO must manage the data quality according to certain operating procedures. The followings are some systems and methods for reference purposes.

1. **Understand the objectives of digital transformation and set up an accountability system**

Before managing data quality, the CDO must first understand the digital transformation objectives and then successfully sort out the data governance modules relevant to the different business scenarios.

After understanding the digital transformation objectives, the CDO must set up an accountability system for the responsible persons in the technology, business, and data analytics teams. Then the CDO may clearly define the roles of every team during the digital transformation and tasks assigned to each member of the internal departments, implementing the workflow of personal accountability, a compilation of reasons and improvement so that the relevant teams and members attach great importance to the quality of data, forming firm support for the businesses.

2. **Align the quality of data with business performance indicators to support business results**

One of the reasons for the poor quality of data is the failure to align the quality of data with the business objectives and only focusing on the quality of data alone. In other words, the emphasis of the data governance results lies in the presentation of data logic and publishing the truth of data while neglecting the consideration of data quality from the business perspective. A clear sorting out of the relationship between data quality and business performance also facilitates the development of an accountability system for data quality.

In the data governance process, if the data governance team only focuses on the accuracy of data to be raised from the original 80% to 90% without considering any business improvement with such optimization, it leads to the business analysis team only seeing the comprehensive data indicators and governance path from the data results, completely neglecting the business logic behind the data. Ultimately, it results in a low usage rate for the data governance results without enabling the businesses. Increasing market share involves different dimensions of key indicators, including financial performance, operating performance, and customer service. The data governance team must have a sufficient understanding of these business indicators.

We must use the business results to enhance the data quality instead of presenting the data themselves. Having familiarized themselves with market operating rules of digitalization, the frontline business staff emphasizes data analysis value while making certain decisions. However, at the same time, they also consolidate their personal industry experiences to carry out a comprehensive analysis. Data with pure technical terms cannot help the business staff quickly understand its significance. The data governance presented to the frontline business staff must also contain certain business characteristics. The CDO can only better direct and advance the functions achievable by each module and allocate them to the responsible persons by understanding the relationship between data quality and business objectives.

We may sort out the relationship between the quality of data and the business performance indicators in the three following ways:

(1) Elucidate the business requirements

Before the beginning of data governance work, the data team must elucidate the string of ideas of each business and product line, uncover the requirements of different business lines and sort out the data governance work in each phase from the perspective of business requirements and according to the relationship between business logic and quality of data.

(2) Align the quality of data with the business indicators

Determining the data quality with business performance indicators can help the data team verify the effectiveness and accuracy of the data quality. The data team must develop a feedback mechanism for the data analysis results used by the business department and validate the relationship between business performance indicators, analysis of the decision-making process, and the fundamental quality of data. As the data management leader, the CDO must ensure a correlation between the data governance process and results, key business indicators, and business logic.

(3) Develop an unusual data rectification and investigation system as well as an accountability mechanism

Data quality must be continually tested in the data governance process according to its influence on business objectives. At the same time, the start of new businesses leads to changes in data volume, and the emphasis and methods employed in testing data quality must also be adjusted.

13.5.2 Build a Data Analytics Model and Devise Improvement Plans for the Quality of Data

In the data management process, the data team must differentiate, diagnose, repair, and improve the data in the entire life cycle from generation to application. The data team must build a data analytics model for the entire life cycle of data applications and devise improvement plans for the quality of data with business objectives at its core to facilitate the ease of validation of the quality of data by the data team and the business analysis team, providing intelligent recommendations over the data applications of the business analysis team.

1. **Analyze the current quality of data and identify the influence of the quality of data on business value**

After the business objectives of data governance are set, data analysis can begin. Data analysis penetrates through the entire cycle of data intelligence applications.

By performing validation of the quality of data in the early phase by using the data analytics model, it can lay the foundation for the results of the quality of data. With the validation of the original quality of data to deliver fundamental accuracy in the improvement of the quality of data in the later phase as a measurement benchmark, it can differentiate the influence of the improvement of the quality of data on business value, helping the CDO allocate the budgets for the data management team.

2. **Create a data analytics model by utilizing data analytics tools**

A series of data analytics tools with superior performance can help companies to measure the key business process indicators better and analyze the relationship between the different data sets. A data analytics model, which can be created with data analytics functions, can help the technical data staff and business analysts understand the current data quality in a shorter period. The model can also configure more complex data analytics functions to validate data quality under complex and ever-changing business scenarios.

3. **Devise improvement plans for the quality of data with business objectives at its core**

Sometimes, the CEO may find it hard to figure out why the improvement cycle for the quality of data is long, and the coverage for the quality of data is broad due to the lack of understanding of the relationship between the life cycle of data and the quality of data. Hence, the CDO must first report to the CEO and devise improvement plans for data quality with business objectives at its core while managing data quality. There are several ways below to devise improvement plans for data quality.

(1) Determine the improvement goals for the quality of data

The CDO can determine the data quality strategy, sort out the business and data quality indicators that can realize business value, and build a corresponding mechanism according to the business processes, ensuring data governance results.

(2) Determine the execution plans

The CDO must determine the solutions for the quality of data according to its improvement goals to decide whether the final results of such solutions should be kept within the data team or defined as a service-sharing model. The CEO must also identify the data quality governance in specific business sectors and fields to determine the proportion of data governance work allocation between the internal development team and suppliers.

(3) Implement the precautions

Different business teams may have different interpretations for the same data set, and two different data sets may be interpreted with the same semantics. So, the data governance team led by the CDO must have the correct understanding of the meaning of the same data set in different business units, create the business rules and safeguard the metadata management. While we summarize and link the internal data, the third-party data, the partners' data, integrator's data, and network wide open data, the data governance team must build a set of models to appraise and track the sources of the third-party data and look for the reasons of inconsistent data sources from the data pool that seem to be complete, accurate, and timely. The data governance team must also verify the authenticity of the external data and build confidence and trust with them. Although the business staff may not understand the technical issues arising from the data governance process, the CDO can construct a set of complete data quality training systems to help them understand the fundamental data, differentiate the data formats, and define the data.

The purpose of orientating the improvement plans for the data quality with the business is to achieve the long-term goal of enhancing the business value using data. Such plans should be devised and rolled out by the CDO or CTO/CIO. The improvement plans for the quality of data can help the data governance team to build awareness of the concept of "Any management of the quality of data should begin from the perspective of the business and create business advantages." The management of data quality needs the CDO to proactively organize the closed-end data, expand the external data, and constantly form the data circulation usage model if it wants to build a "closed-end circulation" model. Companies can better determine market needs and predict the results of data-driven decisions.

13.5.3 Estimate the Cost of Data Quality and Return on Investment

The level at which companies can achieve their digital transformation is often dependent on budgets, akin to the results of data quality management. Before developing and implementing critical strategies that concern the survival of companies, the CDO must first evaluate the expected effectiveness and roll out measurable performance indicators to the relevant staff, determining the expected returns and contributions.

1. **Estimate the cost of data quality and return on investment**

The initial and subsequent investments in the digital transformation of companies must be maintained within the range of reasonable return on investment. The CDO must plan for the followings in advance: application of digital technologies (hardware infrastructure, data analytics tools, cloud servers), selection and recruitment of talents to manage the quality of data, human resource costs of data integrators and system integrators, relevant business costs of the data quality plans, maintenance costs of business disruption and system downtime.

2. **Comprehensively set every level of indicators for costs and profits**

While estimating the cost of data quality and return on investment, the data governance team must fully record the costs of improving data quality and the profit indicators. Under such permissible circumstances, it must also set up every category, such as high, middle, and low, that affects costs and align it with the upper, middle, and lower threshold values of estimated costs. While setting the threshold values for the data quality between the data governance team and business managers, it must be noted to align the technical level and completion schedules of improving the data quality with the business indicators.

After the completion of the management of the quality of data, and before reporting to the business executives of varying departments such as the CEO or CMO, and COO, the CDO can conduct a self-examination in the internal data management team, review the logic of business data, figure out the areas that may contain issues and recalibrate the approaches and methods to accomplish the management of the quality of data.

For companies with urgent needs for digital transformation, managing data quality is a long-term project oriented toward the business, generating assets with data-driven business value. First, while performing the management of the quality of data as the internal driver of digital transformation, the CDO must not solely contemplate the governance methods from the data perspective and must also dive deep into the uncovering of the correlation between data semantics and business indicators, building an accountability system for the quality of data and ensuring its effectiveness. Second, the CDO must verify the data governance results by using the data analytics model at any time and devise improvement plans for data quality, ensuring the steady progress of data quality management. Lastly, the CDO must also develop plans between costs and profits based on data quality management, ensuring an alignment of the data assets with digital budgets.

13.6 How Does a CDO Review the Algorithms?

In the digital era, algorithms are critically important to the business growth of any company, and it is also the key to implementing digital transformation and building competitive advantages. IT engineers or data analysts may describe an algorithm as a set of rules formed by data operations. From the business value perspective, the algorithm is a type of approach to capture business opportunities and enhance business insights. On top of being used for product commercialization and applied to business analysis, it provides much convenience to the front-end business department.

With the development of digital technologies in the data intelligence era, algorithmic businesses trigger intelligent decisions of a much higher level ever seen. Large companies utilize advanced data analytics and algorithmic models to enhance their competitiveness and reinforce their leading market positions. Some companies may set up an internal high-profit department for product commercialization and business operations using data assets. Hence, it is necessary to employ stringent methods to ensure the accuracy and creditworthiness of the algorithms and data analytics.

Despite the relative importance of algorithms toward business value, for the managers of the respective departments, such as the technical department, data analysis department, and business application department, there are still some difficulties for them to use the algorithmic review and applying algorithms to the business. As an important driver of digital transformation, the CDO must proactively explore the value of algorithms in driving businesses and elevating the consumer experience. The CDO must be clear about the approaches of algorithmic review and driving business growth with algorithms and understand the key points of algorithm-driven businesses.

13.6.1 Procedures in Reviewing the Algorithms

In the digital transformation process, the capability of data technology directly affects the results and effects of business analysis. By relying on a series of analytics models constructed by high-level algorithms, it can enhance the accuracy and predictability of business analysis. That is also why many companies have focused on algorithms and models during their digital transformation.

It is of utmost importance for the CDO to review and manage the algorithms. A review can be conducted in the seven following ways, namely a clear understanding of the types of algorithms, creating the concept of algorithmic service business, constructing the workflow for synergistic collaboration, devising a practical algorithmic model management framework, multi-dimensional algorithmic review, full management of algorithmic market, and creating algorithmic incentive models, as shown in Fig. 13.3.

1. **A clear understanding of the types of algorithms**

During managing algorithms, the CDO must first understand the types of algorithms. There are mainly three algorithms: statistical, mining, and AI deep learning. Second, the CDO must understand the industry models closely related to the algorithms. In other words, it is the big data analytics model derived from integrating the algorithms with industry application scenarios and implementing business processing with the results.

2. **Create the concept of algorithmic service business**

The algorithm team reports to different departments, such as IT, operations, or marketing, for companies with different degrees of digital transformation.

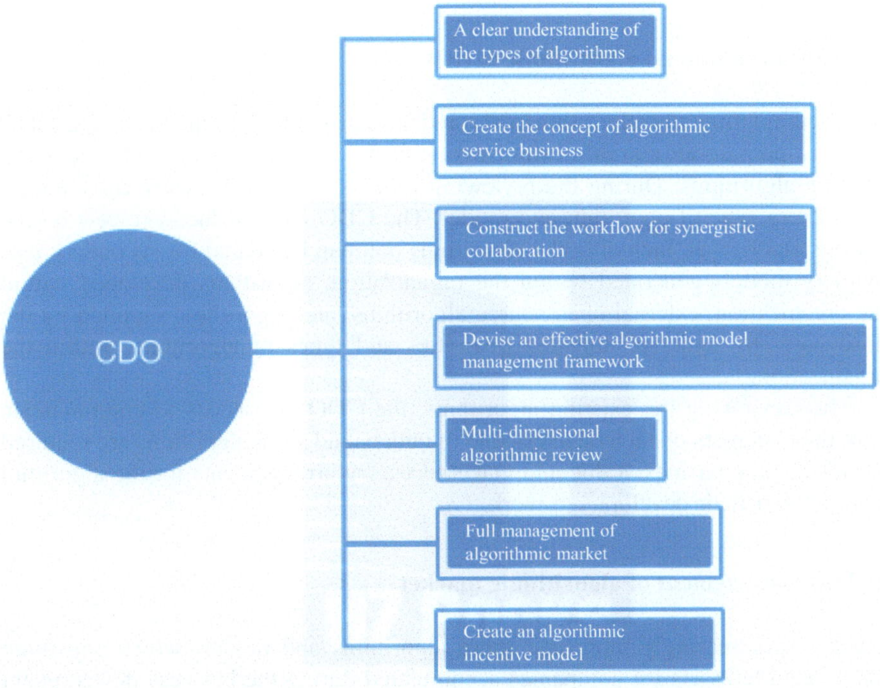

Fig. 13.3 How does a CDO review the algorithms?

And some algorithm teams led by the CDO report to the CEO in the end. In the digital transformation process with the highest objective of "value-realization of business," regardless of which department the algorithm team reports to, the ultimate service object should be the business department and not the IT department.

3. **Construct the workflow for synergistic collaboration**

After having a clear understanding of the organizational relationship of the algorithm team, the CDO can then lead his team to conduct the development of algorithms and models. Before developing algorithms, the CDO must develop the workflow of the algorithm team and reasonably devise plans for the data use, process management, technical deployment, and staff deployment, creating a synergistic, effective and collaborative work unit.

4. **Devise an effective algorithmic model management framework**

With the proliferation of the use of algorithmic and modeling technologies by many companies nowadays, these professional technologies form the intangible assets of companies undergoing digital transformation. The CDO needs to devise an effective management framework to manage these intangible assets, for example, the model validation and testing model, environmental allocation uploading model, and model upgrade solution.

5. **Multi-dimensional algorithmic review**

After completing the algorithm and model management framework, the CDO needs to prepare an algorithm directory with the algorithm team and review the existing algorithms. During the reviewing process, the CDO must clearly understand every type of algorithm and model. The CDO can conduct a review on the various algorithms, including the algorithms that can be shared for secondary use, industry models generated within the organization, algorithms developed within the organization, external open source algorithms, and algorithms supplied by the third party by understanding the quantities and types of algorithms within the organization.

After reviewing the existing algorithms, the CDO also needs to communicate with the managers of each business line to understand what algorithms are required to enhance the business value and make necessary arrangements for the algorithm team to start their development work.

6. **Full management of algorithmic market**

There are increasingly more and more algorithms and models which constitute the intangible assets for companies accumulated during the business development process. The CDO needs to properly manage these algorithms, construct a management showcase platform and place the different types of algorithms and models with varying characteristics on a common platform to create an algorithmic market.

The CDO also needs to develop a one-stop service comprising algorithms' development, uploading, downloading, and applications and determine how the third-party team can develop and collaborate the platform algorithms. During managing the algorithmic market, the CDO needs to prioritize the order of algorithms according to the companies' future growth, providing references about the staff deployment, resource allocation, and budget distribution in the next step.

7. **Create an incentive model for algorithmic development**

With the rapid development of artificial intelligence and the constant use of computing power and data, algorithms dive deep into every type of vertical need, contributing to objectives and measurable profits for companies. Building an incentive model for algorithmic contributors can allow more people to participate in the development and construction of algorithms.

13.6.2 How Does a CDO Drive Algorithmic Business Growth?

Today, algorithms have become part and parcel of the daily lives of everyone. In the future, algorithms may encompass all industries, generating and realizing value to create profits for every company. This type of trend is known as the "algorithmic business." It is also key for the digital transformation of companies to utilize algorithms to drive business growth.

1. **Develop algorithmic business strategies and allocate basic resources**

Algorithmic business is an effective motivation in the industrial Internet of Things era. Significant algorithmic applications can improve the decision-making process and automated operations. In the digital transformation process, the value of algorithms is pivotal to any successful transformation. Hence, the CDO needs to develop the algorithms with the senior management to drive the business strategies, roll out the programs in the entire company, and allocate resources to the algorithm team for the development and maintenance work to uncover the value of algorithms in driving businesses.

2. **Develop a scalable platform and benchmarking architecture to support algorithmic breakthroughs in the future**

Marching along with the mainstream of disrupting industries with algorithms, companies must quicken their pace to develop a scalable platform and benchmarking architecture to support the large volume of requirements to drive the algorithm-enabled businesses, enhancing the interactive level of automation at the same time if they want to gain competitive advantages in the future.

13.6.3 Precautions in Driving Algorithmic Business Growth

In driving algorithmic business growth, the CDO must understand the relevant concepts and measures, duly adjusting the work of the algorithm team.

1. **The algorithm is commonplace in the entire life cycle of the project**

With the unabating rise in the popularity of digital transformation for companies, it is a market acknowledgment of the value contributed by algorithms in driving business growth. Algorithms, however, are not a new phenomenon, and they have existed long ago in the market operations process for companies. The project's early phase algorithmic functions are mainly for meeting business requirements. And in the medium to long-term phase, it is the achievement of intelligent management (refer to Fig. 13.4) with machine learning algorithms, which autonomously accomplishes the business goals. Algorithms are the secret weapon in constructing control systems, marketing automation, and marketing campaign management. It has played an important role in the financial service industry recently.

Many components, such as processing engines for complicated matters, stream processing, advanced analytics, and business intelligence (BI), are depending on the algorithms to find answers. Algorithms are widely used in business analysis, deciding on product pricing, insurance claims, and other important information. With the broad applications of low-cost sensors and IoT equipment, there is a rapid spike in the speed at which data is obtained. As a result, the value of algorithms is substantially enhanced. The vital role of algorithms in enhancing business

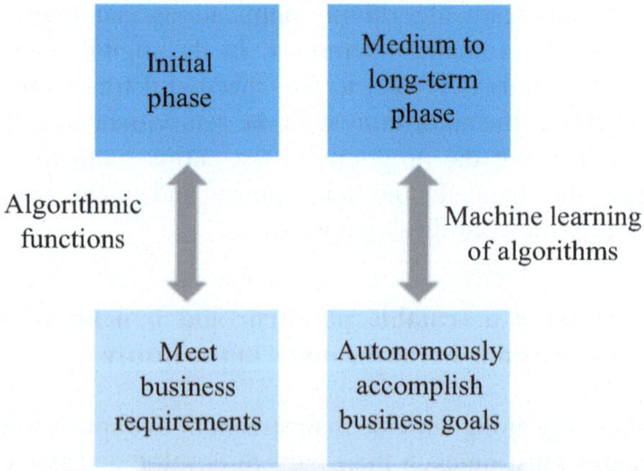

Fig. 13.4 Precaution 1 in driving algorithmic business growth

value and capturing business opportunities has also been uncovered through data processing, analysis, and applications. With the constant hard work of many developers, algorithms have become more intelligent and effective while uncovering new business values. With the deepening of digital progress, intelligent algorithms have garnered stronger support. They are beginning to optimize business results by automating the distribution of business objectives.

Hence, the CDO can lead the algorithm team to use the algorithmic functions to explore and meet the business requirements in the early phase of business applications of algorithms. In the medium to a long-term phase of digital transformation, the CDO can also lead the algorithm team to develop the machine learning approach, achieving the autonomous accomplishment of business goals.

2. **Algorithms can optimize business results**

Algorithms can automate many sectors, including the internet, social media, and mobile business. Intelligent hardware and software algorithms increasingly perform automated target searching and self-learning to optimize business results. The algorithm team led by the CDO must record the decision-making rules and critical processes to determine which areas can be automated and develop specific algorithms to achieve automated decision-making that be applied across the various businesses, as shown in Fig. 13.5.

3. **Algorithms can monitor the development trends of data and reinforce the capabilities of companies to counteract the challenges of technological transformation**

The rapid development of digital technologies has enabled a constant improvement in the interconnectivity between people, companies, and intelligent equipment. Besides, data has also quickly grown in geometric progression. Despite the quick changes in technologies, algorithms can still enhance companies' capabilities to capture business opportunities, help companies monitor their data, and reinforce their capabilities to counteract the challenges of technological transformation by utilizing their agility and adaptability, as shown in Fig. 13.6.

Companies must be agile and adaptable to capture business opportunities. In addition, companies also need to employ and increase the technologies of non-manual systems to identify business opportunities. Algorithms can identify the relevant trends of many data streams more accurately and effectively. And companies can monitor the development trends of new technologies and improve the response speed and agility of businesses by using algorithms.

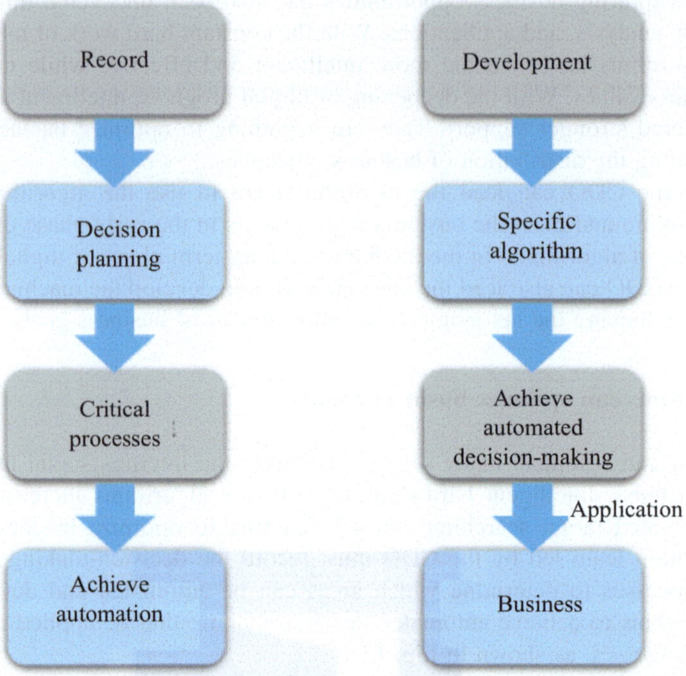

Fig. 13.5 Precaution 2 in driving algorithmic business growth

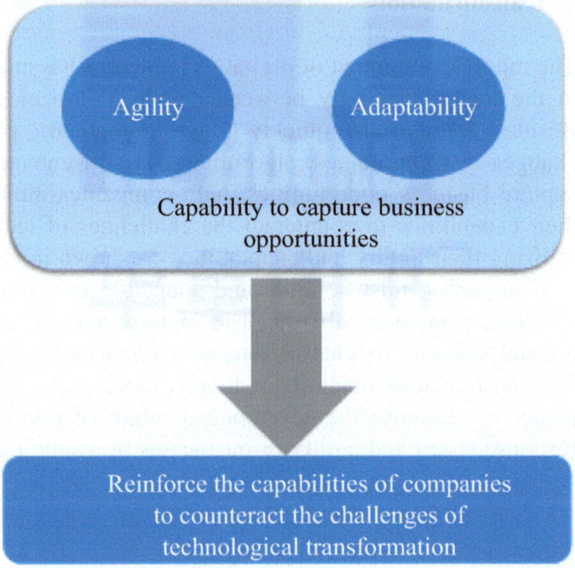

Fig. 13.6 Precaution 3 in driving algorithmic business growth

How Does a CTO/CIO Control Digital Transformation? 14

Regardless of standardizing data specifications or bringing in data technologies, the implementation results of digital transformation will be affected to a certain extent. All these require the CTO/CIO to control in an overall manner. Apart from having many relevant technological capabilities and closely monitoring the latest development trends of technologies, the CTO/CIO must also emphasize how to select solutions for digital transformation, review the data assets and organize the technical team.

14.1 Requirements of Digital Transformation for a CTO/CIO

The CTO/CIO is the highest-ranking individual in the technology area of companies. Most CTOs/CIOs have a technical background with a niche in employing technologies to meet customer needs. Many companies believe that an outstanding CTO/CIO is either an extraordinary product expert or a technology expert dedicated to R&D. Digital transformation gradually disrupts the traditional definition of CTO/CIO. They must not only focus on technologies, infrastructure construction, and IT operations/maintenance but also have a deep understanding of the alignment of technology with the businesses to drive digital transformation for companies.

14.1.1 Self-improvement

The CTO/CIO, with the critical designation of the technology chief, can refer to the five following recommendations to further improve themselves in the digital transformation process.

X. Ma, *Methodology for Digital Transformation*, Management for Professionals,
https://doi.org/10.1007/978-981-19-9111-0_14

1. **Learn digital transformation in a systematic way**

Long ago, the responsibilities of the CTO/CIO in the IT department were primarily in the R&D of management and control software, achieving online business processes, and ensuring superior interactive results from the software. They were also responsible for selecting suppliers and ensuring more efficient software development. However, digital transformation depends on empowerment or enabling models to meet the digital requirements of companies. For example, the CTO/CIO needs to empower his business staff using digital approaches, enabling them to complete their tasks more efficiently or enabling companies to achieve their business goals quickly.

2. **Understand the digital transformation methodology**

In the past, the growth models used by IT personnel were mostly the agile development methodology and project management methodology. But the requirements of digital transformation are based on data innovation. The IT personnel may be too reliant on a certain path over time, and they unconsciously develop the products using the methods at which they are best. Hence, the CTO/CIO needs to change their way of thinking to understand the digital transformation methodology.

3. **Take the initiative to perform innovation**

Formerly, the IT personnel were more focused on upgrading technologies, while digitalization achieves the overall business goals based on digital methodologies. It requires the IT personnel to change their habits of getting passive instructions and take the initiative to perform innovation.

4. **Adjust the frame of mind to counteract the challenges proactively**

Having ascended to the designation of CTO/CIO from technical staff, the CTO/CIO may have dedicated his life to his specialty area for many years and accumulated a solid technical background. Digital transformation, however, requires a different capability model. The CTO/CIO should not rely on his traditional thinking and methodologies to resolve the issues faced in digital transformation. Despite certain similarities in the technologies employed in the digital era, the specific execution details are deceivingly different.

5. **Specific system awareness**

Some CTOs/CIOs understand digital transformation by employing the fragmentation method, which is severely lacking in the systematic execution methodology. They do not have the slightest idea of which areas to emphasize and which not to emphasize during the implementation process of the project result. These uncertainties may cause companies to miss innovation and the chance to succeed.

14.1.2 Countermeasures

As shown in Fig. 14.1, the CTO/CIO must perform the followings during the digital transformation process.

1. **Broaden technical vision**

The CTO/CIO must understand the tried-and-tested growth approaches, testing procedures, and platform architecture. Besides, the CTO/CIO must also find the relevant information that can help companies complete their digital transformation, driving the digital transformation for companies faster.

The CTO/CIO must continually broaden his technical vision and fully understand the development trends of every technology and application scenario. By doing this, the CTO/CIO can then counteract all issues at different levels and know which types of technologies to use in different scenarios. In addition, the resolution of many problems still depends mainly on the broadening of technical vision and the experience of resolving issues by the CTO/CIO.

2. **Reinforce technical background**

The CTO/CIO must have an accomplished technical background and rich working experience. The CTO/CIO can only better guide his team by profoundly understanding the tools, workflow, and program design used by his team members.

3. **Strengthen team management**

The core of team management is the management of personnel. The CTO/CIO needs to think deeply about the issues, including how to strengthen his team cohesion and fully deploy the initiative and creativity of his team members.

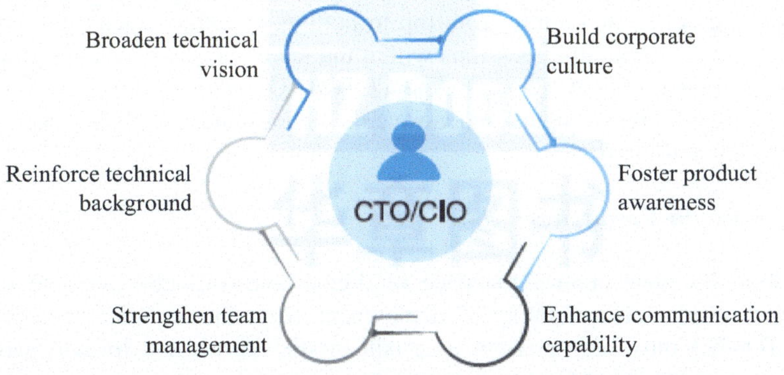

Fig. 14.1 Six capabilities that the CTO/CIO must have in the digital transformation process

(1) Stringently control the development pace of the project and products

Although the CTO/CIO is the highest-ranking individual in the technical area of companies, the CTO/CIO must also perform well in the project management area aside from adequately handling the relevant technical issues. For example, companies' product development requires the CTO/CIO to properly manage the R&D team and control the pace of development, enabling the team to complete product delivery according to plan. If the project is often delayed or the product delivery can only be accomplished with overtime work, it simply indicates that the project management capability of the CTO/CIO is inadequate.

(2) Emphasize the nurturing of the strength of an echelon formation and reserve of talents

To be an outstanding CTO/CIO, it is grossly insufficient to only focus on the development pace of products and projects. Getting support and coordination from the team members is paramount if the CTO/CIO wishes to deliver and launch the project on time. It requires the CTO/CIO to emphasize nurturing the strength of an echelon formation and organizing a team with a powerful fighting spirit and a strong sense of belonging. At the same time, the CTO/CIO must maintain a reserve of talents in the relevant positions to replace any personnel in the key position with the appropriate qualifications in the echelon formation.

4. **Build corporate culture**

The CTO/CIO must emphasize the culture in the technical department and the entire corporate culture. As one of the senior executives of companies, the CTO/CIO is responsible for creating a corporate culture. If the corporate culture is oriented toward technology, it is aligned with the corporate strategic plans. On top of instilling a sense of belonging for the staff, corporate culture can also help to retain talents in companies and further attract suitable talents to join the team.

The CTO/CIO is a yardstick for the technical staff in future growth and a channel to spread the corporate culture from top to bottom. Creating a healthy corporate culture depends on building passions within the team and the leadership imposed on new personnel by the CTO/CIO. And a CTO/CIO must willingly share his vast experiences with his colleagues and elevate the opportunities to further understand the company and industry.

5. **Foster product awareness**

The CTO/CIO must control the pace of digital transformation and the implementation results of technological deployment from the technical perspective. The CTO/CIO must also possess a certain product awareness to safeguard the transformation results at the technical levels.

(1) Place the customer needs in the No. 1 position

The objective of product development is to meet customer needs, while the purpose of product development is to place customer needs in the No. 1 position. It certainly requires the CTO/CIO to not only know about technology but also instill a great sense of passion toward internet products such that the CTO/CIO can integrate the customer experience and the actual needs from the logical, practical, and viable perspective of products, providing the overview of product improvement and guiding opinions. The CTO/CIO often gets customer contact and interaction from the product managers and business staff. During the product development process, the CTO/CIO needs to be more focused on customer experience and product applications than the product managers and business staff. In the product development process, the involvement of the CTO/CIO can help the product managers and business staff to develop products that better meet customer needs quickly.

(2) Select the technologies that apply to product development

There are also certain requirements for the selection of technologies for product development. It does not always mean using the most advanced technologies. While selecting technologies, the CTO/CIO must consider two factors: one is to meet the customer needs, and the other is the ability of the company to invest resources that are compatible with the technologies. The CTO/CIO needs to fully control the selection of technologies and the market positioning of the products to improve development efficiency and reduce the corresponding risks effectively.

6. **Enhance communication capability**

As the highest-ranking individual in the technical area of companies, the CTO/CIO must grapple with the most comprehensive information about technology and communicate and interact with all personnel at each hierarchical level over technology. Hence, the CTO/CIO must have strong communication capability.

(1) Coordinate the internal work

While coordinating the internal work, the CTO/CIO must create good communication and collaboration with the CEO, providing unwavering support for the CEO's work. In particular, the CTO/CIO must provide strong technical support to the ideas proposed by the CEO and help the CEO to recalibrate, infer and improve his ideas until they are implemented.

Second, it is of utmost importance for the CTO/CIO to communicate and interact with the senior management team. The CTO/CIO must conduct appropriate and timely interactions with the COO, CMO, VP of Sales, VP of Marketing, and HRD to reach a consensus over the final strategies, ensuring a common strategic goal across the product development, sales, and operations departments.

Finally, the CTO/CIO must often communicate with the project team members and provide necessary guidance to them. The CTO/CIO must always motivate the internal team members by instilling the company's vision into their minds, ensuring an orderly performance of the assigned tasks with the correct information and decisions. The CTO/CIO must also complete the product development and project implementation with his members on the premise of not lowering efficiencies and wasting resources.

(2) Maintain external relationships

Besides assuming the key role in companies' technical and management areas, the CTO/CIO also needs to be the bridge of communication and interaction between the company and external personnel in many instances, in particular, while aligning the customer needs to the introduction of new technologies. The CTO/CIO must have socializing capabilities to handle existing and potential customers. Apart from communicating with the customers, the CTO/CIO can also help the customers to sort out the new way of thinking and approaches, enabling the customers to become participants and creators and allowing the customers to have a deep understanding of the corporate predicaments through different forms of communication, constructing the original model of user experience and creating incremental values.

The CTO/CIO is the technical façade and the company's technology spokesperson with a solid technical background. While they are adept at communicating with machines, they may not be skillful at communicating and interacting with people. For this reason, the CTO/CIO must enhance their communication capabilities.

14.2 How Does a CTO/CIO Select the Models?

The digital transformation of companies is closely interconnected with the equipment of digital technologies. Companies, however, also face a problem while selecting their digital technologies. That is, finding a balance between technological investment and the bold deployment of advanced digital technologies and mitigating the investment risks to the minimum possible. More importantly, any mistakes in selecting technical models cause companies to incur immeasurable losses.

Being knowledgeable about the development trends of digital technologies and integrating them with business practices is a capability that the digital transformation team must have. As the chief engineer responsible for the overall technical directive during the digital transformation process, the CTO/CIO must select the digital technologies correctly, build the data platform architecture compliant with the corporate development and help companies complete the transformation as smooth as possible. The CTO/CIO can emphasize the following areas to achieve this goal.

14.2.1 IT Provides Infrastructure Support for the Construction of a Data Platform

The data platform is built between the front-end and back-end systems and above the management layer. Its purpose is to consolidate the management and control of the technical platforms and the front-end business data to meet the varying needs of corporate users. The data platform's construction depends on the stable IT technologies at the bottom layer and the multi-dimensional data. Companies can utilize the data infrastructure to perform storage and optimization for system data, social data, and machine logs to drive data applications highly efficiently. The data platform constructed to provide strong support to the digital transformation of companies is closely dependent on IT technical support.

1. **IT determines the implementation methodology for the data platform**

The CTO/CIO can extract, transform, load (ETL), and integrate internal and external data for companies with data warehouse technology, constructing a huge data network. The data platform is constructed under this foundation. The data platform can help the business team to analyze data and reasonably allocate tasks to meet the requirements of the business department. The digital transformation team must also capitalize on IT technologies to optimize the data platform sustainably and assess whether it has attained the expected goals.

2. **IT provides support for the development of a data self-service analysis system**

As an approach to constructing the data platform, IT technologies can help companies implement digital transformation to develop a self-service system with powerful data processing analysis capabilities. It provides data integration technologies that the data analysts or data scientists can use, or other business roles, motivating every staff from each hierarchical level of the company to focus on data with awareness and monitoring the quality of data.

14.2.2 DT Provides Technical Architecture Support for the Construction of a Data Platform

As a fundamental tool for data-enabled businesses, the data platform can enhance the agility of data assets, ensuring their alignment with corporate development and meeting business requirements. The data integration tools in the data platform can achieve data access and operations and provide the basic architecture of data transmission for data analysis, data warehouse processing, standardization of data operations, data migration, master data management, and internet data sharing. DT can provide technical architecture support for the data platform.

1. **CTO/CIO collaborates with the CEO and all departments to jointly create a digital vision**

The CTO/CIO can draw on the valuable experiences of other industries in their construction of the data platform, collaborate with all departments, determine the construction plan for the data platform and provide a technical vision to the CEO, delivering a new industry vision under such a foundation.

2. **CTO/CIO must construct the data platform with business at its core**

While constructing the data platform, the CTO/CIO must allocate the technical resources with the core fundamentals of uncovering business value to build a data platform that can be shared, collaborated, and synergized between the business and technical departments. The CTO/CIO can listen to the requirements of the business department to build the Application Programming Interfaces (APIs) that fit into the data platform architecture and expand the data collection scope in the data platform. They can also develop models suitable for the business staff to analyze their data and enable them to be agile in their decision-making. Afterward, to develop a data tracking system and help the business staff and developers track the data during data analytics applications. At the same time, specific measures to monitor and audit the data must also be administered.

3. **CTO/CIO must optimize the data platform technologies**

The CTO/CIO is responsible for constructing the data platform and organizing and operating the digital transformation team in the digital transformation process. Simultaneously, the CTO/CIO must also ensure that the data platform can sustainably operate, providing endless data analytics application services for the front-end business department. Hence, the CTO/CIO needs to regularly evaluate the optimization capabilities of the digital platform, including operational planning, machine learning, internal audit, model construction, unit of data analysis, intelligent interaction, and other functions of the interconnected systems, to ensure that the data platform can meet the requirements of data sharing at any time.

14.2.3 Issues to Be Noted While Selecting a Data Platform

The following describes several issues to be noted while selecting a data platform from the CTO/CIO perspective, as shown in Fig. 14.2.

1. **Can it save costs and quickly cover the costs?**

The CTO/CIO needs to focus on whether the data platform can trim operating costs as well as whether the business revenue generated by the digital platform can

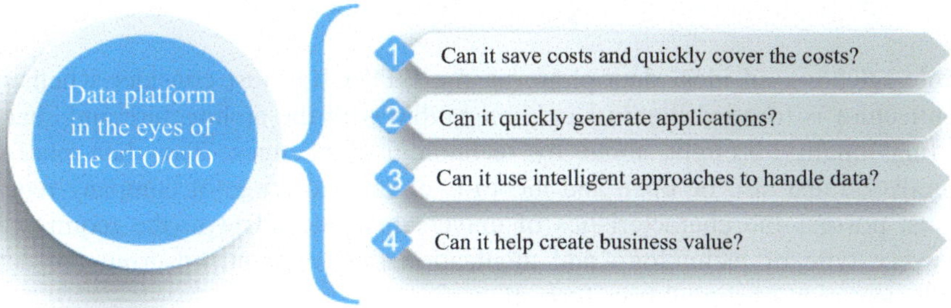

Fig. 14.2 Issues to be noted while selecting a data platform

cover the existing costs. If the digital platform can only play the role of a technical facility without quickly helping companies to cut costs and enhance efficiencies, it has an existential problem. Or in other words, it is still not perfect.

2. **Can it quickly generate applications?**

The digital platform is a sizeable data-driven business system, and a real data platform can help companies quickly develop applications and resolve pertinent issues.

3. **Can it use intelligent approaches to handle data?**

Many digital platforms in the market are merely traditional integration platforms. In other words, they are just an integrator of many tools without intelligent data handling approaches.

4. **Can it help create business value?**

A digital platform is not only a technical product. It can also help companies create business value.

14.2.4 Recommendations for a CTO/CIO in the Selection of a Data Platform

While implementing digital transformation, companies must purchase a data platform that meets their requirements. So as the technology leader in the digital transformation of companies, how does the CTO/CIO select an ideal data platform? This section illustrates the items noted while the CTO/CIO selects a data platform.

(1) A data platform should be open and forward-looking

While selecting an ideal data platform, the CTO/CIO must consider whether its architecture is forward-looking and compatible with the architecture and changes in functionality brought about by technological changes. The data platform, moreover, must also be open and meet the diversified range of company requirements, possess the characteristics of universality, and adapt to the requirements of every type of technology and application development, ensuring the actual implementation of digital transformation.

(2) A data platform should be compatible with all systems

While selecting a data platform, the CTO/CIO must take note of its compatibility with other systems and whether it can seamlessly connect with other business systems, helping companies to reduce data compatibility costs.

(3) The data platform architecture should be standardized

While selecting the technical models, the CTO/CIO must also note whether the data platform is standardized, whether it has installed common functions relevant to the specific industry and whether it can be customized for developing special functions.

(4) A data platform should be capable of controlling operating and maintenance costs

Some time back, the CTO/CIO needed to compile and organize the company-wide meter to build the data warehouse. This type of practice was prone to errors with higher maintenance costs. If the interactive systems field has changed, such systems' analysis and models would need to be redeveloped. More importantly, a good data platform can reduce operating and maintenance costs.

(5) A data platform should be capable of safeguarding data security

Some companies have more concerns over data privacy. They can resolve data security issues with the data security systems constructed by the data platform. They, moreover, can create a data committee to oversee the types of data, data users, and approving personnel for the use of data, developing a rule-based system for data use. While selecting a data platform, the CTO/CIO must focus on safeguarding and maintaining data security with the data committee.

(6) The construction cycle for a data platform must be short

A mature data platform can quickly deploy and shorten its technical architecture's construction cycle.

(7) A data platform should have implementation precedents in the industry

While selecting the technical models, the CTO/CIO must also note whether the selected data platform has any implementation precedents in the industry. An outstanding data platform would have implementation precedents in many industries, providing valuable references and lessons for more companies.

(8) A comprehensive supplier team for the data platform

While selecting a data platform, the CTO/CIO can also consider whether the data platform supplier has a comprehensive team. A comprehensive supplier team can help companies quickly locate the key points of digital transformation and implement the digital transformation program orderly.

14.2.5 Examples of the Selection of a Data Platform

After clearly understanding the significant issues while selecting a data platform, the CTO/CIO can refer to the following examples to help companies procure a suitable data platform.

1. **Project background**

In the digital era, data has become a strategic asset for companies. A particular organization has listed digital transformation as an essential growth strategy, striving to utilize an important component of digital transformation—a data platform to build data assets and a data capability center to drive business innovation and transformation.

This organization has over 70 application systems, and each business department has independently constructed a system based on its requirements. As the data of these systems are not fully integrated, it has led to issues of duplicated development and waste of resources for the organization. This organization must make an apparent breakthrough, transforming the whole organization from many chimney platforms to a data platform constructed to standardize data collection, processing, computing, and services to trim data use costs. On the other hand, it is the top priority for this organization to develop effective data governance and construct a data platform with powerful functionality to manage the colossal volume of data assets and deeply uncover the potential value in the data.
The current state of data of such an organization is as follows:

- Huge data assets, high complexity, and low degree of integration.
- Yet to construct a standardized data benchmarking and management platform.
- Yet to deeply uncover the value of data.

2. **Project objectives**

- Construction of data collection components and data repository
- Construction of data management and analysis components
- A comprehensive and orderly data lake
- Complete the construction of data governance and quality monitoring system
- Provision of data services.

3. **Project scope**

The project scope includes the business data of ERP, CRM, and data from internal and external equipment. The final data scope and system objects shall be subject to the results in the blueprint design phase.

4. **Project schedule**

The projected schedule is X months, beginning from Month Date, Year, and ending on Month Date, Year.

5. **Main tasks and deliverables**

The project is divided into eight phases. The following section details the description of all tasks at every phase.

(1) Planning, tendering, and initiation phase: The main tasks include a survey of the existing state, resource assessment, project initiation, and business tender, while the suppliers need to deliver the project proposals and initiate reports.
(2) Examination of requirements and analysis: The main tasks include implementing an analysis of business requirements, a user manual for the suppliers to submit their deliverables, a list of source system requirements, data specifications manual, and hardware resource requirements manual.
(3) Blueprint design: The main tasks include architecture design, manual of architecture design deliverables required to be submitted by the suppliers (including integration architecture, technical architecture, functionality architecture, hardware deployment architecture), functionality manual, and database design manual.
(4) Construction of technical platform: The main tasks include system installation and deployment, system installation and deployment deliverables required to be submitted by the suppliers, system operations and maintenance inspection manual, functionality manual, and development handbook.
(5) Data lake: The main tasks include all data lakes, deliverables of data lake specifications required to be submitted by the suppliers (including data lake

standards, data lake procedures, and data lake frequencies), safeguarding all data lakes, and meeting the quality requirements.

(6) Data governance: The main tasks include data management across the organization and process construction, data model design, data standards, quality standards, and data management system deliverables required to be submitted by the suppliers (including organization, person-in-charge of process, systems, supporting tools), process and system documents, data standards manual, and data quality-management-review manual; preparation of data standards and specifications for each field, data quality management specifications and review system, requiring the data quality to meet 100% of the requirements.

(7) Model development and service provision: The main tasks include the construction of models in the business fields and model development and design document deliverables required to be submitted by the suppliers.

(8) System acceptance and technical support: The main tasks include the compilation of lists of system functions, preparation of system operations and maintenance reports, training, training materials required to be submitted by the suppliers, operating manuals, operations and maintenance handbook, acceptance reports, and the provision of source code development.

6. **Needs and functional requirements**

This section includes but is not limited to the following business needs or functional requirements.

(1) Construction requirements of data management mechanism

The construction of the data management mechanism is divided into five segments: conceptualization of the construction, data assets management, data standards management, data quality management, and metadata management. The following section describes the requirements of each construction in detail.

1. Conceptualization of the construction of data management mechanism
   - Design the data management organization, develop the data management process and determine the personnel responsible for the data by integrating the current state of the organization's business.
   - Construct standardized data models, data distribution, and data flow solutions, serving as the basis for identifying the objects of data governance.
   - Devise plans for the design of core business fields and encompass the different business modules of the organization, such as R&D, marketing, planning, manufacturing, logistics, quality, finance, and human resource, based on the current survey of the business.
   - Develop the standards and specifications of data objects, such as the definition of a data object, collection specifications, data lake standards, and quality standards.

- Design the relevant processes, such as data standards management, quality management, and quality review, ensuring sustainable data quality improvement.
- The platform must provide an early warning or tracking functionality for data quality issues, performing auto-examination and reminders for the development and ETL coding specifications.

2. Data assets management
   - Asset ownership: Support the ownership departments of multi-level data assets flexibly set up according to the company's organizational structure, providing a sense of belonging between the department and the data set and performing management.
   - Asset classification: Support the management of data assets according to certain classifications, performing management through a tree or mesh structure and quickly retrieving and locating the data assets.
   - Data output: Support the output information displaying the data, including metadata changes, operating frequency of tasks, and duration.
   - Bloodline analysis: Support the bloodline information displaying the data, including superficial bloodlines and field bloodlines from the up and down streams.
   - Permissions management: Support the process application, approval, and retraction for permissions of data assets.
   - Assets overview: Display the corporate data assets in a multi-dimensional and comprehensive manner from the various segments, such as data ownership, usage conditions, and data flow.
   - Statistical overview: Display the total number of projects, meters, occupied storage capacity, consumed storage capacity, the TOP ranking of occupied storage, and other diagrams.
   - Assets query: Support the query of data assets and fuzzy query.
   - Support the import and export (related to permissions) of document formats, such as PDF, Word, and Excel.
3. Data standards management
   - Information architecture management: Support the data standards constructed according to the principles of business fields, business themes, business objects, object relationships, business processes, and business attributes.
   - Template management: Support the data standards managed according to the templates in varying business fields.
   - Logic-based modeling: Support entity-relationship (ER) model management, database reverse engineering, primary/foreign key management, distributed design, and temporary table management.
   - Dimensional modeling: Support the fact tables constructed based on star schema and snowflake schema and support the management of hierarchical dimension tables.

- Materialization of models: Support the business tables created and synchronized with relationship modeling directly in the data warehouse after publication, as well as the fact tables, dimension tables, and summary tables of dimensional modeling.
- Standard calibration: Calibrate the data source entering the data lake according to data standards and generate a list of items that do not meet the standards.
- Publication and synchronization: Support the process operations, such as approval, publication, alteration, and offline data standards, and support the interconnectivity and synchronization between business and data standards.
- Support the import and export of document formats, such as PDF, Word, and Excel.

4. Data quality management
    - Quality rules: Support predefined common data quality rules and specific user-defined data quality rules.
    - Rules calibration: That supports full directory and conditional scanning of data assets and supports quality warning and identification functions.
    - Monitoring of quality: Support the monitoring indicators for creating data quality, set relevant monitoring thresholds, and support warning on data quality.
    - Publication and review: Support the publication of data quality, including common or user-defined quality review dimensions and indicators, measuring the data quality.
    - Interconnectivity of rules: Be capable of interconnecting the data standards and data quality rules during the development of models.
5. Metadata management
    - Metadata collection: Provide the mass collection acquisition function for external metadata.
    - Metadata parser: Possess certain metadata parser capabilities and support the generation of data dictionaries and bloodline relationships.
    - Metadata management: Possess metadata management capabilities, check and maintain the detailed information of data dictionary, possess data bloodline analysis, influence analysis, and other functions.
    - Meta modeling management: Perform refining and management of several contents, including technical meta model, business meta model, data meta model, and management meta model, in companies, enabling each department of companies to find the data they require easily and accurately.
    - Metadata display: Display the metadata from the IT technology and business perspectives if they suit certain scenarios' business maps.
    - Metadata query: Provide a query for the data tables and applications for permissions based on the metadata.

(2) Functional requirements of technical platform

There are sixteen functional requirements for the technical platform. The following section describes each functional requirement in detail.

1. Data collection and storage
   - Support several types of data sources.
   - Support relational database, migration of distributed database, and support incremental migration of documents and database.
   - Support local deployment, data extraction, and retrieval from databases in private and public clouds.
   - Support the non-disclosure of data sources in public networks due to security or networking constraints.
   - Support offline data collection and real-time data collection based on business requirements.
   - Support mass collection of relational databases and real-time collection of server logs and streaming data.
   - Determine the data collection specifications, and the system can support the configuration of data collection strategies.
   - The bottom layer of the file system is the Hadoop Distributed File System (HDFS), which fully supports the upper layer applications of the Hadoop system.
   - Provide automated or manual expansion of storage capacity in Web interfaces, and ordinary operating and maintenance personnel can handle it by themselves.
   - Support the mutual migration of mainstream big data platforms in the market and configured with Web pages without a large volume of manual processing or development of code processing.
   - The shared interfaces for data storage must be universal.
2. Data development, program development, and control
   - Support SQL script editor, including but not limited to the common functions of the editor, such as code formatting, code completion, and highlighting of keywords; support the visualization of the internal structure of SQL commands, helping the relevant staff to understand the semantics of long SQL commands easily; support the concept of SQL components and create templates with the same SQL logic, increasing the reusability of the codes.
   - Support the ETL editor from the graphical WYSIWYG (an acronym for What You See Is What You Get) to achieve the ETL capabilities; support the extract, clean, transform, and load data functions.
   - Support quick generation of ETL codes, make references to preset code snippets, mapping rules, and others; replace manual coding process with intelligent data processing methods and adjustment of parameters, significantly trimming manual participation, enhancing the accuracy of data cleaning strategy, and ensuring the data is correctly processed according to the requirements of the data standards.
   - Provide an integrated development environment with powerful functions; support version control of codes; support coding comparison between any two versions; support multi-user collaborative development, support recycling of codes; support full-text search function.

- Support the control of publication and isolate the development from the production environment for code publication to production items after approval.
- Data development supports a hybrid arrangement of stream processing and batch processing and supports the arrangement of a variety of big data service engines.
- Program task scheduling, including time cycle scheduling and event scheduling based on news channels. Support the setting of dependencies between tasks.
- Program task management, including but not limited to re-execute certain batches of tasks, supplementing data to the tasks, suspending some of the nodes of a running task; real-time monitoring of end-to-end tasks, real-time display of data input/output volume at each node of the task and process incorrect data volume, while the execution results of the task support various forms of notification, such as email, SMS (Short Message Service), instant communication. Provide URL links in the graphical interface (Data Flow Designer), use each type of Stage being pre-deployed to carry out the development of tasks for ETL data processing, achieving the conversion and construction of local data and data cloud with flexibility and convenience, highly efficient management and ease of maintenance.
- Provide enriching data conversion and construction functions and support many types of data.
- Parallel processing capabilities of native data.

3. Data modeling
   - The data modeling tools display and manage the user construction of data scenarios.
   - Support the import, export, and quick duplication of data models based on data scenarios. The main functions include the management of result sets of model-based design, model distribution, and model operations. For unpublished models, it can perform view, revise, delete, and operate functions; for published models, it can also support view and operate functions.
   - Support the import and export of the data dictionary, making it easier to use and achieving accumulated industry experience and duplication across projects.
   - Support the referencing of data elements in the data model fields, apply the data standards directly to the designing of models, ensure the consistency and intelligibility of the data, and ensure that the design personnel can operate according to standardized specifications when faced with data models of different logic.
   - Support offline and real-time data integration and support the schedule of user-defined analysis.
4. Model management
   - Under the constraints of data standards in data model management, ensure that the data models can be sustained and readable.

- Under data standards and specifications constraints, complete the data modeling design, ensuring the data models' consistency, completeness, accuracy, and intelligibility.
- Support met a model management.
- Support hierarchical data management and complete the design of each hierarchy and data field of the data architecture.
- Under the constraints of data standards and specifications, complete the basic information of logic models and the design of storage method for data structure, and support the management of million-level data models.
- Support the import and export of all document formats.

5. API services
   - Support the online open, debugging, and publishing of data services API; monitor the development of APIs and transferable APIs; API development process and use process management.
   - User-defined API flow control strategy.
   - Support the concurrent API capability of 200 times per second for a single instance.
   - Support the business staff to self-define the data services.
6. Visualization
   - Seamless integration of cloud data warehouse services, data lake exploration, relational database, and object-oriented storage services, support the local CSV (Comma-Separated Values), online API, and private data cloud of the internal departments of companies and others, achieving the presentation of a different data source in the same, large visualization screen.
   - The product must be complete, providing comprehensive corporate-level BI and functions presented by agile BI through a single product, a single service, and a single platform.
   - The metadata model can support the business staff in self-service modeling and the IT staff incorporate-level complex modeling.
   - Besides common graphs, visualized representation supports the decision tree diagram, motivation analysis diagram, spiral model, and sun path diagram for predictive analysis purposes.
   - Provide common diagrams and decorations, support the drawing of tree diagrams, relationship network diagrams, and query maps, and support the visual presentation of the results of integration between diagram information and business data.
   - Drag to complete the free configuration and layout of components, WYSIWYG, easily build a large visual screen without programming and free configuration of large screen dimensions based on the projector's resolution.
   - Support the integration with the market mainstream BI tools.
   - Support publishing large visual screens in a public and encrypted way, generate link sharing among other users, and support the transmission of URL parameters in the ensuing period.

- Deliver agile color configurations and page layouts to allow users to understand the different layers and interconnectivity between data.
- Abide by the standardized user authentication and tenant-level authority isolation mechanism, publish a large screen to support the configuration of passwords and tokens, safeguarding user data privacy.

7. Data standards
   - Support information architecture management, construct database themes with standardized access, and manage data assets directories (businesses divided into different categories), data standards, and data models.
   - Support hierarchical business management, table management, data standards management, and self-definition of data standards templates.
   - Relationship modeling: Support ER (Entity-Relationship) model management, database reverse engineering, primary/foreign key management, distributed design, and temporary table management.
   - Dimensional modeling: Support the fact tables constructed based on star schema and snowflake schema and support the management of hierarchical dimension tables.
   - Model transformation: The business tables of the modeling, as well as fact tables from dimensional modeling, dimension tables, and summary tables, all support the creation and synchronization in the data warehouse after publication.
   - Approval function: Support online publication, offline approval operations, and others, support the synchronization between business assets, technical assets, and data assets, and support the interconnectivity of business assets and technical assets.
   - Support the import and export of document formats, such as PDF, Word, and Excel.
8. Quality management
   - Quality statistics function: Display quality warnings and statistical information on quality rules.
   - Directory management function: Support directory management and operating and maintenance rules.
   - Monitoring function of business indicators: Support the creation of three layers of architecture, namely the user-defined business indicators, rules, and scenarios, and monitor data quality.
   - Rules management function: Support the monitoring of rules for basic data quality.
   - Rules operations function: Support the scanning of data sources with multiple engines, all databases, all tables and conditions, and support functions, such as notification warning and labeling of data assets.
   - Rules interconnectivity scheduling: Support the quality of rules interconnectivity scheduling through the task of module development with data.
   - Support the import and export of document formats, such as PDF, Word, and Excel.

9. Metadata
   - Metadata management function: Perform refining and management of several contents, including the technical meta model, business meta model, data meta model, and management meta model, in companies based on the concept driven by a meta model, enabling each department of companies to understand and find the data they require. It is a core capability of constructing a data assets map of companies.
   - Provide the external collection capability, search, and presentation capabilities of metadata.
   - Enable the metadata to be presented according to the physical and business logic.
   - Present the basic metadata of data, including fundamental information, storage information, and permissions information.
   - Provide search and permissions applications for data tables based on metadata.
   - Identify the master data used across different business segments within the organization's business scope and build data and logic models for the master data.
10. Master data management
    - Identify the master data used across different business segments; extract the master data scattered across each application system and congregate them into the master data repository; build data models, logic models, and physical models for the master data.
    - Perform processing and organization of the master data collected according to the corporate business rules and corporate data quality standards, forming the master data that meet the corporate requirements.
    - Determine the approval process mechanism for changes in master data to ensure the consistency and stability of altering the master data.
    - Achieve data synchronization between the business systems and master data repository to ensure every system uses the same master data.
    - Ensure the agility of master data management and provide convenience for alteration, monitoring, and updating any changes in the master data in the relevant systems.
11. Data assets management

As mentioned in the earlier description, we shall not elaborate further.

12. Monitoring function and configuration
    - Support real-time monitoring of cross-network segment, cross-manufacturer, and cross-system data links, support multi-system status information reporting, summarization, and centralized pushing at the monitoring end.

- Support user-defined monitoring links configuration to quickly achieve the layout and source tracking of all links from data production to business applications.
- Ensure timely discovery of industry data link disconnection, delay, and other issues and immediately inform the relevant maintenance staff to perform maintenance work.
- Provide global overview function and display the operating status of all data business lines that have been enabled for monitoring, including the name of business lines, description of business lines, responsible persons, and normal/unusual status of business lines.
- Provide a monitoring function that can view the operating status and warning information of all business nodes in the current business segment on the detail page and the monitoring task nodes and data quality conditions involved in a single business node.
- Provide configuration management function which can view the business segment configured in the back-end configuration. It can quickly activate or close the monitoring function of the business lines and configure the responsible organization commonly used by multiple business segments and the applications involved.
- Provide configuration of panel function. Users can quickly create the processing links of critical data nodes in a visual drag manner. Users can also configure the task nodes already associated with the business nodes.

13. Task monitoring
    - It is primarily used to display the conditions of data indicators of task scheduling.
    - Task management: There are two types of models for the user to choose from—list schema and DAG (Directed Acrylic Graph) model, which supports task cycles, manual tasks, data supplement, operational testing, altering of resource scheduling portfolio, supporting the configuration of reserved CPU, RAM (Random-Access Memory) and GPU (Graphics Processing Unit). At the same time, it can close the unnecessary environment resources and perform similar adjustments to computing resources.
    - Task operations and maintenance: Support the rerun of a single task, rerun of multiple tasks, reconfiguration success, suspend, and other operations. Support the list schema and DAG model. It can view the operating status of the tasks through the operating cycles, operational testing, and manual operations of the tasks. It can also perform a rerun of the tasks, view the operating logs, coding the nodes and characteristics of the nodes.
    - Smart monitoring supports early warning for baseline. It also supports the configuration of the expected completion time for the baseline, and the algorithm automatically predicts the warning duration of each task during the process. If any task crosses the boundary, it triggers a warning, helping users eliminate the glitch in the initial growth phase.

- Smart monitoring supports incident warnings. For the critical tasks that determine the baseline output, if there is any error or slowdown, it immediately generates an incident and automatically decide son the warning objects.
- Smart monitoring supports user-defined warning rules and many types, such as complete, incomplete, error, overtime, and incomplete cycles.
- Support cyclic dependency and monitoring of isolated nodes.
- Support several notifications, such as SMS, email, and instant communication.
- Provide a monitoring dashboard for the model and monitor the operating conditions of the model already deployed.

14. Security management
    - Define the asset classes of data and devise different security strategies for a different asset class, including identification of sensitive data, encryption, and dynamic/static desensitization, ensuring the security of data at the bottom layer in storage and use as well as the security of offline and real-time data during the ETL process.
    - The security class of data is constrained by storage and extraction control, and the data is encoded with a dense marking. Marking is virtually inseparable from the data. When users can only operate the data if they meet the requirements of the dense marking, it improves the security level, further ensuring the legality, rationality, and security of sensitive data access.
    - Automatically recording all access to the databases by the users with the audit log technology can help the technical staff label the users and other information hazardous to data security.
    - Provide comprehensive application of permissions for data—approval—use—remove processes and platform support.
    - User-defined security class of data supports the security class configuration of fields and the authorization of the field classification.
    - Sensitive data: Discover and position the sensitive data based on the security class of data, ascertain its distribution on the data resource platform and automatically locate the sensitive data based on the types of sensitive data, and divide them into different classes and types of data.
    - Data access audit: Record and audit the access behaviors of privileged users, including the access period, and operating contents, remind the privileged users to complete correct operations within the correct period and inspect any infringement behaviors to ensure the security of the data system further.
    - Data desensitization: Including the databases of sensitive information, perform dynamic masking over sensitive information without restricting user access.
    - Support the display and authorization of metadata across organizations and accelerate data sharing among different departments.

15. Smart labels
    - Build a labeling system in the data platform, providing business data OLT (entity-relationship label) modeling functions and functions to produce labels and standardize viewing.
    - Label planning supports multi-dimensional data analysis based on the business entity, supports the presentation of data visualization, and supports the editing of data sets.
    - Support the management of label values and code tables, providing manual input of values, codes, and functions associated with the values and codes.
    - Support the sharing function of labels within the organization, providing the production, management, application, and other functions of public labels/private labels.
    - Provide configuration function for public policy on public labeling pool, and it can configure the visibility of sub-trees and subordinate nodes.
    - Provide the public labels' browse, search, view, application use, and other functions.
    - Provide the approval and authorization functions for the use of applications.
    - Provide the public release and retract functions for the labels.
    - Support synchronized labels between different computing resources, support consolidation of tables during synchronization, support the scheduling and task operations and maintenance of synchronized tasks, support label consolidation of entity relationships scattered across multiple physical tables, and synchronization into a single target table.
16. Intelligent algorithmic tools

The modeling development of machine learning requires the following functions:

- Data loading. Support remote and local data access.
- Data pre-processing, including data migration, data conversion, data quality management, and data source management. Provide standardized data directory functions to support the search and query of data sets or physical data.
- Feature engineering. Perform necessary conversion and processing of data after pre-processing based on the business goals to support the quick achievement of authorization models. That is one of the key functional modules of intelligent algorithmic tools. Support the performing of automated analysis and graphical presentation of data sets based on the mature algorithms of the automated feature engineering segment; support the sharing of data sets and feature engineering.
- Algorithm selection. Algorithm selection is an important procedure in the construction of models, and it can optimize and simplify the model construction process according to its unique model selection algorithm.
- Modeling training. Modeling training is a key procedure for the construction of models.

- Support the adjustment and optimization of super parameters. Contain Prescriptive Analytics, support optimization algorithms, and contain GPU support capability.
- Development management of algorithm models. Development management is managing results, personnel, and projects during model construction.
- Automated development of algorithm models. Provide end-to-end development solutions for machine learning modeling, automatically collect, clean, convert and optimize super parameters during the development phase, support real-time feedback of modeling training results in a visual manner to check on the characteristics of the model; support one-key deployment of models with seamless integration with the model deployment functions.
- Model deployment. The completed machine learning modeling requires deployment to achieve the rating of online or bulk models.
- Regularly perform the model assessment. The administrators deploy the model assets to the production environment and perform updating. Support the activation or locking in of the versions.

(3) Data lake

The data lake is divided into four requirements: data lake objective, data lake strategy, collection method, and implementation of standards.

1. Data lake objective
    - 100% data lake, 100% management of data assets.
    - It can view the data assets' storage locations, contents, and others through the data platform.
    - The system platform must contain the data lake conditions at the end of X month.
2. Data lake strategy: Devise the strategy and plan of the data lake with a survey on requirements, for example, prioritizing the data lake.
3. Collection method
    - Support the synchronization of structured business systems to the data platform with professional tools.
    - Semi-structured/unstructured data streaming supports the access of data platforms through streaming channels.
4. Implementation of standards
    - Assist the organization and every business department in implementing data standards through consulting services.
    - Before the formation of the data lake, it needs to perform data governance (pre-governance) according to the standardized data lake specifications and quality standards of the company.
    - After implementing data standards across every business department, it also needs to perform comprehensive monitoring (post-monitoring) of the quality of the data lake.

(4) Key issues

The leaders of such organizations are very concerned about the following issues. The suppliers must iron out viable solutions for these issues.

1. Data collection and storage
   - Determine the data collection method, period, frequency, increment, and other strategies based on the data transmission influenced by the network.
   - Propose a data lake strategy about the big data, such as OT (Operational Technology) interconnected equipment, three types of data (video, audio, and image); prepare a solution for the formation of a data lake in the initial phase and incremental phase.
   - Determine the hot, warm, and cold data storage, backup approach, and strategy.
2. Data computing
   - Ascertain whether data computing is conducted in the digital platform or beyond the platform.
   - How is data computed? Describe the computing characteristics, approach, and process according to the data types.
   - Regularly stay connected with the users and offer new technologies and functions for the products.
3. Security strategy. Explain what kinds of contents should be recorded for data access and the types of storage for the records.

7. **Acceptance Process and Standards**

(1) Acceptance process

Perform acceptance by the contract ratified by both parties, specific work, and the relevant indicators stipulated in the project implementation process. Party B shall issue an acceptance report for the project, while Party A shall perform the work acceptance.

The acceptance report shall be in force upon the signing and stamping of the official seal by the Project Director of Party A.

(2) Acceptance standards

The project acceptance is divided into four sections: process acceptance, functional acceptance, technical acceptance, and specifications acceptance.

- Process acceptance: Execute acceptance according to the agreement. The acceptance of task completion and stipulated deliverables are listed in the "Results Confirmation," which shall be signed and acknowledged by Party A and B.
- Functional acceptance: Perform acceptance according to the agreement. The acceptance report shall be signed and acknowledged by Party A and B. The

contents of the agreement shall be 100% achieved. If any item fails to meet the requirements, both parties cannot proceed to the next phase of technology acceptance.

- Technical acceptance: The standards are listed in Table 14.1. If all acceptance items meet the requirements, they shall be deemed to have passed the technical acceptance.
- Specifications acceptance: The types and quality of documentation in the project must meet the system requirements of Party A's company project management.

(3) Handling of non-acceptance

In each phase of the acceptance process, it shall be handled with the following provision if there is any non-acceptance due to Party B's reasons.

If the first acceptance test is rejected, a second acceptance test is conducted one month later. If the second acceptance test is still rejected, Party A shall raise a written objection to Party B without ruling out the claim for any compensation of losses. If the third acceptance test is rejected, Party A has the right to terminate the contract and file claims for any compensation of economic losses from Party B.

8. **Service and technical support**

(1) Service contents within the service period

Beginning from the completion date of project acceptance, Party B shall provide a1-year free original manufacturer warranty for the hardware and software.

1. Party B shall provide Party A with free software upgrades, including system upgrades, transfer, troubleshooting, and retesting of relevant procedures and interfaces.
2. Party B shall provide 1-year free on-site technical support. When Party A's engineers face system issues they cannot resolve themselves, Party B's technical engineers shall proceed to Party A's site to conduct servicing and clarify questions until all issues are resolved. If the issues are not caused by Party B, Party A shall pay for the relevant maintenance fees. The specific details shall be negotiated separately by both parties.
3. Party B shall provide 1-year of system on-site inspection services and propose improvement or rectification solutions for the issues uncovered.
4. Party B shall perpetually provide the following services to Party A.
   - Regularly in contact with Party A, introducing new technologies and functions of their products.
   - Party A has the right to access Party B's technical support network for technical support, and the right is perpetual.
   - Party B shall provide support by telephone and email for technical or system usage and business issues. If necessary, Party B shall also provide on-site technical support.

Table 14.1 Table of project acceptance standards

S. No.	Acceptance item	Acceptance standards	Meeting the requirements	Remarks
1	Satisfaction of functionality	100% meet the industry requirements	Yes	
2	Reliability of system functions	100%	Yes	Perform more than 3 times of forwarding and back testing for all functions. The success rate must be 100%
3	Usability of system performance	100%	Yes	
4	System response time	In the range of seconds	Yes	The query and statistics for presenting over 100 million items should reach a response in seconds
5	Data lake rate	100%	Yes	Including SAP, external equipment, and each system data
6	Data governance	100%	Yes	Including data standards, data quality management system, and implementation of system functions
7	Data security	100%	Yes	Including but not limited to classification, segmentation of data, including data security management system, data life cycle control, and security prevention technology approach
8	Data storage and computing	100%	Yes	Including but not limited to online computing query, extensive data streaming computation, big data offline computation, and distributed storage system

(continued)

Table 14.1 (continued)

S. No.	Acceptance item	Acceptance standards	Meeting the requirements	Remarks
9	No. of bugs affecting system operations	The no. of bugs affecting business operations must be 0; the no. of bugs after improvement must also be 0	Yes	All bugs discovered during the project term must be eliminated
10	Interface standards and adaptability	100%	Yes	All components can be seamlessly replaced with Hadoop open-source components without additional development or adaptation

- Provide free technical support hotline services so that Party A can directly contact the technical support center of the software manufacturer for technical support.

(2) Relevant service provisions

Party B shall be designated to liaise with Party A's service engineers and provide a 24-h hotline. Party B shall not change the designation to liaise with Party's service engineers without written acknowledgment from Party A.

Party B's technical department shall directly provide party A's technical support. If Party B's technical department cannot directly resolve the issues, it shall seek other assistance. The fees incurred shall be borne by Party B.

(3) Service levels and response time

The technical services proposed by Party A are divided into four priority levels, as shown in Table 14.2. Party B shall respond according to the priority and provide direct technical support.

(4) Service assessment standards

Party B's service assessment standards evaluated by Party A are divided into six sections, as shown in Table 14.3.

Party A shall conduct an acceptance test for every maintenance and warranty service carried out by Party B. A deduction shall be initiated according to the accepted standards if the acceptance test is rejected. If there is an accumulation of two acceptance tests being rejected, Party A has the right to terminate the contract and request Party B to compensate for the relevant economic losses.

Table 14.2 Table of service levels and response time

Level	Circumstances	Response
0	System breakdown, unable to activate the system or refuse to connect, Party A cannot access any system service, Party A's business operations are significantly influenced	7×24 telephone contact. After receiving the call, respond within 1 h and resolve the issues within 4 h
1	The system's main functions are not working properly, significantly influencing the normal operations of Party A's business; the main system is unstable, with frequent cyclical breakdowns	7×8 telephone contact. After receiving the call, respond within 2 h. If it is an email, respond within 4 h. Resolve the issues within 8 h
2	The main system contains glitches, but it still can fully operate. Certain influence on the normal operations of Party A's business	5×8 telephone contact. After receiving the call, respond within 4 h. If it is an email, respond within 1 working day. Resolve the issues within 3 working days
3	Requesting enhancement on product performance; the product functions, installations, or configurations require support with virtually no influence on the business operations of Party A; non-system related glitches	5×8 telephone contact. After receiving the call or email, respond within 1 working day. Resolve the issues within 1 week

Table 14.3 Table of service assessment standards

S. No.	Acceptance item	Acceptance standards	Penalty
1	Response time for glitches	Abide by the service levels and response time	Failed to respond promptly. Deduct X% of contract value per occasion
2	On-site arrival time	Abide by the service levels and response time	Failed to arrive at the site promptly. Deduct X% of contract value per occasion
3	Time duration to resolve the glitches	Abide by the service levels and response time	Failed to resolve Level 1, 2, and 3 glitches. Deduct X% of contract value per occasion; if Level 0 glitches are not resolved within 3 h, deduct X% of contract value per occasion; if they are not resolved within 24 h, deduct X% of contract value per occasion; if they are not resolved within 48 h, deduct X% of contract value per occasion; if they are not resolved within 72 h, Party A has the right to claim compensation for relevant economic losses from Party B
4	Regular on-site inspection service	Issue a comprehensive on-site inspection report and summary	Failed to issue an on-site inspection report. Deduct 1% of contract value per occasion

(continued)

Table 14.3 (continued)

S. No.	Acceptance item	Acceptance standards	Penalty
5	Training (Upgrading)	Users grappling with basic operations and troubleshooting skills; with training records	No training or failure to meet the training requirements. Deduct X% of the contract value
6	Customer satisfaction level	Customer assessment of service quality	Customers are not satisfied. Deduct X% of the contract value

14.2.6 Technical Score Sheet for Data Platform Suppliers

Regardless of the data platform being constructed by the IT team in the internal departments of companies or procured from data platform suppliers, the company's technical capabilities shall be first determined. It is of paramount importance to have a set of assessment standards for evaluating the technical capabilities of the data platform suppliers. A technical score sheet for data platform suppliers, Table 14.4, is provided for corporate references.

14.3 How Does a CTO/CIO Govern the Data?

In the digital transformation process, companies must first clear the data chimneys involving specific data governance. The objective of data governance is to guide businesses. A mature data intelligence administrator would first penetrate from the application perspective and maintain a holistic view of the dimensions of data governance, completing the job of data governance in phases with the project formats and integrating several application requirements into data governance. At the same time, the CTO/CIO must also properly control the changes in business scenarios as well as changes in the IT systems.

Regardless of the corporate technical staff, business staff, middle and senior management executives, or data service providers, all must be completely aware that data governance is an ongoing and long-term job. In the initial phase, its objective is to resolve certain application problems. But the long-term data governance process requires an inspection of the technical architecture to determine whether it can sustainably maintain long-term stability and operate stably according to the original intent of building the architecture. Simultaneously, the results generated by the data must be validated with actual application scenarios. In the data governance process, a single result does not conclude that the data governance is ineffective or very effective. Data governance is a systematic engineering project that requires the participants' deep understanding and involvement.

Table 14.4 Technical score sheet for data platform suppliers

Assessment item	Assessment factor	Score	Assessment standards
Overall corporate capability	Corporate capability qualification	5	Contain big data software development capability (non-procurement capability) and can provide the relevant copyrights, patents, technical specifications, and other certificates for big data
	Application case	5	Contain successful application cases and the relevant certification for good operations (acceptance report). Every provision of 1 case gets 1 point
Understanding of requirements of products and technical solutions	Understanding of requirements	5	For the full orderly formation of data lake and understanding of requirements: complete understanding (3 pts), clear understanding (2 pts), general understanding (1 pt.), non-understanding (0 pt.); Devise a work plan to fulfill the requirements of objectives: fulfill (2 pts), slightly fulfill (1 pt.), unfulfilled (0 pt.);
Understanding of requirements of products and technical solutions	Understanding of requirements	5	The overall platform architecture is built based on the open-source system framework (Hadoop): yes (3 pts), no (0 pt.); Provision of open interfaces: yes (2 pts), no (0 pts)
		5	For the objectives created by the data governance mechanism and understanding of requirements: complete understanding (3 pts), clear understanding (2 pts), general understanding (1 pt.), non-understanding (0 pt.); For the understanding of work concepts in achieving the objectives: fulfill (2 pts), slightly fulfill (1 pt.), unfulfilled (0 pt.)
	Product and technical solutions	7	Collection and storage functions Support multi-source, polymorphic collection—a total of 1 pt., assess as appropriate; Support real-time and mass collection—a total of 1 pt., assess as appropriate; Hot, warm, and cold data storage and backup and strategy—a total of 2 pts, assess as appropriate; The initial formation of the data lake and incremental data lake solution—a total of 3 pts, assess as appropriate

(continued)

Table 14.4 (continued)

Assessment item	Assessment factor	Score	Assessment standards
		11	Data development and functional integration development environment: perform comparison from the perspectives of agility, synergy, and ease of use—a total of 3 pts, assess as appropriate; Task scheduling capability: perform comparison from the perspectives of execution cycle, incident scheduling, and others—a total of 3 pts, assess as appropriate; ETL capability: whether employing graphical ETL editor—a total of 3 pts, assess as appropriate; Whether using sub-storage and computing solutions—a total of 2 pts
		4	Intelligent analysis capability Smart label system: whether the construction of the label system meets the business requirements and the functions to manage the labels—a total of 2 pts, assess as appropriate; Intelligent algorithmic tools: observe the development process of algorithms, automated development, and deployment of functions—a total of 2 pts, assess as appropriate
		4	Data service function Any provision of data service directory and permissions management functions—a total of 4 pts, assess as appropriate
		4	Monitoring of operations and maintenance function Any provision of standardized operations and maintenance monitoring and control platform for early warning, perform an inspection on particle-size monitoring, such as operations overview of the platform, task monitoring, and early warning—a total of 4 pts, assess as appropriate
Understanding of requirements of products and technical solutions	Product and technical solutions	4	Security function Any provision of identification of assets, labeling, permissions control, desensitization sharing, security auditing, and other functions—a total of 4 pts, assess as appropriate

(continued)

Table 14.4 (continued)

Assessment item	Assessment factor	Score	Assessment standards
		11	Data management function Data assets management: perform comparison from the perspectives of asset classification, bloodline analysis, assets search, and others—a total of 3 pts, assess as appropriate; Data standards: construction and verification of data standards—a total of 2 pts, assess as appropriate; Data quality: perform inspection on the definition of data quality specifications, rules verification, publication, assessment, and other functions—a total of 2 pts, assess as appropriate; Master data management: perform inspection on the identification, cleaning, modeling, publishing, and change management of data—a total of 2 pts, assess as appropriate; Metadata: perform inspection on the analysis, management, presentation, search, and other dimensions—a total of 2 pts, assess as appropriate
Implementation capability	Project management capability	10	The overall implementation plan complies with the actual situation of the companies; explicitly clear in the work arrangement and deliverables of each phase; Specific quality management and control standards, effective measures; Science-based project risks identification and prevention mechanism; Appropriate project scope management, change management approach; Science-based training and knowledge transfer plans Note: points are appropriately assessed based on references from an on-site technical presentation
	Team capability and supply of digital talents capability	10	The project managers must have over ten years of project management experience of three investments worth more than CNY1 million; Reasonable allocation of project members; It must help Party A's team to enhance its digital capabilities; It can help Party A to optimize its digital team and provide recommendations for potential talents

(continued)

Table 14.4 (continued)

Assessment item	Assessment factor	Score	Assessment standards
After-sales service	Product service	3	A definite feedback approach for product issues; Comprehensive response standards (SLA: service-level agreement) for product issues; Provision of a functional upgrade for product standards Note: points are appropriately assessed based on on-site technical presentation
After-sales service	Technical support	3	Provision of remote or on-site technical support services throughout the implementation scope of the project within 1 year from the date of final acceptance of the project; Tracking of operating results in the ensuing project and provision of problem diagnosis services and recommendations for system optimization; Provision of lifetime technical services according to the service standards Note: points are appropriately assessed based on on-site technical presentation
Narrative and Q&A	Narrative	2	The business narrator has outstanding professional capabilities to highlight the key points of the process and make the narrative easy to understand—0–2 pts, assess as appropriate
	Q&A	2	Compliant with the requirements with no apparent deviation, maintaining consistency before and after the narrative with no apparent logical errors—0–2 pts, assess as appropriate
Total		100	

14.3.1 Procedures of Data Governance

Data governance is, in essence, a systematic process and must be executed under the premise of service application scenarios. In the data governance process, the CTO/CIO needs to prepare the plans in advance for the possible use of application scenarios, employ these business scenarios for constant testing, and direct the technical department to conduct the data governance work to ensure the effectiveness of data governance.

Data governance is generally divided into four steps.

1. **Data integration**

The first step of data governance is data integration. In other words, it is the integration of external data with internal data in the management systems of companies. Data integration must completely encompass the business scenarios. The working principles of data integration are the integration of business data in different channels by utilizing all types of data tools to maintain stable operations in a long-term manner.

Under the circumstances that no one is maintaining data integration due to staff turnover or business restructuring, data integration must be carried out in a standardized way on the one hand. On the other hand, the lack of any business scenarios can be supplemented with professional data tools to safeguard the complete clearance of passage for the data, paving the way for a firm foundation for system maintenance and business changes in the ensuing period.

2. **Data governance**

After completing the integration of global data in the companies' internal and external departments, data governance is required in the next step. First, it requires the design of a data governance model, including the construction of data standards. The construction of data standards must dive deep into the products and business systems to deliver a robust foundation for data intelligence management in the ensuing period. Data standards include standards in varying areas, such as data application standards, business data standards, and data practice standards.

3. **Data service**

Data service is prepared for the use of scenarios.

The construction of a data platform undergoes the integration process from partial to global data, encompassing all business systems in companies. Based on a colossal volume of data, specific data services a reformed according to different business scenarios and product categories. These data services can provide user profiles, group labels, and others to the business department and support marketing campaigns. Besides, data services also include the analysis approach, algorithm models and user segmentation, and data clustering capability.

4. **Data security**

Besides fulfilling the use of internal departments of companies, data also generates interconnection with external parties as a result of business collaboration. Hence, it is of paramount importance to safeguard data security. On top of the data platform architecture, different security configurations can be set up with different data types. The data originating from different systems can be properly protected with the data security service centers created in varying layers with a protection mechanism from the data platform. During the data sharing with external parties, the secured mutual interaction of data privacy can be accomplished with the public spaces constructed in the data platform.

In conclusion, data security can be accomplished with specific mechanisms in the data platform. The data platform can build a platform for the external export of data. Given the different types of data and the relevant measures devised according to the privacy level, the data can be stored in a relatively safe and controllable environment such that all staff from different departments can share and mutually interact with the internal and external data in the data platform.

14.3.2 Standardized Construction of Data Governance

Setting and rolling out data governance standards help companies better conduct data governance.

1. **Rolling out administrative regulations on data governance**

Regardless of the finance, retail, or traditional industries, these mature industries would have a set of relatively complete data standards. And the data is also defined from the business characteristics in the industries. This set of data standards is commonly used in industries, and companies can also use industry standards as a reference for their data governance.

2. **Opinions and guidance on data governance**

With the advancement of digital waves, relevant data governance standards are constantly evolving. For data governance, the Chinese government has also launched some reference opinions as important references for companies performing data governance.

3. **Full-encompassing data**

Full-encompassing data includes three areas of content: full-encompassing data governance, full-encompassing data structure, and business segment.

Full-encompassing data governance refers to constructing systematic data governance tools while pondering over data governance. The data governance model constructed by the data governance team must fit perfectly into the functions of the digital platform, while the data governance team must also consider the data acquisition approach, data types, contents, and data application approach simultaneously. These can provide a new way of thinking to improve the data governance model and adjust the data governance directive.

Full-encompassing data structure includes the traditional data warehouses and the processing of relational databases. The conceptualization of data governance should begin from the applications. As data governance structure becomes increasingly complex, the encompassed area also becomes increasingly broad.

Full-encompassing business segment encompasses all business scenarios by data governance, including conventional business data, such as bank loans, savings, and wealth management business, and more refined business contents, such as banks' educational, financial products, and tourism-based financial products.

With constant changes to consumer scenarios, new business segments continually emerge with increasingly more directions for data governance. It, however, requires companies to carry out data governance comprehensively.

4. **Applications drive data governance**

The objective of data governance is intelligent applications. Data governance and data applications must continuously integrate and transition together. Data governance needs to have an objective. The data governance standards and methods must be prepared at the beginning of the implementation process before gradually moving out with applications in mind.

14.4 How Does a CTO/CIO Organize and Form a Data Team?

In recent years, the volume of data in many industries has been increasing exponentially. Regardless of the retail companies being deeply rooted in the internet industry, the digital operators providing technical support and marketing services for intelligent applications, or the traditional industries with strong technical capabilities striving to achieve digital transformation, they have all consecutively formed a data team.

In the digital transformation process, the data team is undertaking significant work. We must not only complete data transfer and sharing, data tracking, R&D of models, and other technical work, but also coordinate with the business department to complete data reports and intelligent data services applications. Hence, digital transformation needs to have an effective data team.

There are two main construction methods for a data team. One is an outsourcing model, collaborating with professional data service providers, while the company constructs the other. We shall not further elaborate on the former method. The following section introduces the noteworthy issues for constructing a data team.

14.4.1 The Formation of Members in a Data Team

The data team is constructed with enormous efforts and heavy investments by companies. Its main duty is to collaborate with the business department under the data platform architecture to complete the operations and maintenance of data and intelligent applications. The main duty of the technical staff is to research and develop data products, enhancing the convenience of using the data by the business staff. The business staff changes the business requirements and feedback the application data to the data staff, providing the basis for product upgrading and R&D.

The core members of the data team and their job duties are described in the following section.

1. **Data platform bottom-layer architecture construction team**

The data platform bottom-layer architecture construction team comprises data development engineers, data platform architects, and operations and maintenance engineers. They are mainly responsible for the construction of the fundamental architecture of the data platform. The data development engineers are responsible for constructing, adjusting, optimizing, maintaining, and upgrading the Hadoop, Spark, and other systems.

The data platform architects are responsible for the design of the bottom layer of the data platform, technical route planning, and maintenance of the scalability of the data platform, ensuring the support of requirements of data storage and computing for every business by the data platform architecture; the operations and maintenance engineers are responsible for the daily operations and maintenance of data platform. The operations and maintenance engineers are the core members of the data team, and they are also key personnel for constructing a stable, reliable bottom layer of the data platform architecture.

2. **Data operations management team**

The data operations management team comprises data development engineers, mining engineers, and warehouse architects. After completing the construction of the bottom layer of the data platform architecture, these personnel are responsible for accessing, pooling, and cleaning data and other construction work revolving around the data center. Among them, the data development engineers are responsible for the access, cleaning, processing, pooling of data, and other management work, providing strong data support for the data analysis of senior management. The data mining engineers are responsible for the mining of valuable contents in the data and inserting them into the data center for the provisional use of the data analytics team; the data warehouse architects are responsible for the data business planning of the architectural design of data warehouses.

3. **Data intelligence application team**

The data intelligence application team is primarily comprised of business analysts and modeling analysts. This team utilizes the large volume of enriching data services provided by the data operations management team to develop data analytics intelligent applications, delivering decisions and opinions about more aspects of data for the R&D/upgrading of products and expansion of new businesses. The business analysts set relevant indicators according to the business insights to meet the data analysis requirements of the business department, delivering more basis for the decisions made by the business staff. The modeling analysts build data models according to business characteristics and key data factors, elevating the data utilization rate for intelligent applications.

14.4.2 The Working Approach of the Data Team

The work of the data team is composed of the following two parts. The first part is the construction of the fundamental technical architecture for data, while the second part is the provision of data services and data modular products for the products and businesses of companies under the data platform architecture. The fundamental technical architecture for data is to deliver a reliable, stable data storage and computing platform for multiple data applications in the ensuing period.

The data intelligence-analytics management team is mainly responsible for the access, integration, cleaning, pooling, storage, management, and analysis of internal and external data of companies, filling up the relevant data to the data platform architecture according to certain business requirements and regulations, and form a data center for the internal departments of companies on top of the data platform. In addition, it also allocates professional data mining and modeling capabilities, providing multi-dimensional data analysis and intelligent application services for the front-end business platform.

At the same time, under the collective operations of the data team, aside from meeting the data requirements of the business staff, the data platform can also deliver data analytics and a basis for decision-making for the operations department, marketing department, and corporate management.

14.5 Common Decision-Making Mistakes of a CTO/CIO on Digital Transformation

The CTO/CIO not only needs to help companies to complete the construction of the bottom layer of the technical architecture, but the CTO/CIO must also consider the compatibility between the bottom layer of the technical architecture and the businesses to provide support for the digital transformation of companies from the technical perspective.

It is inevitable for the CTO/CIO to make mistakes in their decisions during the digital transformation process. The three common types of mistakes are illustrated below.

(1) The bottom layer of the technical architecture is incompatible with the front-end business requirements, forming an IT vicious circle that is impenetrable.
(2) Indistinct positioning of roles in the technical department.
(3) The digital transformation process excessively emphasizes technological investments, leading to outrageous investments with no apparent business value creation.

14.5.1 The Formation of an IT Vicious Circle

If the digital transformation team, particularly the technical department responsible for data governance, fails to completely clear the passage of internal and external data, it generates an IT vicious circle.

As the front-end business scenarios constantly change, the business department must respond to user requirements anytime. Meanwhile, the business department continually spells out all requirements to the technical department; even if some business requirements are simple, they do not require technical staff assistance but straightforward data governance processes or procedures. The technical department often has no choice but to respond to these crude and simple requirements at any time because the data governance is not completed comprehensively. The technical department can hardly find time to develop more complex applications. Under such circulation, the technical department slips into an IT vicious circle and cannot get away from it.

The IT vicious circle can be attributed to companies having constructed an incorrect data platform architecture. On top of failing to showcase its value, the data platform cannot form an enclosed loop for data, and the bottom layer of the data architecture is not rectified. As a result, the IT department cannot effectively resolve issues through the incorrect data platform. Over time, the IT vicious circle continues to evolve, creating more and more problems along the way.

14.5.2 Indistinct Positioning of Roles in the Technical Department

The indistinct positioning of roles in the technical department is one of the most common mistakes made during the implementation process of building a data platform. Take a simple example. Someone is washing, chopping, and buying vegetables in a central kitchen. A restaurant can receive a few thousand customers a day. If the central kitchen is not built properly, however, the entire process is not complete. The chef may have to be responsible for buying and washing vegetables, even inspecting the warehouse for two days. In the end, the talents' skills are misused—the technical talents are working on things that do not require their technical skills.

Many companies have allocated loads of IT staff. But their job duties and division of labor are rather indistinct. Available talents are ineffectively utilized, resulting in a waste of human resources.

Furthermore, there is an inaccurate positioning of the job duties of technical talents, enabling the technical talents to over-participate in non-technical work, which is completely irrational.

14.5.3 Huge Technological Investment But No Apparent Business Value

Another common mistake made during digital transformation is the inability to directly generate business value even with bigger investments in digital transformation and a strong technical team in the internal departments of companies. There are two reasons for such a situation.

One reason is that IT and DT are not integrated. If there is no DT in the internal departments of companies, it is impossible to achieve integration between IT and DT. In the internet, IT era, the IT investments at the business level have become more comprehensive along with corporate growth, even to the extent of being saturated. But there are fewer relevant talents in data-driven businesses. It clearly illustrates that companies are more inclined to invest in the IT area rather than the DT area of digital transformation. It simply just cannot achieve the objectives of data-driven businesses.

The second reason is that the IT staff are working on DT-related tasks. While the IT staff are adept at coding according to requirements, the DT staff are more accomplished at using data-driven businesses. If the IT staff are assigned DT-related tasks, it is easy for them to make unnecessary mistakes. As the IT staff lack the DT way of thinking, they can only develop a large quantity of all types of IT systems to drive digital transformation for companies. However, such action impedes the development pace of transformation—data barriers exist between different types of systems leading to the failure to form an enclosed data loop.

15 Insights from Alibaba's Digital Transformation

As an advocate and pioneer in digital transformation, Alibaba (abbreviated as "Ali") has led the industry in successfully achieving digital transformation. The immeasurable benefits of its successful transformation have encouraged many companies to delve into digitalization proactively. The digital transformation of Taobao, in particular, has provided endless references and takeaways for other companies. This Chapter further outlines these contents.

15.1 Data Use and Digital Advancement Process of Taobao

In the digital transformation process of Taobao, data use and digital advancement have all undergone several different development phases. These experiences would offer more significance to the references for other companies striving to implement digital transformation.

15.1.1 Five Phases of Taobao's Data Use

The data use of Taobao has undergone five phases, as shown in Fig. 15.1. The following section introduces them, respectively.

1. **Carry out refined data-based management**

In this phase, Taobao still has not used the data yet. The operating items were getting more complicated with the company's continuous development. And Taobao realized that it needed to carry out refined data-based management.

X. Ma, *Methodology for Digital Transformation*, Management for Professionals,
https://doi.org/10.1007/978-981-19-9111-0_15

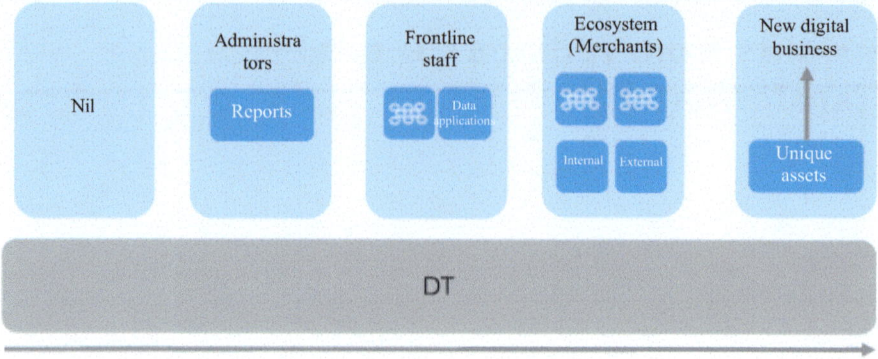

Fig. 15.1 Five phases of Taobao's data use

2. **Data-based consumerism with the administrators at its core**

The data users at this phase are mainly the administrators from the company departments. The technical team uses the data to generate reports and operating dashboards to support the administrators in making decisions.

3. **Data empowerment of frontline staff**

This phase is the beginning of the data empowerment of frontline staff. Taobao could advance to this phase because many decisions were made by the frontline staff, not the administrators. If the frontline staff were not empowered, making any decisions would be virtually impossible. The items generated in this phase were no longer straightforward reports but rather complex digital applications, enabling the productivity of the frontline staff to climb several times to even tenfold.

4. **Empowerment of the ecosystems**

Taobao advocated the empowerment of merchants in this phase. The significance of empowering the ecosystems was to enable the merchants to grow better. The capabilities and value of the platform would increasingly grow only with the positive development of the ecosystems. To put it simply, DT advocates the concept of altruism, always showing concern for the customers.

To enable its merchants to operate their products better and enhance the objective of service quality, Taobao launched over 100 digital applications, which employed the latest R&D. On the one hand, it could enable the ecosystem of merchants to grow sustainably, delivering better services to the end-users and enhancing the user experience. On the other hand, it could also increase the degree of dependency of the merchants on the platform. From the perspective of the platform, its advantages would be more apparent if the stickiness of the platform is high.

The merchants and the platform were mutually driving and integrating such that the merchants would find it hard to adapt once they left the platform. The platform has empowered merchants to earn more profits and increase their operating income.

5. **Generation of new digital businesses and digital economy**

Companies generate large volumes of unique data during their digital transformation process. Once this data has accumulated to a certain scale, it can generate new digital business carriers.

15.1.2 Six Phases of Alibaba's Digital Advancement

Ali has experienced six phases of digital transformation. The following section briefly describes these phases.

1. **Employ scattered data to resolve issues**

The first phase consists of slowly growing the business with the business systems. Each department would employ fragmented data in this phase to resolve some issues.

2. **Employ data to help the operations management executives to make decisions**

In this phase, Ali built several business intelligence tools. The technical department employed these tools to provide operating reports to the operations management executives and help them make decisions, making more straightforward management tasks.

3. **Data empowerment of frontline staff**

In this phase, Ali empowered the frontline staff with data, enabling the frontline staff to autonomously complete the preparation of reports and simple development of applications. At the same time, Ali also provided data services for them, helping the frontline staff to enhance their productivity.

4. **Employ the technical architecture of the digital platform to service its internal departments**

In this phase, Ali began to employ the technical architecture of the digital platform to provide services for its internal departments. With the provision of digital tools and applications for its frontline staff, Ali has enabled them to complete their work more efficiently. A job that required 10 persons to complete in the past would only need 1 person now.

5. **Provide services to the external parties with data development**

After increasing the productivity of its staff, Ali entered the next phase of development to provide services to external parties with data development. In this phase, Ali made two important decisions: First, it decided to empower the merchants, and second, it decided to empower the ecosystems. While empowering the merchants and ecosystems, Ali also increased the stickiness between the platform, merchants, and ecosystems.

In the ensuing period, Ali constructed an open data platform. Each data company could develop all kinds of digital applications with the data from this platform. Ali empowered its ecosystems. While empowering its ecosystems, it utilized the ecosystems to empower itself.

6. **Define data to create business models**

In this phase, Ali was striving hard to create its business models. More specifically, it is the definition of data. For example, creating an exclusive business model belonged to itself. Based on these data, Ali could provide loan services and deepen the collaboration of its supply chain. If the digital system were utterly based on the data of a data company, the result would be the emergence of a new billion to trillion-dollar company. Ant Financial Services is the new business carrier wholly built on top of the data architecture.

In conclusion, of the unique takeaways from Ali's six development phases, we can clearly understand the milestones of data value and the unique characteristics of data in the varying development phases. Due to space limitations, the description above was not a complete narrative of Ali's entire digital transformation process. We hope to provide valuable references for companies implementing digital transformation with the above examples.

Nowadays, many companies' digital transformation has stagnated at the phase in which the operations management executives rely on the reports to make decisions, and it has yet to advance to the phase whereby the frontline staff is empowered. These companies, particularly the listed companies, would need to advance to the next phase as soon as possible.

15.2 Learning References from Alibaba's Digital Transformation

In the exploratory digital transformation process, Ali has undergone different development phases, for example, the evolution of technical architecture, organizational structure, "urgent" businesses, "fatigue" technology, misallocation of talents, and the evolution of data culture. Sorting out the advantages and disadvantages of these development phases would provide more significance to the references for companies with digital transformation.

15.2.1 The Evolution of Technical Architecture

Ali's data platform architecture has evolved from its initial independent data tools, such as BI. In the initial period, Ali did not use any reports, and it only began to employ BI tools to analyze the data when each business unit gradually generated analysis requirements. After that, Taobao's business requirements grew increasingly. To counter these requirements, Ali started to allocate relevant tools for data governance and big data clusters, resulting in the proliferation of varying types of tools.

To better resolve the issues, Ali needed to organize the different types of tools into an integrated platform. In the operating process of the integrated platform, Ali found some deficiencies in the platform.

1. **The management and control of data quality, as well as applications, did not achieve intellectualization**

There were often data errors during Ali's use of the integrated platform. Hence, the IT team had no choice but to deploy large numbers of engineers to manually ensure the accuracy of the data analysis results and the effects of data governance. There were still data errors, and the maintenance costs were very high.

2. **Failure to quickly generate deep, intelligent applications**

While the static data applications generated by such a platform mainly were reports and precision marketing, user profiles, and others, the platform could not quickly generate deep, intelligent applications, such as dynamic profiles, intelligent operations, and other applications. Besides, the development costs of the platform were comparatively higher.

Given the issues above, Ali gradually evolved from an integrated platform to a data platform. The whole evolutionary process and characteristics of each phase are shown in Fig. 15.2.

15.2.2 The Evolution of Organizational Structure

Ali's organizational structure has experienced six evolutions, as shown in Fig. 15.3.

First phase: The business department was responsible for raising the requirements, while the IT department was responsible for meeting them. But both departments were independent of each other.

Second phase: The business department was responsible for raising the requirements, which would be fulfilled by two departments from the IT department, namely the data department and the traditional IT department.

Third phase: The business department would set up an IT department and a DT department beneath it, while the IT department would add a data management department.

Evolutionary phase	Independent tool	Integrated platform	Data platform
Requirements	Data analysis requirements	Integration of many data tools	Requirements for intelligent applications
Outputs	Reports	Reports + infrequent static analysis applications; User profiles, precision marketing	Reports + infrequent static analysis applications + intelligent applications; Intelligent global marketing, intelligent stock replenishment, dynamic profiles, and other AI applications
Characteristics	CEO's operating reports	Manual data, a large volume of manual processing; Easy data errors, many chimneys	Global clearing of chimney data, intelligent safeguarding of data quality

Fig. 15.2 Evolutionary process and characteristics of each phase of Ali's data platform

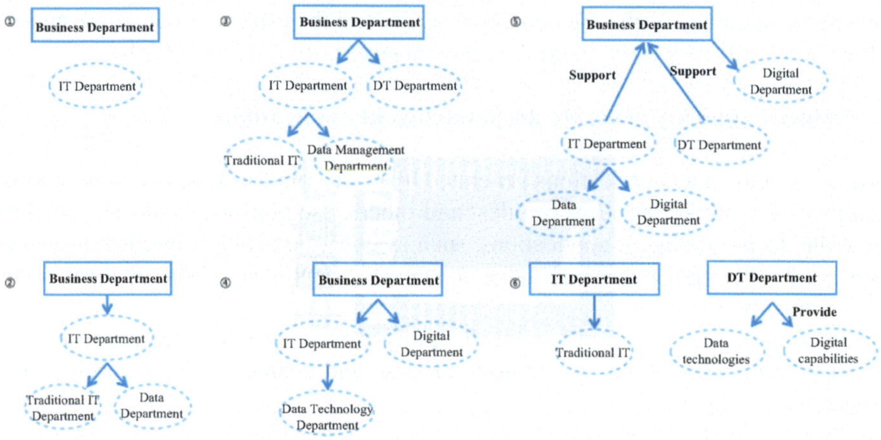

Fig. 15.3 Six evolutions of Ali's organizational structure

Fourth phase: The business department would set up a digital department and an IT department beneath it, while the IT department would set up a data technology department beneath it.

Fifth phase: The business department would retain the digital department, while the original IT and DT departments would support the business department. The IT department would set up a data department and digital department beneath it.

Sixth phase: The IT department would be responsible for the traditional technical support, while the DT department would provide data technologies and digital capabilities.

The phases given above were the six evolutionary milestones of Ali's organizational structure. During this period, Ali executed the splitting of different departments and attempted different organizational models, gradually developing into the organizational structure it has today.

Some companies may want an exact replication of Ali's organizational structure to "save time and reach their objectives in the fastest possible way." This move, however, would not be able to resolve their pertinent issues. Companies should design their digital organizational structures suited to their growth based on specific conditions under the foundation of making references to Ali's organizational structure.

15.2.3 Business Innovation Models

During the constant evolution of the organizational structure, Ali's business department needs to continually innovate to enhance corporate performance, which is "business urgency." But business innovation requires strong back-end support. The IT department often could not promptly respond to the business department's requirements for several reasons, such as continuous changes to requirements and exorbitant costs of innovation.

In general, the followings are scenarios that cannot fulfill business innovation.

1. **Hard to describe the requirements, and the products are viewed as poor**

For some business requirements that are hard to describe, the IT department believes that the business requirements of the products do not meet the market demand, that it is "hard to describe the requirements, and that the products are viewed as poor." Sometimes, business requirements are hard to be precisely described in words. Once the IT department is faced with such an issue, the speed of response slows down, and business innovation stagnates.

2. **Exorbitant costs of innovation**

Although the business department may clearly describe some business requirements, the development costs are exorbitant if the traditional IT development approach is still being used, resulting in the requirements not being passed at the product review session. Companies need to prioritize every project while creating them. As the budget is limited, some projects with exorbitant development costs may be shelved.

3. **Long cycle and slow response**

Long project execution cycles and slow response speed may also lead to the unresponsiveness of business innovation. The process of business innovation is shown in Fig. 15.4.

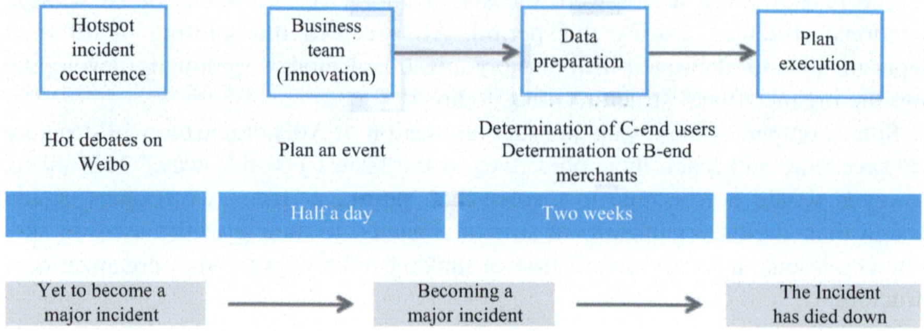

Fig. 15.4 The process of business innovation

Hotspot incidents often fuel hot debates on the internet. It is an excellent opportunity to launch marketing activities.

To launch marketing activities amid the hotspot incidents, the operations staff must have much preparation work in the early stage. The execution cycle is relatively long, so they often miss the best moment. For example, some operations staff want to roll out a marketing event for some hand phone products.

But the premise of such an event is plan execution, and they face the data issue to complete the specific plan execution. As the marketing event may encompass hundreds of millions of users, the operations team needs to precisely figure out the C-end users, analyze the types of B-end merchants that are suitable to participate in this event simultaneously, and screen through the SKUs. These works need to be validated by data, and the operations staff needs to analyze the data to determine the executable conditions at varying phases.

(1) Determination of C-end users

The operations staff need to determine the users with the best possible chance of purchasing a hand phone in the initial phase when the hotspot incident was in the limelight. For example, the users that have coincidentally browsed hand phone products recently.

(2) Determination of B-end merchants

The operations staff need to conduct a preliminary screening for merchants that are suitable to participate in this promotional campaign, and they also need to conduct another screening for a second time based on the specific requirements of the campaign. In the end, a group of merchants is shortlisted.

(3) Determination of SKU

The operations staff needs to screen through hundreds of millions of SKUs with the employment of data to filter out those SKUs that are suitable to participate in the marketing campaign.

As can be seen, this simple marketing campaign also requires data support. The marketing process needs about two weeks to determine these three types of participants with data analysis. But after two weeks, the simmering heat from the incident has subsided. This type of innovative opportunity has often disappeared due to long execution cycles.

Companies striving for their digital transformation can compare with Ali's model of business innovation to deploy digital technologies, optimize the business innovation approach of their business department to trim the costs of business innovation, and shorten the time for business innovation.

15.2.4 Manifestation of Technical Value

The technical department is supporting the development of the business department. Some IT staff may be disheartened in the long-term work with low efficiency, and the reason may be that they are doing work that cannot raise their value daily. The specific performances are depicted below.

1. **Preparation of reports**

The most common job in the data department is the preparation of reports. It often uses Excel and other office software or coding SQL to analyze the data. The preparation of reports limits the career development value of the IT staff.

2. **Mistakes made in the manual screening of data**

The IT department is using the data with traditional data warehouse technology. Regardless of reports, models, or intelligent applications, they all lack data quality maintenance. Many companies ensure the quality of data with manual maintenance.

Once there are errors in the data, the technical department employs a manual approach to look for the reasons for errors in the colossal volume of data fields and indicators. There are many types of reasons for data errors, however. It may be due to the change of definition of a field in the technical module of the business system, causing a change in the data indicators while the superiors are working on data applications. Or it may be due to incomplete data computing or the improper training of models leading to data errors. It needs the deployment of a large number of IT staff to complete the screening of data errors using the manual approach or little tools, spending a long time to complete the job.

3. **Cover up the shortfalls and gaps**

The longer a company exists in a going concern, the more data applications are generated, and the reports, applications, or models also generate data results. If there is any staff turnover, in particular those positions in charge of the development of data applications and data products, the new technical staff may not be able to understand the coding written by the prior staff, so they cannot rectify the data smoothly.

The more data errors appear in the company, the more shortfalls and gaps the IT department needs to cover. As the technical department has to spend plenty of effort and time to cover up the shortfalls and gaps, they often find it hard to have extra time to develop new applications.

4. **The work value is not being recognized**

Companies employ traditional technical architecture to generate mostly reports or presentation-based applications. Even if the applications developed by the IT department are superior and the value generated is unexpectedly more, they are merely additional decision-making tools for the department that generates the businesses. The high value generated by the business may be attributed to the correct decisions made by the business staff or may also be attributed to the high accuracy of reports. It is hard to differentiate which has a more critical effect than the other. Companies cannot be sure that the increase in business value is credited to the technical department as the work value cannot be measured. In addition, these reports are difficult to help companies to decrease their costs and increase their revenue. Despite having a larger volume of work, the IT staff continues to work daily without having any means to measure the value of their contribution. Besides, their work value is also not being recognized.

The technical team is often not recognized as it performs simple and repetitive work. Taobao had experienced a long period of development before it could successfully overcome this dilemma, enabling the work value of the technical team to be fully recognized. After that, the morale of the technical staff was substantially boosted in a dynamic environment. The technical and business departments can only have a future if companies implementing digital transformation can accomplish this remarkable turnaround.

15.2.5 Reasonable Allocation of Talents

In the digital transformation process, Ali was also muddling up the technical talents and digital talents. Today, the allocation of talents in many companies is mainly divided into business staff and technical staff. Often, the technical staff only provides technical support according to the requirements and views raised by the business staff. And the most critical job description of the technical staff is to write codes of the highest quality in a highly efficient way. Like most companies, Ali also made a grave mistake of not dissecting another type of role from its technical talents—digital talents.

The primary job duty of digital talent is not to write codes but rather to quickly identify business problems and creatively resolve them with a data applications approach. Technical talents may create the solution, or digital talents may even create them.

Ali was not very sure about the subordinate and hierarchical relationships of the technical and digital talents. It had previously allowed the technical talents to lead the digital talents. The way of thinking in work execution between these two parties was very different. On the one hand, the technical talents were pursuing to achieve the business value in a highly efficient manner. On the other hand, digital talents were pursuing to creatively look out for the existing issues in the business and resolve them. Allowing the technical talents to lead the digital talents would have a detrimental influence on the efficiency of the digital talents. After a lengthy trial and error, Ali finally set up an independent working model for both the digital and technical departments.

15.2.6 The Evolution of Data Culture

In the digital transformation process, Ali had undergone seven phases in the evolution of data culture.

1. **Not believing in the digital capability**

When Ali announced that it wanted to implement digital transformation in the early period, many people had little faith in the project. Some business departments and key decision makers strongly objected to this plan because they needed a more reliable way to achieve their performance amid their heavy responsibilities to hit all business indicators. Digital transformation is, however, a holistic strategy for the company. The business department had no other alternatives but to spend vast amounts of effort and time on digital transformation while undertaking heavy pressure to achieve business targets. With wide uncertainty about the success of digital transformation, it was very natural to harbor skeptical views. Most people were worried about the business performance being substantially affected since the senior executives had ordered that the digital transformation work should not affect the business performance.

2. **Discrimination against digitalization**

There were various reasons for the discrimination against digitalization from the business staff. Ali expressly stipulated that every department would try to use the digital approach to manage their businesses, and the business staff should expend part of their efforts to coordinate with such innovations. It was discovered during the innovation process that the results were however far from ideal. It was attributed to the incorrect decision to use a control approach to drive digitalization at the beginning of digital transformation, allowing the IT to perform the DT's work. The business department also spent much time and effort coordinating the digitalization work. But the results were not ideal, and the business performance was also greatly influenced.

3. **Countering digitalization in a mechanical way**

Coordinating with digital innovations was a hardcore task strictly assigned by the organization. As every department had important work to complete, some staff might consider doing it for its sake. Frequently, this type of thinking was the scariest part.

4. **Generating the awareness of data applications**

In this phase, data has a supplementary role most of the time. The business department could sense the value of data partly because of the significant value data had created on one or two business assignments. The business staff also mainly employed the traditional way of resolving issues in this phase. Only on some occasions would they think about integrating their issues with data. Ali had created a cultural belief for data. Once the lower and upper hierarchy of the company was confident about data, the development of digitalization would advance to the next phase, that is, the data-oriented phase.

5. **Data-oriented phase**

This particular phase was named the data-based operations in the internal departments of Ali. When the business department encountered problems or wanted to carry out business innovation, they would first consider using data to raise efficiency. They would delegate the mechanical work to the digital applications for processing and gather their energy to spend on more innovative work. In this phase, the business department had a healthy awareness of digital operations and would take the initiative to carry out business innovation with the data approach. And in this phase, the proportion of using the data approach versus the traditional approach was half each. For some companies, this ratio is already very encouraging. The advancement to the next phase would depend on a sufficiently fast and agile response to data in this phase.

6. **Cannot survive without data**

While entering this phase, business innovation was inseparable from data. In other words, most of the work had already been built on top of the foundation of data. It was also part of the reason Ali positioned itself as a data company. Ali would not be able to operate normally without data. During this phase, the whole organization of Ali was very reliant on data. The working efficiency of each department was also very high. It slowly became a habit for the company's lower and upper hierarchy to use data to resolve their issues. The employment of data resolution would always be a priority in the face of problems. The rest would be resolved manually. This type of data application would directly penetrate the next phase, which is the development of cultural beliefs for data.

7. **Development of cultural beliefs for data**

Regardless of managing the existing business, developing a new business, or even setting up a new company or business department, from the senior to middle to lower management, all people would unconsciously perform relevant business activities using the data approach.

Part VII

Critical Tools of Digital Transformation—Data Platform

For the subject of digital transformation, it is often not enough to understand the significance and other theoretical knowledge—a full understanding of the critical tools of digital transformation, the data platform, must also be accomplished.

A data platform is the core of a digital platform. Simply put, it is the fundamental technical architecture of digital transformation or its carrier. Hence, it is paramount to understand "the past and the present" of the data platform for companies striving to achieve digital transformation. Companies need to have a deep understanding of the development phases of a digital platform, interpretation of the digital platform under varying roles, the contents created by the digital platform, and implementation methodology for a digital platform.

16 The Development Phases of a Data Platform

A data platform is a technical architecture that generates value from data-driven businesses. In 2019, it was known as a "data platform" in the first year of a new digital era, and every internet company has competitively launched its data platform.

So, under what context is the data platform proposed?

What is the strategic significance of proposing a data platform?

What is a real data platform? How to define a data platform?

What are the misconceptions about the data platform during its construction process?

What are the key elements of a data platform?

How should companies construct a data platform?

16.1 Strategic Significance of a Data Platform

Under the backdrop of Ali's digital platform strategy of "large digital platform, small front-end platform," every giant internet company has begun the exploration of the data platform with its unique advantages, providing services to external parties.

What reasons drive internet giants to proactively recalibrate their organizational structures and focus on creating a data platform? Why do every internet company compete with each other to deploy a data platform which is a strategic high ground?

1. **The origin of the data platform strategy**

In reality, Ali began to employ the digital platform model to meet business requirements at a much earlier period. It officially announced its digital platform strategy in 2015. The principles of a digital platform strategy are to accumulate the tools

X. Ma, *Methodology for Digital Transformation*, Management for Professionals,
https://doi.org/10.1007/978-981-19-9111-0_16

and technologies commonly used in different businesses and set up a professional digital platform department. By doing this, new business requirements will no longer need to be redesigned, avoiding the waste of resources deployed in duplicating functional construction and maintenance.

Constructing agile, ever-changing organizational and business mechanisms is the strategic core of Ali's data platform construction. The leading companies in every industry have also begun to proactively explore the data platform and digital transformation, constantly striving to achieve the intellectualization of production operations and management by utilizing the data intelligence approach.

At the end of August 2018, Tencent made a public announcement to transform its organizational structure by forming a technical committee steering the creation of a technical digital platform in the future. Meanwhile, JD.com, Huawei, Meituan, and other internet companies in different industry sectors have all started a radical change in their organizational structures, proactively paving the way for constructing a data platform. As of now, the concept of a data platform has gradually become a reality. The business model enabled by data intelligence, servicing the customers with lower costs and higher efficiencies, is slowly being recognized. With further data platform development, a new wave of digital transformation is becoming a mainstream trend.

2. **The strategic significance of the data platform**

When the development of companies reaches a certain scale, it is commonplace for resource wastage and duplication in functional construction. Companies must consider the issue of how to maintain their core competitiveness and uncover new businesses. The data platform is of utmost importance to many companies.

After completing the data platform construction, it can standardize the data and achieve the standardization of data storage, sorting out data assets that can be flexibly deployed for companies. The data services the data platform delivers are unique and reusable assets for companies. In addition to functioning as an accumulation of businesses and data, the data services can reduce the duplicated construction of each department and many projects and help companies develop a differentiated advantage in the ultracompetitive business environment.

Amid the rapid development of mobile internet, regardless of the traditional manufacturing industry with decades of industry experience or the newly emerging internet companies, they face the same "predicaments" in their internal and external environment. Beyond the companies, mobile internet has provided enriching consumer product usage scenarios, and new demands have emerged. But the response speed and service capabilities of companies cannot keep up with the pace of the consumers.

Each organization and department has erected barriers in the internal departments of companies due to many business systems. As the data systems, such as CRM and ERP, cannot be interconnected, they cannot achieve effective communication between many departments and provide standardized, precise company services. The high-value data related to many types of users can only revolve around a single system in the internal department, failing to showcase the value on a standardized platform. It leads to inadequate innovation in the internal departments of companies and fails to provide better customer service.

If it continues to go on by doing this, companies could be booted out of business in the ultracompetitive business environment. Ali acutely singled out the corporate dilemma and learned important lessons from its failure to effectively employ a "shared business department" in the early phase of the process. The rigid requirements for all business platforms to interface with an "intermediate organization" in a mandatory manner did not work.

Hence, the "digital platform model" created by the "large digital platform, small front-end platform" organizational and business mechanisms has become a favorable breakthrough in Ali's digital development, spurring many internet companies to develop their digital platform strategies. Through the data platform, Ali recorded the product requirements of the users in their searches and timely pushed relevant product information to them. One of Ali's objectives was to pour huge investments into the data platform's construction. The notion of utilizing historical corporate data to generate value has increasingly been acknowledged as the growth path of many companies and the companies' objective in their dedication to constructing the data platform.

While initiating a new project in many companies, the business department often raises the requirements, followed by the technical department to carry out design and research. By doing this, it increases the costs of communication between the departments. On the other hand, it also exacerbates the severe phenomenon of data silos in each business system.

With increasingly escalating user requirements, the operations staff faces many business issues. It becomes imperative and urgent for companies to resolve several issues, including enhancing the system software's response speed, mining the users' potential requirements, improving user satisfaction, and trimming communication costs between varying departments.

Consequently, data governance has become a daily routine for many companies. With localized, unilateral development of data governance, the idea of a data platform was born. Alongside the pioneering implementation of a data platform by the adventurous Ali, data sharing has become the core of the construction of a digital platform strategy.

The digital platform strategy is not a pile of pure technical concepts. But instead, it is the accumulation of core capabilities, data, and user information of the companies with the shared services approach, avoiding duplication of construction in every business department and reducing the costs associated with new businesses such that most of the business requirements are fulfilled by the business team. This type of model that integrates data and businesses not only achieves the circulation of internal and external information of the companies but also enhances the innovative capability in the internal departments. While meeting the existing and potential requirements of the consumers at the same time, the value of data has been mined continuously, striving to gain a foothold in the ultracompetitive markets.

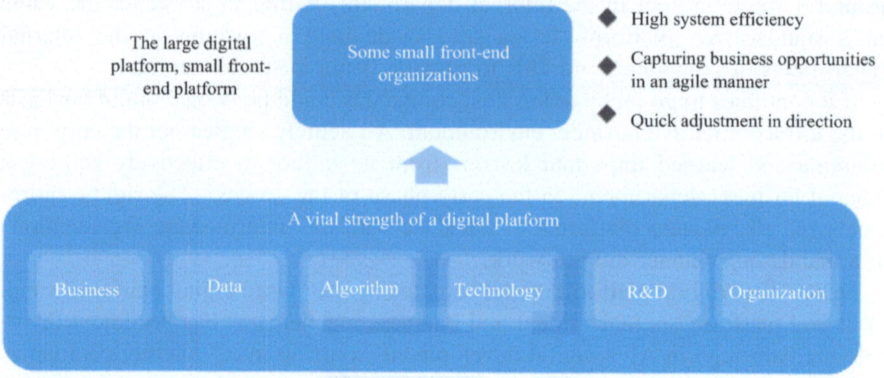

Fig. 16.1 The digital platform strategy is an important strategic measure to achieve digitalization for companies

There is a pivotal significance to proactively creating a data platform for companies' long-term development.

(1) Disrupting the traditional vertical data architecture

A data platform can help companies quickly respond to market demands and enhance the capability to capture market opportunities for companies. It is favorable for companies to set up agile organizations and make quick adjustments to the organizational structure according to market conditions. It is also favorable for companies to gather their strengths to make correct decisions, simultaneously saving labor and material costs, as shown in Fig. 16.1.

(2) Redefining IT and DT

Constructing a data platform can disrupt the corporate tree construction model, avoiding duplication of work in the IT department and effectively controlling corporate operating costs. It redefines the IT working model. While quickly responding to the customer requirements, the data platform avoids the burdensome procedures of describing the business requirements in the business department, effectively saving communication costs and improving the business precision level to facilitate the business and technical departments in their collaboration of developing DT applications. As can be seen, the data platform can enable the different positions of the companies to perform their duties and optimize the allocation of human resources.

16.2 How to Define a Data Platform?

What is a data platform? What types of capabilities does a data platform contain? Which are the application segments of a data platform? What are the construction descriptions in a data platform? We shall answer some of these questions in the following section.

16.2.1 Multi-dimensional Interpretation of a Data Platform

A data platform is a new transformational architecture. It is an organic, integrated platform for the sharing of capabilities. And it is a new type of concept in the construction of technologies.

1. **A data platform is a new transformational architecture**

In the past 30 years, companies' data management has been based on traditional IT architecture. Whenever the technical department was resolving issues for the business department, it required building a new system. Each system was independent of the other, with the sole purpose of meeting a single business requirement. It not only undermined a considerable amount of effort from each department but also did not enable data interconnectivity between every system and resulted in a failure to utilize the more robust data capabilities.

In addition, the IT supplementary management system was more focused on data collection, and each system acted like a data silo independent of the other. In the internet era for new industries, companies must quickly respond to the rapid changes in their external environment, building multi-dimensional data to reshape DT applications. The traditional architecture was not suitable to be deployed in the current market, while the data platform has disrupted the traditional IT data management architecture in the past 30 years. Figure 16.2 showcases the value of a data platform.

The working principles of a data platform are akin to a restaurant fulfilling customer needs, and data is like basic food. Several systems, such as CRM, ERP, and other systems, dissect the data into varying categories and place them in different databases (central kitchens). The data is cleaned correctly with the data governance technology, while certain data with special requirements are further processed.

With the processing approach given above, the data is ready to be supplied to the business or technical staff. It is similar to the food types that are properly classified and cleaned before handing them to the chefs. The business staff performs data grouping according to the varying requirements. That is, perform modeling on the data. The data generate different applications through modeling, showcasing the application products that align with the user requirements after further enhancement by visualization.

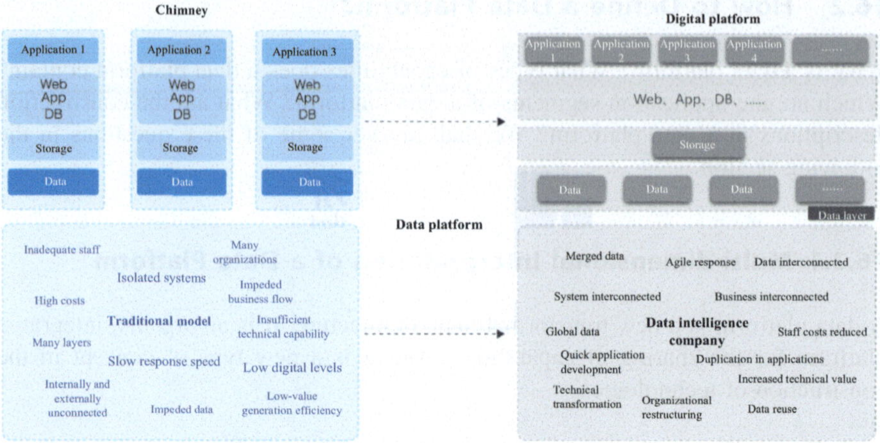

Fig. 16.2 Value of a data platform

Before the emergence of the data platform in companies, the generation of application products must also undergo several processes, including data governance, cleaning, and modeling. But it only formed the processing chain for this type of product. Unfortunately, data was not synchronized, and barriers like the chimneys were erected. Although there might be some overlapping between the new business requirements and the products manufactured in the past, companies still need to start afresh.

In the era of IT management systems, the development cycle was about 3–6 months. There must not be too many changes during the implementation phase. In other words, the requirements could not be timely adjusted according to changes in the business. The R&D for this application was slow with a long development cycle, but there might also be duplication in the construction of common functions, resulting in a waste of resources for companies.

The construction of a set of complete data platform systems is equivalent to the building of a one-stop, integrated central kitchen. The system prepares and properly processes the food, while the business staff only needs to directly tap on the "Order" button, generating customized applications for the customers. Companies can enhance their competitiveness and maintain market positions by utilizing powerful data platform services.

2. **A data platform is a sharing platform for capabilities**

Previously, companies often emphasized the functions in the initial application development phase. The functions of each application would have a certain degree of duplication. Companies had different definitions of these duplicated functions and did not accumulate these common functions.

The data platform focuses more on the sharing of capabilities during the development of applications to quickly meet the varying requirements. The data platform collects the data in a standardized way and generates standardized data after the cleaning process. After that, it performs storage for the data to form the big data assets layer. These data services based on achieving business objectives are unique to companies. On top of having the capability of reusing it, it is also the accumulation of corporate businesses and data. This type of data service can help companies mitigate duplication in construction and diminish the collaborative barriers between departments, helping companies enhance their competitiveness.

3. **A data platform is an organic, integrated platform**

The data platform is an empowerment platform consisting of models, applications, tools, and technical assets, as shown in Fig. 16.3. A data platform not only generates technical capability, data capability, assets capability, application capability, and system capability but also generates value for companies. A data platform's core lies in empowering business departments and users with quick responses to external requirements.

The data platform is a new generation of architectural data concepts. The working principles are based on the initial objective of creating applications. After performing data integration, the final presentation of the result is a platform with data applications. With the ever-changing consumer requirements, a data platform oriented to the technologies is difficult to respond to external requirements quickly.

The data platform is not an end-to-end technology platform; it focuses more on using the business end and reflecting on business value. As the traditional export model of API capability required technical transfer in the middle layers, it

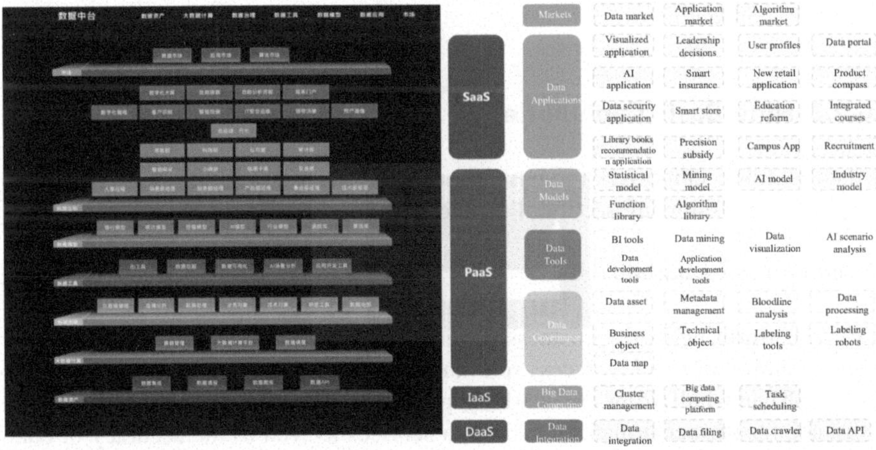

Fig. 16.3 Data platform architecture

could not generate the applications quickly and efficiently, failing to meet the ever-changing corporate requirements. Building a data platform with API interfaces is merely one of the construction steps in building a complete data platform.

The construction of a data platform requires the multi-dimensional coordination of every department in a company. It is an organic, integrated entity of the business, technology, and assets. It is not a single-faceted modular portfolio.

4. **The data platform is a new type of concept in the construction of technologies**

As a new type of concept in the construction of technologies, the data platform shatters the traditional corporate concept of construction based on functionality and integration. Previously, companies would first need to construct a basic technical architecture to create products and then add the application functions. This construction concept is more suitable for those companies with stable product models, and this is not the best option for those non-standardized companies with ever-changing application requirements and applications as their initial objective. Using applications as the core of the construction concept is perhaps the key to maintaining long-term vitality for companies. The construction of a data platform helps companies to roll out a radical change from the traditional application construction approach.

In the past, companies deployed various management systems to enhance their efficiency. These management systems could only deliver single-faceted references in the areas, such as basic data management, and simple business analysis, for the decision-makers. This type of construction concept based on integration could not empower businesses. There was a diversified range of data applications with the occasional generation of a huge volume of temporary, real-time, and fragmented requirements. The data models would need to be often recalibrated with changing business emphasis. It would not be able to respond to the requirements promptly by merely connecting every management system account.

16.2.2 Nine Basic Capabilities of a Data Platform

A data platform empowers the business with nine basic capabilities, as shown in Fig. 16.4. The following section illustrates them in detail.

1. **Data service capability**

A data platform helps the business department to build a working platform. The business staff can quickly access relevant services, such as data extraction, analysis, push, and pull from the working platform. The data platform can provide assurance for the performance of the data services as well as the accuracy of data.

The data platform can perform processing, governance, segmentation, modeling, and labeling of the data. The data platform is like an ecosystem platform, and

Fig. 16.4 Nine basic capabilities of a data platform

it can continually generate data services according to business requirements. These data services can be extracted, recorded, monitored, and audited.

2. **Data application development capability**

The data platform can deliver personalized data exploratory and analysis tools to the working staff in different business positions. It can also generate data interfaces under such a foundation and empower the business staff to perform data analysis. The business staff can explore and discover the data value, conducting in-depth application development according to the requirements. These applications can become independent products.

3. **Data processing capability**

The data platform provides strong technical support for data collection, governance, integration, and synchronization, achieving seamless interconnectivity and data sharing.

Business scenarios need different computing platforms of varying scales to process the colossal volume of data. Constructing a data platform can help the business staff to manage the computing capabilities according to the application requirements at any time.

4. **Data development capability**

The data platform's analysis, mining, and cleaning tools can help upstream and downstream companies and external users directly develop applications. The data platform can also perform silly packaging for the upstream and downstream tools, helping companies share data and applications pertinent to the users of different sectors.

5. **Self-learning and automated improvement capability**

With self-learning capability, a data platform can empower the business staff. The data platform can continually overlay its capabilities and perform a virtuous circle and backflow for the corporate data and assets, empowering businesses and technologies and forming a self-learning platform that is continuously growing.

6. **Assets accumulation capability**

The high-value assets in the internal departments of companies can be accumulated through the data platform, providing more support for corporate grow thin the future. The accumulation over time can help companies to enhance their competitiveness and be ahead of other companies in the digital transformation.

7. **Data quality auto-tracking capability**

During the usage process, many different departments and roles use the data. The data governance system becomes increasingly more complicated as each department defines varying data indicators, labels, and usage methods. Once the data cannot be tracked leads to front-end data errors. Ultimately, it affects companies' decision-making, incurring huge costs for them. The data platform, however, can avoid such a scenario. Data quality intelligent tracking and bloodline analysis can ensure the quality of data.

8. **Data integration capability**

With a constant rise in corporate businesses, there is an exponential increase in the internal and external data generated during the growth process. Hence, the interconnectivity of data is also increasingly important. As companies' computing power is rather limited with barriers erected between different data sets and the formation of data chimneys, they cannot convert their data resources into the driving power for their businesses, severely wasting them. The data platform performs standardization on the data, achieving seamless data integration. And the back-end technical department can support and fulfill the requirements of the front-end business department.

9. **IT system & DT system risk isolation capability**

Several systems, including OA, ERP, CRM, and other IT systems, play a pivotal role in the collection and management of data for companies. The purpose of constructing IT systems is to help companies manage and store data. The purpose of constructing the DT systems is to help companies to enhance their efficiencies, deepen their services and achieve intelligent, streamlined management. The objectives and positioning of these two systems are entirely different. If the systems are not properly utilized, it leads to a divergence of data applications. Consequently, the data platform's construction can help companies isolate the data risks to ensure that the systems are unaffected.

16.2.3 Three Types of Applications of a Data Platform

The following section illustrates the three types of applications of a data platform in detail.

1. **Help the business department to perform data analysis flexibly**

The data platform has solved the business department's issue of inadequate technical capabilities in data analysis. Before the emergence of the data platform, the business department could only seek help from the technical department for the analysis requirements because it lacked the necessary technical capabilities. The communication and coordination between the business, technical, and analysis departments would use up huge amounts of time and effort, distracting the technical department's limited attention.

The data platform has disrupted the complex formats of data. It can perform real-time integration and analysis of the internal and external data of companies as well as structured and unstructured data, resolving the issue of data extraction during the data application process and thus achieving data sharing. The data processed and compiled through the data platform is directly exported to the application end of specific business scenarios, such as in the insurance industry. The insurance company can roll out personalized marketing solutions with customer feedback in the data platform. The data platform can create a breakthrough for the business department in the technical area of data analysis such that the business staff can freely perform data analysis at any time.

2. **Help the technical, business, and external departments to create applications flexibly**

In the DT era, meeting user requirements is the priority objective for most companies' production operations. Companies must utilize the data platform's quick response, exploratory, and mining capabilities to meet user requirements with intelligent applications developed to create more profits.

The internal technical and business departments of companies and even external parties like the suppliers and others can respond to the user requirements in a timely and efficient manner based on the applications of the data platform, directly resolving the business issues. The data platform can help companies to build a sharing platform for the ecosystems of the industry, servicing the staff in the internal departments of companies as well as the upstream and downstream corporate clients.

3. **The technical department can constantly construct the capabilities of the application, accumulate data assets and asset values**

On top of interconnecting the businesses, technologies, and assets, the data platform consolidates the fragmented, messy, and duplicated data into an orderly, contextual data asset. The technical department can generate a sustainable application development capability by utilizing the data assets, while the new applications can generate data to be feed backed into an enclosed loop.

In summary, the new applications that rely on the data platform's construction can help companies achieve real-time, automated, and intelligent data applications.

16.2.4 Confusion of a Data Platform—Fake Digital Platform, Imitated Digital Platform, and Enclosed Digital Platform

Today, the data platform is particularly popular with many companies in their implementation of digital transformation. Many so-called confusing "data platforms" have surfaced in the market, as shown in Fig. 16.5.

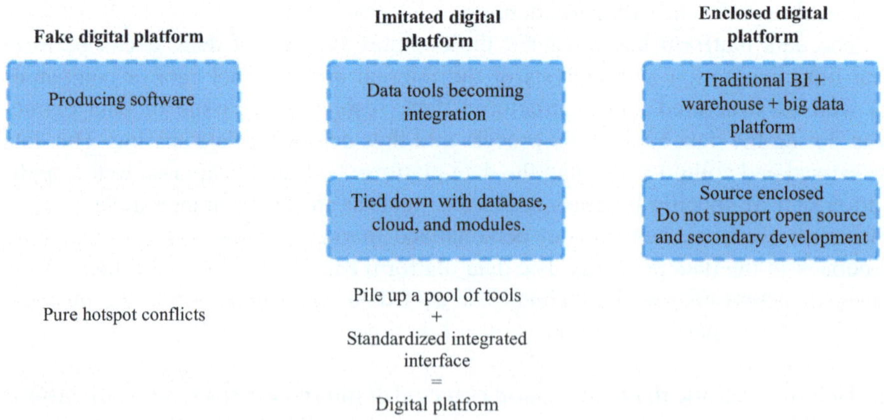

Fig. 16.5 Confusion of a data platform

1. **Fake digital platform**

The products of some software manufacturers have a certain similarity with the concept of a data platform. Then they just announced that it is a data platform. This type of "data platform" is hollow and shallow, and it is a fake digital platform that cannot meet companies' application data requirements. The provision of software services is merely one of the parts of constructing a data platform.

2. **Imitated digital platform**

Some companies integrate data tools, including BI (Business Intelligence), reports, warehouses, ETL, and computing platforms, and define the system's final formation as a data platform. Before the popularity of smart phones, many people did not clearly understand them, thinking they could only be used to take photographs, make calls and play games. Some merchants jumped at the opportunity to roll out products with camera and video-recording functions, defining these as smart phones to be sold to consumers. Currently, many "data platforms," including the fake platforms, are taking advantage of the gaps in similar awareness, defining the tools that are consolidated from the stacking piles as a data platform and resulting in confusion about the concept of a "data platform." From the sole functionality perspective, the imitated digital platform can perform operations like cleaning and analyzing data. But the imitated digital platform can only resolve part of the issues faced in the digital transformation of companies, and it cannot perform deep data applications. The integration of data tools is not a data platform.

3. **Enclosed digital platform**

An enclosed digital platform is a type of platform that contains higher risks. This platform type has two characteristics: First, it is not agile. When a company chooses the option to carry out digital transformation with an enclosed data platform, it also needs to purchase other components. For example, the company can only use the cloud system under the umbrella of this type of digital platform. Second, it does not support secondary development and open-source content. As the name implies, an enclosed digital platform is a closed-end system. The consumer market, however, needs an open digital platform. Hence, it should also be open to the upstream or downstream.

The CTO must be particularly cautious while selecting a data platform, and the CTO should not be distracted by the confusion of a digital platform. If the type of digital platform is incorrectly selected, it will not only raise the transformation costs of companies but also lead to companies missing opportunities for digital transformation. The digital platform is akin to the foundation laid before the construction of a house. If the builder only finds out that the foundation is unstable after a certain phase of the construction project, the CTO needs to demolish everything and start afresh.

16.3 Ten Misconceptions About the Data Platform

With the ever-expansion of corporate scales and diversity in business development, the senior management of many companies is increasingly focusing on utilizing data to enhance their businesses' innovative and operations management capabilities. Hence, the data platform that can reinforce the data utilization rate and enhance the working efficiency of each department slowly emerges.

The data platform is closely correlated to companies' business growth, organizational structure, and degree of informatization development. Consequently, it is incorrect to perceive the data platform as a tool, a big data analysis approach, or an organizational structure.

There is no standardized definition of a data platform in the market, and different people have different definitions of a data platform. The following section depicts ten data platform misconceptions, as shown in Fig. 16.6. It can help companies to have a deeper understanding of a data platform, preventing them from making avoidable mistakes.

1. **Big data BI analysis tools = Data platform**

The value of a data platform lies in the presentation of business growth progress and directions by using data and employing data to drive business development, innovative products, and management efficiency improvement. And the big data BI analysis tools only use data to present the business contents, and it is a type of conclusion for the data analysis of businesses. On the one hand, big data BI analysis tools cannot achieve management and product innovation with data. On the other hand, the data platform can integrate into various areas, such as data collection, data governance, data mining, model construction, visualized analysis, and application development, for companies. It also can filter data through the enclosed loops in the corporate businesses and products, drive business innovation and apply data more comprehensively, mining the value of data.

2. **Big data clusters = Data platform**

Many companies have built distributed big data clusters to resolve the issues of storage, recovery, and highly efficient computing operations of the colossal volume of structured and unstructured data. But a data platform is not equivalent to big

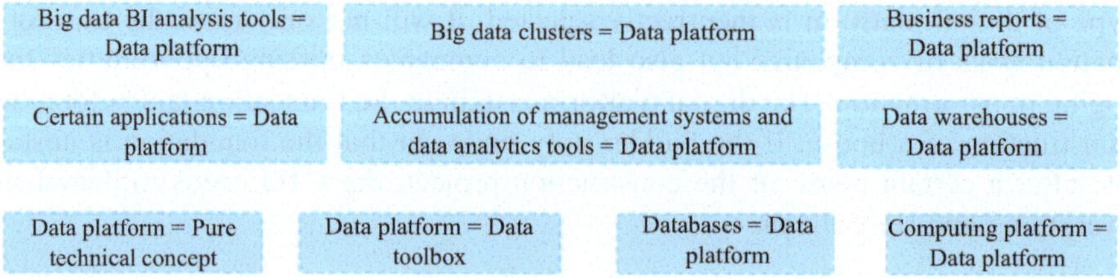

Fig. 16.6 Ten misconceptions about the data platform

data clusters, and the big data clusters are only a part of the technical architecture used for data storage and computing operations during the construction of the bottom layer in a data platform. A data platform is created after integrating all available resources and accumulating the capabilities of the business and technical departments.

3. **Business reports = Data platform**

In the daily operations of companies, a series of business reports, including cost reports, expenditure reports, financial budgets, and financial analyses, play a pivotal role. In corporate management, business reports are confined to the management and monitoring of the internal departments of companies. They have rather limited roles in the external departments of companies, such as customer maintenance, tracking of requirements, and business and product updates. The data platform can not only streamline the passage of companies' internal resources and achieve the sharing of resources, but it can also support the sustainable innovation of products and quickly fulfill user requirements. In comparison, business reports only reflect a small part of the value of the entire data platform.

4. **Certain applications = Data platform**

Alongside the deep penetration of mobile internet in people's daily lives and workplaces, there are increasingly abundant Apps that elevate the quality of personal life based on the mobile network. Besides, many corporate-level applications boost operations management efficiency and enhance corporate competitiveness. There is a broad spectrum of celebrations for every dimension of application. Unfortunately, these independent applications are not data platforms.

The data platform acquires data from the databases in the business platforms and supports the intelligent applications of the business platforms with the results obtained from cleaning and analyzing the data. These intelligent applications then convert the new data stream generated by the users into an enclosed loop. As can be seen, the applications provide R&D data for the data platform, while the data platform delivers more support for business innovation and enhancement of applications.

5. **Accumulation of management systems and data analytics tools = Data platform**

Companies gradually add on different management systems according to their business or management requirements during the operations management process. These systems aim to increase the working efficiencies of all staff. Their simple data statistical function can also collate the basic management data for companies. Companies utilize the data analytics tools to perform analysis on the data in the management systems and then feedback the analysis results to each operations department, relying on this type of "data platform" to provide more guidance and opinions to the corporate management while saving the fees of engaging a professional data platform provider.

Contrary to their belief, this is not the real significance of having a data platform. Combining management systems with data analytics tools is not the cure for the issue's root. This type of accumulation cannot clear the passage of data interconnectivity between every department without optimization and consolidation of common resources. It is incorrect to say that the company has deployed a data platform, let alone provided comprehensive services for its digital transformation.

The data platform is not a set of software systems, and it is also not a standardized product. From the corporate perspective, the data platform supports the company in achieving its business objectives and helps it to accumulate businesses.

6. **Data warehouses = Data platform**

Some people believe that the construction of a data platform is based on ETL,[1] the loading of data from the business systems after being selected, cleaned, and transformed into the data warehouses. The fragmented, messy data with different standards can be combined. But the traditional approach to data processing would only create bigger data silos. A data warehouse needs to duplicate the data source based on document storage. It also has computing capability, providing storage functions for other computing systems.

The data and storage in a data platform are isolated from each other. A data platform does not contain data originating from all types of documents and APIs in the business systems. A data platform contains the adapter for these data sources, equivalent to building interconnected pipelines directed at different data sources.

Data warehouses are a critical component of a data platform and essential metadata sources. Data warehouses, however, are not equivalent to a data platform.

7. **Data platform = Pure technical concept**

A data platform is neither a purely technical concept nor a tooling concept. It contains many aspects of content, such as data sharing services, centralized governance of data assets, and reshaping business applications with data. But the data assets are basic raw materials in constructing a data platform. After cleaning, mining, analyzing, and packaging, data assets can form models that provide data services for companies and empower their businesses with data, helping them resolve multi-dimensional issues. At the same time, reshaping companies' daily operations management models with data can help companies resolve the root of several issues, including wastage of resources, exorbitant staff costs, and slow business updates.

[1] ETL refers to extracting, transforming, and loading data from the source end to the objective end.

A data platform can empower the business by utilizing data, achieving the value-realization of the business. The applications behind it are information technology. The construction of a data platform requires the intervention of technical aspects, including the utilization of different big data processing technologies to perform interconnection in series for the data at the bottom layer, together with the employment of different data analytics technologies, such as modeling and algorithms, to integrate the specific business-related data. It also includes communication, sorting out, deployment of the business department, organizational adjustment of the management departments, and changes in the management models. Hence, a data platform is not a purely technical concept, and information technology is only a tool to achieve the value of a data platform. Companies can only achieve digital transformation and broaden their profits if they truly understand a data platform's essence.

8. **Data platform = Data toolbox**

The toolbox, with a consolidation of data analytics products, analysis tools, warehouse tools, and others, is not a data platform. As the functions of each tool are interoperable and interconnected while individually independent, there is no consistency in the synchronization between varying tools.

The architecture of a toolbox is only part of the entire phases of constructing a data platform, and it can only exhibit the effects of each tool, thus acting as a simple support for decision-making and reporting references. In the initial phase of the construction of a data platform, there is a serious consideration for the seamless interconnectivity of every phase to ensure data maintenance and quality in the ensuing period. If there are any changes to the data in a certain phase, the data should be rectified promptly in other phases. Otherwise, it would lead to errors in the decision-making process, causing huge losses and repercussions for companies.

Some large internet Chinese companies purchased several data technology products from abroad. But it did not achieve the effects of tool integration during the actual operations process. Despite some favorable application results in a particular phase, the final data results were still mired in errors. The reason was that the production chain could not be standardized in a coordinated manner, while the barriers to data maintenance were comparatively higher.

Given the issues above, the traditional resolution was to produce all kinds of intermediate tables. It would, however, generate other issues. Constructing and maintaining intermediate tables would need sustainable investment in time and resources. Besides, it was also difficult to maintain them manually. When the corporate business had reached a certain scale, the intermediate tables could not be repaired, and the data could not be backtracked when there was a need to change the intermediate tables or there was some staff turnover.

As the pioneer in raising the concept of a data platform, Ali has performed much work related to the abovementioned issues, for example, developing a data bloodline analysis system, sorting out the bloodline relationship of data, and maintaining the accuracy of data applications. To maintain data consistency, companies must develop more complex applications to ensure data quality. A data platform is not a data toolbox as a result.

9. **Databases = Data platform**

Some quality software products are equipped with databases of add-on analysis functions, mainly providing business computing functions. This type of database is not a data platform. The analysis data used in such a database is only part of the data pool in the whole company, and it is not global data, so it cannot mine the global value. In addition, companies would accumulate slightly more data systems with differing development cycles of informatization. Databases are only a system at a lower level than a data platform and cannot form a complete data platform.

10. **Computing platform = Data platform**

A computing platform does not have a robust data governance system. So, it cannot generate applications and achieve the interconnectivity and sharing of data. Hence, it is not a data platform.

16.4 Recommendations for the Construction of a Data Platform

To date, data has become the core resource to enhance the competitiveness of companies. Companies must fully showcase the potential value of data during their growth process, turn data into corporate resources and improve their management models with the existing corporate issues exposed by data.

The objective must be ascertained first before constructing a data platform. What types of results can be achieved by constructing a data platform? How much is the budget for the construction of a data platform? The CEO and the board of directors must devise a comprehensive plan related to the data platform construction.

The construction of a data platform requires a standardized data source and data pooling applications. It needs to integrate and analyze the different data sources, delete the duplicated data, mitigate the duplication of data construction and share the data to enhance the business's response efficiency and achieve the objective of reducing costs and boosting efficiencies.

The corporate misconceptions about the data platform result in escalated construction risks. The construction of a digital platform requires considering the compatibility issue, and it must also transform the technical architecture and update its new product system. If there is any error in constructing the digital platform, there are derivative issues with the applications generated by the digital platform. The price to pay for a reconstruction of the digital platform is enormous. Hence, companies must ensure that their data platforms are correctly constructed, focusing on the migration of each construction entity.

The data platform is a complete data program and resolution concept constructed by Ali's repeated validation and trial under the foundation of a complete data system. As many leading companies or SMEs lack a colossal volume of complete data foundation, they cannot forecast the potential issues and find it hard to design digital platform products that align with their corporate growth. The professional data platform construction team can integrate their advanced technological experience with industry development, ensuring the accuracy and scalability of the construction of the digital platform.

16.5 Common Failures in the Construction of a Data Platform

Many companies can easily hit the realm of misconceptions while constructing their data platforms, leading to an eventual failure. Several common failures in the construction of a data platform are illustrated below.

1. **Construct the data platform into a data warehouse**

Many companies construct their data platforms for the sake of constructing. Hence, there are many emergencies of fake and imitated digital platforms in the market. The most common failure is constructing a data platform into a large data warehouse. This type of "data platform" falls under an imitated digital platform category, and it only plays the role of a data warehouse and does not contain all the comprehensive functions.

2. **The data platform does not contain any compatibility features**

A data platform must be constructed according to the business characteristics of the company itself. Some companies may purchase their data platforms off the shelves. However, this data platform is not equipped with customization features and cannot keep pace with the corporate growth, meeting the business requirements. Suppose the data platform of a company ignores the coordination between various organizations, such as operations and management, and purely relies on the technical capabilities of the data platform. The eventual results generated from the operations model of this type of digital platform be diminished.

3. **Construct the data platform into a system**

Many data platform providers in the market are selling systems, and companies often find that the results are far from ideal after using them for some time. A data platform is only an approach to achieving digital transformation while boosting performance is the objective of digital transformation for companies. Companies need to build their digital transformation capabilities and performance improvement capabilities by utilizing this approach of having a data platform.

Interpretation of the Role of a Data Platform

17

As the saying goes, a thousand readers have a thousand Hamlet. Similarly, the value of a data platform interpretation by different roles in the internal departments of companies is also different. We analyze the interpretation of a data platform from the five perspectives of a managing director, CEO, CTO/CIO, IT architect, and data analyst.

17.1 A Data Platform from the Perspective of a Managing Director

In the modern digital economy, constructing a data platform to enhance business value for companies is gradually becoming a mainstream trend. As the highest-ranking leader and strategic commander of companies, the managing director must not only understand the value of data, but the CTO/CIO must also have a clear understanding of the core technologies to achieve value-realization for businesses, that is, the data platform.

With the constant changes in the market environment, there are changes to the digital transformation path and the implementation methodology. From the data management platform in the initial phase to the customer data platform in the ensuing phase, and then to the data platform that is very popular now, these tools have become essential equipment in their exploration of a digital transformation. Meanwhile, the managing director must closely monitor the market development and proactively understand the "past and present" of every methodology amid the deployment of a strategic digital transformation.

The data platform is a nascent resolution of digital transformation for companies. The managing director can clearly understand the value of a data platform from the two following points.

X. Ma, *Methodology for Digital Transformation*, Management for Professionals,
https://doi.org/10.1007/978-981-19-9111-0_17

1. **Service value of a data platform**

A data platform must service specific businesses and optimize the user experience to meet business requirements. Based on the user requirements, a data platform reshapes every phase of procurement, R&D, production, sales, and consumer traceability with data and technical approaches, enabling "data-driven businesses and data generation by businesses" and truly undergoing the implementation phase to achieve digital transformation for companies.

2. **Interconnected value of a data platform**

Companies implementing digital transformation can utilize the data platform to achieve the interconnectivity between technologies and businesses, seamlessly clear the data barriers, helping companies to streamline their business management.

Compared with the traditional approach of collecting user data through a survey company, big data processing has several characteristics of high efficiency and quick feedback. Companies can better achieve the objective of "data-driven businesses" through a data platform. While implementing digital transformation, companies must continually gather many data sources and build a data platform with users at its core, delivering a diverse range of capabilities for the front-end businesses with data models and applications generated from the data platform.

It is clear that in the initial phase of digital transformation for companies, it is a priority for the managing director to construct the data platform with users at its core, leading the companies to implement digital transformation.

17.2 A Data Platform from the Perspective of a CEO

As the highest-ranking individual in digital transformation for companies, the CEO needs to ascertain the role of a data platform in the digital transformation process, understand the core capabilities required, and utilize the data platform to achieve a successful transformation.

The CEO can interpret a data platform from the following perspectives.

1. **A data platform achieves the accumulation of assets**

Against the backdrop of the strong unfolding of the digital platform concept lies the true requirements of digital transformation for companies. For the CEO, a data platform's first value is asset accumulation. In light of the waves of digital transformation, if the CEO still employs the traditional IT construction concept in allocating a set of software systems for each category of products in the data management and application areas, it leads to a huge wastage of resources for companies, failing to enable the accumulation of data assets.

A data platform performs standardization and retention for the reusable business logic and the business data that can be accumulated, truly achieving the accumulation of corporate data assets, modeling assets, algorithm assets, data intelligence application assets, and membership assets. By doing this, it not only cuts down the repetitive costs of front-end businesses but also enhances the value of data-driven businesses.

2. **A data platform quickly responds to requirements**

In the modern ultracompetitive landscape with users at its core, quick response to user requirements is the most vital competitiveness for many companies. This capability can help companies gain a first-mover advantage in business warfare. The CEO needs to ponder how to be more precise and smarter while resolving user issues. Coincidentally, a data platform contains this capability, and it can quickly respond to the constant changes in front-end businesses. The data platform delivers powerful support for front-end businesses based on the customized innovation of data and the perpetual evolution of data feedback, as well as by utilizing the colossal volume of data storage, computing, product packaging, and other capabilities. The agile organizational feature and the platform-based architecture of the data platform can flexibly and quickly respond to any changes in the requirements of the business units.

3. **A data platform helps companies to reduce costs and enhance efficiencies**

In the full-blown explosion between big data analytics and applications, the CEO must not only ponder over how to drive businesses with data, but the CEO must also consider how to construct a set of complete systems for companies, achieving data-enabled businesses and delivering better services with lower costs and higher efficiencies during the innovation process. A data platform can help companies to form a complete enclosed loop between the bottom layer of the fundamental facilities, the digital platform, and the top layer of businesses, building a data intelligence-management application system from top to bottom with the fundamental framework of businesses, services, data, and assets. In addition, it can also help companies construct a strategic system with monetizing data assets, add value to the applications, ensure that companies can quickly accumulate data assets and generate the organizational capability of data amid the ever-changing, complex business environment, and help companies to make wise business decisions and enhance their operating efficiencies.

17.3 A Data Platform from the Perspective of a CTO/CIO

The CTO/CIO is the planner and designer of the technical architecture of digital transformation for companies. From their perspectives, new technologies in the digitalization era can be used to collect customer data, iterative and innovative products, improve service quality and enhance operating efficiencies. To truly achieve data-enabled businesses, a data platform must be constructed.

Amid the ever-changing markets, constant upgrading of product models, difficulty in achieving daily user growth and facing obstacles during the execution of uneven operating models, creating a data platform with a business-driven objective is pivotal for companies to get any breakthrough during their digital transformation process.

The CTO/CIO can interpret a data platform from the following perspectives.

1. **A data platform can centralize the focus of IT staff**

In the internal departments of companies, the IT staff's IT resources and focus are limited. In general conditions, two kinds of work deplete the energy and focus of the IT staff: large volumes and burdensome data analytics work and large volumes of data governance work. Constructing a data platform can help companies shatter the data chimneys between different systems to safeguard data quality. The data platform automatically resolves the issue of data quality with its technical approach, freeing up the heavy workload of the IT staff and enabling them to conduct R&D on more complicated applications with an abundance of energy and focus.

2. **A data platform can achieve the transition from data support to data-driven capability**

For the CTO/CIO, another value of a data platform lies in the achievement of transition from data support to data-driven capability. In the past, IT was more like a support department for business requirements. The business department raised the requirements, while the IT department employed all approaches. Sometimes, however, the requirements of the business department were not very clear. As the business department was not very confident of the ultimate results of such requirements and what types of value they would generate, the business staff would often alter the requirements. The business staff was clueless about the overall requirements themselves. With the constant requirement changes by the business staff, the IT department had no choice but to repeat the development and maintenance processes and completely being confined to a passive position. In the end, the IT department only played the role of supporting the business department.

Through the architecture of the digital platform, companies can build the data applications model with data-driven businesses at their core. The IT department can treat data-driven businesses as its goal, servicing the entire project. The digital staff can understand the business department's requirements, helping it innovate. The process of this business innovation is driven within the entire project, enabling the IT staff to have a holistic view of the whole situation while developing certain application scenarios. While companies are rolling out data-driven project development, the IT staff can understand the whole project's value and the business department's requirements more precisely. Hence, data-driven businesses significantly enhance the IT team's working efficiency and business value.

17.4 A Data Platform from the Perspective of an IT Architect

Having a crystal clear understanding of the value of a digital platform for companies helps the IT architect understand the architectural design of the digital platform created by the CTO and have a clear sense of the actionable plans during the process of constructing a digital platform, ensuring that the construction path of the digital platform is not off the track.

Technologies are used to service businesses. From the analysis angle of enhancing the response speed to the front-end businesses, the IT architect can ascertain the value of a digital platform from the following points.

1. **Accelerate the mining of data value**

The IT architect can utilize the data platform to quickly respond to the requirements of the front-end business department and integrate several resources, such as digital technologies and data, delivering a type of operations mechanism for product innovation and the empowerment of businesses to serve the front-end business department better.

2. **Simplify the data usage process**

A data platform not only can quickly develop applications and rapidly mine the data value, but it can also help the business department respond to user requirements faster. While the business staff queried about certain data results in the past, they would have to go through many burdensome technical phases, which made it very difficult for them. With modular and customized data services, the data platform can quickly meet the data requirements of the business department, elevating the response efficiency toward requirements in a holistic perspective.

3. **Standardize the bottom layer of the data architecture**

Companies develop different application products and allocate different product development project groups according to the varying business requirements during the operating process. As these application products depend much on the entire system architecture designed by the IT architect, it is very critical to address the following questions: whether the architecture is stable, secure, and highly efficient and whether it facilitates the use by the product development project group and the business staff.

Long ago, the product development project group might have employed the data models and services within the systems designed by the IT architect during product development. But they were unclear about the data structure and standards at the bottom layer. The product development cycles were different; some were delivered very quickly with good quality, while some were delayed in their development and could not keep pace with the market requirements. It illustrated that a standardized allocation mechanism for data models and services was required during the product development project group's product development. This type of technology is known as a data platform.

In the initial construction phase, the data platform has cleaned the multi-domain data and categorically stored it properly, delivering a standardized sharing capability according to the data services generated by requirements and the reusable data. It ensured the quality of data in the early phase of the project development and mitigated the repetitive work of bridging the gaps and altering the architecture by the IT architect in the later phase of the project.

The IT architects need to understand the data platform as a builder of the data platform architecture. They must not simply perform a consolidation of the modules that can be shared, such as products, users, and data permissions. Instead, they must integrate all data sets from the entire business and build a platform to resolve the business issues with the foundation of business development at its core, backed by the support of digital technologies. Hence, the IT architect must standardize the business vision from the various perspectives of the strategic concept, data thinking, application theory, design data map and application map, and devise development plans for the data platform, fully mining the potential values of data and businesses during the process of constructing a data platform.

At the same time, the IT architect must understand that a data platform provides business solutions. A digital platform must be equipped with a diversified range of agile responses, relying on the complete, clean data at the bottom layer to generate modular data services and products and delivering sustainable drive for the front-end businesses by integrating the business characteristics. That is not only an executive rule for the IT architect to implement the digital platform, but it is also a key essential testament to the capability of empowering businesses with their data.

17.5 A Data Platform from the Perspective of a Data Analyst

In the era of digital economies, companies need to respond to user requirements quickly. This type of quick response requires utilizing the strength of the platform.

The data platform technologies can implement data analysis, including consumer purchasing behaviors, consumer scenarios, and buying preferences of consumers, seamlessly interconnect the data between each business system and product line, performing computing, storage, and processing of data to generate data products and services to achieve the intelligent applications of data truly.

Analyzing and mining the data's value is a data analyst's job description. For the data analyst, the value of a data platform is mainly exhibited in the four following points.

1. **Achieve data interconnectivity**

A data platform can clear the passage for data silos to form an enclosed data loop and build corporate data assets, providing stable, sustainable production capabilities for data-enabled businesses. The data platform can also present global data, making the analytics dimensions more comprehensive and the analysis results more accurate for the data analysts.

2. **Reduce the preparation time for data**

A data platform performs standardized data processing and storage and creates varying layers of data assets. The different layers of data assets can deliver off-the-shelf data application services for the business staff, data analysts, and others who require the data. While analyzing certain requirements, the data analysts do not need to clean the data again. They can directly select the data they need from the varying layers of data assets.

3. **Focus on complex data analysis**

Before constructing a data platform, the data analysts and IT technical staff may encounter such an issue: As they are always countering with the simple data analytics requirements of the business department, they do not have extra energy to analyze more complex business issues. After the construction of the data platform, the data applications built on top of the digital platform architecture provide a great convenience for the business department to use the data. The business staff can autonomously complete simple data analytics tasks independently without assistance from the technical staff and data analysts. Hence, it provides more time for data analysts, enabling them to focus on analyzing more complex business issues.

4. **Changes to a single-point business do not influence the overall result**

On top of achieving data interconnectivity, a data platform assures the data analysts of their ensuing data analytics tasks. Even if there are changes to the data in a certain business module, the data analysts only need to make slight adjustments to ensure the accuracy of the analysis without affecting the final results.

As the person who bridges the gaps between the front-end business requirements and the back-end multi-dimensional data relationships, the data platform perceived from a data analyst's perspective is mostly the construction of three layers of platform initiated from the angle of application analysis, as shown in Fig. 17.1.

In the layering structure of the construction of the data platform, the storage of data and the core technologies of the computing layer reasonably integrate the big data technologies in the data platform. This layer mainly performs the integration and storage of the information management data with varying orientations and segments in companies' internal and external departments. It conducts classification

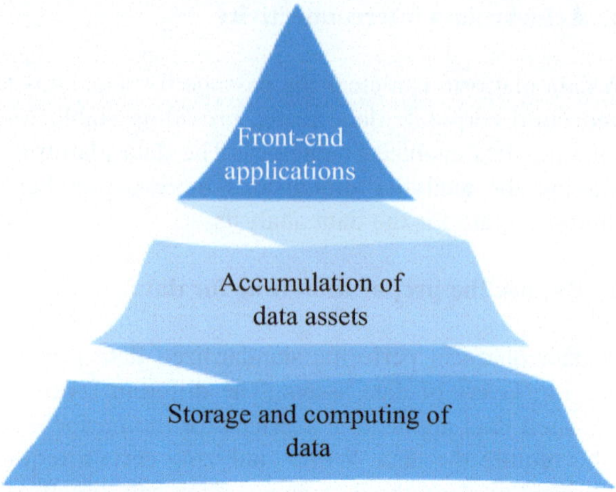

Fig. 17.1 The construction theory of three layers of a data platform from the perspective of a data analyst

and processing of data by utilizing digital technologies, such as distributed computing, enabling the data to become structured, logical, and contextual information and laying the foundation for accumulating data assets in the second layer.

From the data analyst's perspective, the layer of data assets accumulation must first perform the access, integration, and pooling of data from companies' vertical businesses and build a public data center according to the different business segments, organizational structure, and analysis dimensions. And then, it must reconstruct the data system according to the business characteristics, customer attributes, and other varying features, integrate intelligent labeling, intelligent algorithms, and other technologies to construct a data extraction center. Finally, it must also perform data analysis and management according to the different requirements to construct the data map. After the whole process of creating data assets, it facilitates the overall use of data by the data analysts in the ensuing period.

Take an example of the data platform of a bank. First, connect the internet data generated by the bank businesses, such as savings, loans, CRM, wealth management, credit cards, and mobile banking, to the data platform. Next, divide the data into different categories, including transaction, wealth management, risk control, customer, financial products, and other modules, creating a public, open, shared, and transferable public data center. Afterward, perform algorithmically and label processing on each module of data packaged by the bank, forming systematic data and creating a data extraction center for the front-end applications. In this process, the technical staff conducts R&D on the data according to the different business requirements. The R&D process must standardize the varying data indicators to construct different models.

For data analysts, the front-end applications layer is more familiar and is also the area to showcase their results. Mainly completed by the data analysts, the front-end applications layer showcases the data analysis results of the varying data products. Different industries have different business characteristics, so their data products are also different. For example, the bank may have network branch profiles, wealth management products, and user profiles. The launching of these products is still dependent on data analysts.

The core of the front-end applications layer lies in analyzing business scenarios to form all types of applications. The data analysts perform data analysis in the layer of data asset accumulation according to the business requirements and mine the data value to develop application products for companies' daily operations and business expansion. With the ever-changing business scenarios for the consumers, the data analysts must deploy the data services at any time according to the changes in scenarios to enable the front-end businesses. It is critical to safeguard the quality of data, which is also a data platform's value.

The data platform completely changes the traditional analytics models and deployment, resulting in a single-handed conclusion. It drives many corporate departments from top to bottom to perform resource consolidation and analyzes the user requirements from the perspective of global businesses, resolving business issues and enabling every department to collaborate and fight the business war. The data analysts are no longer fighting the battle alone without back-end support. They are now backed by a powerful data platform architecture, from which high-quality data services and data materials can be deployed, shared, and extracted at any time. Besides, they can also focus their energy on researching the front-end business issues, enhancing the overall operating efficiencies of companies.

Five Elements of a Data Platform 18

The five elements of a data platform are data, business, algorithm, application, and organization, respectively. These five elements must properly execute the data platform's basic requirements, which is key to helping companies reasonably employ the digital platform.

18.1 Data

With the rapid development of the mobile internet, the volume of data has exploded exponentially. Companies of varying scales and categories are facing data quality issues. Besides, the ever-changing user requirements and business scenarios have also escalated the complexity of data. Companies often need to collect data from external channels when using data. However, the reliability of the sources and structure of these data is not assured. The danger of data credibility has been a common issue faced by many companies. In the digital transformation process, companies must perform certain measures to resolve data quality issues to ensure the final results. When corporate businesses are affected by the low quality of data, companies can perform certain measures to manage and improve the data quality.

18.1.1 Building a Data Asset Management System

The CDO is the corporate data asset management driver and plays a pivotal role in data governance and quality enhancement. The CDO must lead the data governance team to execute certain strategies and measures to share data across varying departments and standardize data definitions, enabling companies' internal and external departments to use the data easily.

X. Ma, *Methodology for Digital Transformation*, Management for Professionals,
https://doi.org/10.1007/978-981-19-9111-0_18

1. **Sorting out the data sources**

There are four data sources: IT systems, external systems, supplementary internet recorded data, and data integration. The following section elaborate son them in detail, respectively.

(1) Data from IT systems
The IT systems here refer to the information management systems in the internal departments of companies. Companies must perform interconnectivity and data organization within multiple IT systems in the internal departments.
(2) Data from external systems
The data from external systems refer to the data from the various partners, such as suppliers, partners, and integrators of the companies. Pooling these data together can help companies to create a global data center, assessing the overall operating and management conditions of companies from the holistic perspective of data.
(3) Supplementary recording of public internet data
If companies' internal and external systems cannot completely meet the business requirements, companies can perform a supplementary recording of public internet data, often known as "data filing." For example, perform labeling concerning the usage characteristics of certain products and acquire the public internet data with a legitimate technical approach to enrich the user data.
(4) Data integration
Collaborate with other data suppliers using a legitimate and reasonable approach or perform data integration with all types of legitimate data markets. Any organization can acquire such data through legitimate means, from the service providers' data to the online stores' data to the industry and commerce data.

2. **Develop data management regulations**

Companies implementing digital transformation must develop a set of data-driven business regulations, specifying data export, data usage object, data approval process, and data applications in detail to effectively manage the data, enabling companies to achieve the objective of data-enabled businesses.

3. **Create a data directory and manage data assets**

A data directory can help different departments to share data. While maintaining the data directories, the managers of the data governance team, such as the CDO, can build a business convenience usage mechanism to assess the governance conditions of the upstream data, record the usage conditions of the downstream data in analysis applications, and track the circulation of data in different products at the same time. Building data directories can help the data management team identify potential data quality issues.

4. **Build compliant data**

Companies must perform data storage and management in a categorical manner, such as managing master and organization legacy data. They must also extract common attributes from the different data types, including safeguarding data privacy, issuing data definitions, and monitoring data resources. At the same time, data can originate from diverse sources, indicating the risks of using data. If the data is not managed properly, it poses certain risks, such as breach of contract, and infringement of privacy, during the process of using data. As companies' business lines are increasingly complex, companies need to assess more security issues relating to data use. Companies implementing digital transformation must set up a designation to control the risks of data, or even a department, if necessary, to manage data loss, data privacy protection, and companies' data reputation.

5. **Set up a data management committee**

Setting up a data management committee illustrates that companies are very concerned about data asset management. The duties of the data management committee are to develop a data asset management system to monitor and manage the application conditions of the data assets with a set of standardized and regulatory systems, that is, to monitor the progress and value of data-enabled businesses to deliver pertinent recommendations for the digital transformation of companies.

Regardless of the technical experts of the IT department or the key managers of the business department, they are more concerned over the value of data. The data management committee must liaise with these key players interested in mining data value to perform data management together, enabling the frontline teams.

6. **Roll out data asset management methods**

Despite being an important asset for companies, there is a diverse range of corporate data. Companies implementing digital transformation need to employ certain data management methods to manage it.

18.1.2 Constructing a Data Quality System

Along the journey of employing data intelligence, data chimneys and information silos are prevalent. Due to the design defects in the top layer and historical reasons, there are severe issues over data barriers in every business system and management system of companies. In addition, the data between every system is incompatible and cannot be integrated for various reasons, including the different technologies used, varying technical levels of development teams, non-standardized development platforms, and tools lacking in the standardization of data management specifications. The data cannot be shared, leading to unnecessary wastage in data storage and management costs.

Under the mainstream concept of data governance, "construct, govern and apply," data governance merely focuses on data facts and logic. It is only carried out to complete the governance objective, and it cannot form an enclosed data loop or a sharing model. The data governance results cannot help the business department to achieve the business goals and uncover more business opportunities. In some companies, the data governance job is completed manually, and some research personnel with certain technical capabilities expend much energy sorting the data manually. On the one hand, it causes a waste of human resources and time. On the other hand, it is easy to result in manual omission without assuring the accuracy of data, posing a danger to data credibility.

Consequently, tracking the data sources, standardizing the data definitions, classifying the data storage, and deleting the invalid data can trim data management costs, mitigate the legal risks of data applications and lower the product maintenance and development costs for companies with digital transformation.

How to govern data correctly?

1. **Compile business rules and regulations, and standardize data definitions**

In the digital transformation process, it is of utmost importance to have a common understanding and interpretation of data for companies. The issue of data quality often refers to the same data sets being interpreted as different objects or different data sets being interpreted as the same object. Regardless of business or technical metadata, it is imperative to determine the data definitions according to the business characteristics to enhance the data quality. Companies can direct their data governance team to employ certain data management application processes to complete the sorting out of business rules and regulations and standardize data definitions.

2. **Track the sources of external data**

Against the ultracompetitive market environment, the direction of data applications for companies is no longer restricted to internal data. More importantly, the focus has shifted to third-party data, and it has become one of the elements in the analysis of solutions. The partners, suppliers, or open internet data can enhance the company's new business value. Meanwhile, relying on the traditional data governance approach cannot track the true data conditions and cannot ensure a fixed data source even if it can ascertain the data quality. Hence, the data governance team must build a viable model to ensure the accuracy of external data.

3. **Acknowledge the key data indicators that affect the business**

The key data indicators in the business scenario are business requirements, business processes, and performance. It is necessary to use certain corporate performance indicators to measure whether a certain type of product and service can meet market requirements. Incomplete and inaccurate data can result in customer complaints. Thus, it is paramount to sort out and ascertain the various data indicators, such as customer turnover rate and KPIs.

4. **Analyze the data quality of critical businesses**

After determining the key data indicators that affect the businesses of the internal departments of companies, the data governance team also needs to understand the data quality supporting the systems and procedures of key business processes. In the sorting process, the data governance team can employ data analytics tools to predict the data analytics models to understand the data quality in a shorter time. And it can also create the procedures per the data repository operations to meet the high-level, cross-application data analysis requirements.

5. **Create an automated data management and regulation system**

In the era of digital economies, many companies are advocates of digital transformation. But many of these companies' data systems cannot help them achieve digital transformation. The data governance team must create an automated management system, direct the data governance to the entire process of data applications and build a distinct automated feedback mechanism between performance assessment, analytics decisions, and the quality of basic data to feedback on the data governance results with the business outcomes.

6. **Evaluate the influence level of data quality on the business**

Utilizing professional data quality analytics tools, the data governance team can evaluate the data quality and identify unusual data to perform the pertinent data processing work. Measuring the influence level of data quality on the business can help companies detect data with no value and eventually enhance data quality.

On top of that, the evaluation of data quality should be a long-term feature in the process of data applications. Once companies have decided to implement a digital transformation, they must regularly assess the influence level of data quality on their businesses and carry out relevant adjustments to the critical components and approaches of the data quality assessment in light of the emergence of new business scenarios.

7. **Listen to and communicate with the business requirements, and govern the data in a pertinent manner**

While cleaning and governing the data, the data governance team must first not be unrealistic that they can immediately resolve all issues with data governance.

Instead, they must seriously listen to the data requirements of every department, devise actionable plans with effective communication and explore the potential data issues in the internal departments, delivering necessary support for analysis and decision-making.

8. **Construct a data quality dynamic-perception platform and monitor the progress of data governance**

The data governance team usually synchronizes the progress of every data processing through regular meetings or small group discussions. Without a clear understanding of the progress of data governance from the reports of regular meetings, the data governance team can construct a data quality dynamic-perception platform. The data quality dynamic-perception platform can determine the data quality performance according to key businesses' KPIs and operating processes. In certain areas that require adjustment, the data business analysts can communicate with the CDO to recalibrate the governance paths and critical items.

Mature data business analysts can help companies manage and proactively monitor and enhance data quality. The data quality dynamic-perception platform can help companies to manage data risks and create opportunities with lower operating costs.

9. **Develop a mechanism for learning, sharing, and training**

The division of work for every member of the data governance team is different, while the data modules processed are also different. The data quality issues encountered by every person are different, and a single person alone may find it very hard to resolve them. Hence, the team manager needs to develop learning, sharing, and training mechanism. The team members can share the data issues encountered with other team members, discuss the solutions of data governance together, and help all team members to boost their capabilities.

10. **Avoid the "IT vicious circle."**

If the data governance team does not completely interconnect the internal and external data of companies, the requirements of the business department cannot be met at any time. The data governance team then slip into an "IT vicious circle." First, the business department must respond to the ever-changing front-end business landscapes at any time. Meanwhile, the business department constantly raises all work requirements to the technical department. Even if some business requirements are so simple that they do not need assistance from the technical staff, they only need simplified data governance processes. As the data governance is still not very comprehensive, the technical department has to respond to the low-end requirements at any time.

With the constantly changing business landscapes, user requirements must be fulfilled at any time. As the technical department is too busy countering the low-end requirements of the front-end business department, it leads to a slow response. The results are far from satisfactory, even to the extent of delaying business opportunities. With a continual circulation by doing this, the technical department slips into an IT vicious circle with no chance of redeeming itself.

18.2 Business

All technical investments that cannot drive business growth are considered wasted resources for businesses. The businesses encompass every department, varying roles, and different business scenarios of companies. As the requirements are constantly changing for front-end users, businesses are also changing simultaneously.

Digital businesses disrupt and reshape the entire business system with digital technologies to create new forms of businesses- intelligent businesses. Intelligent businesses provide convenient and smart operating processes for companies with visible digital technologies, enabling the realization of value for businesses. Digital technologies supporting intelligent businesses, such as the data platform, deliver services for companies in an invisible form. These visible and invisible technologies jointly constitute the foundation of digital transformation for companies, as shown in Fig. 18.1.

Technical investments that can promote economic activities and produce gains must be able to drive the operations of varying business scenarios. In the era of digital economies, the technical investment of intelligent business is mainly in the data platform.

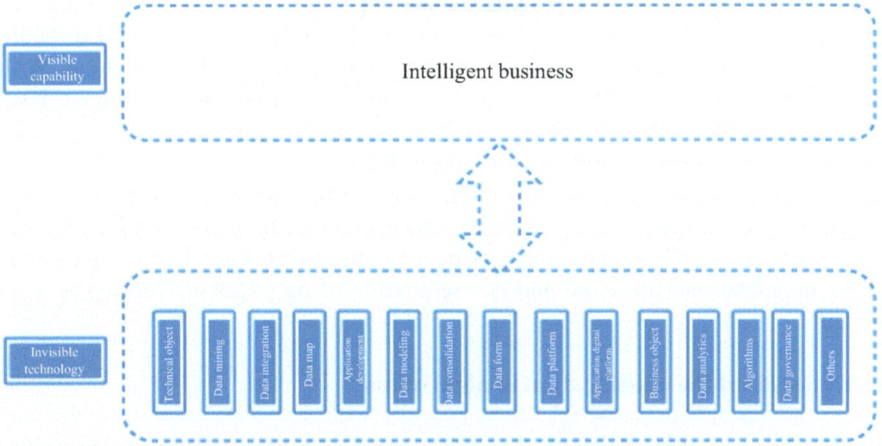

Fig. 18.1 Digital transformation—visible capability and invisible technology

As a key technology of digital transformation for companies, the data platform can perform restructuring in terms of several business factors, including internet users, IoT equipment, corporate business logic, and business units, enhancing the efficiency of the overall digital business and achieving the objective of record revenue for companies.

1. **Reinforce the logic capabilities of digital businesses**

A clear understanding of digital business logic can help companies significantly enhance data and information application results. And this is also the main source of technical improvement. Companies employ digital technologies to standardize and automate business processes, enabling a more efficient application process for digital businesses. It must be coordinated and supported by the logical capabilities of digital businesses. In the digital transformation process, companies must nurture the logical capabilities of digital businesses to enable their teams to apply these capabilities to business innovation and product R&D proactively.

2. **Set up digital business units**

In 2020, the senior executives must also have digital leadership capabilities apart from the common ones, such as financial and administrative capabilities. Under the leadership of the senior executives of the companies, the digital technology architects set up the architecture of digital business units, enhancing the digital business capabilities of companies.

18.3 Algorithm

In the digital business environment, it is imperative to embrace algorithmic businesses to drive the growth of digital economies. But for these senior executives of companies, applying the algorithms to commercial businesses is still difficult. Today, it is a roaring trend to drive business intelligence with algorithms. With these ferocious waves of development, algorithmic businesses herald a higher level of automation for decision-making. Every company is beginning to shift its focus to the development and application of algorithms.

In the next 10 years, over half of the large companies worldwide will utilize advanced analytics and exclusive algorithms to enhance their competitiveness. For these companies, it is exceptionally critical to understand the value of algorithms in the organizational structure and devise a string of packages of working process systems.

1. **Understand the classification of algorithms**

The construction of a data platform needs to build application algorithms according to the different characteristics of the industries. Common algorithms are generally divided into data statistics, data mining, and artificial intelligence. Data statistics includes common statistical algorithms; data mining performs interrelated analysis of data, typical cluster analysis, correlation analysis, and others; the core of artificial intelligence is machine learning. Artificial intelligence includes statistics, probability, basic data mining algorithms, and other fundamental content. It constantly improves its functional performance by reorganizing, restructuring, and relearning.

2. **Reporting the relationship of algorithms in the organizational structure**

The algorithm models shall service the businesses but not the technologies. There are generally four types of reporting relationships in the organizational structure.

(1) The CDO directly manages the person responsible for the algorithms.
(2) Some companies may have assigned various designations, such as Chief Analyst, Chief Algorithm Officer, or Chief Scientist, allowing them to lead the team in researching and developing all types of algorithms.
(3) The algorithm team reports the algorithm models to the IT department.
(4) The algorithm team reports the algorithm models to the operations and marketing departments.

All the reporting relationships above cannot achieve the expected results of the algorithmic applications. All algorithmic information shall be reported to the business department, not the traditional IT department. The algorithm team can collaborate with the business department, researching and developing the types of algorithms to drive the growth of companies. At the same time, the algorithm team needs to create directories for the existing algorithms and ascertain how the existing algorithms work.

3. **Develop a set of complete work processes**

Companies must develop a set of complete work processes for algorithms.

(1) The algorithm team must integrate the personnel, processes, data, and technologies to form a collaborative, effective unit to apply the algorithms to different businesses.
(2) The algorithm is a type of intangible asset. It is a must to construct an effective algorithmic model management architecture, create algorithmic directories simultaneously, and review the existing external open-source algorithms and algorithms supplied by third parties.
(3) It is necessary to develop unique algorithms to manage the algorithmic markets, prioritize the arrangement of algorithms to be developed in the future, allocate the human and external resources based on the priority of arrangement and prepare the budgets in advance, seizing the first-mover advantage in the algorithmic markets.

18.4 Application

Companies must develop exclusive data application systems based on different customers. It is abbreviated as the data radar. The data radar not only can help companies quickly make decisions, but it can also enhance working efficiency and reduce operating costs. Companies develop all kinds of applications during the digital transformation process.

18.4.1 The Effects of Digital Applications

Different types of digital applications can help companies resolve various issues.

1. **Direct companies to perform decision-making**

   Digital application systems contain many types of applications. Some applications can help companies record and extract data and perform analysis on the data, while others can perform deep mining when the volume and quality of the user data have reached a certain level. Companies can use the results of these real-time data analytics and mining applications for quick decision-making.

2. **Deliver more sales opportunities for companies**

   Digital application systems can deliver the required information for companies in real time. Companies can concisely understand user details from varying dimensions and showcase these results in different forms to uncover more sales opportunities and mine more potential customers. Digital application systems not only can help companies to develop user relationship management systems, but they can also help companies to maintain their customer relationships and meet the personalized requirements of their customers. Companies simultaneously have full control over user resources in the constant pursuit of improving user satisfaction and sales performance.

3. **Enhance corporate management efficiency**

The digital management of companies utilizes computers and network technologies, as well as the employment of digital means. On the one hand, digital application systems apply advanced management concepts in real applications, helping companies to perform decision-making faster and more accurately, enhancing corporate management efficiency, and avoiding any delay in business opportunities due to long decision-making and hard decisions. On the other hand, companies can effectively manage many different types of data sets generated during their development process with the digital application systems, enhance the authenticity of data, accelerate the exchanges and transmission of data and information and perform data processing for varying businesses, achieving a highly efficient digital management.

4. **Reduce corporate operating costs**

Innovative digital application systems can help companies to reduce their operating costs. Companies perform analysis with the digital application systems and recalibrate their development strategies and objectives according to the market movements, avoiding the pursuit of blind development under the circumstances of not clearly understanding the market demand.

Through digital application systems, companies can analyze the purchase intent of the customers, purchasing behaviors, purchasing frequency, and acceptable purchasing budgets, further segmenting the customers based on these factors and performing pertinent product sales.

Digital application systems can analyze the relevant product data, helping companies understand the market demand for such products and determining the R&D direction for the products to cut down on development costs.

18.4.2 Constructing a Digital Application System

There are currently many digital application systems in the market. Companies of different industries and scales have different requirements. If the construction of the applications cannot meet the corporate requirements, it not only fails to showcase the effects but may also bring about unnecessary problems for the companies. Hence, companies must construct a digital application system that is suitable for themselves by integrating their growth initiatives, strategic objectives, company scale, personnel structure, industry characteristics, and product features.

1. **Integrate the six-map planning method to construct digital applications for companies**

While constructing the digital application system, companies can consolidate the six-map methodology in Chap. 11 and performance appraisal and assessment from the six perspectives of strategy, business, requirement, application, algorithm, and data. The six-map methodology is the construction process of a digital application system.

2. **Create an application construction status of low costs and high efficiencies**

Many companies are hesitant to construct an application system because the costs of developing each application are very high. While constructing the digital application system, companies must develop an application development system with technical means, such as a data platform, to simplify the application development process and make it seamless and convenient, cutting down the development costs.

3. **Develop a completely digital application system**

Digital application systems can help companies resolve issues. The applications of many companies contain certain issues. Some companies may have large investments, but the R&D of applications cannot showcase intrinsic value. It is attributed to the fact that companies do not develop a good digital application system. They fail to reinforce the interrelationships between each application, and they only perform the R&D of applications in a fragmented and random way. It results in data silos of each application and makes the common functionality not reusable, wasting maintenance costs in the ensuing period. Consequently, companies need to consolidate their own experiences to develop a complete digital application system, reinforcing the interrelationships between each application to help companies generate applications rapidly and effectively, which are used to enable the front-end businesses.

In summary, while constructing the digital application system, companies must not only refer to the six-map methodology but also create an application construction status of low costs and high efficiencies. Besides, they must also seamlessly interconnect the data between each application system, developing a complete digital application system to provide a powerful drive for the digital transformation of companies.

18.5 Organization

Relying on digital technologies to comprehensively enhance agility, decision-making capability, staff participation, creativity, and autonomy is an urgent requirement for the digital transformation of companies. The major themes, such as interactivity and creativity, demanded by the era of digital businesses have pressured companies to construct a compatible organizational structure and staff allocation from the top management layer to the bottom basic layer. Hence, emphasizing user responsiveness, agile organizations that sort out the professional capabilities of members and professional digital talents are the standard configurations of digital transformation for companies.

18.5.1 Unlocking the Construction Approach of an Agile Organization

Each traditional organization and agile organization have its advantages. The traditional top-down organizational structure has an edge in consistent delivery and thorough execution of information and resources. And the new type of agile organization with tasks as its objective emphasizes more on the degree of responsiveness and the professional capabilities of its members. The construction of the capabilities of an agile organization cannot be created with a single attempt, and companies need to employ different approaches to achieve it if they want their organization equipped with data analysis and intelligent decision-making.

1. **The data analysis department is becoming a cross-functional department**

The data department formed the organizational structure of a traditional company, the IT department, and the business department. Each department would roll out the tasks according to its functional definition. The positioning of the roles between the senior and lower-level staff and departments, mainly command and control, as the key architect of corporate digitalization against the backdrop of digital transformation, the data analysis department, developed by data scientists, data modelers, and data analysts, transformed from an independent department to a cross-functional department with a diverse range of skill sets. With the empowerment of data scientists' capabilities in each team, the team members can adequately plan according to the task requirements, flexibly handle all issues arising from the execution process, respond promptly and collaborate to complete the tasks.

The traditional organization model relied on the varying positions of the data technical processing staff, such as data scientists, data modelers, and business analysts, to complete specific projects. From the initiation to delivery of a project, it would require many data technical professionals to complete every project phase. In the present digital era, these cumbersome processes and working models with long development cycles are phased out to deliver personalized analytics solutions for customers.

The working model of an agile organization emphasizes the joint efforts of the organization members to create the analysis contents. The cross-functional team can play multiple roles. It is, however, an absolute necessity for all team members to have data integration capability, data analytics capability, and knowledge in the business field. This type of cross-functional, agile organization can be dispersed and concentrated, facilitating the sharing of resources. At the same time, the agile organization can also quickly complete the iterative upgrading of projects according to the relevant requirements, meeting the ever-changing analysis requirements of the front-end users.

2. **The organization members must be equipped with the dual capabilities of business and data**

The agile organization disrupts the traditional organization model of attaching individual job descriptions for every designation under each superior resulting in very little knowledge of the job descriptions of other designations. Unlike the traditional organization members' fixed job duties, the agile organization members' job duties are comprised of cross-functionality. This unique feature is particularly apparent for data analysts and front-end business staff.

The job description for a data analyst is generally divided into two segments with different job descriptions: business and technology. The data analysts in the business segment are often deployed in the marketing, sales, and operations departments. Their job descriptions include preparing summary reports, plans, and solutions according to the data. The data analysts in the technology segment are usually deployed in the IT and data departments. They can be further subdivided into algorithm engineers, visualization engineers, and others according to the work phase. The job descriptions of the data analysts in these two segments are independent. While the data analysts in the technology segment have no idea about business, the data analysts in the business segment also have no idea about technology.

In the mobile internet era, the front-end business scenarios are constantly changing, and it only points to the fact that the data sources are complicated, and the processing phases are cumbersome. Besides, computing methods are also continually evolving. The data analysts in the business segment must first embrace the blind spots of technology, decide on the dimensions and fields of the data analysis based on the business logic of business requirements and counteract the varying business fields with different data indicators. The data analysts in the technology segment face non-assurance of data quality and patchless key fields, failing to fulfill business analysis requirements due to the lack of business understanding.

Under the agile organization model, the data analysts in the business segment that only know about marketing but not technology, as well as the data analysts in the technology segment that only know about technology but not the business principles, can all accomplish the interchangeability and interaction of varying roles by organizing training and the accumulation of project experiences to truly achieve the capabilities of a "data scientist."

3. **Construct an organization system equipped with description, diagnosis, prediction, and early warning capabilities**

The unique agility of an agile organization does not mean that the internal organization is disorderly and out of control. Under the foundation of effectively building each department's interconnectivity and interactive capabilities, the agile organization still needs to construct a set of systems that facilitate quick and effective completion of digital tasks. That is the organization system equipped with description, diagnosis, prediction, and early warning capabilities, helping companies to be more orderly, highly effective, and more precise during the implementation process of digital tasks.

In the phase of requirements description, the project manager must be very clear about the objectives to be achieved, set the results to be attained in each phase during the completion process of the tasks, and monitor the completion conditions at any time during the implementation process. Suppose the indicator of task completion at a certain phase is 95%, while the actual completion value delivered on time is only 85%. The team must conduct a diagnostic analysis, analyze the reasons that fail to achieve the target from the data sources and gradually take the necessary measures to achieve the objective. As there are many data sources, the team is burdened with loads of analysis tasks that may involve correlation analysis, classification analysis, outlier detection, and other phases. This type of irregular analysis task needs predictive analysis capability. The predictive capability is one of the capabilities that an agile organization must contain, and it can help the team build a precise predictive model for the routine and repeatable processes to predict the project's delivery time and other variables. The agile organization also needs to build the early warning capability to display an early warning signal when certain peak values are reached in the project, guiding the team to carry out the countermeasures.

An organization system equipped with description, diagnosis, prediction, and early warning can help companies create a standardized workflow model to standardize the project-based workflow, safeguarding the orderly execution of each project and task.

18.5.2 Equipping Digital Professionals

An agile organization is indispensable for the digital transformation of companies. Its concept originates from the Special Forces, and it is a fighting unit assembled by companies to achieve digital transformation. This organization has a certain degree of autonomy where the frontline executives can autonomously complete the tasks after understanding the intent of the tasks assigned. An agile organization requires team members to have certain professional experiences and capabilities and complete tasks efficiently and precisely in a highly complex business environment. Although an agile organization is not limited in scale, it is often built with the following important roles, as shown in Fig. 18.2.

1. **Data research engineer**

The data research engineer must be familiar with the big data development platform, well-versed in the big data research tools, capable of employing all types of big data development technologies to perform data development and good coding habits and equipped with certain architecture capabilities.

2. **Data applications engineer**

The data applications engineer must grapple with the popular mainstream front-end and back-end development technologies, be familiar with the application development framework, and be well-versed in integrated skill sets, such as significant data application architecture and performance optimization.

3. **Data intelligence scientist**

The data intelligence scientist must grapple with common data mining and analytics tools, including machine learning, deep learning, and other advanced technologies, capable of effectively applying them to business scenarios and resolving real customer issues.

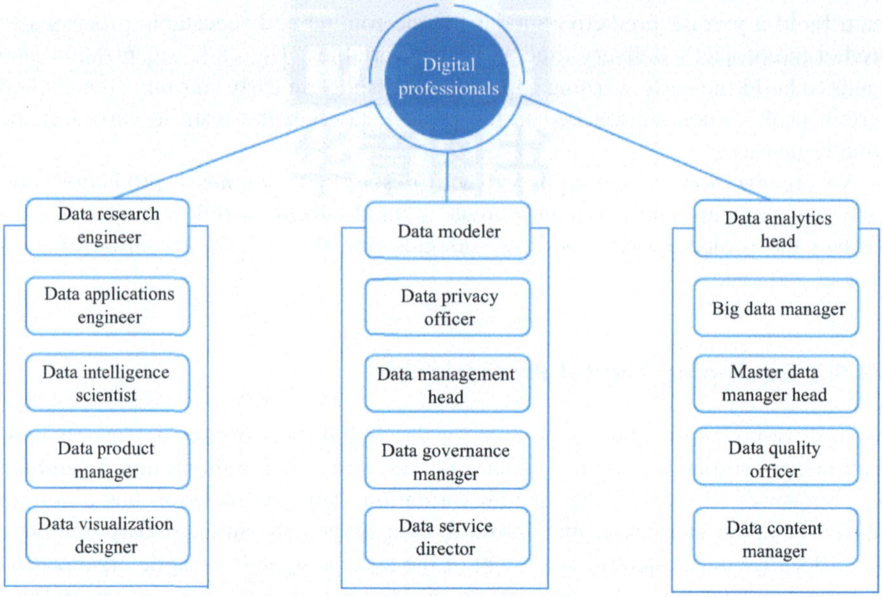

Fig. 18.2 Digital professionals that an agile organization should be equipped with

4. **Data product manager**

The data product manager must grapple with the data technologies, be familiar with the customers, and have a unique business understanding and concept toward data, fulfilling the customers' interests with tangible or intangible data products and optimizing the data and business values in the end.

5. **Data visualization designer**

The data visualization designer must grapple with data interaction or visual design capability, possessing strong interactive senses and impeccable aesthetics with cost control to produce deliverables with the full process, high-fidelity interaction, and visual experience quality.

6. **Data modeler**

The data modeler must grapple with the data technologies, understand the business requirements and possess several capabilities, such as holistic architecture, model design, data research, streamlining of operations and maintenance, and deliver highly usable and scalable data in a low-cost and highly efficient manner.

Aside from the staff described above, companies can also designate other positions according to requirements, including data privacy officer, data management head, data governance manager, data service director, data analytics head, big data management head, data quality officer, and data content manager. The designation of these staff enriches the talent construction for the companies, meeting the varying aspects of human resource requirements of companies.

19 Implementation Path of a Data Platform

It is most important to enable a true data platform implementation to achieve digital transformation. After properly preparing the necessary work in the early phase, including data governance, system construction, talent allocation, and others, the next step is the essential implementation of the data platform. Companies must first grapple with the three key factors in the construction of the data platform: having a correct data construction approach, a clear understanding of the construction concept, avoiding the construction misconceptions of the data platform, and achieving digital transformation with the lowest costs possible.

19.1 Design Concept of a Data Platform

As the most popular technical platform in the modern era of digital economies, from the proposition phase to the first response and then becoming an inevitable approach for traditional industries to implement a digital transformation, the principles and construction concepts behind the architectural design of a data platform remain unchanged and universal despite the fact of not having a standardized definition yet. Strictly speaking, it changes the processing approach of "converge, interconnect and apply" to the data construction model of "apply, interconnect and converge" to achieve the highly efficient innovation of the front-end businesses with reusable data assets. Under such guidance, per the corporate scale and characteristics, the construction approach of a digital platform that fulfills the needs is developed.

19.1.1 Three Key Factors in the Construction of a Data Platform

Based on the usage value of the data platform, the construction must be equipped with three indispensable key factors.

X. Ma, *Methodology for Digital Transformation*, Management for Professionals,
https://doi.org/10.1007/978-981-19-9111-0_19

1. **The governance of data assets**

When the market inventory of companies becomes smaller against the backdrop that the traditional, uneven operating model can no longer bring about economic growth for companies, the construction of corporate informatization is urgently placed on the daily agenda. The electronic management systems help companies to recalibrate the organizational structure and deployment of informatization in the preliminary phase. Meanwhile, external market expansion is still being compressed, and simple marketing promotions no longer work. The most significant advantage of a data platform is digitally driving the front-end businesses to innovate and reduce internal costs quickly.

Maintaining data and delivering data services to drive business growth are often managed by the IT department of companies. Coupled with the business characteristics and utilization of digital technologies, the IT department can incessantly supply the "ammunition" to the "frontline" business department. Among them, the accumulation of data assets is of paramount importance. Hence, the early phase of the data platform construction requires pooling companies' internal and external data through traditional information management software and new data integration technologies and presenting all data resources based on review and planning. In addition, it also requires interconnecting and compiling the data with big data development tools, including exploring the data bloodline relationship and safeguarding data security.

The governance of data assets largely depends on data model management, which can help the digital platform standardize the naming of data fields and develop a standardized development specification, achieving effective data identification. After multiple rounds of data governance, it can form data assets reusable for companies. In addition, there are differences in the construction of the data platform with software technologies of every company, as their businesses and products are different. Consequently, there is no universal or standardized data platform architecture. In constructing the data platform architecture, companies must comprehensively consider their data volume and business characteristics under the foundation of their information structure.

2. **Sharing of data services**

After constructing the bottom layer of the technical architecture of the data platform and creating the data assets that can be deployed, companies still need to construct the data models according to the requirements of the business department to deliver the data intelligence services that can be standardized, deployed and shared to the front-end business teams. The shared data services can provide safe and reliable technical support with convenient operations, standardized specifications, and versatile scalability and deliver label extraction for the front-end users, R&D of products, customer services, marketing campaigns, and others to provide data references for the different applications, such as precision marketing and user profiles.

3. **Data intelligence applications**

The final application directive of a data platform is to provide efficiency improvement, cost reduction, and a key driving force for the business innovation of companies. Hence, data intelligence applications have become the touchstone to validating the capabilities of a digital platform after completing the bottom layer of the technical architecture of the data platform and the work of data governance. It examines whether the data platform can pass the data capability test, including real-time query capability, batch processing capability, report presentation capability, data security capability, data management capability, helping the business staff to complete the intelligent extraction and applications of data and assisting companies to grapple with the mainstream trends of digital transformation and devise the relevant development strategies.

The data engineers and business staff can achieve the self-service processing of data within the digital platform and accelerate the pace of data-driven businesses based on the data platform's interactive model and standardized data processing procedures. At the same time, the standardization of correlation analysis and analysis results of all types of data provides companies with a more objective analytics dimension in the data intelligence application area.

19.1.2 Planning and Design Concepts of a Data Platform

How to decide whether a platform is a data platform?

What types of capabilities should a data platform be carried?

We shall explore the design concepts of digital platform architecture by seeking answers to these two questions. From the author's perspective, the significance of a data platform lies in the provision of incessant business and product innovations for the users as its construction objective and the conversion of all resources, such as the back-end management systems, to a sustainable and reusable capability for the front-end businesses. Regardless of the internet giants converting to 2B businesses, providing export of technologies and industrial transformation, the traditional IT manufacturers that have been immersed in the information sector for many years, or the technology startups constantly working hard in the corporate digital services, these companies need to think deeply over these two questions while drawing up the solutions for a digital transformation.

1. **Sort out the basic business relationships to provide a holistic view for the construction of a digital platform**

While constructing a data platform, companies need to assess their business characteristics and data volume. Before constructing a data platform, companies must first sort out their business relationships in the internal departments and ascertain the construction directive.

For example, the data department must collaborate with the business department to sort out the business types, business domain boundaries, basic business services required by every business domain, and interconnectivity standards between the business domains. Then they can develop or improve the standardization of business capability benchmarks, operations mechanisms, business analysis approaches, business execution framework, and the organizational structure of the team that provides operational services.

The holistic business map created after sorting out the basic business relationships can help the construction staff of the digital platform architecture and the front-end business staff to understand the business standards and requirements better. The holistic business map can guide the data department in constructing the data platform and provide the implementation, management, and control standards for constructing the data platform architecture.

2. **Emphasize the accumulation of capabilities and maintain the scalability**

The construction, improvement, and applications of the data platform architecture must emphasize the accumulation of data capabilities and the scalability of the construction of the digital platform, providing more data support for the future expansion of companies and the R&D of new products to enable the companies to move ahead of their competitors sustainably. But the accumulation of data capabilities cannot be achieved overnight, and it must undergo the process of partial to global optimization and gradual improvement during its applications.

As the consumption attributes of industries are different, the operational emphasis of companies is also different. The operational emphasis of the apparel industry, with high inventory and high consumption, is on the supply chain. In the operational model of a traditional apparel company, the data at the frontline marketing end was not updated in real-time, and it could not provide timely data support for the supply chain. Consequently, the priority task for the apparel industry to implement digital transformation was to integrate the data at the supply chain end and achieve real-time data updating at the marketing end. After completing the data updating of the supply chain and the marketing end, the non-core business departments of the apparel company, such as the marketing department, operations department, and management department, can gradually implement digital transformation until they have achieved a complete transformation for the entire company.

Other companies can also implement digital transformation according to their business priorities, beginning from a partial segment to construct an adaptable, scalable data platform to meet the data requirements from part to whole businesses.

Despite undergoing the sorting out of business relationships in the early phase and the specification of implementation standards of the digital strategies, the fact whether the digital platform meets the application requirements of companies in the end and is capable of bringing about how much contribution value to the front-end businesses still needs to be validated during the business application process.

19.2 Building the Data Organization Capability

The ultimate objective of every company participating in competitive markets is sustainable growth. When a company's development reaches a certain scale, its growth is restricted by bottlenecks due to the environment or its conditions. Undoubtedly, it does not mean that the company just stagnates forever. As long as it can resolve the issues hindering its growth, avoid declining performance, and develop new core competitiveness with the driving force for development, it can still achieve sustainable growth.

In the era of digital economies, new digital technologies have become the main driving force in enhancing sustainable competitiveness among companies. Digital transformation has become a favorable advantage for companies to seek business breakthroughs in the digital era. And whether companies can create data organization capability is an important consideration for a successful digital transformation.

In traditional management, the yardstick of success in companies is having the correct strategic initiatives and outstanding organizational capabilities. Organization capability refers to the ability of the team to showcase the overall fighting force, apparently surpassing the competitors in certain areas and creating higher value. And in the present time of digital waves pounding on every industry, the key factor of success for companies is no longer their inimitable organization capability but rather the implementation of management and control of data organization capability for data management and applications.

In implementing digital transformation, companies need to understand precisely that the extraction process of data value is not an issue at the technical level. Instead, it is a conceptualization model of data applications, or in other words, an organization's capability. From the management level to the frontline team, all company staff must ponder several questions, including where the data should be required in the company, how to acquire data, and how to use the data correctly. By resolving these three questions, companies have embarked on the exploratory process of showcasing the data value. This process requires synergistic collaboration between multiple internal departments of companies, presenting their individual effects.

In the digital transformation process, companies need to perform the followings: empowerment of technical innovation, business guidance, proper processing of the relationships between all types of data in the internal and external departments, enabling the bottom layer of the data architecture to be more enriching; setting up the relationships of data convergence and dynamic correlation between the business department, technical department, marketing and operations departments; joint construction of data capabilities and data services between every department on the data and business levels; developing consolidated, standardized data standards and enhancing data quality under the circumstances of uneven industry standards.

The data organization capability of companies is reflected explicitly in the following areas.

1. **The data issues and conditions of companies**

Companies must have a clear understanding of their data volume, data value, and data application rate. They must also know whether these data can create data assets beneficial for corporate development and assess whether it is well worth mining with digital technologies. Companies must ascertain the data storage conditions and utilize their organization's capability to accumulate, mine, and utilize the data.

2. **The interconnectivity and application capability of external data**

Some applications involved in dynamic data, such as the changes in consumer scenarios, and trend analysis of industry development, do require external data support. Hence, interconnecting external data to achieve internal and external data sharing is a necessary organizational capability for companies during the development process.

3. **The capability to integrate data with business scenarios**

There are many different acquisition channels and application directives for data. For example, the C-end consumer data can be acquired from all types of consumer scenarios, while the B-end production data can be acquired from the information management systems at the workshops and applied to the business department, management, and operations departments.

Some data exhibits a significant boost to enhance productivity and reduce costs of the internal departments, while some data can deliver support to product R&D and business expansion. Some data can also be used to mine the value of cooperative customers, while some data can enable the marketing department. Some data can, even to the extent, complete the integration of upstream and downstream industry chains, providing recommendations of merger, integration, and investment of companies for reference purposes. It is a requirement to consider from the perspective of front-end applications to reflect the value of data. First, consider what types of data organization capabilities a company should be equipped with to allocate the resources, deploy the technologies, and converge the capabilities, including capital infusion, brand building, talent nurturing, and introducing technologies, helping companies to deepen their drive for digital transformation.

19.3 Comparison of Data Construction

With the arrival of the significant data era, the integrated data construction approach can no longer completely handle the data processing tasks for the big data industry. It has constructively opened up new opportunities in the innovation of the data construction approach within China. The emergence of the data platform is perfectly aligned with the development of Chinese digital technologies and the ever-changing market environment.

19.3.1 Traditional Integrated Data Construction Approach

Take the example of a certain company below to review the traditional integrated data construction approach. This company has been an ongoing concern for more than 10 years. But it still has not resolved the data analytics requirements. Hence, it purchased some BI tools. Since that, its data volume has constantly been rising.

Again, it purchased some big data platform tools. In the ensuing period, its data has become increasingly complex and difficult for governance.

Consequently, it installed some data governance tools. And then, with the increasingly higher requirements for data synchronization, this company also purchased some data synchronization tools. Overtime, more and more data tools have been purchased by this company. As these data tools have a single function each, they cannot meet the ever-changing application requirements of the business department.

It was because most of the available products in the market had a single function when the company was purchasing the information management system. The market could not offer a standardized, structured, and scalable information management system from the overall perspective.

Although the integrated data construction approach could resolve some data management issues, each system could only resolve its problems as the information management systems purchased by the company were from different manufacturers with different models as well as the definition and solution for the same business within the systems were also different from each other. The data within the systems could not flow freely and interconnect with each other. For example, databases, ETL tools, data mining tools, data analytics tools, and others were all traditional approaches for companies to implement information management. As various manufacturers produced them with different models, they could only unilaterally resolve several issues, such as data storage, loading, mining, and analytics.

Take another example of a certain bank with good technical capabilities. While it has a bigger investment in information management, it was equipped with at least seven to eight types of information management software in the data application chains, such as business and operations data. For the bank, the biggest obstacle was the employment of different products on different chains with inconsistent data standards between different systems, severe data silos and lacking customized data products leading to a big disparity in the directions of data applications. For example, even though the data governance was comprehensive and correct while the construction of data models was also accurate, it could not determine whether the issue was related to data synchronization or the data at the bottom layer was not cleaned properly. As this type of integrated data construction approach was lacking in a holistic recording of the data actions, the data errors could not be tracked, leading to the project's failure with no accountability. Hence, companies were unsatisfied with information management products.

In addition, the products introduced by foreign information system software manufacturers have been particularly popular, with high credibility in constructing information and comprehensive segmentation of information management products. However, each company only focused on its product functionality and design with virtually no accountability for the overall application of data. For example, the company selling its ODS system was only concerned with its products' optimization and service improvement, while the software manufacturer selling the data warehouses was not concerned over the seamless interconnectivity of its products with other information systems. The software manufacturers were not providing the products from the perspective of data applications resulting in many issues, such as weak data interconnectivity, frequent data errors, and low data application values, faced by the domestic companies after installing their software.

19.3.2 The Data Construction Approach of a New Data Platform

The services of many business systems, including online shopping platforms and payment platforms, under the umbrella of a certain e-commerce giant, were provided by databases. With the launch of the Double 11 shopping festival, the transaction volume at the geometric level triggered higher requirements for the internal storage of databases, and it signified a procurement expenditure of hundreds of millions of CNY. Hence, this e-commerce giant relies on business expansion and fulfillment of requirements as its market growth has transformed itself into a technology research company, beginning its autonomous R&D on databases. During this process, the value of a data platform architecture has been uncovered simultaneously.

Overall, it is no longer viable to use foreign information software systems because of the extremely high data complexity and vast areas of data applications within every industry in China.

In the digital era, as a supporting platform for the digital transformation of companies, the data platform disrupts the traditional integrated data construction approach, meeting the requirements of mining the value of the colossal volume of data for companies. For companies, the priority value in constructing a data platform is that data errors can be backtracked to their origin. At the same time, business reports, data dictionaries, operational reports, and others can complete data tracking, analysis, and rectification through the digital platform. It not only provides a clean base of data for data applications of the business units, but it also frees up the technical staff from handling simple tasks.

19.4 Principles and Concepts in the Construction of a Data Platform

A data platform is an inevitable product of the business model from the IT age to the DT era, and it is also an unavoidable outcome of a paradigm shift from process-driven to data-driven. The parallel alignment with a data platform utilizes data evidence or decision-making capability to build a data service concept, ultimately achieving digital transformation for companies.

The construction model of a data platform truly disrupts the traditional construction model of the data architecture, beginning from the data and information to focus on the integration of specific conditions of the business department and reasonably employing the corporate resources to enhance service efficiency.

19.4.1 Traditional Principles and Concepts in Constructing a Data Platform—"Construct, Govern and Apply"

The traditional data architecture construction model does not emphasize the integration of specific conditions of the business department. It purely abides by the data concept of "construct, govern and apply"—construct the data architecture first, then perform data governance followed by applying the data to applications. For example, companies perform construction from the IaaS (Infrastructure as a Service) level to different PaaS (Platform as a service) levels to the DaaS (Data as a Service) level and then to the SaaS (Software as a Service) level. Some companies inevitably trek the incorrect path during the construction process of traditional data architecture. Some of them first employ cloud technology to perform data migration to the cloud and then interconnect the data, govern the data, and prepare the reports before developing all types of applications. This type of construction concept usually needs a longer cycle. Companies may suspend their construction when they cannot visualize the business value after constructing it for a long time.

Companies need a more agile approach to construct the data architecture and use the results to validate the scientific properties of the construction approach. But that begins from the perspective of data applications, considering how to govern the data.

19.4.2 New Principles and Concepts in Constructing a Data Platform—"Apply, Govern and Construct"

The new construction model of the data platform is to sort out the directive of data applications to drive data governance and construct a complete data platform architecture in the end, quickly responding to the ever-changing business requirements of companies. Figure 19.1 compares the new and traditional principles and concepts in constructing a data platform, showcasing the principles of the construction concepts of data architecture.

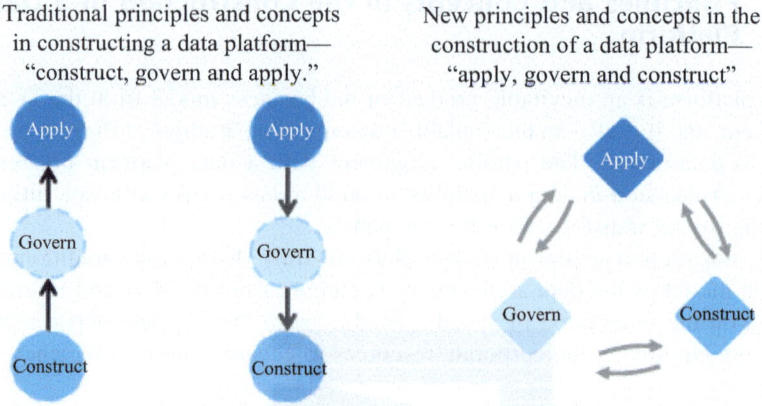

Fig. 19.1 Comparison between the different principles and concepts in the construction of a data platform

Companies can adopt the principles and concepts in constructing a data platform architecture from the three following points.

1. **Sort out the strategy map, business map, and application map**

During the construction of a data platform, some companies cannot utilize the data resources to mine the portion that can enable the business to have record revenue and fail to achieve the expected results. Hence, the relevant staff must sort out the data applications and resolve all issues faced by the business department to reduce costs, enhance efficiencies, and get record revenue during the data platform construction. At the same time, the digital team of companies must construct the strategy map according to the corporate development plans and then construct the business and application maps according to the directive and dimension of the business growth, concisely governing the data with the application map and managing the entire data system.

2. **Use the application map to drive back the data map and determine the path of data governance**

During the investment in staff and capital allocation after sorting out the application map, companies can first organize part of the data to perform governance based on the application map in light of limited resources and labor to construct the data map. In the digital transformation process, those that decide on resource deployment and capital allocation are often the senior management executives, who usually neglect the role of data analytics. Hence, the CDO must communicate with the senior management executives to ascertain the staff allocation and resource supply to the data governance team to provide a smooth path for data governance.

The CDO can relay the confirmed path of data governance to his subordinates via several means, such as email, video conferencing, or brainstorming, enabling the technical and business staff to be familiar with the contents and requirements of data governance, enhancing the beneficial value of data and spreading the scope of influence of the data.

3. **Use data applications to drive the construction of the new data platform architecture**

While constructing a data platform, some companies may be concerned that the data platform creates new "chimneys." As a result, the construction of the new data platform architecture must fulfill the characteristics of being open, scalable, and long-term. Given the open data platform architecture, the list of technical functions and applications can be added or deleted alongside the business growth. This type of new data platform architecture avoids the scenario where there are constant changes to the architecture that affects the flow and application of the data at the bottom layer because of the need to adapt to the requirements of the front-end business department during the application process. Its high level of flexibility and scalability can help companies perform data governance and applications at any time, truly achieving digital transformation.

It is evident that the traditional principles and concepts in the construction of the data architecture of "construct, govern and apply" can no longer meet the user requirements, while the new principles and concepts in the construction of the new data platform have gained widespread mainstream adoption by all types of digital transformation.

19.5 Pitfalls of a Data Platform

Although the market has increasingly acknowledged the data platform, the participants lack an understanding of the system and are rather clumsy in handling some key issues.

1. **Three misconceptions of data governance**

During the construction of a data platform, data governance is a critical component for the measures to the quality construction and outcome of the data platform, despite being involved in the early phase of the formation of data assets. Companies must understand the three misconceptions of data governance to avoid treading the long unnecessary path.

(1) Companies can see results of data governance in the short term

The first misconception of data governance is the belief of companies to see results in the short term.

Data governance is a long-term and complicated task, and it is the most fundamental step in the construction process of the data platform. Data governance often seems to have preliminarily worked after many integrations, cleaning, and pooling rounds. But during business applications, it is often found that the data cannot truly be implemented, let alone drive the businesses. Therefore, companies have some misconceptions during the data governance process, resulting in a long data governance process and poor results. One of the reasons for this type of phenomenon is the lack of data management in the internal departments of companies. Though they have great expectations over the value-realization potential of the data, they have no idea how to manage the data intelligently.

In this situation, companies can perform a comprehensive test on the data architecture, data quality, and processing capability with a small scale of data applications, providing the basis for actual data governance in the later phase. After clearly exploring the data conditions, companies can hire professional data platform service providers to devise a feasible data governance solution, direct the technical and business staff to collaborate, and shorten the time for data governance to work effectively.

(2) Data governance is the work of the technical department

The second misconception of data governance is the belief that data governance and the construction of a digital platform architecture are the work of the technical department without any relationship to the business staff and the corporate management.

The digital transformation of companies is a strategic transformation involving many departments, such as the organization, business, and technology. The ultimate objective of constructing a data platform is to enable the business to deliver the driving force to achieve the value-realization of data. The technical staff's long-term focus is on enhancing technical capabilities, so they often neglect the business requirements and pain points. Without considering the business requirements, it deviates from the original intent of constructing the digital platform. Without the support of resources from the corporate digital platform strategies, it is easy for the digital transformation to fail halfway through the journey, being only driven by the technical department with an insufficient driving force.

The business generates data and enhancing data quality is intertwined with business development. As there are more business segments, there are also more data sources. To standardize data quality, it must first standardize the business terms. Loads of business requirements and incomplete data reports lead to errors in collecting fundamental data. Hence, companies must embrace the multi-dimensional organizational structure of the business department, technical department, and even management levels while performing data governance. It can truly implement data governance by doing this.

(3) Data governance is a simple tool allocation and accumulation

The second misconception of data governance is the belief that data governance is only a simple allocation and accumulation tool.

Some companies may believe that the data be clear, orderly, clean, and ready to be used by performing simple "cleaning" with governance tools. It is not true. Data governance includes the organizational structure adjustment, development of governance processes, allocation of tools, implementation of on-site technical staff, and collaboration and coordination of the business department. The prerequisite of data governance is the deployment and arrangement of staff. They can only showcase their effectiveness if the professional and appropriate staff are assigned the appropriate positions. Similarly, companies' data governance can only be effective with specifically clear actions, instructions, and execution processes.

2. **Several misconceptions about the construction of a digital platform**

(1) Construct only a platform

The construction of a data platform is only the beginning of the IT transformation of companies. The construction of a project or a platform cannot resolve all issues companies face during their digital transformation.

A data platform is a key to the digital transformation of companies. Before implementing digital transformation, companies must devise a full set of strategic plans according to the data's scale and applications, perceiving the data platform's construction as a project involving all companies' business processes from top to bottom.

(2) The digital platform architecture is simple without the need to improvise it

Due to limited expenditure, inadequate staff, and insufficient commitment to digital transformation, many companies have resorted to cheap architecture with simple functions at the beginning of the construction of a digital platform before slowly transitioning to technical architecture with complex structure and full-domain data. The simple, open-source software cannot help companies resolve all digital transformation issues. Some professional algorithmic R&D and model construction can only be achieved with technical professionals.

During the construction process of the data platform, companies often need to perform validation on the technical properties of the data platform through some experimental projects. The results of these experimental projects decide on the overall directive adjustment of the data platform architecture with relevant changes to technical upgrading, business recalibration, and organizational transformation.

(3) Construct the data platform based on personal views

The crux of the third misconception lies in understanding a digital platform. The people constructing the data platform often have no idea what a data platform is, do not completely understand the significance of a digital platform, and have no sense of its real functionality. They only follow their personal views and understanding to construct the digital platform. This type of construction concept is misaligned with the ultimate objective. No matter how hard the team has tried, the ultimate results would be far from the original expectation. Many such cases did not succeed in the implementation of the digital platform.

(4) Construction of a data platform for the sake of constructing

The fourth misconception is constructing a data platform for the sake of constructing. Some companies mistakenly treat the data platform's construction as the objective of its transformation. Hence, they construct their data platform to achieve this objective. A data platform is only an approach used to complete digital transformation.

The fundamental objective of completing the digital transformation of companies is to achieve a significant performance improvement, reducing costs and enhancing efficiencies. Achieving this objective requires some tools and approaches. That is akin to studying. We wish to acquire more knowledge by studying and understanding the world more insightfully. So, the book is a tool while studying is an approach used to acquire more knowledge. It is not the ultimate objective, however. Most people make their decisions or select their options based on the objectives they want to achieve. Once the objective is incorrect, all the following efforts are undoubtedly futile.

(5) A data platform can only meet the short-term business requirements

The fifth misconception is the belief that a digital platform can only meet short-term business requirements. Some corporate leaders believe that the data applications a data platform performs can only meet the current business requirements and cannot meet the business requirements in the next two to three years or even in a longer horizon. It is not surprising that they have this kind of thinking because they are not involved in implementing a data platform. And it causes them to look at the superficial aspect of the issues only without penetrating through the intrinsic core.

The value of technical architecture cannot be perceived with just one look at it. Some common SaaS software can be quickly replaced if it is the incorrect pick, and the costs can be controlled. If PaaS is used as the basic facility of a digital platform, the consequences are very severe if the base is selected incorrectly.

(6) Construct the data platform purely with the IT concept

The sixth misconception is constructing the digital platform using the IT concept, not the DT concept. In the past, the IT concept was reflected in two main areas. One area was that companies built data warehouses instead of data platforms.

Although they used more advanced approaches to manage the data, their IT service department's business models and methodology systems have not changed. This type of management approach could only alleviate the workload of some IT staff. It was not a digital platform driving the businesses and could not change the service approaches and business models. Even though companies have constructed a digital platform, it only benefitted part of the IT staff.

Another area was the stereotype, thinking that all things could be developed completely individually. It was a terrifying way of thinking. The technology industry has its specialties, and each production phase has complexity. Quite a few companies invest in the procurement of ERP software now. But long ago, many companies believed they could develop their own ERP. But the results showed that the things they created were ineffective, even wasting a large amount of labor and time, particularly the opportunity costs. The losses were immeasurable for the business units that would urgently require to be changed.

If companies want to launch their own DT applications, they need two essential conditions. First, it is time. Companies need to have sufficient time and energy to research and develop systems. The long cycle of R&D may have caused companies to miss the opportunity of implementing digital transformation. Companies must never forget that it is the priority objective to respond to business requirements quickly. Second, it is the team. The R&D of DT applications requires a team to dive deep into each development phase.

(7) The data platform system is too technical

The seventh misconception is that the data platform system is too technical. Some companies purchase a lot of IT systems. As they selected the incorrect tools, the business value was not apparent. It was reflected not only in the digital platform but also in all business lines. Some companies have close to a hundred systems that have been developed or purchased over the last decade. Today, many of these systems are no longer positive assets, becoming burdens for these companies. But these companies have no solution on hand. They are often confused by all sorts of perplexing historical issues. Under this situation, the top priority is to jump out of the issue as quickly as possible. Otherwise, the issues would be entangled in a disorderly manner, with no clue where to begin resolving them.

Even though the technical systems are getting increasingly professional, they still cannot meet the business requirements. That is a type of common misconception. A technical system includes all professional terms, such as big data, artificial intelligence, business system, and digital platform. If the research is conducted in a segment for longer, it becomes more professional. But the other areas may be more enclosed. In other words, companies do not consider the business perspective while constructing their systems. It is also one of the reasons why the business department is not satisfied at all. Even though the concepts proposed by everyone are very professional, there is a gap of misunderstanding the real meaning expressed by everyone.

An operating company's essence is to orient itself to the business, which, in turn, orients itself to the users. Hence, it is always user-centric and not the individual profession at its core. Though everyone knows this, they revert to their old ways of doing things during the specific execution. That is why many companies are losing out to internet companies in terms of the degree of intellectualization despite having invested more in technical areas than internet companies. As everyone is getting more professional, wide gaps are increasingly more prominent, failing to achieve a flat, integrated system with users at its core.

Part VIII

Case Studies of Digital Transformation

The emergence of new types of digital organizations, including new retail, digital bank, and digital campus, illustrates the urgency of traditional industries to strive for digital transformation. The waves of digital transformation have pounded from the demand end to the supply end. In the digital transformation process, every company has its characteristics. We share some of the case studies below, hoping to inspire everyone.

20 Marketing Cloud Intelligence Helps New Retail Companies Achieve Transformation

There are four phases of marketing development for new retail companies: from independent marketing campaigns to capturing business opportunities by utilizing the information management system and precision marketing, and finally to achieving an enclosed loop for automated marketing revolving around the user assets.

These four phases reflect the increasingly higher degree of emphasis from the new retail companies on marketing, particularly Phase IV. Utilizing the huge volume of user data to achieve an enclosed loop for automated marketing has become an issue of great concern among new retail companies. And the Marketing Cloud Intelligence coincidentally can help the new retail companies to resolve this issue.

20.1 Project Background

The four phases above of marketing development experienced by the new retail companies are shown in Fig. 20.1.

In Phase I, companies record and manage the business opportunities that may be involved within the management system but are not yet involved in real marketing. It is more broadly to use the hotspot incidents, business opportunities, or specific projects as real opportunities to roll out independent marketing campaigns.

In Phase II, companies roll out the management systems, such as the CRM system, which mainly aims to strengthen sales information management. As customer requirements are constantly changing, mining customer requirements can help companies to generate more business opportunities. Hence, companies track and record the full life cycle of customer product use to capture business opportunities. While reaching the second phase of marketing development, companies are beginning to have an objective of consciously managing the customers, including the lead for customer repurchase.

X. Ma, *Methodology for Digital Transformation*, Management for Professionals,
https://doi.org/10.1007/978-981-19-9111-0_20

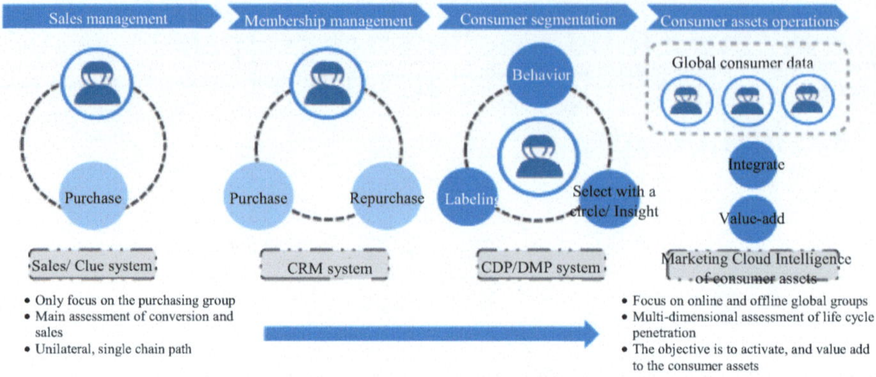

Fig. 20.1 The four phases of marketing development for new retail companies

In Phase III, precision marketing is on the daily agenda. With the application products of user profiles, companies can perform segmentation based on the user profiles and propose recommendations of different products according to user preferences.

In Phase IV, companies can operate the users as their assets and form a fully automated enclosed loop for marketing, providing feedback on product sales and marketing results to form an automated feedback loop. Companies can constantly utilize intelligent systems to enhance user value during this process. If this section is conducted properly, it enhances the company's value.

In Phase IV, companies must implement intelligent marketing to enhance the user assets and execute with a fully automated enclosed loop approach. For new retail companies, it is critical to complete Phase IV of intelligent marketing.

20.2 Analysis of Pain Points

Nowadays, majority of new retail companies have constructed their marketing teams with a diverse range of marketing techniques. The marketing teams do marketing according to the different consumer scenarios, but they cannot quantify the marketing results. Every company is doing precision marketing without precisely targeting the correct consumer groups. Many companies cannot precisely and systematically devise their marketing campaigns and stagnate at point-to-point marketing. For example, they perform precision marketing for a particular business.

Most new retail companies do not understand how marketing tools can generate data, and they also have no idea how to extract the value of data, let alone know how to synchronize the data generated with other phases. Hence, they cannot perform connected, holistic data value mining.

The precision marketing of several new retail companies has fault lines between the different layers. Simply put, it is to perform marketing at a certain phase only. Consequently, it is extremely difficult to achieve the cycle from the preliminary processing of data to the deepening of value mining and then flow back to the businesses to achieve a comprehensive marketing process with a data application system. As long as data cannot flow back to the original cycle, a sustainable showcase of the effects of data cannot be assured.

20.3 Solutions

Given the requirements of new retail companies in the marketing area, Guoyun Data has designed a Marketing Cloud Intelligence solution, as shown in Fig. 20.2. This solution can perform the management of labeled members to enable marketing.

1. **Membership management function of Marketing Cloud Intelligence**

(1) Acquire membership information

The customer acquisition cost of a new retailer is very high. If the users do not repurchase sustainably, the membership value utilization rate diminishes, increasing companies' customer acquisition costs. Hence, a quality marketing product often enables many members to perform repurchases sustainably, and it also boosts the stickiness and loyalty of the members.

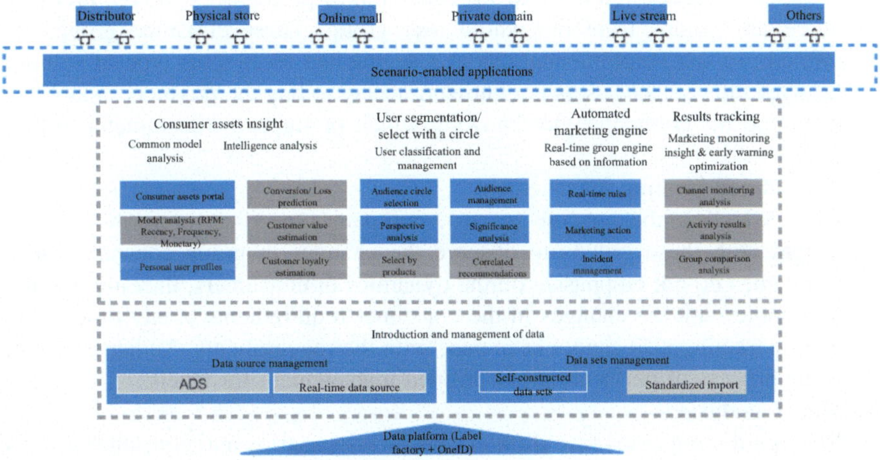

Fig. 20.2 Marketing cloud intelligence solution

(2) Consumer segmentation
Consumer segmentation refers to the criteria selection based on labels, such as user behaviors, achieving streamlined membership management, helping companies deliver precision services according to the different user requirements, and enhancing the members' retention and repurchase rates.
(3) Manage consumer assets
Consumer assets management refers to the process by which a marketing campaign is performed again after the members have made repurchases. It is an extraction process of the members' value after the new retail companies have acquired the customers.

2. **The construction logic of Marketing Cloud Intelligence**

(1) A systematic data architecture
The first step of Marketing Cloud Intelligence completed in a data platform is constructing a systematic data architecture, ensuring data stability.
(2) Data labeling architecture
While constructing the data platform, companies classify all user data and label them by attributes. Marketing Cloud Intelligence can perform the extraction of labels.

The digital team performs group selection by extracting the user labels, equivalent to all members' segmentation. Take the apparel industry as an example. It can be further segmented as lady, jacket, shirt, and suit customers. As some users have specific requirements on the models, colors, and other attributes of a shirt, they can be further subdivided according to their preferences.

Group selection refers to the classification of preferences and requirements of certain groups from the whole user group. These classified groups are offered product recommendations at a segmented level. This type of solution resolves the issues of users not knowing where to buy the products suitable for them and the companies not knowing which products to recommend to their users.
(3) Streamlined labeling management
After selecting the specific groups, companies need to perform audience insight with these groups to observe the changes in group consumption. If companies do not emphasize on the dynamics of consumers, they are not able to grapple with the changes in the consumer requirements at any time, while their marketing also cannot keep pace with the requirements. Audience insight is the process of performing streamlined management for labels.
(4) Model analysis
New retail companies face different business scenarios and consumer groups. By building models under the foundation of deeply understanding the user requirements, it is beneficial for companies to position their products and observe their users, helping companies to achieve streamlined marketing.

Many labels describe the users, including sex, age, height, constellation, occupation, family members, spending power, economic power, perception of value, hobbies, and interests. User profiles can be constructed with these labels, making the marketing work more precise.

3. **The core function of Marketing Cloud Intelligence: Membership depth model**

A membership depth model can enable users with no consumer records, potential spending power, ordinary members, repurchasing members, and loyal members to form an enclosed process. Every phase has a different marketing plan. In the early phase, when the users have not become members, companies can escalate marketing intensity, stimulating consumption through promotional campaigns, issuing discount vouchers, and other methods. When new customers become old, companies can continually provide more profound services to enhance the users' loyalty for repeat purchases.

20.4 Final Results

The marketing techniques of traditional retail companies have low member retention rates at their physical stores. The consumers just purchased the products and left the store, making it very difficult to retain them. As the online and offline systems are not seamlessly interconnected, the retention rate of online members also cannot be controlled. Marketing Cloud Intelligence can perfectly resolve this issue. Thousands of physical stores in the retail industry with millions of members can utilize Marketing Cloud Intelligence to achieve the transformation.

1. **Achieve multi-platform data interconnectivity and precisely reach the users**

Marketing Cloud Intelligence provides all types of marketing intervention programs by integrating the data in all online and offline channels through a data platform. Some users prefer to order their products at the official website, while some have a habit of visiting physical stores. Some users even adore accessing the e-commerce platform. Marketing Cloud Intelligence can easily interconnect these data regardless of the platforms to reach users precisely.

2. **Select different users and provide precision services**

Marketing Cloud Intelligence can provide services in a more precise manner according to the selection criteria of the members. For example, delivering pertinent product recommendations based on the members' preferences, such as brands, types of services, and types of products.

3. **Interconnectivity with multiple brands drives repeat purchases from the users**

For companies with multiple brands under their umbrella, Marketing Cloud Intelligence can help them achieve interconnectivity with multiple brands, driving repeat purchases from the users. For companies with only a single brand, Marketing Cloud Intelligence can also uncover the potential requirements of the users by optimizing the label of user behaviors. In short, Marketing Cloud Intelligence can enhance the users' spending power and help companies maintain their users simultaneously, reinforcing the users' brand awareness.

Building a Marketing Intelligence System for New Retail Companies

21

New retail companies adhere to users' principles, restructuring the interpretation of "People, Goods, and Scenarios" and providing brand new consumer products and services.

The critical technical aspect of a new retail model lies in constructing a data platform. Some retail companies have constructed their data platforms with a global data center, which ultimately integrates the online and offline data, creating a complete Marketing Intelligence System.

21.1 Project Background

Founded in 2004, a certain retail company specializes in international and domestic brands, distributorship, and supply chain services. It has become an integrated supply chain services platform with integrated brand operations, channel expansion, logistics integration, and trade financing. With over 600 staff, its annual transaction value has surpassed CNY 2.0 billion. It has more than 20 subsidiaries, holding companies, and over 30 service brands under its umbrella. With the ever-changing market environment and rapid expansion of the company's scale, it has encountered several bottlenecks in recent years and management requirements, including customer expansion, precision marketing, financial management, staff costs, mall operations, and customer service efficiency, are constantly increasing rapidly.

In the face of these circumstances, this retail company has enhanced and optimized business performance by constructing a data platform. By disrupting the original information silos of the company, the data platform has provided the driving force for its business innovation and growth, fully exploring the cross-business applications between varying departments and deeply uncovering the data and business values.

X. Ma, *Methodology for Digital Transformation*, Management for Professionals,
https://doi.org/10.1007/978-981-19-9111-0_21

21.2 Analysis of Pain Points

Many retail companies are constantly facing several issues, including the failure to achieve any breakthrough for their sales performance, failure to interconnect all channels seamlessly, failure to achieve streamlined operations, lacking agility in their supply chains. It is also not an exception for this retail company. Its pain points include the common issues faced by the industry with individual characteristics. For example, the external purchase of many types of software does not yield any positive effects, the IT department is too tired to counter the simple requirements, and the results cannot be assured.

It is a commonplace for the retail industry to have high online customer acquisition costs, low customer traffic at the physical stores, personalized customer requirements, and other issues. The pain points of its overall development are illustrated below.

1. **The overall consumer spending is waning; the traffic dividends are disappearing; the customer contact point is fragmented**

We can visually get a rough sense of the influence faced by the retail industry with data. In 2019, the total retail growth in society was slightly lower as large technology companies monopolized consumer traffic. The number of active buyers of a certain technology company was 693 million, while the number of daily active users of a certain internet company was 1089 million. The contact point for consumers is scattered around all types of fragmented scenarios, such as social media and short videos.

2. **Online and offline direct selling stores and franchising stores are all independent of each other and fail to form an entire chain path**

Companies do not coordinate their online and offline stores that operate independently from each other. Aside from the failure to interconnect their membership data, some stores from the same company are even in competition with other stores. As direct selling stores and franchising stores are virtually discrete, they cannot create an overall customer experience. The management of the physical store is solely reliant on the store manager's working experience and sensory feel without any support from data.

3. **Lack of global data and failure to achieve streamlined operations**

Under constantly rising costs, companies can only perform streamlined operations to enhance their repurchase rates with their existing users. If companies do not have a global perspective, they cannot perform deep profiling with their users, thus failing to provide personalized services. If the results of the traditional marketing campaigns cannot be feed backed, it is impossible to achieve streamlined operations.

4. **Lack of agile supply chain and failure to make quick response toward the user requirements**

The traditional model of a string of "Production, Supply, and Sales" cannot meet the market requirements of a diversified range of customers and fail to provide caring, personalized service experiences for the users. Besides, inventory, distribution, and logistics efficiencies are still yet to be enhanced.

Apart from facing the overall development issues of the retail industry, there are also many issues in this company. As the company is strong in its business and weak in its technical capabilities, it still cannot resolve many of its issues with the external procurement of several software products and services. Some of its issues include difficulty acquiring customers, severe loss of old customers, difficulty implementing the marketing plans, failure to achieve muti-contact marketing and user profiles, and failure to perform global marketing.

This retail company has many brand distributorships and various business departments. Any simple requirement raised by the business department requires building many data interfaces to link the data applications. While the requirements of the business department are fulfilled, there are new changes to these requirements with the constantly changing consumer scenarios. The technical department is often fatigued to counteract the frequent requirements, expressing dire disappointment over the lackluster results.

This company urgently needs a comprehensive, integrated retail data platform architecture to break the information barriers of every business department. Then it may enable the staff in each department to extract the relevant data in a standardized data platform, implement data sharing, resource sharing, seamless interconnectivity, and free toggling between data and resources to ensure a standardized and highly efficient corporate management.

In addition, amid the complex, ever-changing market environment and the ultracompetitive industry, this retail company needs to construct a data platform with services at its core to optimize its corporate management and drive business growth.

Project construction objectives

The construction objectives of a data platform by this company can be divided into several points from the technical perspective.

(1) It requires drawing up the business data management specifications, standard systems, and data security access mechanisms to provide security safeguards to data access.
(2) It requires being equipped with data intelligence search technology, database metadata management technology, graphical visualization technology of metadata processing, and multi-database data distribution synchronization technology. These technical capabilities not only can facilitate the business staff to perform data intelligence search, but they can also easily perform effective management for data storage, enabling the data browsers to quickly access

the data structure of the company with a visualization approach and delivering synchronization functionality for the extraction and application of data.

(3) Research and develop multi-dimensional data diagnosis algorithms, algorithms for detecting and eliminating data redundancy in databases, unusual, automated detection algorithms for business indicators, helping the data users perform smart diagnoses with these algorithms, enhancing data quality, and supporting the R&D of data tools.

(4) Be equipped with enriching visualization components. As there is comparatively more working staff in the company's different operations, management, and business areas, the construction of a data platform needs a good interface experience, capable of presenting information, positioning the requirements, and the necessary visualization components to support decision-making.

(5) The construction of the data platform must also support third-party integrated applications, helping the third-party applications quickly perform seamless interconnectivity with the data platform and helping companies better grapple with the data conditions of the third-party applications.

(6) This retail company's colossal volume of retail data needs to determine comprehensive data specification standards through the data platform, creating multi-dimensional data management specifications and data management standard systems.

(7) Deliver an integrated management system with several functions, such as quick extraction, self-service analysis, and portal customization, to business staff. Deliver tools, such as visualized operations and maintenance and automated processing, for technical staff. Deliver all warning assessment and decision-making support techniques for management staff.

(8) Develop the intellectualization process of monitoring business data, helping the working staff to perform smart analysis according to the actual usage process of data and dynamically adjusting the rule parameters during the management process, hence, constructing the data platform can help the company achieve intellectualization during the existing and future data application process.

It utilizes professional data platform technologies to drive digital transformation and achieve the company's strategic objectives to create a data platform perfectly aligned with its strategic requirements.

21.3 Solutions

This company has been striving to transform itself from a traditional trading distributor to a service provider with shared businesses, building a highly efficient, scalable value network business ecosystem. As shown in Fig. 21.1, it is a data platform architecture with full functionality constructed by the retail company. It enhances the company's management efficiency effectively, trimming operating costs and inspiring more business potential.

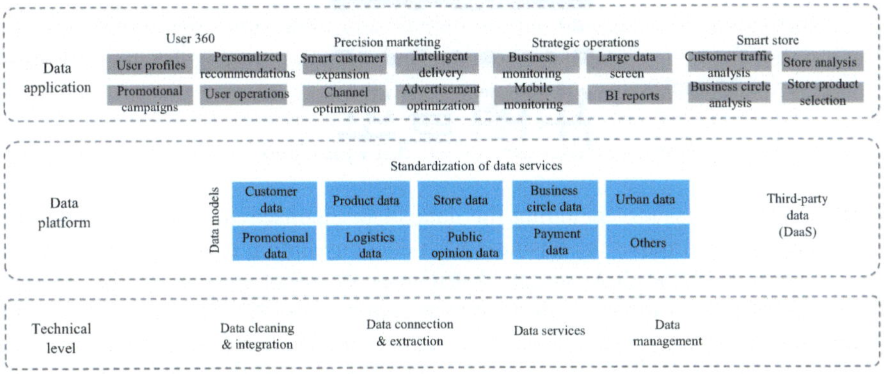

Fig. 21.1 Data platform architecture of a retail company

In the early phase of the project, this company carried out detailed and accurate requirements and data surveys to lay a solid foundation for the construction of a data platform, the construction of a data assets system, and the building of data services in the later phase. Utilizing a clear digital platform infrastructure and architecture, detailed and accurate data assets system, and multi-dimensional data services, this company's smart retail data platform provides strong support of digital platform technologies for most of its business systems, directly hitting the business's pain points.

1. **Requirements survey**

The emphasis is on the process connectivity between each business application system, the interface level of information, and the specific scenarios and challenges for data sharing. Surveying the data entry channels and export paths of every business line requires providing the types of tasks supported by data and the types of external data required to enhance the departments' working efficiencies.

It also requires collecting and analyzing several issues and requests, such as data sources, data collection and synchronization, data computing and storage, task deployment by data, data application products, data control permissions, and the application system of each business line.

In addition, it also requires collecting and analyzing other issues and requests, such as the organizational structure and division of labor, core business processes, core business indicators, core business systems, and business data control permissions, of the responsible departments for each business line.

2. **Data survey**

Based on the business requirements and objectives of the data platform project, the technical team shall start from its existing business systems and data, perform the core processes of the business modules (such as survey, refining retail, inventory, distribution, finance, and supply chain), and understand the significance of data charts. Then they may support data and decision-making for the designed architecture and analysis scenarios.

3. **Construct the basic architecture of the data platform**

There are various issues, including the data silos, inconsistent data standards, and weak capability to enable the business with data circulation that exists in the business ecosystem of the downstream distributors, business systems in the internal departments of the companies, third-party e-commerce platforms, and offline retail stores. This company comprehensively accesses the data from business systems in its internal departments and the data of third-party platforms, such as JD.com and Tmall, through the construction of the basic architecture of a smart retail data platform (refer to Fig. 21.2). By doing this, it quickly and precisely improves the data standard system and information maps, safeguarding the eventual rolling out of the financial and platform data applications on schedule. Besides, it also sustainably optimizes and expands the scope of applications based on the foundation of the solid self-circulating capability of data in the data platform, providing more data support for the new businesses and products developed by the company.

4. **Construct a data assets system**

During the initial phase of the construction of a data center, the prime focus of the construction of a digital platform is helping companies to perform collection, interconnectivity, and storage of data on different platforms, delivering a high-quality data foundation for the construction of a standardized, comprehensive data center.

As shown in Fig. 21.3, the business team of this company also connected the data from each business system (e.g., supply chain system, storage system, offline

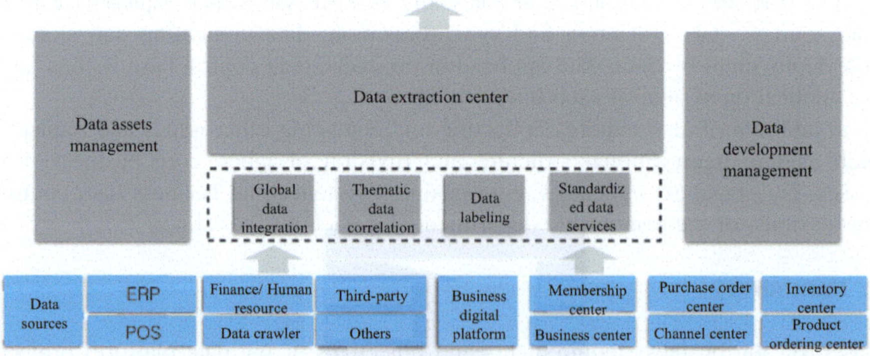

Fig. 21.2 Basic architecture of a data platform

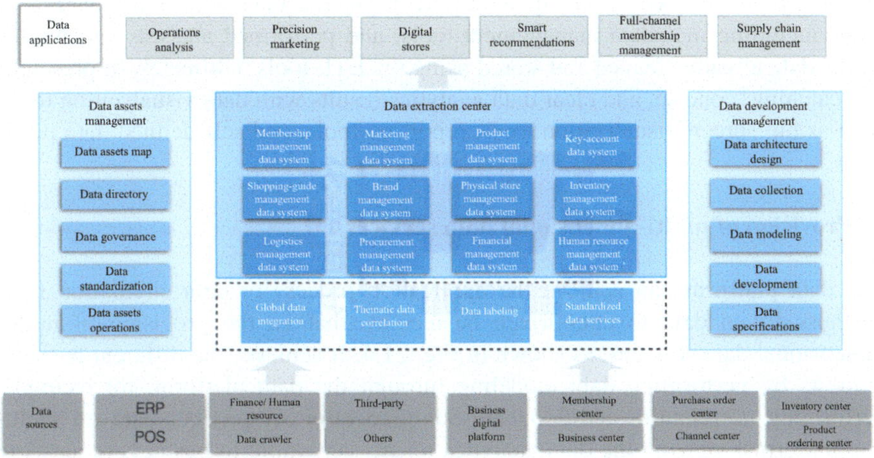

Fig. 21.3 Data assets system

retail stores, third-party e-commerce platforms) to the data center, standardizing all data pooling. After completing the construction of the back-end technologies with different data analysis and mining tools, it performed adjustment, extraction, synchronization, and other operations on the data at any time according to the constantly changing front-end business requirements. The final phase provided more reference opinions for adjusting business systems and product R&D based on the rich, strong, multi-dimensional data foundation. It also adjusted the product applications promptly according to the varying business requests, and timely performed collection and cleaning of data in the applications and stored it in the data center initially constructed to achieve the objective of data circulation between the data collection end and the data usage end.

This company deployed many systems for collecting, synchronizing, and deploying data to achieve data storage, interconnectivity, data applications, and data intelligence objectives. While constructing the data platform, it first built a basic platform and then exported and integrated the operating data of the front-end business systems, including CRM, OA, WMS, OMS, and other systems with extraction tools of the business system. After that, it manually reported and recorded the data into the system and performed integration and coverage of the data from various channels, such as JD.com, Gome, Suning, Pinduoduo, Tmall, and Xiaohongshu, with external API interfaces. And then, it performed data pooling at the bottom layer and stored the data in a self-constructed private cloud environment.

In addition, this company interconnected all the data distributed in the third-party platforms, including Tmall and JD.com, and integrated all data from the same type and series of products in different platforms. After integration, it first performed data storage using the distributed big data storage system, offline big data computing system, and accurate, real-time big data computing system, forming a big data platform. After that, it processed the stored data with data governance tools, including metadata management tools, and performed analysis and mining on the data already cleaned and stored using the ETL tools. Ultimately, it presented eye-catching, concise, and clear data analytics results with data visualization tools, such as big screen visualization tools, reporting tools, and self-defined data portal tools.

5. **Provision of multi-dimensional data services**

The data platform can achieve the application process of data circulation from business-driven data to data-driven businesses, that is, the provision of multi-dimensional data services, as shown in Fig. 21.4. It achieves the different business requests by performing data modeling through the data platform, for example, performing correlation, addition, and summarization of product data on multiple platforms, viewing the data analytics results according to business requests to deliver footfall to the offline stores or online flagship stores and provide marketing references.

Let's take a look at another example. Monitoring of financial data and configuration of early warning quota can be performed through the data platform. Once a certain quota is reached, it can be directly audited by the highest senior management, simplifying the burdensome process of approval between departments. By doing this, it not only streamlines the company's operating processes but also saves time and labor costs. The same working principles can also apply to the company's other departments. For example, it can also dispatch an early warning when the sales revenue reaches a certain amount.

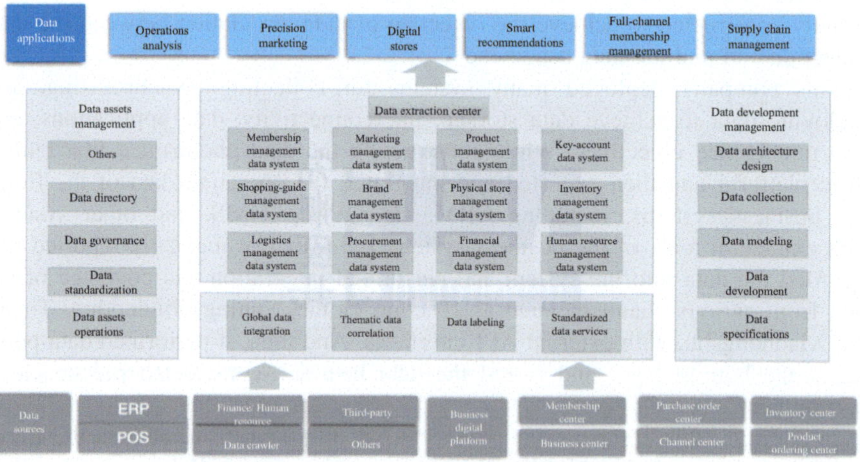

Fig. 21.4 Multi-dimensional data services provided by a data platform

With the solid self-circulation capability of data, the smart retail data platform can perform analysis on a full range of varying scenarios, including the annual operating conditions of the company, quarterly/monthly operating conditions, operations, promotional expenses and conversion, warehousing logistics, and supply chain conditions, questions and answers from the customer service department, labor costs, capital expenditure, back-end expenditure, enhancing the efficiency of every business scenario, mitigating manual intervention and helping companies to achieve the operational decision-making and business digitalization of the business intelligence system.

21.4 Final Results

The integration and management of data in the smart retail data platform can be achieved with the three core construction components, including constructing a basic technical architecture, creating data assets, and developing data intelligence applications. Then we may construct a standardized data marketing system, comprehensively interconnecting the different business components, including merchants, supply chain, inventory, membership, and e-commerce. Then, all the staff carries out standardized actions and centralized plans by data.

1. **The interconnectivity of multiple platforms creates a data center**

The smart retail data platform performs cleaning and processing of business data generated from the business systems, external distributors, offline retail stores, data input, deletion, and storage of third-party platforms to form a data center.

2. **Create intelligent applications for the business staff and drive business enhancement**

According to the requirements of the business systems, the smart retail data center performs classification, abstraction, Induction, and summarization of data from each business module, constructing standardized data standards and data maps and forming the decision-making system of a digital platform. After the work enhancement by the data quality and the work assignment with the data logic map in the earlier section, it sorts out the business models and original data indicators according to the requirements proposed by each front-end business department and develops application products that can be expanded and enhanced. Under the support of the self-circulation capability of data with strong functionality and outstanding quality, the business staff can perform optimization and adjustment of the business systems and products at any time according to the user requirements to drive the enhancement of business performance.

3. **Capable of analyzing data in multiple dimensions, truly achieving data-driven businesses**

The smart retail data platform helps this company achieve comprehensive coverage and standardized management of business data and simultaneously creates the self-circulation capability of data. Companies can invest more efforts in business innovation, truly achieving data-driven businesses.

4. **Strengthen the stickiness of members and understand the operating conditions to achieve streamlined operations**

By integrating its business development and current operating conditions, companies reinforce the stickiness and activity of members with the user (member) profiles, membership management, and online/offline integration to avoid the loss of any member. They also analyze the indicators (sales revenue, volume, gross profit margin, repurchase rate, staff efficiency per personnel, efficiency per space unit, and brand) to build a terminal operating analysis model with advanced analytics functions, such as analysis, algorithms, modeling, and early warning. Streamlined operations can create multi-dimensional labels, including group, product, store, and channel, laying the foundation to enhance the precision of marketing and utilizing digitalization to boost the products and operating efficiency of the channels to develop the digital competitiveness of companies.

A Renowned Retail Company Creates an Industrial Internet Platform

22

A renowned retail company has made a crucial breakthrough to overcome its sales bottlenecks by constructing an industrial internet platform. It has finally created a data intelligence business of its own.

22.1 Project Background

Although we are already in the midst of the digital era, many companies have yet to begin their digital transformation. Unfortunately, their operating approach is still very traditional. For example, they still depend on supply chains, traditional distributors, and offline stores to generate sales for their products. In the ultra-competitive retail industry, particularly those oriented to C-end customers, many companies are in danger of bankruptcy if they cannot transform rapidly. Some slow-moving companies have even exited the retail scene.

22.2 Analysis of Pain Points

A certain retail company is a renowned, leading giant in the industry. Its sales revenue has been ranked first in the industry chart for an extended period. With decades of historical milestones, this company's brand is well-known in the industry. Its operating approach, however, is still very traditional, over-relying on the supply chains and distributors. Thus, it still cannot overcome its sales bottlenecks.

1. **Its traditional and single-faceted sales channel was not able to acquire user data**

Long ago, the company only participated in the market competition as a brand merchant. It sold its products to the C-end users through various channels, including distributors and offline franchises. Hence, its sales channel was traditional

X. Ma, *Methodology for Digital Transformation*, Management for Professionals,
https://doi.org/10.1007/978-981-19-9111-0_22

and single-faceted. It was not concerned about collecting user data and failing to integrate it from upstream and downstream industry chains and their internal departments to perform smart marketing.

2. **Its sales revenue was stagnating without achieving any breakthrough in its sales bottlenecks**

Its traditional business model helped the company to achieve a sales revenue of CNY 20 billion annually. Despite standing firm in the first position in the industry, its sales revenue stagnated without fulfilling its ambition of gaining more market share.

22.3 Solutions

Given this company's current conditions and requirements, Guoyun Data has proposed the following solution.

First, prepare the six major maps after a survey analysis.

And then reconstruct the data intelligence business model to implement digital transformation.

Last but not least, bring in digital systems and internet systems to construct an industrial internet platform.

Through the digital industrial internet platform, the company successfully transformed from a brand merchant to a platform merchant with significant improvement in product sales. This company not only could sell its products on the platform, but it could also sell its partners' products, proudly achieving a sales breakthrough from CNY 20 to 50 billion. Hence, it has constructed a data intelligence business model. And this type of business model is known as the S2B2C model.

1. **S-end (supply chain end)**

The company could sell not only its products but also the products of other companies through the digital approach of quick matching the external products. By utilizing the construction of a smart supply chain digital platform and employing the intelligent stock allocation and replenishment system, the types of products have surged while the inventory has substantially dwindled.

2. **B-end (channel merchant)**

Through the digital platform, the distributors, suppliers, and super individuals with a certain user foundation are all connected, enabling more companies and individuals to become channel merchants that jointly serve the C-end users. All types of channels are enabled (distributors, agents, e-commerce platforms, super individuals, physical stores), lowering the barriers to entry for selling products on behalf of the original manufacturers.

3. **C-end (user)**

More data on user behavior can be collected with a digital platform, while the construction of a complete user assets system can facilitate the company to better allocate its products and services to the users at its core.

Product sales channels have grown, and the sales system has also expanded. Under the S2B2C model, the company has tens of thousands of sales channels, and it is all feed backed to the S-end via the collection of user data and composing of user profiles.

22.4 Final Results

The transformation of this business model is completely based on digital capabilities, and it can be known as a data intelligence business with the two following characteristics.

1. **Expand the depth of the traditional business structure**

The company can recommend more relevant products to its users by understanding the product characteristics with the digital approach. Transforming from a brand merchant to a platform merchant, the company altered its excessive reliance on the survival model of key accounts' orders. Today, in addition to serving key accounts, the company can also service a colossal volume of small clients, significantly enhancing its product sales from the overall perspective.

2. **Expand the width of the traditional business structure**

In the past, the company purely relied on distributors and agents to push its products. There were limitations in the incomplete management. Today, the company enables its external capabilities with digitalization, expanding the width of its sales structure.

A University Builds a Digital Campus 23

Data analytics has become an essential means of making scientific decisions. Decisions and actions purely based on experience and intuition have gradually disappeared. Big data is becoming a new highlight in corporate competition. Every industry has to use big data technologies. Companies not concerned about the data-driven business model eventually become obsolete in the market.

23.1 Project Background

A digital campus is a vital construction objective in the era of Education Informatization 2.0. The new era has bestowed upon the education informatization a new mission. The era of Education Informatization 1.0, with a greater emphasis on the IT systems, construction of business systems, and accumulation of a colossal volume of data, has also brought about many worrisome issues for universities. The document "Action Plans of Education Informatization 2.0," printed and issued by the Ministry of Education of the People's Republic of China, concisely illustrates the reconstruction of the educational ecosystem under the strong support of new technologies, including big data and artificial intelligence.

In the era of Education Informatization 2.0, universities need to focus more on integrating every system and using data to fully reflect the value of data, drive the management of informatization and enhance the application levels. Meanwhile, the government has developed an overall framework for the smart campus, and data platform construction has been included in the plan as the critical mission for every high school.

X. Ma, *Methodology for Digital Transformation*, Management for Professionals,
https://doi.org/10.1007/978-981-19-9111-0_23

23.2 Analysis of Pain Points

A certain university has implemented the construction of informatization for many years. Its internal departments are mainly comprised of the library management system, student orientation system, teaching system, student management system, OA system, and payment system. It has ten business data systems, including industry research data, fixed assets data, logistics data, further education data, human data sources, university-enterprise collaboration data, recruitment and employment data, online internet data, and all-in-one card data.

These systems are maintained and implemented by more than a dozen manufacturers. Hence, there are many different data rules. In addition to the many different types of systems, many systems have been used for over a decade. The updating of data has been suspended, with many data issues unresolved. With the improvement of technical concepts, many outdated systems could not meet the requirements of new emerging businesses. This university wishes to roll out innovation with its data, and few manufacturers can meet the university's requirements when facing technical and capital issues.

The university has higher requirements in the data management area. In the internal departments of the university, the teachers and students need to use more than a dozen systems that are not interconnected. The system data is primarily stagnating in the phenomenon of "too many, fragmented, messy;" the definition of the data fields is not standardized, and the data is very messy.

Besides, the university also has higher requirements in data intelligence applications. Along with the constant deepening of education reform, the university needs to achieve an intelligent and personalized education to help the students grow in a conducive environment. The university also needs to manage its teaching and administrative staff better and safeguard the security of its students.

23.3 Solutions

To achieve a "smart campus," the university has launched a university-enterprise collaboration with Guoyun Data. By utilizing the construction solution of a smart campus as well as the technical architecture of a data platform, the university has constructed the data assets layer, extensive data storage computing layer, data governance layer, data tools, and models layer, standardizing the user center, achieving a comprehensive smart service platform integrated with the "generation, learning, research, innovation" of the big data and thoroughly resolving the various issues, including data silos, data mess, simple application analysis.

The comprehensive smart service platform integrated with the "generation, learning, research, innovation" of big data has supported the basic requirements for professional teaching and achieved horizontal expansion. Teachers and students can initiate interdisciplinary and cross-domain research using big data technologies. At the same time, the "smart campus" has formed a set of complete data systems, fulfilling the university's many areas of data requirements. Guoyun Data

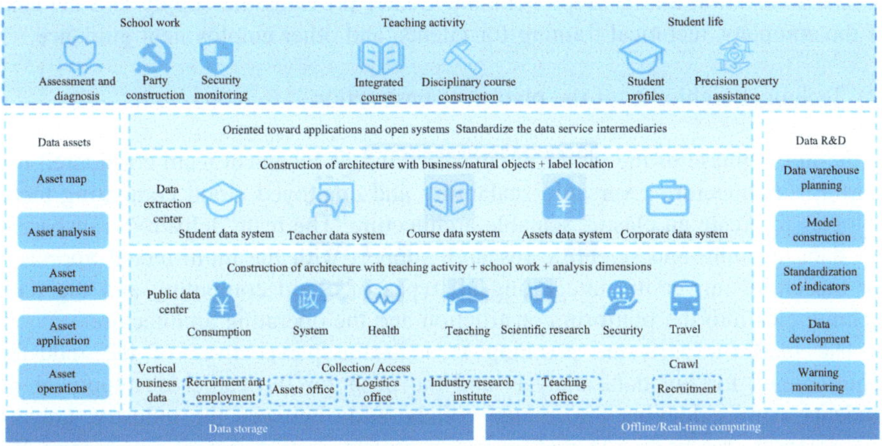

Fig. 23.1 Overall architecture of a smart campus

has created an "ecosystem in four environments" for the university, which is a new representation of a new teaching model, providing personalized, dynamic learning services for students.

Through the "smart campus" system, the teachers and students can promptly be aware of all activities and information within the university. Relying on the smart campus, the university can easily achieve multi-dimensional data perceptions, real-time business insight, and decision-making, comprehensively enhancing campus information and intellectualization. The construction architecture of the university's data platform is shown in Fig. 23.1.

1. **Construct the basic platform with the "generation, learning, research, innovation" of the big data**

(1) Construction details of the basic platform

The platform contains the followings: big data theory guidance, technical operations, big data application analysis of relevant courses, big data cluster construction, big data computing experimental environment construction, big data training lectures, and big data nurturing of teaching qualifications.

The applied scientific research projects include various models of scenery monitoring, emergency command, tourism public opinion monitoring, and traffic prediction.

The platform construction also includes precision learning support applications.

The big data-IoT experience center contains IoT solutions, including smart healthcare, smart transport, smart office, and future education; IoT technical displays, such as smart central control system, holographic images, and 4D cinema; IoT case presentations, including voice interaction and human–machine interaction.

The Innovation and Entrepreneurship Center provides the supply and demand of the company, technical training for talents, and other employment guidance.

(2) Technical highlights of the platform construction

In the initial phase of the platform construction, the technical team considered the platform architecture's versatile scalability and employed cloud computing technologies to create an elastic, scalable architecture. The team delivered transparent big data teaching and scientific research support with the multi-tenant approach for the entire university, integrating all types of cloud computing and big data technologies into the platform construction and the operating architecture.

The platform performs planning through the perspectives of the industry requirements for big data analysis and the push for the career development of students, truly achieving the mutual collaboration between the industry, university, scientific research, and real operating projects with apparent advantages. By importing the artificial intelligence architecture and capabilities above the existing functionality, the platform fully showcases the symbiotic capabilities between the data and big data platforms, profoundly mining the professional profiles of the students, teachers, and university and perceiving all scenarios and equipment within the university. The constant online updating of information from all personnel, resources, and activities in a real-time manner within the university helps all personnel in the university to grapple with its dynamics at any time, intelligently recalibrating all types of activities.

2. **Develop open, shared data services with big data at its core**

Based on the varying service requirements, Guoyun Data has also set up a set of complete data systems for the university, encompassing all data on the campus, including data collection, data processing, data services, data applications, and every phase of the data chain, providing data services covering the entire chain for the businesses and management within and beyond the campus.

(1) Analysis of the technological principles of constructing a data system

This data system accesses the data based on the business systems and extracts the data to the computing platform. And then, it forms an architecture with the properties of "business modules + analysis dimensions" through the One Data system to construct a "public data center." From the business requirements perspective, it constructs student, corporate, and teacher data systems. After in-depth data processing, the business value can be realized and applied to the products and services. Finally, it provides standardized data services with the standardized data service intermediary, One Service.

(2) Highlights of the construction of a data system

With big data at its core, the university's data system emphasizes the accuracy, availability, scientific and systematic properties of the data and the big data applications provided by the platform with "generation, learning, research, innovation" of the big data. It is, thus, not only a virtual platform. The development of an open system for the application of data with the design concept of having big data at its core has ensured the smooth development of new big data applications in interdisciplinary fields, delivering scientific, systematic big data learning and a research environment for big data researchers throughout the university.

The construction of the data system with big data at its core can accelerate the applications of new technologies, cut development costs, and mitigate the duplicated construction of systems. Within the university, colleges surrounding the University City, and the education field of the whole province, the open, shared services can readily achieve big data processing, publishing of data service results and innovation of data applications, thoroughly mining the internet data and the intrinsic value of the colossal volume of unrelated data in the social data released by the government.

(3) The data system enables the data services

The data system has laid a solid foundation for constructing a data assets center. The data assets center integrates the data from dozens of business systems in the university and utilizes the filing system to compile the manual and new data, assuring the comprehensiveness of the data. The big data storage computing center performs collation and analysis of the data acquired by the university, clears the barriers between the data, and enhances the response efficiency of the data. After that, it stores the valid data in the big data storage computing center without contacting the original informatization structure. The highly secure, stable, and high-performance computing platform then ensures a response from the data computing in seconds. By sorting out and developing the data standards with the data governance approach, it enhances the quality of data, uncovering the shortfalls hidden in the original systems to avoid any disadvantages and foster the advantages.

The university has built a series of D-Apps, such as teaching recalibration, integrated courses, comprehensive management of campus, library book recommendation system, peer profiling system, and student profiles.

The library book recommendation system integrates student information, a library book management system, all-in-one card data, online usage data, and performance data. In the past, the library book system could only perform a single function of borrowing and returning library books. To date, it can recommend library books to students according to their behavior, economic conditions, learning conditions, and other attributes. Besides, it can assess students' conditions, such as their psychological states, according to their borrowing and reading behaviors. If there is any issue with any student, the relevant responsible person can be informed at the first instance for early intervention.

3. **Explore a brand new teaching model of an ecosystem in four environments**

The learning navigation system of an ecosystem in four environments has completely disrupted the static learning navigation of traditional teaching, delivering dynamic, personalized services for the students. The navigation system can help students to configure their learning contents and learning processes in an agile manner. It is a paradigm shift that shatters the fixed, linear, and single-faceted approach of traditional teaching, truly accomplishing personalized learning and a diversified range of learning models.

Apart from the convenience provided to the users to browse the contents, the eco-learning navigation system also provides smart navigation strategies, including analysis of user behaviors, knowledge association, and learning recommendations, to the students according to the data mining algorithms of the university, recommending different courses for the students according to their learning habits, learning conditions, hobbies.

This system helps students plan their learning paths and flexibly select their choice of courses. The smart navigation strategies behind the system provide the status prompt for learning units and content roaming function for the students, and it also sets learning objectives with relevant testing and assessment.

The learning navigation system of an ecosystem in four environments has invented a new educational concept with collaboration between the university and an enterprise, exploring a brand new teaching model for the university with strong support from big data technologies. The intellectualization of the learning navigation system of an ecosystem in four environments can remind the teachers of the changes in the teaching curriculum, helping them optimize their teaching plans. Driven by big data technologies with a good fit in the course teaching model, the teachers can always control the students' learning pace, and the school can also obtain timely feedback on the teachers' teaching quality. This system presents the nurturing plans for the students in the entire university with the navigation approach, displaying the current progress and teaching results in a real-time manner, using data to quantify the intangible nurturing of talents, intelligently controlling the educational directives of the university, and effectively optimizing the quality and efficiency of learning and teaching.

23.4 Final Results

1. **Destroy the data silos and effectively manage the colossal volume of data in the university**

The solution of a "smart campus" has effectively resolved the collaborative issues faced by the university, clearing the passage of data silos between the business systems, proactively driving every type of business flow, and delivering overwhelming convenience for the university's information management system with the accomplishment of "convergence, interconnectivity, application and intelligence" of the data.

2. **Develop intelligent applications to achieve smart decision-making**

Every department utilizes intelligent applications to successfully achieve smart decision-making, significantly enhancing each department's working efficiency and quality. The innovative applications, such as early warning prediction mechanism, security perceptions, public opinion monitoring, recruitment and employment recommendation guidance, and peers data mining, have further accomplished the objective of "having unparalleled foresight in knowing the future dominated by the powerful data," becoming a classic role model in the construction of the new generation of smart campus for that province.

3. **Construct the data sharing mechanism to innovate the teaching model**

The "smart campus" has built a basic platform with the "generation, learning, research, innovation" of the big data under a new approach of "three integrations and four dimensions," smartly creating a new teaching model. In addition, it has also created open, shared data services with big data at its core.

An Urban Merchant Bank Builds a Digital Bank

24

The banks' informatization construction began in the 1990s of the twentieth century, and the technical informatization deployment of most Chinese banks was implemented comprehensively. In the DT era, however, the banking industry's data intelligence performance lagged behind the e-commerce industry.

24.1 Project Background

Alongside the significant influence on the macro-economy with various factors, such as the commercialization of interest rates, and downward pressure on the economies, the banking industry is facing unprecedented challenges. It has become a consensus within the industry to inject intelligent capabilities into the development of the banking industry by utilizing smart technologies and employing the digital innovation of advanced e-commerce models. The banking industry needs to quickly transform itself from the IT age of original process informatization and automation to the DT era of data intelligence and data-driven businesses. The retail financial data platform architecture is shown in Fig. 24.1.

The development of the retail banking industry has already become a concerted strategy for the entire banking industry. In the retail banking industry, 46% of the profits have been contributed by 40% of the scale. With a strong bargaining power and a dispersion of risks among individual customers, it has become an essential business for every bank. Under the immense competitive pressure from the large professional banks, the regional banks, in particular, urgently need to enhance their retail banking efficiencies and customer experience to integrate a full-chain path and streamlined management.

X. Ma, *Methodology for Digital Transformation*, Management for Professionals,
https://doi.org/10.1007/978-981-19-9111-0_24

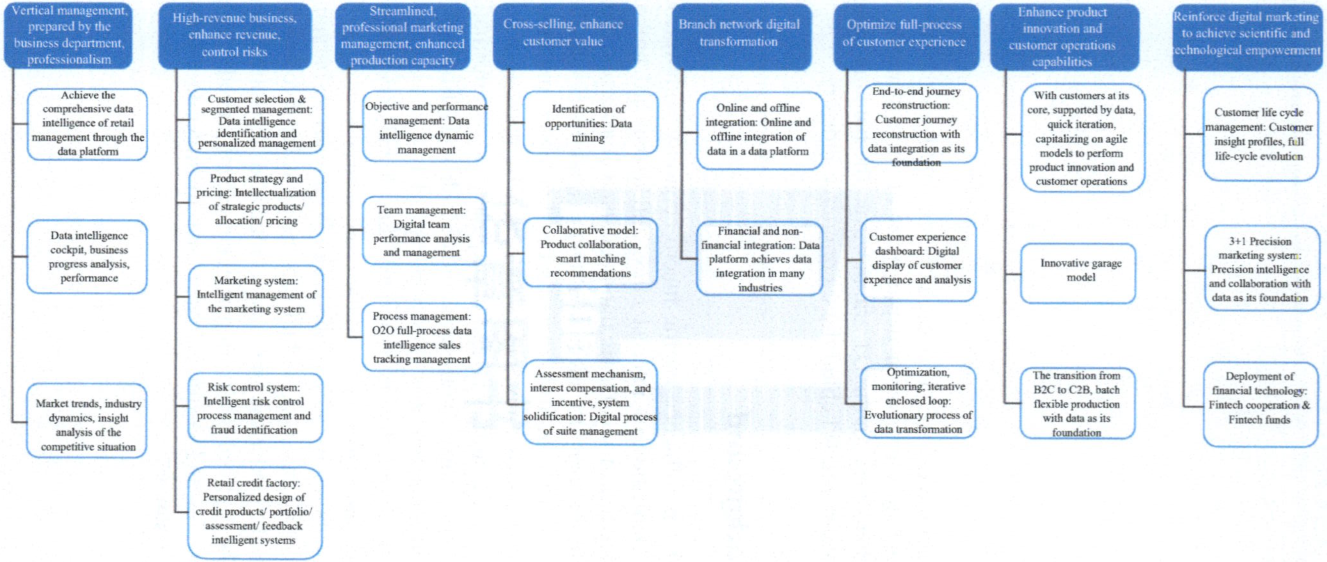

Fig. 24.1 A retail financial data platform architecture

1. **The financial technology disrupts the competitive order of the traditional banks**

The rise of online shopping platforms has delivered a more and better-personalized consumer experience for the users. Besides, it has prompted the continual innovation and upgrading of payment methods and platforms. And correspondingly, it has raised the requirements at the mobile end of the financial businesses. Online banking has gradually supplanted the former simple counter-service of the financial business.

With the rise of online shopping, the payment platform has disrupted the competitive order of the traditional financial institutions and activated the customer service models and product application models, urging the traditional banks to begin upgrading their product layouts and service models with the lever based on users and digital technologies as the core.

2. **Strong demand from users of in-depth operations of regional banks**

Some large traditional banks with certain strengths have also proactively dipped their toes into digital transformation, providing many cross-selling services to retain existing customers. For the representatives of regional banks—urban commercial banks and agricultural commercial banks, their advantages lie with the core users within their regions while not engaging in a fierce battle with the four major Chinese banks and the fintech giants.

Hence, the first step is to secure their foothold in the existing customers, performing in-depth operations in a pertinent manner for the regional banks. In the specific implementation process, the digital team must consider retaining their users with digital technologies and appropriately mine the other users in the region, striving to achieve a victorious battle in the regional areas.

3. **The widespread use of personalization in financial services be the core of the future development of banks**

In the future, the core element in the development and operations of banks is the customers. The banks can only secure their foothold in the competitive market for a long period if they can meet customer requirements. The different characteristics of the products, such as convenience, real-time, degree of control, and customization, are the prime emphasis of future product research and services in the financial sector.

Customer product requirements continually change along with the internet development of the financial industry. The satisfaction level of personalized customer requirements will be the predominant competitive force for banks in the future. This type of service capability, however, cannot be accomplished without a comprehensive data platform and agile organization. Some banks can roll out a new series of hot-selling products in a matter of days, while some can only do that in months. That is the difference generated by digital capabilities.

4. **The trend of financial digitalization has become mainstream**

Some Chinese fintech giants, ING Bank (Netherlands) and DBS Bank (Singapore), have achieved their digital transformation objectives. Traditional Chinese banks have also been proactively implementing digital transformation. The four major Chinese banks are enormous, so their digital transformation needs more time to validate the varying processes gradually. Although the size of the banks limited by shares is bigger at large, they are very powerful such that their digital transformations are also more versatile. The regional commercial banks and agricultural commercial banks can place their focus on building a unique bank with local characteristics.

The success or failure of a digital transformation strategy is highly dependent on the level of commitment and dedication of the senior management of the banks. Banks' digital transformation can only be sustainably driven to achieve the objectives with strong support from senior management.

24.2 Analysis of Pain Points

The digitalization waves have brought about an influence of exceptional proportion to the entire banking industry. The former "deep-rooted" banking industry has no other option but to transform its growth models. As part of the entire banking industry, regional banks are naturally not an exception.

1. **The overall development requirements of the banking industry**

(1) The priorities of a production system in banks are stability, consistency, and security. Lacking adaptability cannot meet the varied requirements of frontline business scenarios.
   - The batch working model is a centralized business processing, a huge volume of centralized data.
   - It cannot support the local business requirements of the branch systems.
   - The rolling out of new businesses is lagging behind the rest.

(2) There is a massive volume of business data in the internal departments, but the data is scattered in each application system, unable to form a holistic view of the data.
   - The data of each system is isolated and not integrated.
   - It cannot create a system and mechanism to collect external data systematically.
   - Cannot achieve a deep insight of customers and cannot manage in a streamlined manner.

(3) The rolling out of financial products and marketing campaigns are not supported by data but rather by many years of experience resulting in a low conversion rate.

- Lack of data support of the market and customer requirements and fails to understand the trends of the customers and market in an insightful and timely manner.
- The marketing approach to financial products is still very rough without precision.
- Lack of interaction between financial products and the market and fails to evolve to adapt to market demand quickly.

(4) The channels are discrete without creating an overall customer experience.
- Lack of the full-chain contact collection of online and offline customer data and fails to create a global customer experience and feedback.
- Weak coordination between online and offline business services.
- No channel profiles and fails to provide personalized services according to customers' preferences.

(5) The intellectualization of the branch network has to be enhanced.
- The branch network is too traditional, or the products are very plain, or inadequate to provide professional services.
- The branch network operations are passive, and their intellectualization must be enhanced.

(6) Retail operations management is traditional without capitalizing on the global aspect promptly.
- Cannot timely update the pace of the business.
- The in-depth global understanding of the business conditions lacks data support.
- The marketing feedback is insufficient.

2. **The development requirements of a certain urban commercial bank**

As a certain urban commercial bank did not interconnect the online and offline data, several issues occurred in various areas, including product sales management, marketing development of online stores, and customer retention.

(1) Lacking in the standardization of product sales management

While implementing the digital transformation, this urban commercial bank did not interconnect its internal data, which was severely isolated in every system resulting in its failure to create an enclosed data loop. Consequently, product sales lacked standardized management, failing to ensure a highly efficient implementation. There were pain points in the enhancement of sales revenue.

(2) Lacking in precision marketing of its branch network

As this urban commercial bank lacked basic data labels, there was inadequate data interconnectivity between the internal departments. The marketing development of the branch network was also lacking in local characteristics. Coupled with an unclear understanding of the surroundings of the branch network, the marketing campaigns developed by this urban commercial bank were not precise at all, in particular failing to perform a comprehensive collection and analysis of the business groups (especially the sole proprietors) in the surrounding area of the branch network.

(3) Lacking in customer loss prevention model

It was lacking in the customer loss prevention model when the fixed deposits had matured and failed to provide early warning for potential customer loss. Besides, it failed to promptly follow up with customer requests, especially in the special analysis area of familial customers, and no model was available to be used. Hence, it failed to consolidate the marketing activities to assess the operating results of the familial customers.

24.3 Solutions

Integrating its development conditions and business growth requirements, this urban commercial bank has integrated its internal and external data resources to construct a data platform. It has also performed optimization in many areas, including the construction of an agile bank system, the building of in-depth customer profiles, design, and marketing of financial products, enhancement of full-channel customer experience, improvement of intellectualization of branch network, and full control of operations management of the financial business sector with the data platform. Hence, this urban commercial bank has created a model generated by the business-driven strategy, and it not only spurs business growth but also enhances the business scale and performance. The data platform architecture of this urban commercial bank is shown in Fig. 24.2.

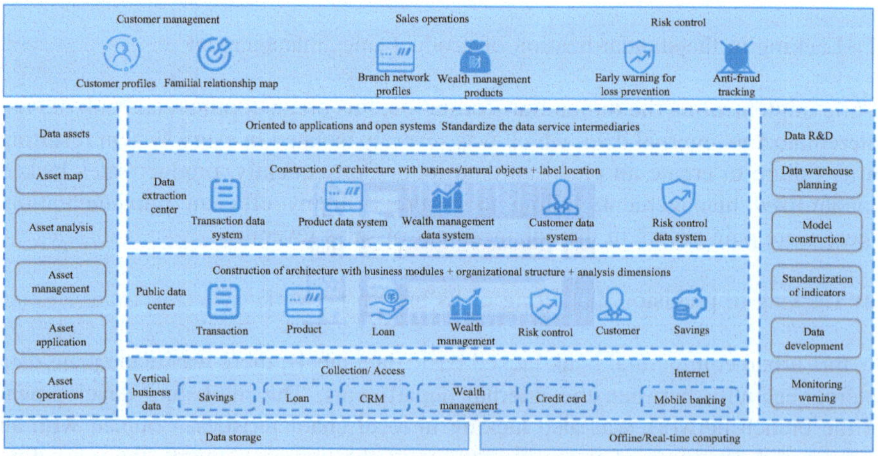

Fig. 24.2 Data platform architecture of a certain urban commercial bank

In the initial phase of the project, Guoyun Data needed to have a comprehensive, in-depth understanding of the strategy of this urban commercial bank. Only by doing this could it ensure that the directive and emphasis of the digital transformation were correct and compliant with the strategic intent of the bank. With the conducting of a survey, Guoyun Data divided its strategy into four areas: customers, products, channels, and operations. Every area consisted of specific, measurable objectives and distinct strategies and measures. And coupled with the existing IT conditions, specific digital transformation work was implemented.

1. **Create an agile banking system**

First, Guoyun Data constructed a digital platform with highly efficient and quick data processing capabilities and built an agile banking system with the data platform as its foundation. After that, it integrated the stable back-end architecture with the data platform architecture to deliver data intelligence for the front-end businesses and quickly roll out more personalized customer services.

And then, it developed a comprehensive backup/recovery strategy, security control mechanism, monitoring process of operations management, and malfunction processing approach to ensure the system's security and stability. A digital platform can deliver the convenience of business operations, the simplification and standardization of technological expansion, and the easy operation of system deployment.

2. **Collect global data from customers and construct in-depth profiles**

Integrating the existing development conditions and the business development requirements of the bank, Guoyun Data constructed a standardized data platform by fully utilizing the current internal bank data and external data resources. It analyzed some specific business scenarios within the industry, mined the potential value of data, and constructed in-depth customer profiles according to the acquired data, achieving streamlined management and enhancing the business scale and performance to drive business growth further.

3. **Support the design and marketing of financial products**

Capitalizing on the global data center, the bank performed integrated analysis for the market data and competitive products data, designed and rolled out a digital system about the financial products to construct profiles for financial products, facilitating the bank to perform control over the precision marketing, smart risk control, and pricing strategy. The digital system of financial products facilitated the formation of the feedback interconnectivity mechanism between the products and the market, enabling the digital iteration of the bank's products and services.

4. **Enhance full-channel customer experience**

Utilizing the data platform architecture, the bank collected the online and offline full-chain customer data and interconnected the online and offline business services. By launching R&D of the early warning on the customer loss model and providing cross-selling services to the existing customers, the bank can mitigate the loss rate of old customers. It can also optimize its channel services according to the customer data-expansion product category and rich product functions.

5. **Boost the intellectualization level of the branch network**

Creating a full ecosystem of branch network and professional branch network with the data platform, the bank performed a system layout with the surroundings of the branch network, grappled with the customer data, and fully encompassed the surrounding regions of marketing, constructing intelligent models for the branch network with intellectualization and proactive attributes to boost the operating efficiency of the branch network.

6. **Global cockpit operations management**

On the issue of the construction of a cockpit management platform by the decision-making team, the decision-making level of the bank could understand the global data of the bank through cockpit management, analyzing the bank operations in a real-time and dynamic manner, and managing the current conditions to devise the marketing strategies.

24.4 Final Results

The bank has successfully achieved its digital transformation by revolving around the six components: the construction of the data platform, data interconnectivity, sales management, customer experience, branch network management, and the decision-making mechanism.

(1) The data platform provides stable, scalable, and agile technical support for the bank, facilitating later development of data governance and intelligence applications.
(2) The interconnectivity of the online and offline data, as well as the internal and external data, helps the bank to construct a global customer data center, which showcases the full outline of the bank data, providing intangible benefits to all its staff in the different departments, including business, technical, management, operations, customer services, and other departments, to view the data overview.

(3) The product sales management system helps the bank standardize the product sales data so that the bank can understand the customer circumstances, customer preferences, and product sales conditions holistically to recalibrate the sales and product research directives in a pertinent manner.
(4) The early warning for customer loss model helps the bank to retain its original customers. The bank's business staff can deliver compensation recommendations with the customer loss data, acquire new customers from the old customers, effectively reinforce the interaction between the bank and its customers, and strengthen the customers' stickiness.
(5) The intellectualization of the branch network management completely alters the "confusing sentiment" of the bank's branch network management. The bank can provide personalized services by utilizing its branch network's operations data. At the same time, the intelligent management model of the branch network achieves a full encompass of the branch network surroundings such that the bank can operate the branch network in a comprehensive, real-time, and intelligent manner.
(6) The cockpit management can help the bank's decision-makers to grapple with the data conditions from an overall perspective, understand the operating conditions of the bank and monitor the bank's operating data from the bird's eye view such that they can adopt a long-term vision and a holistic control over the varying aspects, including developing the bank's marketing strategy and management reinforcement.

Architectural Diagrams of Digital Transformation Solutions for Nine Major Companies

Case Study I: A certain listed retail company creates the application of the "Superpower Store Manager"

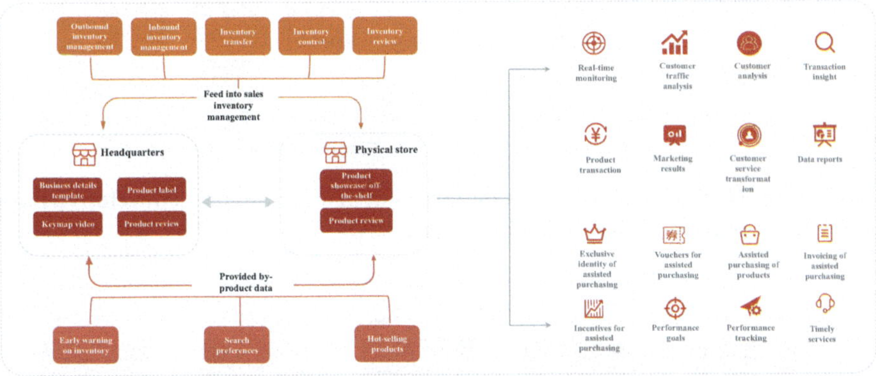

X. Ma, *Methodology for Digital Transformation*, Management for Professionals,
https://doi.org/10.1007/978-981-19-9111-0

Case Study II: A certain university constructs a personalized smart education platform

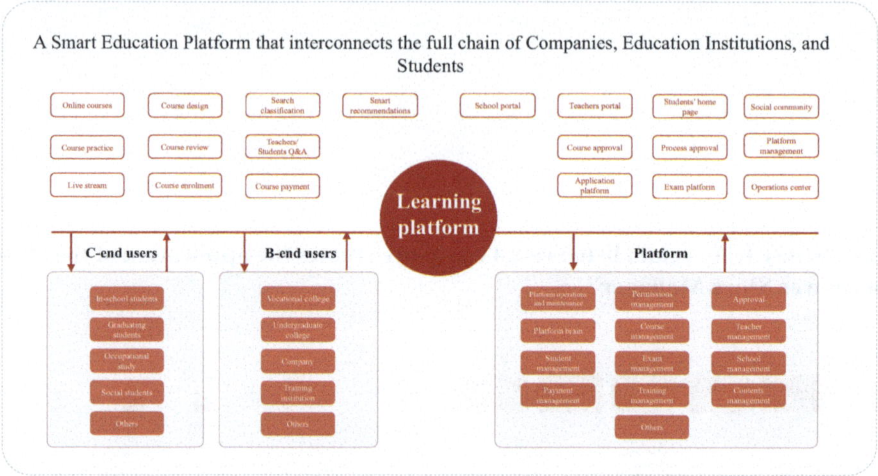

Case Study III: The retail business department of a certain bank develops a data platform to achieve digital transformation

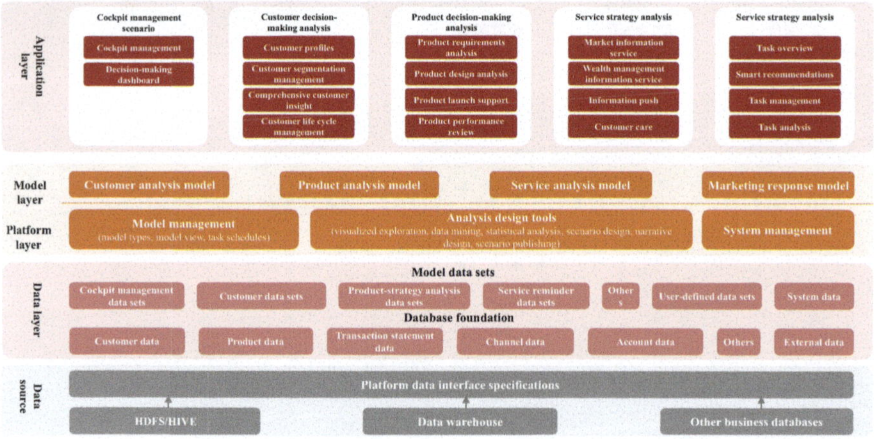

Case Study IV: A certain technology giant creates a data platform to achieve digital transformation

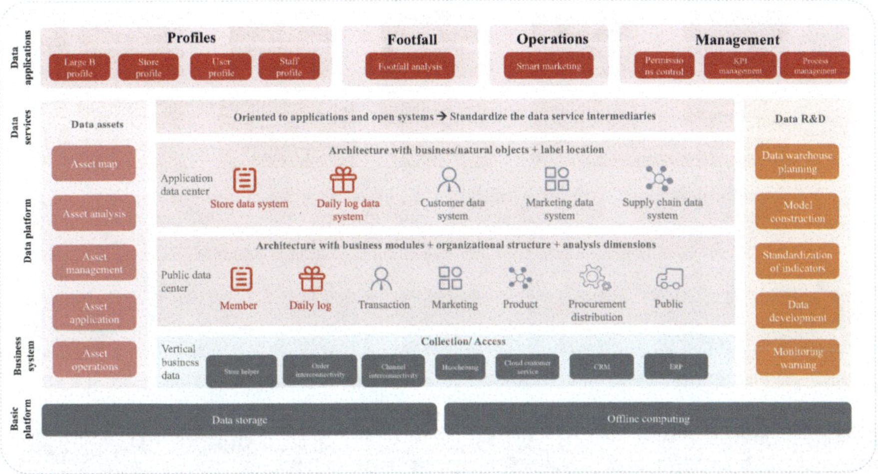

Case Study V: A technology unicorn constructs a data platform to achieve digital transformation

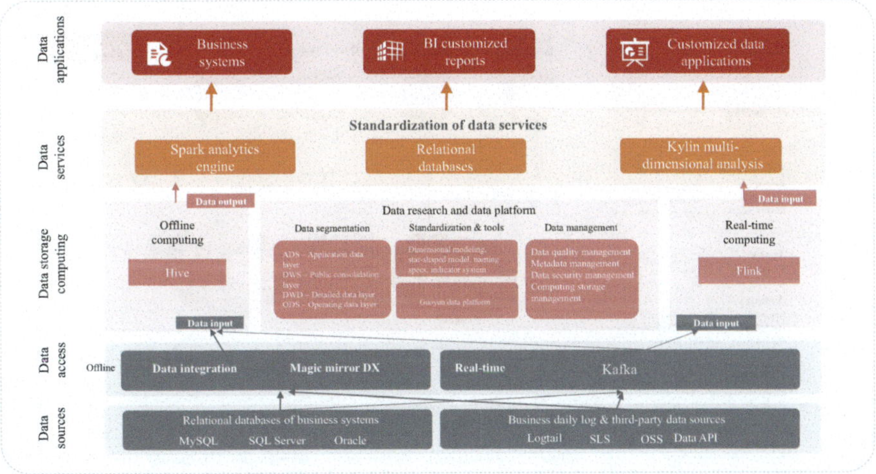

Case Study VI: A certain government builds a data platform for the dairy industry to create a unique digital economy

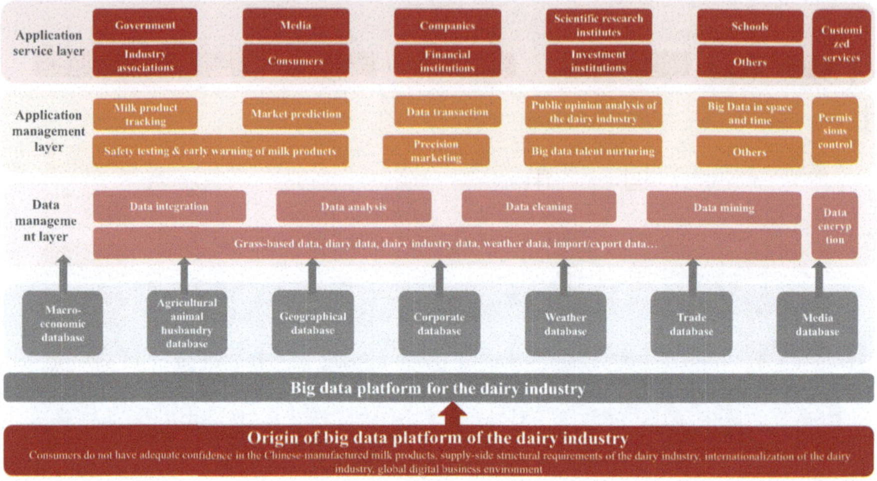

Case Study VII: A certain manufacturing company builds an industrial internet platform through a data platform

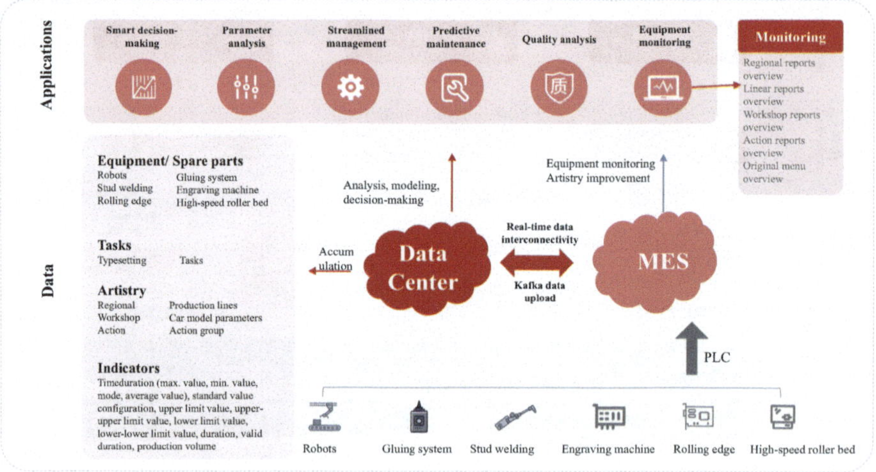

Case Study VIII: A certain mobility service company constructs a smart digital transport system through the smart mobility platform

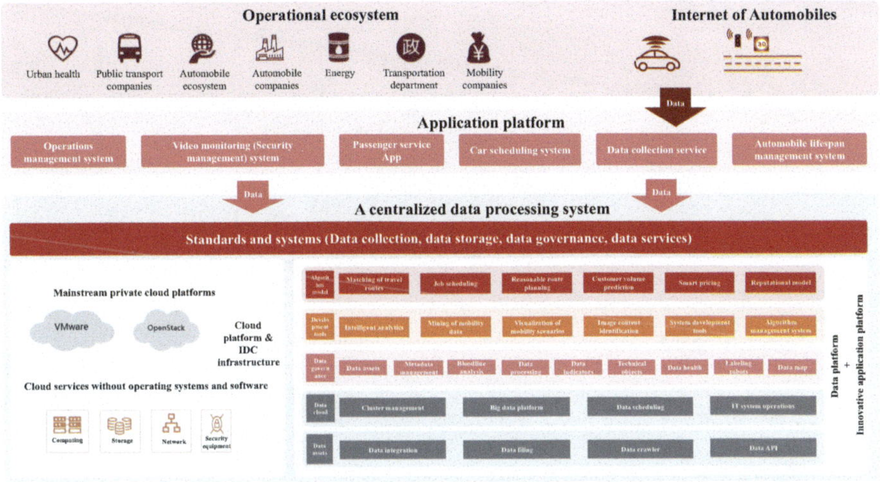

Case Study IX: Construction of a digital talent system

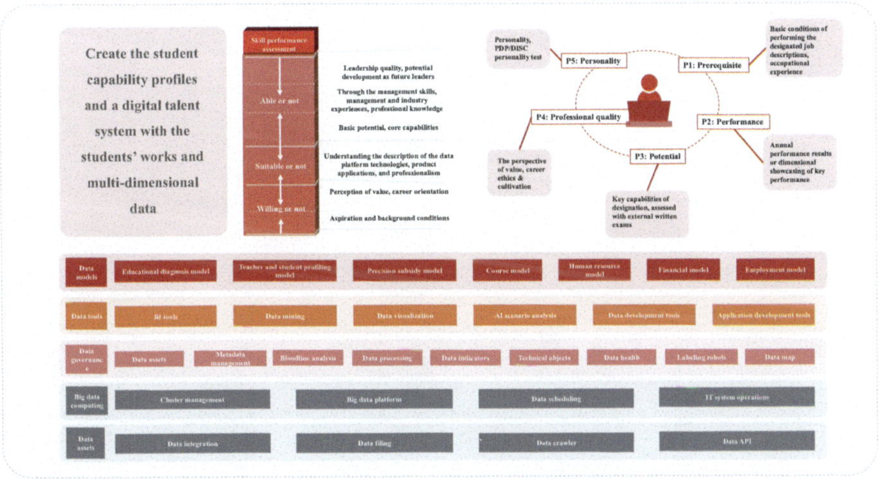

The manufacturer's authorised representative in the EU is Springer Nature Customer Service Centre GmbH, Europaplatz 3, 69115 Heidelberg, Germany. If you have any concerns regarding our products, please contact ProductSafety@springernature.com

Printed and bound by CPI Group (UK) Ltd, Croydon, CR0 4YY
01/10/2026
02225851-0011